ECONOMIES OF SIGNS AND SPACE

SCOTT LASH AND JOHN URRY

SAGE Publications
London • Thousand Oaks • New Delhi

SAGE Publications Ltd
6 Bonhill Street
London EC2A 4PU

SAGE Publications Inc
2455 Teller Road
Thousand Oaks, California 91320

SAGE Publications India Pvt Ltd
32, M-Block Market
Greater Kailash – I
New Delhi 110 048

Published in association with *Theory, Culture & Society*, School of Health, Social and Policy Studies, University of Teesside

British Library Cataloguing in Publication data

Lash, Scott
  Economies of Signs and Space. - (Theory,
  Culture & Society Series)
  I. Title II. Urry, John III. Series
  301.01

  ISBN 0–8039–8471–5
  ISBn 0–8039–8472–3 pbk

Library of Congress catalog card number 93–86216

Typeset by Photoprint, Torquay, Devon
Printed in Great Britain by The Cromwell Press Ltd,
Broughton Gifford, Melksham, Wiltshire

CONTENTS

PREFACE

We are immensely grateful to the following for their comments either on the ideas contained in this book or upon the manuscript itself: Nick Abercrombie, Ash Amin, Ulrich Beck, Alistair Black, Sarah Franklin, Michacla Gardner, Anthony Giddens, Robin Grove-White, Colin Hay, Suzette Heald, Kevin Hetherington, Martin Jay, Bob Jessop, Ulrich Jürgens, C.W. Lui, Celia Lury, Saskia Sassen, Dan Shapiro, Joost van Loon, Sylvia Walby, Alan Warde, Brian Wynne and especially Nigel Thrift.

Chapter 5 is based on an interview study of the London culture industries carried out by Nick Abercrombie, Celia Lury, Dan Shapiro and Scott Lash. Each researcher wrote a paper on the industry he or she investigated. The chapter is a reworking in the context of this book of Scott Lash's unpublished overall report which drew on all these papers.

1
INTRODUCTION:
AFTER ORGANIZED CAPITALISM

Who now reads Marx? After the decade of leveraged buyouts, global concern for the ozone layer and above all the collapse of communism in 'eastern Europe', is there any writer now more dated, more of a 'dinosaur', than Marx? The 1980s have surely sealed Marx's coffin for good and confined him and his monstrous works to the dustbin of history. Even if we are not at the end of history, we are surely at the end of his history, based as it was on the analysis of the unfolding contradictions of *industrial* capitalism. That society and those contradictions have unequivocally gone for ever.

And yet there is another Marx, not so much the theorist of industrial capitalism, more the first analyst of 'modernity'. This was the Marx we employed in *The End of Organized Capitalism*, the Marx who at the astonishing age of 30 provided analysis of how with modernity 'all that is solid melts into air'. And there is a further Marx who may have much to contribute to the analysis of those changes in social structure that seem to be sweeping all before as we approach the turn of the twenty-first century. This analysis is to be found in volume 2 of the now maligned *Das Kapital*.

These turn-of-the-century changes increasingly play themselves out in the ethereal processes of time and space. Volume 2 addresses, and is subtitled, *The Process of Circulation of Capital*. If production happens at one time and at one place, circulation allows that production to vary – as commodities are cast adrift and acquire mobility to flow through changing spaces at shifting times. It is in the first part of this volume that Marx addresses the circuits of capital, of how one form of capital metamorphoses into another. There are three circuits, of money-capital, of productive capital and of commodity capital. Productive capital in turn consists of the means of production or constant capital and labour power or variable capital. There are thus four types of capital involved in these processes of circulation: money-capital, commodities, the means of production, and labour power. They move through space and they work to different and changing temporalities.

Contemporary Marxists have adopted similar analyses. Only they, and this is their originality, have taken Marx's abstract model of the circuits of capital and have concretized it. They understand that circulation takes place in real, substantial geographical and social spaces. And in terms of time, they understand Marx's abstract model concretely. With Marx one might assume that the same model would apply across the entire history of capitalism. His four types of capital would always circulate or move in circuits in a historically unchanging manner.

In contradistinction, though, contemporary Marxists introduce temporal variation with something like the following periodization (it is the one that we adopted in *The End of Organized Capitalism*). First, in nineteenth-century, 'liberal' capitalism, the circuits of the different types of capital more or less operated on the level of the locality or region, often with relatively little intersection or overlap. Second, in twentieth-century, 'organized' capitalism, money, the means of production, consumer-commodities and labour-power came to flow most significantly on a national scale. The advanced societies witnessed the appearance of the large bureaucratic firm, vertically and in some cases horizontally integrated nationally. There was also the replacement of locally based craft unions by industrial unions whose territorial basis was 'stretched' to cover national dimensions. Commodity markets, capital markets and even labour markets took on significance across the scope of entire national economies.

Third, in the more fragmented and flexible types of production that accompany the 'disorganization' of capitalism, this circulation takes place on an international scale. At the end of the twentieth century circuits of commodities, productive capital and money qualitatively stretch to become international in terms of increases in global trade, foreign direct investment and global movements of finance. This has taken place especially in the 1980s. Foreign trade increased on average by 7 per cent per year while total production of manufactured goods in the OECD countries grew by 3 per cent per year. Foreign direct investment grew that much faster, and had a 20 per cent compound annual increase between 1983 and 1988. As for money capital, the volume of bonds traded internationally rose from $150bn in 1983 to $460bn in 1989; and the volume of trading on international equity markets rose from $73bn in 1979 to $1,212bn in 1988.

This transformed political economy is both 'post-Fordist', in that it succeeded the era of mass production and mass consumption, and postmodern. Three of the forms of capital – money, productive capital and commodities – that we just described as circulating through international space are *objects*. The fourth, variable capital or labour power, is a *subject*. Thus the circuits of capital which Marx described are, at the same time, circuits of objects and of subjects, which are increasingly difficult to distinguish from each other. And in the shift from organized to dis-organized capitalism, the various subjects and objects of the capitalist political economy circulate not only along routes of greater and greater distance, but also – especially with the rise and increasing capacities of electronic networks – at ever greater *velocity*.

This faster circulation of objects is the stuff of 'consumer capitalism'. With an ever quickening turnover time, objects as well as cultural artefacts become disposable and depleted of meaning. Some of these objects, such as computers, television sets, VCRs and hi-fis, produce many more cultural artefacts or signs ('signifiers') than people can cope with. People are bombarded with signifiers and increasingly become incapable of attaching 'signifieds' or meanings to them. Like Georg Simmel's neurasthenic flâneur, the first 'modern subject', people are overloaded by this bombardment of the signs of the city, people become blasé. In this sense, of increased profusion and speed of circulation of cultural artefacts, postmodernism is not so much a critique or radical refusal of modernism, but its radical *exaggeration*. It is more modern than modernism. Postmodernism hyperbolically accentuates the processes of increased turnover time, speed of circulation and the disposability of subjects and objects.

Analyses of such postmodern economics and societies have dominated debate on the left and the right for the last decade. If modernism came to cut away the foundations of the Western tradition with the death of God, then postmodernism proclaiming 'the end of Man' removed even those few foundations that remained. The abstraction, meaninglessness, challenges to tradition and history issued by modernism have been driven to the extreme in postmodernism. On these counts neo-conservative analysts and many Marxists are in accord. In any event not just are the analyses surprisingly convergent, but so too are the pessimistic prognoses.

Now much of this pessimism is appropriate. But it is part of the aim of this book to argue that there is a way out. It is to claim that the sort of 'economies of signs and space' that became pervasive in the wake of organized capitalism do not just lead to increasing meaninglessness, homogenization, abstraction, anomie and the destruction of the subject. Another set of radically divergent processes is simultaneously taking place. These processes may open up possibilities for the recasting of meaning in work and in leisure, for the reconstitution of community and the particular, for the reconstruction of a transmogrified subjectivity, and for heterogenization and complexity of space and of everyday life.

One reason why so many analysts paint such a uniformly pessimistic scenario for the future is because of a reliance on an overly structuralist conception of social process. This conception is prevalent on the political left and right, among structuralists and post-structuralists. In this book we will endeavour to correct this through focussing upon subjectivity, and in particular on an increasingly significant *reflexive* human subjectivity. We shall examine the causes and consequences of a subjectivity engaged in a process of 'reflexive modernization'.

Such an analysis was not to be found in *The End of Organized Capitalism*, which insufficiently examines these economies of space, of how objects and subjects are amazingly mobile and that these mobilities are themselves structured and structuring. In later chapters here we shall investigate the causes and consequences of various kinds of mobility, of migrants moving into the United States and Europe looking for work, and of the enormous temporary migrations involved in travel and tourism.

Contemporary societies are inexplicable without analysis of the effects of such massive flows upon the economies, social structures and modes of cultural interpretation of different societies. It will also be shown that there have been some striking changes in such migration patterns, including the emergence of post-Fordist ghettoes and post-Fordist patterns of travel.

But we shall also see that there are changes as well in the nature of not just the subjects, but the *objects* involved in mobility. They are progressively emptied of material content. What is increasingly produced are not material objects, but *signs*. These signs are of two types. Either they have a primarily cognitive content and are post-industrial or informational goods. Or they have primarily an aesthetic content and are what can be termed postmodern goods. The development of the latter can be seen not only in the proliferation of objects which possess a substantial aesthetic component (such as pop music, cinema, leisure, magazines, video and so on), but also in the increasing component of sign-value or image embodied *in* material objects. This aestheticization of material objects takes place in the production, the circulation or the consumption of such goods.

Such aestheticization is instantiated for example, in production, in which, as we shall see, the design component comprises an increasing component of the value of goods, while the labour process as such is less important in its contribution to value-added. This is true in the sense of increased research-and-development or 'design intensity' of even industrial production. And this increased R&D intensity is often importantly aesthetic in nature, as in clothes, shoes, furniture, car design, electronic goods and the like. Consumer durables feature as a sort of built 'micro-environment', of buildings, rooms, clothes, cars, offices and so on.

So we hope to show that, after organized capitalism, there is such a distinctive 'economy of signs and space'. Contemporary global order, or disorder, is in this sense a structure of flows, a de-centred set of economies of signs in space. But alongside and against these asymmetrical networks of flows there is increasing evidence of a radically other set of developments. There is evidence that the same individuals, the same human beings who are increasingly subject to, and the subjects of, such space economies are simultaneously becoming increasingly *reflexive* with respect to them. Alongside the silent majorities, the small-screen addicts, the 'black hole' of Baudrillard's semio-scape, there are large numbers of men and women who are taking on an increasingly critical and *reflexive* distance with reference to these institutions of the new information society.

Owing partly to an increased pervasion of cultural competencies and partly to a tendential breakdown of trust in the 'expert-systems' of the new order, a growing space enables such a critical reflexivity to develop. This growing reflexivity is in the first instance part and parcel of a radical enhancement in late modernity of individualization. That is, there is an ongoing process of *de*-traditionalization in which social agents are increasingly 'set free' from the heteronomous control or monitoring of social structures in order to be *self*-monitoring or self-reflexive. This accelerating individualization process is a process in which agency is set free from structure, a process in which, further, it is structural change itself in modernization that so to speak forces agency to take on powers that heretofore lay in social structures themselves. Hence for example structural change in the economy forces individuals to be freed from the structural rigidity of the Fordist labour process. That is, it is increasingly a prerequisite for structural economic change, increasingly a precondition of capital accumulation today that the labour force becomes increasingly self-monitoring as well as develops an even greater reflexivity with respect to the rules and resources of the workplace. Hence we address in some depth a developing process of *reflexive accumulation* in economic life.

This book thus is more than just a global sociology of flows – of migrants, of tourists, of communications, images, money, information and time. It is just as much an inter-national and local sociology of reflexivity. Most of the now substantial literature on reflexivity has understood the phenomenon in an almost exclusively *cognitive sense*. Much of this literature has its origins in the sociology of science, in which reflexivity means broadly the application of a theory's assumptions to the theory itself, or more broadly the self-monitoring of an expert system, in which the latter questions itself according to its own assumptions. Sociologists of science of a less committed constructivist persuasion have extended the notion to include – in place of the self-reflexivity of a scientific community – the increasing proclivity of an increasingly individualized lay public reflexively to *question* the assumptions of science and the expert-systems themselves. Subsequently sociological theory more generally has used a still very cognitive notion of reflexivity in discussions of how social agents are able increasingly to monitor and organize their own individual life-narratives and how society itself – via social science – is even more able to be self-constituting. In the chapters that follow we too devote considerable attention to this cognitive dimension of reflexivity. In particular, unlike other analysts, we focus here on economic life, addressing in some detail phenomena of 'reflexive production' and 'reflexive consumption'.

But running parallel to this phenomenon is another probably just as important development in late modern societies. And this is an increasing pervasion of, not cognitive, but *aesthetic* reflexivity. Whereas cognitive reflexivity has its origins in the rationalist and Cartesian assumptions of the Enlightenment tradition of modernity, this other dimension of reflexivity is rooted in the assumptions and practices of aesthetic modernism, in another modernity – not of Descartes but of Baudelaire, not of Rousseau but of Rimbaud. If cognitive reflexivity is a matter of 'monitoring' of self, and of social-structural roles and resources, then aesthetic reflexivity entails self-*interpretation* and the interpretation of social background practices. If cognitive reflexivity presupposes judgment, then aesthetic reflexivity, hermeneutically and with Gadamer is grounded in 'pre-judgments'. If cognitive reflexivity assumes a subject-object relationship of the self to

itself and the social world, then aesthetic and hermeneutic reflexivity
assumes a self which is at the same time a being-in-the-world.

Aesthetic reflexivity is instantiated in an increasing number of spheres of
everyday life. In the economy itself there is an ever growing centrality of
'design'-intensive production in many economic sectors. If knowledge-
intensive production of goods and services is embodied in the utility of the
latter, design-intensivity is embodied in the 'expressive component' of
goods and services, a component having significance from the goods of the
culture industries to the 'managed heart' of flight attendants. Consumer
practices will likewise be grounded in aesthetic reflexivity, as will the
'place-myths' that tourists and travellers construct and deconstruct.
Aesthetic reflexivity is embodied in the contemporary sense of time – in a
widespread refusal of both clock time and any sort of utilitarian calculation
of temporal organization. Aesthetic or hermeneutic reflexivity is embodied
in the background assumptions, in the unarticulated practices in which
meaning is routinely created in 'new' communities – in subcultures, in
imagined communities and in the 'invented communities' of, for example,
ecological and other late twentieth-century social movements. Aesthetic,
then, as well as cognitive reflexivity will be thematized throughout this
book.

Economies of Signs and Space, which is an essay, in the sense of an
attempt, at an empirically grounded *zeitdiagnostische Soziologie*, contains
thus both a sociology of flows and a sociology of reflexivity. As we have
just suggested flows and reflexivity can be substantially contradictory and
counteracting phenomena. But this is not the only possibility. The
individualization thesis, presupposed in the phenomenon of reflexivity, has
been registered in Western social theory of the late 1980s and early 1990s.
In the United States in the pervasion of rational choice theory; in Europe
through the impact of theories of reflexive modernization or reflexive
modernity; and in Britain in ex-Prime Minister Margaret Thatcher's
contentious assertion that there is no such thing as society, but just a set of
potentially entrepreneurial individuals in the context of a strongly empowered nation-state. The notion of individualization is also registered in
Jean Baudrillard's apocalyptic pronouncements of the implosive dissolution
of 'the social'.

We agree in a rather prosaically empirical sense that earlier existing
social structures do have less power in monitoring increasingly autonomous
agency than in the past. But we do not argue that this entails some sort of
end to the value of structural explanation *tout court*. We propose to the
contrary that there is indeed a structural basis for today's reflexive
individuals. And that this is not social structures, but increasingly the
pervasion of *information and communication structures*. We propose that
there is tendentially the beginnings of the unfolding of a process in which
social structures, national in scope, are being displaced by such global
information and communication (I & C) structures. These information and
communication structures *are* the very networked flows, *are* the very

economies of signs and space which are the subject of this book. Thus structured flows and accumulations of information are the basis of cognitive reflexivity. Thus structured flows and accumulations of images, of expressive symbols are the condition of burgeoning aesthetic reflexivity. Thus the conditions of both cognitive and aesthetic reflexivity are economies of signs in space.

This said, the book is divided into four parts. Part 1 lays out the two structuring principles of the book, the networks of flows and the phenomenon of reflexivity. Chapter 2 thus draws on the work of communications geographers to sketch an economy of flows of information, of communications, of money and of capital investment. In the first instance what this yields is an asymmetrical networked set of flows; an institutionally governed set of flows whose hubs are the global cities. What is sketched in is a configuration of flows of material and post-material objects moving at ever greater distances and at ever greater speeds. The result initially of this 'speed-up' and 'stretch out' is an emptying out of content and of previously existing meaning of objects and of subjects as well as of the spatio-temporal nexus in which they operate.

Chapter 3 is the place of a detailed development of the countervailing principle of reflexivity. This takes place via detailed consideration of the work of Ulrich Beck and Anthony Giddens on risk, expert systems and individualization. Here Beck's theses are criticized in their implicit under-socialization, their implicit methodological individualism and Whiggish assumption that society is a 'learning process'. Giddens' argument is criticized in that its core assumption of 'ontological insecurity' leads to an instrumentally rational understanding of human conduct and almost uncritical, virtually Durkheimian understanding of the role of expert systems. Avoiding a certain cognitivist bias in both Beck and Giddens, we attempt to develop the aesthetic dimension of reflexivity, via treatment of Marcel Mauss' and Pierre Bourdieu's effectively pre-cognitive understandings of classifications and the habitus, and via Charles Taylor's arguments on aesthetic and ultimately allegorical sources of the modern self.

Part 2 opens with chapter 4 on the structural conditions of reflexivity. We do so via an analysis of 'reflexive accumulation' in Japanese, German and advanced sector (Anglo-American) production systems. Here we start from the notion, developed by Japanese social scientists, of an 'information structure' which conditions information flow and knowledge acquisition in given production systems. We point in this context to these three modes of reflexive accumulation, arguing that information structures are such in the American and British cases to encourage reflexive *consumption*, while 'corporatist' and pre-modern institutional governance of information structures in Germany and Japan are favourable to much more highly modern reflexive *production* in those countries.

Chapter 5 takes these principles into a more detailed study of the *culture industries*. It highlights a process of vertical disintegration in the film, TV, record, publishing and advertising industries, the conditions of which are a growing aesthetic reflexivity in both the consumption and production of images. Here cultural products are now mainly produced external to the industry's firms, which function predominantly in the finance and the marketing of such products. That is, culture industry firms are becoming, neither commodified nor more like businesses, but more like business *services*. What takes place is an effective de-differentiation of culture and economy in which the advertising industry, a business service, is increasingly involved in producing aesthetic artefacts, while the culture firms themselves become business services.

If chapters 4 and 5 consider the 'winners' in reflexive modernity's two-thirds society, chapters six and 7 address the situation of the 'losers', among the ethnic minorities and migrants of the Western world. Chapter 6 is a socio-spatial analysis of today's 'underclass', who inhabit a space characterized by a deficit of economic, social and cultural regulation. In such spaces the older organized-capitalist *social* structures – industrial labour market, church and family networks, social welfare institutions, trade unions – have dissolved or at least moved out. Only unlike the spaces of the city centres and the suburbs *they have not yet been replaced by the information and communication structures*. The resulting deficit of governance and regulation is the condition of social disorganization of today's black American ghetto, but would equally apply to their white equivalents in British council housing estates, as well as partly explain racism among eastern German youth, where also 'Fordist' and communist/statist social structures have disappeared while the information and communication structures have not yet arrived. Chapter 7 understands post-organized capitalist *migration* in a similar context. Special focus is here on the German case. Here we see that the corporatist institutions, which were the condition (chapter 4) of such effective information and communication structures in production, operate at the same time to *exclude* ethnic minorities and women from access to these very information and communication structures, as well as largely to exclude them from civil society itself.

Part 3 turns to a sustained reflection upon economies of space and time. Chapter 8 is specifically concerned with post-industrialism and with the causes and consequences of the massive increase in the importance of various kinds of services, which are progressively more design-intensive. We show what the nature of work is like in such services, including its heightened reflexive element; what the characteristic modes of restructuring are in both the private and public sectors; and what the consequences are for place of the growth of such services. Use is made of Esping-Andersen's analysis that there are three different trajectories of post-industrial spaces. Overall it is argued that consumer services play a more important role in today's economy of signs and space than has previously been recognized. Such services are particularly symbol-laden and not simply based on information. People, places and social groups are all transformed by the endlessly complex flows of such services.

Chapter 9 is by contrast concerned with the nature of time. Through a critique of existing approaches to the sociology of time it is shown that there are many different 'times'; that what has been taken as emblematic of time in nature, clock-time, is in fact a human construction; and there are many parallels between natural and social times, given that the former is no longer viewed as Newtonian and Cartesian. Particular attention is devoted to showing how social time has changed, with clock-time dominant in the period in which organized capitalism is established and this is now being replaced by time that is increasingly instantaneous *and* glacial or evolutionary. The ways in which both these forms of time connect to reflexivity are examined in detail. Disorganized capitalism thus ushers in a quite distinct configuration of time and memory.

One aspect touched on in chapter 9, namely the increasing importance of travel through time (and of course space), is particularly examined in Part 3. Here we turn to a specific study of flows which occur on an increasingly global scale. Chapter 10 is devoted to travel. We begin by arguing that a constitutive feature of the modern world is mass travel and this needs to be analysed in terms of the category of risk. It is also shown that mobility transforms people's identities. Special attention is devoted to the growth of a reflexivity about the physical and social environment and how this results in a stance of 'cosmopolitanism', in which 'legislators' increasingly give way to 'interpreters'. More generally, we argue that corresponding to disorganized capitalism is a de-differentiation between 'tourism' and many other social practices of the contemporary social world. This is analysed in terms of the particular exchanges involved in tourism, especially that of the exchange of finance for 'visual property' and the supposedly 'aestheticization' of everyday life.

Chapter 11 considers the issue of globalization directly, in the context of three different aspects of social life: money and finance, nature and the environment, and global culture and nationality. In each it is shown that there is a particular configuration of global and local processes involved. Indeed it is argued that global processes presuppose certain local configurations, this being described in detail in the case of the growth of global financial networks. In the case of the environment we demonstrate that the transformed reflexivity about 'nature' has brought in some striking changes in the relationship between it and human activity. We also examine some of the contradictions involved in the reflexive demand to think globally and act locally. Some further arguments about the global are considered in the light of the debate about a supposedly 'global culture'. Here we see that such cultural forms do not obliterate national and local difference but may indeed re-emphasize such particular identities.

A general theme in this chapter and in the final concluding chapter is to consider the transformed character of citizenship in the light of informational and communicational flows analysed here – and what this does to conventional notions of citizenship focussed around the individual nation-state. Indeed we elaborate alternative scenarios that our analysis of the sociology of flows and reflexivity might imply. Either on the one hand, there is an optimistic post-industrial and decentralized informational society full of 'new sociations' detached from the 'traditions' of organized capitalist societies; or on the other, a bleak dystopia of increasingly wild zones deserted by the mobile informational and communicational structures and by the mobile tourists who hurry past to progressively well-defenced symbol-rich tame zones. Whichever of these looks more plausible – and in all likelihood both are proceeding side by side – this book endeavours to recast the categories and theories by which to debate such alternative futures.

The End of Organized Capitalism has been criticized for suggesting that contemporary societies are disorganized rather than reorganized. In this book we demonstrate, hopefully more convincingly, that contemporary capitalism is indeed disorganized. By this we mean that the flows of subjects and objects are progressively less synchronized within national boundaries. So although there are massively powerful organizations affecting each individual country there is no reason why these patterns will be synchronized. And indeed different organizations operate with different times. These range from the instantaneous time of the computer, and the forms of global electronic communication it presupposes, to the glacial time of environmental change where individuals are encouraged to consider the impacts of their actions upon unborn generations of both people and of other animal and plant species. So individual societies are subject to systematic de-synchronization, and in a way so is the globe as a whole. Today's world is a 'risk society' where humans themselves both have created global problems and are increasingly reflexive about monitoring the outcomes and developing at least partial solutions to those problems. And the individualization process so basic to the risk society is dependent on the decline of institutions and the literal end of a number of pivotal organizations. So contemporary life is premised upon the social organization of reflexivity. But of course it is doubtful whether that reflexivity can be organized so as to regulate and minimize the scale of those risks.

There are many topics which this book does not deal with in detail. This is partly because even a big book cannot cover everything; and it is partly because what we might have to say on such topics could be banal. Particular neglected topics include theories of patriarchy, the revolutions in 'eastern Europe', the development of the EC, the burgeoning power of the Pacific Rim (apart from Japan), developments in the state form, the nature of science and technology, and the effects of these various processes outside the north Atlantic rim (again apart from Japan). This is a book about the centre, about the major powers in the new world order, the new global cities, the migrations into and out of that centre, and the theoretical insights and empirical materials appropriate to examining that centre.

But this is not a centre which is in control. Disorganized capitalism disorganizes everything. Nothing is fixed, given and certain, while every-

thing rests upon much greater knowledge and information, on institutionalized reflexivity. People are increasingly knowledgeable about just how
little they in fact do know. Such increasingly uncontrolled economies of
signs and space are inconceivable without extraordinarily complex and
ever-developing forms of information, knowledge and aesthetic judgment.
The unintended consequences of reflexivity – that is, the effect of reflexive
agency on increasingly contingent structure – often lead to yet further
disorganization.

PART 1

ECONOMIES OF OBJECTS AND SUBJECTS

2

MOBILE OBJECTS

The aim of this chapter is to outline a framework for the analysis of flows that characterize late twentieth-century societies. These flows consist of capital, labour, commodities, information and images. In the first section we will present an analysis of a dystopic scenario, the dark side of postmodern political economies. Emphasis in this account focusses upon the increasingly rapid circulation of subjects and objects, of multiple space odysseys, and how as a consequence they are emptied of meaning and significance.

The second section of the chapter is devoted to making a set of substantial corrections to this ideal-typical model. It is shown that this flow of subjects and objects is not as free, not as 'deregulated', as it might seem. Indeed the flows are highly specific to particular times and particular spaces. And these certain times and certain spaces, through which labour, capital and signs flow, are determined by very specific sets of institutions. These latter, which are initially institutions of economic regulation, figure at the same time as institutions of spatial regulation.

Thus in the third section we detail the emergent economic 'core' of the post-organized capitalist order. This core clusters around the control functions centred in the head offices of the global cities of the major transnational firms. The core includes advanced business services, as well as communications services which service this hub. It embraces the mass communications and culture industries of these global cities. It reaches out into the outlying agglomeration surrounding global cities, engaged in the production of telecommunications and computing equipment. To service business and consumers it includes airlines services, aerospace and a significant part of the tourism and leisure industries. This information-saturated, service-rich, communications-laden core represents a major shift from the older order's central cluster of Fordist industries. It is in this new core, and not in restructured older manufacturing sectors, that the

most significant processes of flexible specialization, localization and globalization are developing.

In the final section more detailed examination is provided of the
changing relations between core and periphery especially resulting from
the transformed nature of various global flows, particularly of information
and visitors. Much of the rest of this book consists of an analysis of the
effects of this highly informationalized socio-economic core upon many
other aspects of contemporary culture and society.

EMPTYING OUT: SUBJECTS, SPACE-TIME, OBJECTS

Georg Simmel – arguably the first and most penetrating analyst of
modernity – was a sociologist of time as well as of space. Simmel not only
analysed the relation between subjects and increasingly rapid circulating
objects, but also worked at how ever quicker circulating subjects relate to
each other (1950). Simmel contrasted such subject-subject interactions in
modernity with those in traditional societies. In modernity such interactions are fleeting, intense and diverse (by which he means with many and
with very different types of others), whereas in traditional societies they
are of long duration, diffuse and uniform (that is, with only a few, rather
similar others; see Needelmann 1988). This Simmelian modern circulation
of subjects, by train and on foot in the metropolis, has shifted up several
gears in the postmodern era of mass air travel and ubiquitous motorways.
If relationships in the era of organized capitalism were already ephemeral,
then how much more so they are now. In the postmodern, again only
taking to excess what already is to be found in the modern, not just objects
but also subjects would be depleted of meaning.

The thesis of the postmodern political economy is one of the ever more
rapid circulation of subjects and objects. But it is also one of the 'emptying
out' of objects. For Giddens (1984, 1990), modernization is a process of
'time-space distanciation' in which time and space 'empty out', become
more abstract; and in which things and people become 'disembedded' from
concrete space and time. For example, the city with numbered houses
based on boulevards and the grid structure, in which the high street has its
Benettons, McDonalds and Nexts, is more abstract, more emptied out
than the pre-modern city of winding streets and numberless houses. In the
pre-modern city streets were spaces, not to move through, but to live in
(Mumford 1960). Giddens' theory of modernization via the process of
space-time distanciation does seem to constitute a new departure in
modernization theory by contrast with previous neo-Darwinian forms
which, from Spencer through Habermas via Parsons, understood modernization primarily as a process of structural differentiation and functional
integration. But the newer kind of paradigm is visible also in Durkheim
and Mauss, which traces a lineage from tribal to modern societies via a

similar process of disembedding, of emptying out. For Durkheim and especially Mauss what becomes emptied out in modernization are the categories through which people classify the world. And they also point to a process of spatio-temporal disembedding. They trace, for example, a route of temporal modernization through the particularistic marking of time via seasonal rhythms in tribal societies, to its marking via animal symbols in the Chinese horoscope, to modern calculable time.

And indeed time and space would indeed need to empty out, and become increasingly abstract time and abstract space, for the sort of circulation of subjects and objects that Marx's and post-Marxist political economy describe. Not only does this spatio-temporal ether have to take on an abstraction so that markets can 'stretch' over national and then international space, but so also do the objects which circulate in it. And indeed these objects have become increasingly emptied out of meaning, of affective charge, through the centuries' long process of modernization. Baudrillard contends that the 'crisis of the object' in capitalism came not with the domination of exchange-value, but was already present with use-value (1981). What this suggests is that meaning was already largely disembedded from objects with the domination of use-value. In the symbolic exchange, the Maussian gift relation, of traditional societies the object of exchange was 'peopled', so to speak, with the gods and demons, with the social and political relations of society. As utility dominates, as the functionalism of the object (and modernist architecture shares this charac-teristic with Marxian use-value) takes over from its symbolic significance, particularistic symbols are already disembedded from the object.

In this sense Marx was wrong in characterizing use-value as particular and concrete and exchange-value as general and abstract. Use-value was already abstract, already general, already quantifiable as is readily apparent in theories of marginal utility, and in the preference schedules of rational-choice theorists (Coleman 1990). For Baudrillard exchange-value is a simulacrum of use-value; in this a simulacrum is a copy without an original. Exchange-value is thus a copy of use-value. But when an object is primarily qualified by use-value, it has already lost its meaning, already lost its concrete and particular foundation. In no substantial sense at all is use-value 'original'.

But postmodern 'sign-value' is even more abstract than modernist exchange-value. It is as Baudrillard says a 'simulacrum of a simulacrum'. If exchange-value is already a matter of the calculability of the value of an object in quantifiable units of price, or general utility (cf Simmel 1990), then sign-value breaks even with that possibility of calculation in a sort of 'anything-goes' absorption in the image associated with an object. Sign-value cuts away the last remaining foundations of an already almost foundationless object. It clears away the last traces of territorialization of an already largely de-territorialized object.

Yet the objects in contemporary political economies are not just emptied out of symbolic content. They are also progressively emptied out of material content. What is increasingly being produced are not material objects, but signs. These signs are primarily of two types. Either they have a primarily cognitive content and thus are post-industrial or informational goods. Or they primarily have an aesthetic, in the broadest sense of the aesthetic, content and they are primarily postmodern goods (Eagleton 1989). This is occurring, not just in the proliferation of non-material objects which comprise a substantial aesthetic component (such as pop music, cinema, magazines, video, etc), but also in the increasing component of sign value or image in *material* objects. This aestheticization of material objects can take place either in the production or in the circulation and consumption of such goods.

In production the design component comprises an increasing component of the value of goods. The specific labour process is becoming less important in its contribution to value-added, and the 'design process' is progressively more central. This can be seen in the increased research-and-development or 'design intensity' of even industrial production (see chapter 5 below). This increased R&D intensity is often importantly aesthetic in nature, as in the case of clothes, shoes, furniture, car design and so on. Further, goods often take on the properties of sign-value through the process of 'branding', in which marketers and advertisers attach images to goods. This is normally brought about through the 'symbolic violence' not of the producers but of the business services, but it also occurs through the complicity of producers *and* consumers. Indeed the consumer takes on the role of agent of aestheticization or of branding. For example, the tourist consumes services and experiences by turning them into signs, by doing semiotic work of transformation (Urry 1990c). The tourist aestheticizes, so to speak, originally non-aesthetic objects. He or she turns referents into signifiers. This activity of the tourist is but one sort of demand-side semiotic work that characterizes what Featherstone calls the aestheticization of contemporary everyday life (1991).

Thus we have here an account of a seemingly endless profusion of 'space odysseys', of subjects and objects travelling at increasingly greater distances and speeds. Objects are emptied out both of meaning (and are postmodern) and of material content (and are thus post-industrial). The subjects in turn are increasingly emptied out, flat, deficient in affect. This is mirrored in recent social theory, of post-structuralism which deconstructs subjects, and rational-choice theory which reduces them to calculating unit-acts with preference schedules. Postmodernism (as hypermodernism) is indeed the cultural logic of late capitalism.

Cultural hegemony of the dominant class in pre-modern societies was exercised through symbol systems which were full of meanings, contents, peopled with gods and demons. In modern societies cultural domination has been effected through the already emptied out or abstract ideologies of liberalism, equality, progress, science and so on. Domination in post-modern capitalism is effected through a symbolic violence that has been even further emptied out, even further de-territorialized, whose minimal foundations have been swept aside. This is manifested in space, time and ideology.

Regarding space, if modernist domination is effected through the already emptied out, abstract, codified space of a city gridded horizontally by geometric street plans and vertically by International Style high rise buildings, then postmodern domination is brought about through destroying even these grids as last points of orientation and leaving a space of dizzying disorientation (as Jameson 1984 and D. Harvey 1989 analyse).

Regarding time, in pre-modern societies there is embedded time coded through affectively charged symbols. Modernist domination operates temporally through the already disembedded metanarratives of progress whose causation lies in a driving subjectivity and the ever finer rational calculation of time in both factory and leisure. Postmodern and late capitalist symbolic violence comes through the final nihilism of destroying even these last temporal foundations and reducing time to a series of disconnected and contingent events, as exemplified in the pop video and the advent of the 'three-minute culture'. If modernist time is based on a literary paradigm, postmodernist time is based on a sort of video paradigm, where attention spans are short, and events jumbled out of narrative order via re-wind, fast forward and channel hopping.

Finally, modernist domination operates through 'ideology', through already abstract ideas (compared to pre-modern affectively charged symbols, gods and demons, etc) such as equality of opportunity and socialism. Their symbolic violence takes place through meanings and functions to reproduce the dominant class in the social. Postmodern symbolic violence is effected through forms which are characterized by very little meaning. The media gain ever increasing autonomy and power with respect to the social. They follow their own interests as a specialist 'field' and decreasingly reproduce the interests of the dominant class in the social field. Champagne, for example, endeavours to show that the media come to focus on spectacular events of violence and cultural flamboyance, whose aim is largely to attract viewers (1989). This is a departure from previous modernist media activity which showed a class bias in portrayals of, for example, strikes. Champagne demonstrates not a class bias in the media but instead a 'media bias', in which the media are partial to their own interests as a quasi-autonomous and powerful field. The media, operating through spectacle, at the same time privatize poverty, race and other social problems, and contribute to the fragmentation and comparative marginalization of the social (Balaczs 1991).

In 'modern' capitalism, critique was possible through the massed power of the working class, or through aesthetic avant-gardes, both retrieving meaning in another separate and ideal world. For political avant-gardes this played itself out in a social utopia. For aesthetic avant-gardes this was reflected in a shadow world of metaphysical forms – to which form-conscious figures such as Picasso, Klee, Kandinsky, Franz Marc and Piet

Mondrian subscribed. The problem is that the 'burn out' of aesthetic and political avant-gardes in postmodern political economies appears to leave no obvious way out.

THE SPATIAL INSTITUTIONS OF CAPITALISM: THE NEW CORE

Until now we have been speaking, in effect ideal-typically, in terms of a dystopic post-modernization. In this section we shall suggest that this account has to be significantly modified but by no means rejected. It will be shown that what this account ignores is that the free-flow of subjects and objects on a global scale is significantly determined by and mediated through a set of very specific institutions, the institutions of 'economic governance'. Williamson has argued that economic transactions in capitalism typically take place through the 'market', between firms, or are interior to 'hierarchies', or large, bureaucratic firms (1975). More recently, other analysts have investigated further institutions of economic governance, such as the state, trade unions and corporatist mechanisms and communities (Schmitter 1988; Campbell, Hollingsworth and Lindberg 1991). It should also be noted that these institutions of economic governance are at the same time institutions of spatial governance and crucially channel the mobility of people, money, goods and information.

In this section we will, firstly, show how the ideal-typical model must be corrected for the existence of such institutions of governance; secondly, trace some of the modal changes in such institutional mediation as we move into the post-organized capitalist economic order; and thirdly, begin to outline the nature of a new 'core' of the post-organized capitalist order.

The old Fordist, organized capitalist core was characterized by a set of producer networks clustered around a heavy-industrial hub of the motor, chemicals, electrical and steel industries. Finance, services and distribution functions were either subordinate to, or driven by, this industrial production function. This old order has been significantly undermined by two processes. The first is the disintegration of the old core with finance, distribution, property, service, and knowledge and R&D functions each taking on their own autonomy. The second is the formation of a new core, one in which 'the post-industrial tail of the old order begins effectively to wag the Fordist and industrial dog'. The new core is clustered around information, communications and the advanced producer services, as well as other services, such as telecommunications, airlines and important parts of tourism and leisure. Spatially, many of these services are centred around global cities, located in vast agglomerations, whose industries feed these services. In terms of economic significance, the most important development in localization is what we might call 'globalized localization'.

How then are these flows of objects and subjects, of capital and labour, regulated through economic institutions? Markets themselves are important institutions of governance. The shift to market governance in the West and the world as a whole developing from the late 1970s, though carried out under the heading of 'deregulation', was not a change to an absence of regulation but a change to market regulation. The irregular spatial distribution of markets as institutions leads to massive deviations from the 'free' international flow of subjects and objects. Goods, labour, money and information will not flow to where there are no markets. For example, with the devastation of economic governance by the state in eastern Europe, market governance has not automatically sprung up to take its place. In eastern Germany the short- to medium-term result has been the rapid decline of most forms of economic governance. The outcome has been, not a shift from state to market regulation, but an overwhelming *deficit* of regulation. There has been the emptying out of economic space of many institutions. This has been followed by an emptying out of population; by a massive population outflow to western Germany where institutions of governance, and jobs, are present in much greater density.

The same can be said of the black ghetto in the USA. The ghetto in organized capitalism rather closely resembled the classic ghetto in which a minority ethnic group was forced to inhabit a particular space containing a reduplication of the central institutions of the wider space of the dominant ethnic group. The disorganized capitalist ghetto does not reproduce this sort of dominant institutional space. Instead the institutions empty out of the ghetto. Many institutions of economic governance migrate away. Markets of all sorts, including labour markets and the small corner shop, the pizza parlour, the sports shop, the bank branch vanish. So do hierarchies as large plants relocate beyond the suburbs. State governance declines, as the welfare state apparatus comes under fire; and its very physical presence, in drug abuse clinics, libraries, funded schools and social workers distributing supplementary benefits, disappears. The hollowing out of the American ghetto is particularly tragic because these same institutions of economic governance double as instances of spatial, social and cultural governance. As with eastern Europe there is a deficit of institutional regulation and it is followed by an outflow of subjects, as the major inner city ghettoes experience depopulation (Wilson 1987; Wacquant 1991; and chapter 6 below).

According to various analysts these institutional transformations on the periphery of today's world economic order are largely caused by changes taking place within the core (see Sassen 1988, 1991; Mulgan 1991). Particularly central to such transformations in the core are changes in capital markets. Three major interlinked processes have characterized the now consolidating new shape of contemporary capital markets. These are securitization, deregulation and electronification.

'Securitization' means that debt takes place not through loans from banks to industry, as was pervasively the case in organized capitalism, but through industrial firms borrowing money through the issue of equities. In this, banks underwrite share issues. This initial transaction between the financial institutions and industrial borrowers constitutes the 'primary' market in securities. The 'secondary' market in securities is that in which these created instruments of debt are traded. It is the initial securitization of debt which has enabled the massive increase in opportunities for trading in instruments of debt (Daniels 1991: 156). By 1985 the market value of equities on the New York exchange was £1,302bn, that on the Tokyo exchange £648bn, and that on the London exchange £245bn (Hepworth 1991: 133). Particular changes have affected the commercial banks which have come to take on investment banking functions and have, further, become the biggest players on the primary market in securities. This has resulted in a considerable diminution in the temporal duration of the risks undergone. Here a bank's exposure time is limited to the time it takes to distribute the issued securities on the secondary market, which itself is further shortened through the use of electronic trading and information networks (Daniels 1991: 156).

Further securitization of debt is on the agenda with the continuing deregulation of American banks. In the USA, the Glass-Steagal Act of 1933, prohibiting commercial banks from engaging in investment banking functions in underwriting securities issues, continues to be effective (Hepworth 1991: 143). Such restrictions were loosened in 1981 with the large scale introduction of international banking facilities. This enabled American banks to avoid Glass-Steagal restrictions in their international banking activities, and enabled New York to recapture some 10 per cent of the Eurocurrency banking market (Daniels 1991: 156). Such relaxation may be extended to domestic activities, if the plan to reform America's finance system passed by the banking Committee of the House of Representatives on 28 June 1991 becomes law. The plan enables commercial banks not only to engage through affiliates in underwriting, but also to sell insurance, and to spread their branches across state borders (*The Economist* 6–12 July 1991: 14).

The most significant cause of securitization has been the rise of pension funds and insurance companies as investors. In 1986 at the time of the City of London's Big Bang, the total assets of private pensions funds in the USA was $1,250bn, in the UK $243bn, in Japan $145bn, while only $48bn and $12bn in Germany and France respectively (Hepworth 1991: 141). Public pension funds in these countries as well as in Sweden are also heavily invested in securities (Heclo 1974). Such institutional investors – pension funds, insurance funds, unit trusts – at the beginning of the 1990s controlled about two-thirds of the shares in quoted British companies. Norwich Union, for example, controls an estimated £18bn of such resources, invested in 400–500 different companies. Such institutional investors are often accused of 'short-termism' and cast in the function of high-rollers in the world of casino capitalism. Funds do not typically engage in short-termism in the sense of the frequent selling of securities in one company to buy them in another, and keeping funds invested in one company for months at a time. Indeed the recent 1990-1 spate of involvement of fund managers in intervention in the governance of corporations where they are major shareholders would be an indicator rather of 'long-termism'. Short-termism arises specifically in the voting decisions made by fund managers in the face of takeover bids. Such decisions would reflect a 'cut and run' attitude towards the firm only in cases where the bid price was above the level where the fund would be able to refuse (*The Guardian* 11 July 1991: 15, interview with Mike Sandland, head of investment for Norwich Union). The failure of so many highly leveraged buyouts at the end of the 1980s makes large numbers of such exorbitant bids less likely in the 1990s.

The irony is that the growth in pension funds and insurance, stemming from the massive organized-capitalist development of private and public welfare state provision, comes to play a key role in a cluster of structures which dismantle and displace the organized capitalist framework itself. That is, what played primarily a demand-side function in the outgoing economic era comes to play a supply-side function in the present. In any event, along with investment banks and securities companies, pension funds and insurance companies become major and characteristic actors on the restructured capital markets. All four of these major players are providers not of loans but of financial *services*. Likewise individual consumers are also following suit. In the world of personal finance, individuals are using financial institutions not as repositories for their savings as creditors, but as providers of services so that their savings indirectly find their way into equity holdings.

Alongside securitization, capital markets have undergone considerable deregulation. There have been two major steps in this direction. The first, at the end of the 1970s, was the abolition of exchange controls on most major currencies. This enabled the development of substantial outward portfolio investment. By 1986 Americans held $102bn of foreign securities while foreigners held some $277bn in US stocks. Whereas the British have been leaders in foreign direct investment in the USA (some $100bn in 1990), the Japanese have led the way in terms of outflow of 'portfolio capital'. In 1983 Japanese firms and individuals held only $16bn of stocks and bonds in all foreign countries. In 1985 this figure increased to $60bn, 78 per cent of which was issued in the USA. For Britain the lifting of exchange controls in 1979 enabled the proportion of pension funds invested in foreign securities to increase from 9 to 23 per cent by 1986 and the proportion of insurance companies holdings to increase from 6 to 13 per cent. In 1986 the proportion of outflow of pension fund portfolio capital was then 23 per cent for the UK, 10 per cent for Japan and 3.6 per cent for the USA (Hepworth 1991: 140).

The second deregulatory step took place in the 1980s and opened up dealing privileges for financial institutions, most importantly as members of foreign stock exchanges. This was the key component of London's Big Bang in 1986, paralleled by similar changes in most of the advanced countries. Several processes have been involved in this: first, large multinational industrial companies came to be quoted on stock exchanges in a number of countries; second, it was made easier for financial institutions to buy substantial proportions of shares in industry on stock exchanges in other countries; and third, foreign securities companies, usually affiliates of major commercial banks, were able to underwrite share issues of domestic industrials, to distribute these shares on secondary markets and to otherwise deal in these secondary markets, often becoming members of stock exchanges in foreign global cities.

This last process has been slower to develop in Japan although this has now changed. By 1983 only six foreign securities firms were licensed to deal on the Tokyo stock exchange, although 77 companies at that time operated residence offices to collect information from the exchange. By contrast Japanese securities companies at that point operated 96 branches in 17 other countries. Most affected by this was the City of London. In the nineteenth century London, and London's investment banks, had already been the entrepôt through which other national governments had processed their securities issues onto international markets. Just before Big Bang in 1986, international lending was dominated by London. For example, British owned banks and subsidiaries of foreign banks in Britain held some 25 per cent of all international claims booked in countries reporting to the Bank for International Settlements. This was more than double that held by banks operating in the USA and Japan. Moreover London accounts for some 30 per cent of world Eurobanking and 40 per cent of the worldwide business of Japanese banks and 25 per cent of that of US banks is booked through their London branches and subsidiaries (Daniels 1991: 163). In 1986 just after Big Bang, as much as 60 per cent of the stake in London securities firms was foreign owned (Hepworth 1991: 141). Yet at the same time British investment banks increased enormously their number of foreign offices, some such as Schroeders coming to employ as much as 60 per cent of their total staff abroad (Daniels 1991: 156).

The third major change in capital markets, 'electronification', has enabled the making of new secondary markets for trading in securities. Thus computer trading systems compete with national stock exchanges. By 1985 the turnover in equities trading on the American NASDAQ (National Association of Securities Dealers Automated Quotation system) was the third highest in the world after New York and Tokyo. Stock exchanges, both 'physical' and computerized, compete for business through their provision of a market. What they offer to 'subscribers' or members is information relevant to equity trading, and a licence to engage in such trading. Firms which provide on-line information support computerized dealing networks. For example, the Reuters network is 'piggybacked' by several of these, the most prominent of which include on-line financial information services like Telerate and Quotron in the USA and Extel and Datastream in Europe (Mulgan 1991: 30). Information provided through these channels includes share prices collected from a number of international exchanges; company related data, such as annual reports; financial news, such as changes in interest rates; and more general political and economic information (Hepworth 1991: 137–8).

Telecommunications also transform other banking functions. Thus SWIFT, the international banking network, links together some 1,000 banks, handling for example transfer of funds from accounts in one bank to those of another. Telecommunications have become so important to banks, that for majors like New York's Citicorp they have constituted the third most substantial cost category after salaries and accommodation (Daniels 1991: 159; Mulgan 1991: 229–31).

Salaries though are still important because electronic banking and securities dealing are more labour-intensive than is immediately apparent. Leased networks require computer switching and data processing centres, 'and large banks have several of these scattered throughout the world. These switching centres are located typically in suburbs, outside of major cities where the rents are too high, and they make use of relatively inexpensive female labour. For example, ADP's computer centres are not in New York but in New Jersey and NASDAQ's data processing centre is in Turnbull, Connecticut (Hepworth 1991: 140).

* * *

So far then we have considered some dramatic changes in the nature of especially capital markets. But even more important than these in the regime of spatial governance particular to disorganized capitalism is the continuing importance of hierarchies. This might sound contradictory given our claims regarding the disintegration of such hierarchies (in Williamson's (1985) sense) into relations between smaller firms carried out through market transactions (see Lash and Urry 1987; and chapters 4 and 5 below). But the changing relationship between markets and hierarchies in the advanced societies today is complex and contradictory, as the following points demonstrate.

First, small 'disintegrated' firms are clearly not the only important economic form in disorganized capitalism. Indeed the necessity for constant innovation and the increasing unpredictability of product markets have two effects on economic governance. Either there is the dis-integration of functions of large bureaucratic, hierarchical firms, such as marketing, sales, research and development, production of intermediate and primary materials, onto the market. Or there is the disaggregation of such functions interior to such large firms, so that movement of infor-mation and employees (and this includes promotion in internal labour markets) begins to take place along horizontal rather than vertical lines (Aoki 1990; Coriat 1990; Kanter 1984). These are discussed at length in chapters 4 and 5 below.

Second, the decline of the national state in the process of globalization means that 'hierarchies', especially in transnational firms, have a more enhanced role to play in the new economic arrangements. In this sense the more pronounced profile of hybrid forms of governance such as sub-contracting, alliances or joint ventures does not imply a decline in the power of hierarchies. Instead this would seem to be emblematic of an enhanced role for hierarchies, but now as political actors, as political space is left to fill with the decline of the national state. Hierarchies thus take on quasi-political status and themselves carry on foreign relations with other firms, concluding 'treaties' in joint ventures and alliances. This increased power of such meso-economic hierarchies is especially visible in Japan, as subcontractors are increasingly brought into the orbit of the parent corporation. The latter themselves are ever more free, as they become increasingly transnational, from the power of the Japanese state and MITI and from the *zaibatsu* (O'Brien 1989).

Third, even where there are enclaves of flexible specialization, or at least vertically disintegrated networks of small firms engaged in transaction-rich linkages of market exchanges, there is often a large transnational firm at the hub of such networks, and most exchanges are with such firms. For example, in business services the large numbers of small firms are often engaged in transactions with head offices of major industrial transnationals in global cities. In the culture sector the very large number of small firms, including one-person firms, also commonly transact with the 'majors' in the record industry or movie industry. In high tech a large number of exchanges appear to be between small and large firms. Even in the classic flexible specialization regions it may not be much different. In for example the Stuttgart region, firm sizes in the machine tool industry are not small but commonly middle sized, of between 100 and 500 employees. And the firms they transact with are usually not local firms at all. More typically they export product to firms out of the region and more often out of the country (Herrigel 1988). Also in the Third Italy, many of the transactions are between the admittedly very small (under 10 employees) manufacturing firms and very large hierarchical distributors such as Benetton. Thus as critics of the flexible specialization thesis such as Amin and Robins have argued, hierarchies retain much of their power, and in important instances gain more power than they had previously (1990).

But finally, hierarchies are not all powerful in disorganized capitalism for a number of reasons. Although hierarchies may be stronger than ever in the macro-relations of political power, they are less significant in the microsociology of work relations. That is, the everyday lived experience of many, if not most of the work force, is substantially changed. Working alone, or working for a small firm which is indirectly dominated by a hierarchy, is vastly different than working for the parent firm itself. Much of the importance of hierarchies is in the ancillary jobs they create in consumer services supplied to highly paid managers of the central offices and the allied business and financial services. Though these workers are ultimately dependent on hierarchies, their everyday life experience is different from that under organized capitalism. In some sectors, such as publishing, cinema, food products and clothing, concentrated distributors take on powers which dwarf those of industrial firms. Some of the most powerful hierarchies are non-industrial. While in other sectors – culture industries, some high tech, clothing – so much of actual production is outsourced to other firms that erstwhile manufacturing companies come to take on more the role of business and finance services and providers of R&D rather than manufacturing proper. Finally, in most sectors, despite the rise of transnationals, globalization has meant that the oligopoly power of individual hierarchies, counted as market share of given national product markets, is diminished, as we previously showed (Lash and Urry 1987: ch 7).

The question of 'markets' versus 'hierarchies' in today's advanced societies is complex, and it makes little sense for one side to argue for the importance of markets and the other for hierarchies (such as Hirst and Zeitlin 1990; Amin and Robins 1990). This is for a number of further reasons: first, the same process of globalization that has given the transnationals power vis-à-vis national states has cut into their power of domination of national product markets; second, the increased power of such organizations as international players is accompanied by the 'hollowing out' of these corporations; and third, the creation of many of the most important disintegrated cutting edge sectors, business services, finance services, and even high tech and telecommunications which themselves have become largely advanced producer services, is conditioned by the very centralized power of the transnationals themselves.

The movement, the flows of capital, money, commodities, labour, information and images across time and space are only comprehensible if 'networks' are taken into account because it is through networks that these subjects and objects are able to gain mobility. Whatever form of institutional governance is dominant, whether markets, hierarchies, the state or corporatism, the subjects and objects which are governed must be mobile though networks. The formulations of economic geography are useful here. Thus Brunn and Leinbach conceive of the 'world as a map of "bridges" of communication and transport, comprising dense networks, sparse networks and blanks' (1991: xvii). The issue for us in this context is what are becoming the modal changes in this mapping in the post-organized capitalist order; that is, where and what sort of the 'cobwebs' of connections on these maps are becoming denser, and which are becoming relatively sparser. Networks are made up of a few basic elements: of 'bridges' or 'links' which connect the points in a network. These bridges stand out in lesser or greater relief from a 'backcloth' or 'support structure'. The entities that move along these links are called 'traffic'. This traffic can be transmitted or not. Communications, including documents, are transmitted traffic. Other traffic is mobile, not through transmission, but via transportation, whether of capital, labour or information. The points connected by links in a network are 'simplices' (Gould 1991: 25–6). Simplices can be individuals, they can be organizations, they can be terminals, transmitters or receivers.

There are six principal 'media' used in telecommunications to move information from one place to another along such bridges and nodes. Such information consists either of electronic signals or of hard copy information. Each medium is more or less valuable in terms of cost, speed of transmission, accessibility to small users, volume of information that can be delivered ('bandwidth'), and reliability.

The six media are, first, *transportation*. These include mail and express services, and are cheap and accessible to small users, but slow. They are important for original copies of documents. Second, there is *wire cable*. The advantage is sturdiness, the disadvantage is the low volume of information that they can carry and hence they cannot carry enough information to transmit images. The third medium is *co-axial cable*: bandwidth is large enough to carry images as well as voice and data. This is reliable but expensive. The fourth is the *micro-wave channel* which has a large bandwidth and is cheap, but is unreliable in that signals can be intercepted and affected by atmospheric conditions. Recent successful use of microwave is in cellular telephones. This medium is better suited for mass, than point-to-point, communications (Abler 1991: 31–2). *Earth satellites* involve cheap transmission and are well-suited for isolated areas. For example, INTELSAT (International Telecommunications Satellite Organization), which began in 1964, involves 100 countries and has over 400 earth stations (Janelle 1991: 62). Finally, there is *fibre-optic cable* which has a large bandwidth. It can simultaneously handle some 40,000 conversations, and transmit 246 bits of information per second (Janelle 1991: 61; Mulgan 1991). Fibre-optic cables also boast superior signal quality, but their problem is expense. And their advent is not at all favourable to isolated areas, either in the Third World or rural areas in advanced societies.

Given the context of these new technologies, the transition from organized to disorganized capitalism brings with it processes of globalization, localization and stratification, which we shall now address sequentially.

The paradigmatic media of mobility during the epoch of organized capitalism were railroads, telephone via wire cable, postal services and later road networks. All of these brought 'time-space convergence' and 'time-cost convergence' mainly on a *national* scale (although their role in the British Empire should be noted). By contrast the paradigmatic mobility media of disorganized capitalism are fibre-optic cable, satellite communications and air transport. These have led to time-space and time-cost convergence on a *global* scale.

Early organized capitalism in the second half of the nineteenth century saw the creation of national railway networks. These themselves were one of the preconditions of an effective mass national postal network. And just prior to the First World War the constitution of effective national telephone networks followed. In the US the interconnections of all these are exemplified in the career of Theodore Vail who was chief executive of

AT&T from 1878 to 1887 and from 1907 to 1919. Before 1878 Vail was Superintendent of Railway Mail Operations for the US Post Office. In the decade leading up to World War I, he was at AT&T the chief initiator of the integrated national telephone network (Abler 1991: 37).

Time-space convergence brought about by 'space-adjusting technologies' refers to the diminution of time it takes for mobility from one place to another. Organized capitalism's transport via railroads, autoroutes and a postal service dependent on trains led to just about as much saving of mobility time between two relatively small towns as between two large ones. However, contemporary airlines drastically alter this state of affairs. Now time-space convergence basically lowers the time it takes to get between major airports, whereas in Europe travel between places with minor airports is often faster by train. Space-adjusting technologies in the post-organized capitalist era mean that travel from a major city in Britain, Germany or Italy to, for example, Paris (the most thickly 'cobwebbed' air hub of all Europe) takes less time than travel to a provincial town in their own country. 'Time-cost convergence', the diminution in cost of communications of a certain length between places, is now globalized rather than nationalized as satellite and fibre-optic cable forge links between global cities in different countries rather than connecting places within a country. 'Relative location', that is, how one is connected, becomes more important than 'absolute location' (Brunn and Leinbach 1991: xvii).

We will now consider localization in the context of these technological shifts. Telecommunications networks globally are thickest within Europe and between north America, Japan and Europe, that is, along the most important trade routes. But they are as conspicuous within the confines of the global cities, on the level of the area about the size of a 'local loop' telephone exchange. Sometimes this thickening of circuit and switching capacity of networks is in particular locations within these cities. New York, perhaps the most 'wired' city in the world, contains the world's largest urban teleport, providing bulk access to micro-wave, satellite and fibre-optic transmission channels. This provides circuitry to a set of effectively strategic 'smart buildings' with the latest inter- and intra-office telecommunications facilities, from express courier pick-up boxes to satellite dishes (Abler 1991: 33). Smart buildings such as the Empire State Building and the World Trade Center serve as nodes for the New York Teleport's network. The entire New York agglomeration has been a focus for investment in fibre-optic cable, of which there are more than a half dozen systems (Daniels 1991: 164; Mulgan 1991: 65).

It should be noted that this sort of localization is different from that spoken of by Piore and Sabel (1984). It is a localization, not in the traditional and pre-modern utopia of the Emilia-Romagna, but in the much more cosmopolitan and international networks of global cities. In terms of the cutting edge of contemporary capitalism, this disintegration is proceeding in the advanced services of the major cities and the high tech feeders of these cities on the periphery of these same agglomerations. Thus it is not that disorganized capitalism pits markets versus hierarchies, but that it signals, at least in the medium term, the victory of *both* markets and hierarchies over other, state, corporatist and associational, forms of governance which were much more prominent in organized capitalism.

This may also help illuminate a key debate among economic geographers. In the late 1970s and early 1980s analysts associated with the notion of 'restructuring' such as Massey argued that firms were undergoing a process of spatial dispersion of their various production functions, such as research and development; skilled manual work; office work; unskilled assembly and the like in various mostly national (but also international) locations (summarized in 1984). In our earlier arguments for spatial dispersion the analyses were very much in line with Massey and such restructuring theorists (Lash and Urry 1987: chs 4 and 5; and see Bagguley et al 1990, for a thoroughgoing examination of this 'restructuring' research programme).

More recently, however, it has been argued by Scott and by Storper and Christopherson that there are agglomerational concentrations in emergent sectors in vertically disintegrated districts (Scott 1988b; Storper and Christopherson 1987). Involved here has been a two-step process in the change of production systems, which transforms the classic Fordism of the vertically integrated and spatially concentrated plant such as Ford's River Rouge complex. The first step was the spatial dispersion of the still vertically integrated firm along the lines of the 'restructuring' thesis. The second was that the firms themselves disintegrated vertically and then reconcentrated spatially in the market-rich networks of certain urban agglomerations (Storper and Harrison 1990).

The contradiction here, however, is only in the theories. In the real world both processes occurred simultaneously (Mulgan 1991; Garnham 1990; Sassen 1991; Sklair 1990; King 1990). The spatial dispersion of the vertically (and functionally) integrated firm, most significantly on a global scale, occurred at the same time as the growth of vertically disintegrated economic districts in the major agglomerations. The former process causes the latter. The very spatial dispersion of these transnationals, along with their qualitatively larger post-industrial component, gives rise to a massive need for telecommunications and advanced service inputs (see Castells 1989). The gap came to be filled by vertically disintegrated firms in the advanced producer and some consumer services.

Moreover, the computer and telecommunications equipment companies on the peripheries of these agglomerations integrally link together this cluster of disintegrated manufacturing firms, advanced services and head offices. Such telecommunication companies are huge. For instance, in 1985 BT (British Telecom) had 245,000 employees, sales of £6.9bn and assets of £9.2bn. It was fifth on the Times 500 Index in capital employed and sixth in profits. Its investment programme was £1.7bn per year. Its three main feeders in the telecommunications equipment industry at that point – GEC, Plessey and STC – each had sales between £2.1 and £2.5bn

(Garnham 1990: 136). Moreover, the frontiers dividing the telecommunications and computer industries are quickly breaking down. Indeed one
reason for the decision to deregulate telecommunications in the USA was
so that AT&T, through its equipment subsidiary Western Electric, would
be able to compete with computer giant IBM on world markets (Garnham
1990: 151). Further the culture, or mass communications, industries are
becoming increasingly less distinct from telecommunications – with the
digitalization of international news networks, of television (now broadcast
through analogue electronic signals) and its possible transmission through
fibre optic cable. Thus, although images, printed words and voice are input
and output, what comes in between in a future Integrated Services Digital
Network is a 'single intermingled bit-stream' (Garnham 1990: 137). The
airlines and aerospace, whose military research has led to so many of these
innovations and much tourism and leisure, complete the profile of this
information-soaked and service-rich, communications-laden core of the
post-organized capitalist economic order.

CORE AND PERIPHERY

This interlocking set of processes entails a transformed stratification of
core and periphery, one that differs both from the classical paradigm of
bourgeoisie and proletariat, and also from the world systems theory of the
stratification of nations. In our account the core comprises the heavily
networked more or less global cities, as a 'wired village of non-contiguous
communities'. And the periphery consists of isolated areas in the same
countries, in the former eastern Europe or in the Third World. In terms of
time-space convergence, the disparity between core and periphery in a
restructured world order is, we think, likely to grow greater.
    Moreover, globalization, where its tentacles do reach, should not be
understood as any sort of symmetrical process. Stratification into powerful
and relatively powerless is partly decided by who is doing the transmitting
and who is doing the receiving of information. Information is usually
transmitted from those places in which the cobwebs of communication
media are thickest. Even between advanced countries there are enormous
differences on this count. For example, as late as 1983 the USA constituted
38 per cent of the world's total telephone stock. The US postal service
delivered 320 million pieces per day, about four times as much mail per day
per individual as in western Europe (Janelle 1991: 58).
    Likewise, in 1981 44 per cent of all books translated were from the
English. In that year some 18,000 books were translated from English into
other languages, and only about 1,200 books were translated into English
(Janelle 1991: 57–8). In terms of mail, phone calls, faxes, television
programmes, radio shows and movies the advanced Western countries,
and overwhelmingly the two Anglo-Saxon cultural giants (in influence,
though surely not in value), transmit disproportionately more than they

receive. This is most stunningly evidenced in the international press agencies, in which only four truly world-wide companies are operative – AP and UPI in the USA, Reuters in Britain and Agence-France-Presse (AFP). These agencies are large organizations, AFP comprising 171 full-time journalists and 1,200 stringers in 167 countries and territories. AFP is made use of by 12,000 newspapers and 69 national news agencies. It sends 3 million words per day by cable, radio and satellite. Information is collected world-wide by the agency journalists and channelled into Paris, where it is sorted, rewritten and translated into other languages before retransmission throughout the world (Janelle 1991: 60). In all organizations, institutions and fields, such as the firm, the university, the family and the 'field' of social scientists, more information transmission stems from those with power located near the core while those at the periphery tend to be on the reception end.

Habermas has built a corpus of social theory which in large part understands power to be a matter of the acceptance or rejection of transmitted communications in the form of speech acts (1981). Habermas' focus is on cognitive and moral utterances to which the potentially subordinate either assent or dissent. But many of the global transmissions analysed above are statements neither of fact nor of values, neither descriptive nor prescriptive utterances, but they are rather utterances which have more of a 'poetic' function (Habermas 1987; Jakobsen 1960). They do not exercise power immediately through the acceptance of such speech acts by receivers. Narratives and music in popular culture typically operate through such a poetic function. *Dallas*, *Dynasty*, American movies and Anglo-American pop music achieve their effect, not so much through the acceptance of utterances, but from communications constituting the very media within which one assents or rejects. That is, information communicated from the core as poetic function affects not so much what those on the periphery will classify, but their very classificatory categories themselves. This poetic discourse from popular culture affects the self much as 'muzak' does. That is, it is there, it is pervasive, but it is not the object of judgment – one does not assent to it or reject it.

This poetic discourse is perhaps sinister by comparison with cognitive or moral discourse. In both of the latter people have the right to reject statements. The former however affects us on a bodily level, without us having that right of acceptance or rejection. Poetic discourse is constitutive of the rituals through which we operate. It creates the very least mediated universals through which people from now many nations communicate. Globalized popular culture, functioning as poetic discourse, thus becomes everybody's 'elementary forms of religious life'. It imparts form to an unreflected, relatively immediate and internationalized habitus.

Moreover, not only are networked flows of communications highly stratified, so too are the equally networked flows of subjects. The professional-managerial classes of the advanced societies are the most footloose. They circulate at greater distances back and forth on holiday and internationally at work. Here they perform the sort of advanced services which can be separated from the means of service production, such as consulting, finalizing a merger, checking out a recently acquired foreign subsidiary, giving papers at international conferences and so on (experiencing David Lodge's 'small worlds': 1983). Thus for this class social life is intrinsically partially 'touristic' (see Urry 1990c). Moreover as 'gentrifiers' in urban centres they consume tourist-like services while more or less at 'home'. The intermediate classes of skilled manual workers and more routine white collar work (the middle third of the 'two-thirds society') have been tourists largely on fixed holidays in the summer. So they circulate back and forth once per year, in the case of Britons to the Mediterranean, or increasingly to Miami. The new post-organized capitalist, largely immigrant, underclass do not circulate but move. And they tend, with the occasional trip back to country of origin, to stay. They come to perform the low value-added services that the global city's new upper class consumes (Sassen 1988). The one-third of Third World immigrants (and now also 'second world' immigrants) 'shine the shoes', in the words of Noam Chomsky, of the two-thirds in the two-thirds society.

3
REFLEXIVE SUBJECTS

We have just outlined the changing economies of signs and space in the wake of organized capitalism. We have examined the accelerated and ever wider-ranging trajectories of objects (goods, capital, money, communications, commodities) as well as subjects (labour, immigrants, tourists) in the recent past. The scenario painted is exhilarating yet its implications are disturbing. They are that this acceleration, which simultaneously 'distanciates' social relationships as it 'compresses' time and space, is leading to an emptying out of both subjects and objects. This accelerated mobility causes objects to become disposable and to decline in significance, while social relationships are emptied of meaning.

In this dystopic scenario the Marxist left, Harvey and Jameson for example, and the 'semiotic left', such as Foucault and much French social theory, are very much in accord in their analysis of commodification. For those who took the 'linguistic turn', it is the growing tyranny of disciplinary practices; of 'logocentric', or 'phallocentric' signifying practices. Moreover, in this shared dystopic quasi-evolutionism, the politics of Marxism and deconstruction are joined by more conservative forces, who see this socio-cultural process of emptying out from the standpoint of a firm set of 'foundations' from the past, be they the Judaeo-Christian tradition (Daniel Bell), Classical Antiquity (Allan Bloom, Leo Strauss) or the family (Christopher Lasch).

In our view this spatialization and semioticization of contemporary political economies is less damaging in its implications than many of these writers suggest. This is because the implications for subjects, for the self, of these changes is not just one of emptying out and flattening. Instead these changes also encourage the development of 'reflexivity'. The modernization and postmodernization of contemporary political economies produce, not just a flattening, but a deepening of the self. Such a growing reflexivity of subjects that accompanies the end of organized capitalism opens up many positive possibilities for social relations – for intimate relations, for friendship, for work relations, for leisure and for consumption.

This chapter then is concerned with analysing such reflexivity. It is primarily theoretical (empirical treatment will be developed in later chapters). There have recently been two very influential and crucial treatments of this increased reflexivity in contemporary societies – Ulrich Beck and Anthony Giddens. This chapter will scrutinize and draw upon these two contributions. Our argument will be that both theorists miss an entire dimension of the reflexivity of the contemporary self in their particular concentration on the cognitive dimension of reflexivity. It is the aesthetic-expressive dimension of the modern self which they omit to analyse. Further, their notion of the self is not sufficiently 'embodied', the self is structured too much along the lines of the ego. Their idea of the subject is an entity that reflexively controls bodies rather than as something which itself is bodily. The alternative aesthetic and bodily notion of reflexivity of the contemporary self that we propose will then be developed, drawing importantly on the work of Marcel Mauss and Charles Taylor.

In each case – Beck, Giddens, ourselves – there is an homology between agency and structure. That is, to each of these three notions of reflexivity as agency there corresponds a vision of socio-cultural structure, in other words a vision of modernity. Corresponding to Beck's subjectivity is a notion of the modern as the Enlightenment project, of Elias, of Habermas. Correspondingly, the other side of Giddens' agency, grounded in his notion of 'ontological security', is an idea of the modern as juxtaposed to tradition, much in the paradigm of the classical sociological theory of Durkheim, Tönnies and Parsons. At the same time corresponding to our more aesthetically based reflexivity is the notion of the modern as a cosmopolitan spatial heterotopia, the modernity of Baudelaire, Simmel and Benjamin.

Incidentally, we would not suggest that the cognitive dimension of reflexivity is an insignificant aspect of social processes and social change today. Moreover, the idea of reflexivity in both its cognitive and aesthetic senses will feature throughout this book in our discussions of the changes in the structure of the firm, the labour process, industrial relations, the production of images, the nature of post-industrialism and tourism, time and globalization.

We will turn first to Beck's concept of the 'risk society'.

REFLEXIVE MODERNIZATION: THE RISK SOCIETY

Beck lays down a challenge to the doomsday scenarios of postmodern political economy by developing the concept of reflexive modernization. He argues that the solution to the negative consequences of late modernity is not the rejection of modernity but its radicalization. Late modernity not only brings commodification and the domination of techno-scientific instrumental rationality, but also opens up possibilities for individuals to reflect critically on these changes and their social conditions of existence, and hence potentially to change them.

Beck argues that we are in the midst of a transition from an industrial society to a 'risk society' (1992a, b). We are moving from a social situation in which political conflicts and cleavages were defined by a logic of the distribution of goods to one in which these cleavages are increasingly defined by the distribution of 'bads', that is, of hazards and risks. Societies constructed around the distribution of goods were national societies. The risk society by contrast knows no national boundaries, as for example the effects of Chernobyl spread over much of Europe (six years later the consequences are still being felt in parts of the Lake District in north west England). The risk society is the demise of the national society; it is the world of the Brazilian rain forests; the world in which the use of fire extinguishers in India, for example, affects the ozone layer for everyone else (Beck 1992a: 42).

The risk society is not a class society since the rich are also subjugated to ecological hazards. In practice however the poor are the worst affected, and the result is especially a sharper international cleavage between the Third World and the advanced societies. Third World countries often quite rationally decide that the remedy of prevailing economic misery is more important than the abstract issue of cosmic destruction. The consequences are that their populations will be hit hardest by environmental degradation, especially if they function as the world's 'dustbin'. The result for the advanced countries, besides ozone layer problems, may be a veritable exodus of 'eco-refugees' and 'climatic asylum seekers' into the wealthy North in future decades.

In place of the class-versus-class cleavage of industrial society, the risk society is more likely to pit sector against sector. Sectors may be 'risk winners' such as chemicals, biotechnology, the nuclear industry and many heavy industrial sectors. Or they may be 'risk losers', such as the food industry, tourism, fisheries, some of the retail trade and many services. Beck stresses that the risk society is also importantly an industrial society. It is the industrial sectors, often those stemming from the nineteenth and earlier twentieth centuries, which have created massive environmental hazards. Further, even if the majority of individuals in the advanced countries consume and produce 'semiotic' rather than industrial goods, nonetheless the absolute amount of goods that are industrially produced and consumed is greater than ever in the advanced and especially in the developing countries.

Beck's analyses are based on a three-stage periodization, of pre-industrial, industrial and risk societies. Each of these three types of society contains risks and hazards, but there are qualitative differences between the types of risk involved in each.

In pre-industrial societies, paradigmatically, risks were not 'man'-made. They were 'natural', such as from childbirth, famines, epidemics, crop-destroying weather. And if they were synthetic, such as casualties in war, they did not follow directly from techno-economic progress.

Modern industrial society, 'which brings uncertainty to every niche of existence', changes all this. Hazards and risks are no longer 'externalized' onto the gods or fate; that is, external agents can no longer be held accountable. There is instead a new modern social accountability for the consequences of hazards and risks. Beck notes that modernity 'finds its counter-principle in a social compact against industrially produced hazards and damages, stitched together out of public and private insurance agreements'; this social compact which simultaneously involves a 'consensus on progress' gives rise to a 'normative system of rules for social accountability, compensation and precaution' (1992a: 61–4; 1992b: 98–100). The insurance principle understands hazards to be 'systematically caused and statistically describable'. What this amounts to is a sort of 'security pact' which, through 'making the incalculable calculable', 'creates present security in the face of an open uncertain future' (1992a: 33–4; 1992b: 100–1).

Beck reserves the title 'risk society' for those societies in which, first, risks become the axial principle of social organization, and second, take on a very specific form, becoming incalculable, uncompensatable, unlimited and unaccountable. In contemporary risk societies this social compact, this security pact of an earlier modernity, is shattered. The present age of 'nuclear, chemical and genetic technology' is instead an 'uninsured society' with diminishing protection. The risk society brings down all of the 'four pillars' of industrial society's risk calculus.

The first, compensation, is impossible with global irreparable damage which cannot in principle be limited. The second, precautionary aftercare, is precluded by the impossibility of anticipatory monitoring of results. The third, limitation, is violated by the time-space dimensions of contemporary ecological catastrophes, events of wave upon wave without an end, affecting also future generations. The fourth, accountability, faces demise with the great increase of difficulty in enforcing the 'polluter pays' principle (Beck 1992a: 27–8; 1992b: 102–3). The consequence is a sharp erosion of industrial society's social compact, instantiated in the new dissensus on the value of progress, the crisis of today's welfare states and the new tendency to externalize risks again onto some sort of mythic *fortuna*.

What sort of theory of modernization is at issue here? Beck's chronology is of pre-industrial societies, industrial societies and more recently, risk societies. In the nineteenth and earlier twentieth centuries, industrial societies were undergoing a process of 'simple modernization', while in risk societies this modernization becomes 'reflexive'. For Beck, simple modernization is only partially modern. Simply modernized societies contain many feudal or estate-society (*ständisch*) characteristics. Like previous analysts such as Renner, Beck understands trade unions and associations of monopoly capitalists largely in a *ständisch* sense, and these bodies are to be displaced by modernization's process of individualization. Further, the classical nuclear family of industrial society is still importantly *ständisch*, itself to be transformed by the individualization process. Even in the risk society many *ständisch* residues exist, for example in the still important monopoly on scientific knowledge and power exercised by guilds of scientists, engineers and technicians.

If modernization in industrial society was simple, that in risk society is reflexive. More precisely, only part of risk society's modernization is reflexive. Indeed that modernization brought about by decision-making and institutions dominated by techno-scientific elites is not reflexive, but extends the worst excesses of the dark side of earlier simple modernization. On this count Beck differs with Giddens who understands even this sort of modernization as reflexive. For Beck only modernization brought about by the critique of these elites is reflexive. And full modernization is impossible without modernization becoming thoroughly reflexive.

The axial principle of the risk society is knowledge. Beck's account however differs from Bell's vision in seeing scientific–technical elites as being on the side of the villains, as 'risk winners'. The implications are the transformation of the political sphere. Beck speaks of an alliance between the scientists and capital. But if the latter were the hegemonic fraction of the ruling class in industrial society, it is the former who are so in the risk society (Beck 1991). The result is the transfer of political power from parliament, parties and legal institutions onto corporate bodies of scientists, operating, for example in Germany, through the Society of German Engineers and the Institute of Standards. The pervasiveness of their power is embodied in legislation, for example in the Atomic Energy Act, in which the problem of necessary precautions is defined as corresponding to 'the state of technology'. This sort of definition is decided in the 'Guidelines' of the German Reactor Safety Commission, an advisory body to the Minister of the Environment, and comprises representatives of the engineering societies (1992a; 1992b: 106–9).

Such powers for the interests of science may have been more acceptable in an earlier age in which a normal logic of theory and experimentation held force. But nuclear reactors and test-tube babies are only 'testable' after they have been built. Testing, in the risk society, has to occur *after* application; production must precede research. This anticipatory application of a scientific problem before it has been fully explored erases the 'boundary between laboratory and society' in the risk society, and this technological monopoly becomes a 'monopoly on concealed social change' (1992a: 156; 1992b: 108–9).

Where then will the forces of reflexivity come from according to Beck? In *Risk Society* he speaks largely in terms of structure and agency. On this view, with modernization, agents become ever freer from structural determination and are able in effect to reflect upon and change structures. Part of this is bound up with the process of individualization which is so central to the book. And part is as a reaction to the structural-functionalism of Luhmann. More recently, as Beck has entered into more practical, political and policy-oriented engagements, he has come to view reflexivity as a property of institutions (1991, 1992b). What is needed, he claims, is a new set of political institutions, in a political sphere now deprived of its own foundations in the rationality of law, democracy and assumptions of progress; and in a public sphere in which there has been a shift to the quasi-governmental power of research laboratories, chemical factories, courts and editorial offices. Most important in this is the struggle for the symbolic power to define what risk is. What is needed is an American Constitution-like division of powers specifically tailored to the present age. Thus the political constitution of risk society would institutionalize redistributed 'boundaries of scientific proof'. Bodies whose membership cuts across the professions in a true interdisciplinarity would provide a forum for the proposal of systematic alternatives, for dissenting voices and dissenting experts.

This could take the form of a sort of ecological 'upper house', partly structured on corporatist lines, that would constitute a 'public science', a 'second centre for the discursive checking' of scientific results (1991: 51; 1992b: 119). Its composition would be of a set of smaller bodies consisting of science and business, science and consumer representatives, technology and law, and the like. Key here in this recasting of accountability is the division between the producers and evaluators of hazards.

Although Beck does ascribe importance to the new social movements and to enlightened middle-class opinion of the public sphere, pivotal as agents of reflexivity in the risk society are the less well-educated petty bourgeoisie and workers of everyday life. Crucial is 'the fact that everyone between the Alpine cottages and the North Sea mudflats now understands and speaks the language of the nuclear critics' (1992b: 115). A major influence are the institutions of the mass media which create a symbolic language for popular opinion through their 'images in the news of skeletal trees or dying seals' (1992b: 119). Paradoxically, the media do this in spite of themselves through following their own 'postmodern' interests of spectacularization. That is, the unanticipated consequence of the 'spectacle' created by the media is not to trivialize, but to create for public opinion a matrix of affect-laden symbols underpinning the new reflexivity. The paradoxical effect of these postmodern 'dead symbols' is to provide a live and critical domain more in keeping with the symbolic exchange of Mauss' gift society than with the flattened present.

For Beck, then, reflexive modernization comes paradigmatically with the questioning of science through knowledge, or the self-reflection of knowledge on knowledge. The sheer overwhelming nature of hazards in the risk society encourages this. The solution he proposes is thus not a retreat into the mythification of the powers of these hazards, but a reflexive radicalization of modernity. More specifically, reflexivity paradigmatically arises in attempting rationally to deal with contemporary risks – risks that are incalculable, unaccountable, uncompensatable and unlimited.

Much of the rest of *Risk Society* is devoted to the analysis of how the decline of three particular structures, class society, the classic nuclear family and mass industrial production, leads to a process of individual-ization (1992a: 87–90). This process forces men and women to take decisions over their lives that they previously did not have to take, whether or not to have children, to separate or divorce, how to sort out families in circumstances of second marriages, whether ever to marry at all, whether to prefer the same sex and so on (1992a: 105–24). Also people are obliged to take control over their more flexible work lives (1992a: 146–7). This structurally necessitated decision-taking, being constrained to reflect upon one's social conditions of existence, is the other major dimension of the risk society.

Beck's is a benchmark contribution to European sociology, which forces us to re-think many conventional debates. And yet the cognitive notion of reflexivity that he proposes is bound up with an astonishingly orthodox notion of modernity and modernization. What Beck is essentially analysing is the modern project of the Enlightenment. As in the Enlightenment there is a metanarrative of progress that, despite the three stages, is virtually evolutionist, involving a process of 'detraditionalization'. Further, change for him is not so much structural but occurs through the critique of agency, again like Habermas and the Enlightenment and unlike both Marxist and sociological structural models of modernization. And finally, his notion of critique is not aesthetic or hermeneutic but rational and cognitive. As with the Enlightenment and Habermas, cognitive critique is a means towards moral and political change. The very notion of *Lernprozess*, seemingly ubiquitous in German social science and in enlightened public life confirms this (1992a: 177–88). Beck, an enthusiast of Rilke and Gottfried Benn and an essayist and prose stylist himself of some considerable distinction, quite well embodies aesthetic reflexivity as a source of the modern self. But paradoxically his theory of reflexive modernization almost wholly neglects this aesthetic dimension. And yet in the increasing reflexivity about the environment that characterizes the risk society, people's attitudes and sensibilities are aesthetically and expressively formed, as the history of English romanticism shows (see Bate 1991 on Wordsworth's ecologism, as well as Urry 1992).

GIDDENS: SELF-REFLEXIVITY IN MODERNITY

The convergences between Beck's theory and the recent work of Giddens are extraordinary. Both break from accepted notions of modernism and postmodernism; they are eminently sociological in their analyses of modernity; they see modernity in terms of a central and increasing place for reflexivity; they are very concerned with the dialectic of 'structure and agency'; they have extensive concern with issues of what Giddens calls 'extensionality', or globalization, and with 'intensionality', or the private sphere, sexuality and love relationships; they identify a central place for the role of risk in contemporary society; and, crucially for us, they leave very little space for the aesthetic, for the bodily, for difference and heterogeneity in their ideas of reflexivity and modernity.

But Beck and Giddens are also very different sorts of sociologists. Beck is partly an essayist and partly a middle-range sociologist of institutions, who has accumulated expertise in the study of work relations and the family. His later inquiries into the sociology of science and the environment are what led to his theory of reflexive modernization which he subsequently read back into his analyses of other institutions and hence general social change. Giddens is the consummate general social theorist. Thus his analyses pursue, in a much greater conceptual depth than Beck, the issues that they share in common. Yet despite Giddens' conceptual acumen, Beck's framework may be of more relevance to the analysis of social change. Whereas Beck's reflexivity leads mainly to the critical change of social structures, Giddens' notion mainly functions to reproduce structures. And whereas Beck's agent reflects on norms and structures of the social, Giddens' agency is increasingly *self*-reflexive, that is, not on the social, but in the organization of his or her personal biographical narrative.

There are four key features of Giddens' generic definition of reflexivity. First, the focus is on the monitoring of the conduct of the self rather than on the nature of the social, although knowledge of social conventions is seen as assisting this monitoring. Second, a very important role in this monitoring is played by knowledge or knowledgeability in the sense that in 'all human activity' in 'all societies' agents can provide 'discursive interpretations' for their behaviour' (Giddens 1991a: 35). Third, Giddens' notion is very much 'strategic', a notion he shares with Goffman, ethnomethodology and Bourdieu, and which stands in strong contrast to Beck and Habermas. And fourth, Giddens uses the term 'discursive interpretation' rather than 'discursive explanation'. This signals his understanding of reflexivity as 'hermeneutic'. Hermeneutics by contrast with positivism is associated with an aesthetic, intuitive tradition in sociology with strong roots in romanticism. However, interestingly, this is not found in Giddens, whose notion of the self is grounded in a very strong positivistic ego psychology.

Giddens' modern and mediated reflexivity takes place by what he calls 'disembedding mechanisms' which bring about 'time-space distanciation'. They are the means by which social relations are disembedded or 'lifted out' from the immediacy of the traditional *Gemeinschaft* and 'rearticulated across indefinite tracts of time-space' (1991a: 18; and see Giddens 1990: 21–9). Disembedding mechanisms are mediated or 'abstract systems'. There are two types of these: symbolic tokens such as money; and 'expert systems' which 'bracket time and space' 'through deployment of modes of technical knowledge' and of social knowledge (1991a: 18; and see chapter 9 below for more detail). Such 'expert systems' incorporating technical knowledge include airplanes, nuclear energy, food, the buildings we live in and so on. If in traditional societies 'trust relations' were between people, in modernity a considerable portion of trust is disembedded and placed in abstract systems, which include forms of social knowledge as well as the media.

In *The Consequences of Modernity* social change is seen as radically 'discontinuist' with two phases, tradition and modernity (1990). In *Modernity and Self-Identity* there is a third phase, of 'high' or 'late' modernity (1991a). On this view, in earlier modernity expert systems played very much the role of 'providential reason', while in high modernity this sort of Enlightenment project has been radically challenged by the 'systematic questioning and doubt' of such expert systems. Hence reflexivity becomes 'chronic revision in the light of new information or knowledge' which itself undermines the certainty of knowledge (1991a: 20).

Giddens also suggests that such institutions are themselves reflexive. For example, he sees the modern state in terms of 'reflexively monitored systems'. Indeed modern organizations are to be understood, not primarily as bureaucracies but in terms of the 'concentrated reflexive monitoring they both permit and entail' (1991a: 16). Giddens is thus unlike Weber in this view of the bright side of institutional rationalization. He is effectively a sort of anti-Foucault in his assessment of the enabling side of discourses such as social science and versions of psychotherapy.

Giddens agrees with Beck's notion of a risk society. He is sceptical of the effectiveness of 'providential reason' because of our experience of the 'erratic and unintended consequences of knowledge infused abstract systems . . . the chronic flow of knowledge into . . . environments . . . creates uncertainties [which] frequently confound the expectations which that knowledge informs' (1991a: 29). For both Beck and Giddens these unintended consequences are the hazards or risks of late modernity's risk society. But Giddens extends the notion of risk to cover wider areas of social life, at work, in one's private life, the chronic 'consideration of counterfactual possibilities . . . in risk assessment'. This for him could be so pronounced that our very understanding of the future is transformed, so that it is no longer an 'expectation of events to come', but is instead understood as actuaries do in their calculation of risks for the purposes of insurance. Thus high modernity's 'combination of specialized expertise and eccentric consequences' leads to counterfactual thought and the centrality of risk. The life course becomes a passage no longer governed by tradition, but a set of passages circumscribed by risks and opportunities (1991a: 79). The use of expert systems themselves such as psychotherapy is again a matter of risks and opportunities. In fact on this view simple social reproduction in high modernity would only be possible under the condition that agents take risks.

There is a conservative bias towards social reproduction, built into this notion of reflexivity. This is grounded in the concept of 'ontological security' which for Giddens is based in a 'sense of continuity and order in events' (1991a: 243). The ontologically secure individual is anchored in the discipline of predictable routine: 'The discipline of routine helps constitute a "formed framework" for existence by cultivating a sense of "being", and its separation from "non-being", which is elemental to ontological security' (1991a: 39).

Ontological security operates for Giddens on three levels: the unconscious, as in the work of existential psychoanalysis; practical consciousness, where the framework of rules or 'social conventions' is accessible to the agent but s/he does not express them verbally or formulate them explicitly; and discursive consciousness where, often via the intermediation of time-space distanciated abstract systems, there is explicit and verbal formulation of these rules. In each case, whether in unconscious and personal relations, whether in practical consciousness, whether in tradition or modernity, ontological security is achieved through these formed frameworks of rules doing a certain work of 'bracketing'. What bracketing does is to create order out of chaos for the individual, to create predictable routine out of anarchistic contingency. The unconscious is fundamental to this. Giddens' view here is grounded in existential psychology, in the ego-psychology of Erikson and more recently in Winnicott's object-relations theory (see Giddens 1991a). Ontological security is grounded in 'basic trust' relations grounded in an 'unconscious sociality' between infant and caretaker. Key here is the transition of the infant from original feelings of omnipotence to its recognition of the other. This is structured by the nurturance of infant by the caretaker and of the initial modes of absence of the caretaker. The transition from omnipotence to the recognition of the other opens up a 'potential space' or field, whose poles at the outset are infant and caretaker as other. If the nurturance and separation relations are sufficiently substantial as well as consistent and ordered, then this field or potential space will itself constitute a relatively stable framework and basis for ontological security (Giddens 1991a: 41; and 1990: 92–9). This potential space, no matter how stable, cannot be constructed other than on the basis of anxiety. Anxiety is the obverse side of ontological security. Anxiety is what is felt when ontological security is shaken. But anxiety, stimulated by the caretaker's absence, is 'a time-space relation' creating this arena for the development of basic trust. This potential space, this arena, this field, which is constituted through Winnicott's 'basic security system', also provides the initial impetus to processes of identification as well as to processes of cognitive learning whereby 'characteristics of the object-world are grasped' (Giddens 1991a: 45–6).

'Practical consciousness' serves as an emotional and cognitive anchor, the 'natural attitude'. That is, the day-to-day routines described in the micro-sociology of ethnomethodology are not merely cognitive but are invested with emotional significance. That is, in order to 'go on' practical consciousness must be involved in constant monitoring of conduct (1991a: 39). Further, the failure of practical consciousness creates unacceptable levels of anxiety, as demonstrated in Garfinkel's social experiments. On this account the routine of day-to-day activity creates a formed framework, a 'protective cocoon' through the bracketing of 'events which could threaten the bodily or psychological integrity of the agent' (Giddens 1991a: 40). When this cocoon is stripped away, as in Garfinkel's experiments, the result is just this sort of anxiety.

This notion of ontological security is extended even to modernity, in which trust is no longer vested in the caretaker, nor in the significant others of pre-modern societies, but largely in abstract systems. In modernity it is these abstract systems which do the work of bracketing. Thus abstract systems such as money, as credit, 'brackets'; it also 'brackets' space, by enabling relations across distances. And expert systems 'bracket' time and space and the knowledge of individuals through the deployment of technical knowledge. And trust in modernity is in these abstract systems which create islands of certainty – and actually reduce hazards – in a world peopled by chaos, risks and hazards. In this way abstract systems function in the reproduction of modern societies.

Giddens' notion of anxiety, as with Durkheim's of anomie, differs from fear (as in Hobbes) in that fear has a clear object, while anomie and anxiety refer to rather more undifferentiated feelings. And while anomie is a property of the social structure, anxiety is a property of individuals. Further, anxiety stands in an important relation to the unconscious. Anxiety is on the one hand unconsciously organized, and on the other, anxiety creates repression which gives decisive shape to the structuring of the unconscious. Moreover, undifferentiated, unconscious anxiety can be attached to all sorts of substitute objects or situations (Giddens 1991a: 44).

However, there is a significant departure from this reproductionist position in *Modernity and Self-Identity* (1991a). In this Giddens systematically distinguishes between (simple) modernity and high modernity. Knowledge and institutions are on this view much less foundational in high modernity, so the possibility of critique is opened up. But at the same time in high modernity, reflexivity transfers from monitoring the social to monitoring the self. It is a theme consistent with what many have seen as the increased individualization of high modernity.

In high modernity the self becomes for Giddens a 'reflexive project'. This involves an enhanced *temporal* element. Modernity's reflexive project 'consists in the sustaining of coherent, yet continuously revised, biographical narratives, . . . in the context of multiple choice as filtered through abstract systems' (1991a: 6). The 'objective time' of earlier modernity is superseded in high modernity by a set of personalized, subjective temporalities in these self-created narratives (1991a: 72; and see chapter 9 below on postmodern time).

This is an emptied out sense of time. Thus self-help therapies are understood as 'methodologies of life-planning', or in terms of 'life calendars' (1991a: ch 6). Thus the reflexive project of the self passes via the mediation of 'abstract systems that penetrate day-to-day life and offer multiple choices rather than fixed guidelines for action' (1991a: 84). The future is understood 'actuarially' instead of in terms of events. Giddens' high modernity rips the foundations out from abstract objective time and internalizes them reflexively as the subjective time of life narratives. Giddens' deracinated reflexivity gives us a temporality and spatiality which is other than classical modernism and of a piece with Featherstone's (1991) 'calculating hedonism' in leisure time. But even this is a positivist time, based heavily in his cognitive notion of reflexivity. Although this notion of time has considerable empirical purchase, there is neglect of the hermeneutic or aesthetic dimension, which itself we would argue partly structures time in late modernity (see chapter 9 below).

If modernity reflects the advanced differentiation of social institutions and relationships, then Giddens' high modernity exemplifies their hyper-differentiation into largely 'internally-referential' systems. This hyper-differentiation is exemplified in the 'pure relationship'. The pure relation-ship is pure in Luhmann's (1986) sense that it becomes an autopoetic system. It becomes autonomous from structures of traditional societies and an earlier modernity. 'External anchors' of either traditional convention or early modern institutions disappear as stabilizers of the relationship. The relationship is connected to no external advantages for the partners, and the partners only draw benefit (through a deepening of intimacy foreign to pre- and early modern relations) from the relationship itself. Trust and commitment are no longer 'geared to established positions' either of families or of modern institutions, but are only geared to the partner and to the relationship itself which is so to speak treated like an autopoetic system (Giddens 1991a: 90, 96). Like the high modern narrative project of the self, the pure relationship is entered into reflexively out of choice and then 'reflexively organized, in an open fashion, and on a continuous basis' (1991a: 91). This hyperdifferentiated pure relationship is a self-referential system. Like the project of the self it involves a 'sequestration of experience which involves few contacts with events linking to 'broad issues of morality and finitude' (1991a: 8). Thus in this overall positive treatment of the contours of high modernity, morality, as with aesthetics, gets short shrift.

Giddens is thus associated with a certain strand of positivism, namely that associated with ego-psychologists such as Erikson. It is also shown in his particular use of object-relations theory. Whereas for example Deleuze and French feminists influenced by Melanie Klein use object-relations to show the plurality and play of an heterogeneous unconscious in face of the homogenizing forces of the ego and 'the Oedipus', Giddens uses them to explore ontological security and the formation of the ego. In his under-standing of the self in terms of the mastery of modernist abstract systems, Giddens considers the self as ego rather than, say, as the Lacanian complex combination of ego and unconscious. He is thus opposed not only to Foucault but also to French and to Anglo-American feminist psychoanalytically-oriented social theory. What they positively value as the heterogeneous play of an unconscious structured by 'complexity' and 'difference', he sees as a threat to ontological security. Whereas French theory and Anglo-American feminism see the ego as a homogenizing and controlling apparatus structured by the 'law of the father', Giddens' ego is the hero of the battle against ontological security and the structuring principle of the reflexive biographical narratives of the high modern self.

Giddens' attraction to ego theory can also be seen in his discussions of cognition and memory. He views the unconscious as being based on memory. And memory develops from perception. Taking his cue from the cognitive psychology and the psychology of perception of the 1960s and 1970s, he argues that perception takes place via universals. It is organized via 'anticipatory schemata'. Such schemata are 'neurologically based formats whereby the temporality of experience is continually processed' (1984: 46–7). Classifications of a higher level of abstraction – which might seem to the reader of Durkheim and Mauss or Kant to be of a different order and cognitive – are primarily a more complex sort of perception. That is, the 'selectivity' of these schemata is 'relatively gross' for the young child, while later children learn the art of coping conceptually with objects which have gone out of sight. Thus much more developed schemata enable 'naming' or 'identifying'. This entails typifying the properties of something and 'relating it to a class of comparable objects differentiating it from other classes' (1984: 47). But as he does this the specificity of the aesthetic, the *dis*continuity of the transition from the aesthetic to the cognitive, from 'nature' to 'culture', is lost.

Giddens' 'ontological security' is also structured though these modes of recall or memory, whether unconscious or part of practical or discursive consciousness, which form in order to protect such ontological security. Unconscious memory as well as the anticipatory schemata, or neurological formats, on which it is based form a motivation to ontological security of the infant. That is, 'the earliest interaction between infant and mother is layered into the development of the "unconscious" '. As the body of the infant 'becomes an instrument of acting in the world', the mother, noted Giddens, quoting Erik Erikson, must ' "become an inner certainty as well as an outer predictability" '. Predictability, continuity, sameness, provide ' "a rudimentary sense of ego identity which depends . . . on the recognition that there is an inner population of remembered and anticipated sensations and images which are firmly correlated with the outer population of familiar and predictable things and people" ' (1984: 53).

It is indeed clear that memory is an important dimension of the unconscious. Notions of the 'return of the repressed' or any sort of temporality would be impossible to ascribe to the unconscious without the operation of memory. A memory-encrusted unconscious has also been analysed by many, including Proust and Deleuze. The problem is that whereas Deleuze's unconscious is nomadic and Proust's is narrative and aesthetic, Giddens' is positivist, cast in a learning model, and resembles the ego. Whereas surrealism and surrealist-influenced French theorists such as Foucault, Lyotard, Derrida and Lacan want the ego – and especially the creative ego – to recast itself rather along the lines of the unconscious, Giddens has recast the id along the lines of the ego.

The positivistic ego psychology fuelling Giddens' analyses of high modernity is exemplified in his treatment of the 'body' which he sees as an entity to be monitored by the self rather than as a constitutive part of what is doing the monitoring. It is also exemplified in his treatments of 'shame' and 'guilt', in which the former emotion is thought to be progressively replacing the latter with the move towards high modernity. Whereas traditional and early modern self-identity was bound up with the guilt of Christian and Victorian values, high modernity is very much tied up with shame. Motivations of action in this are distinguished both from reasons for action and from needs, in that motives – which are tied up with our 'basic security system' – imply a cognitive anticipation of a state of affairs to be realized. When this does not happen the result is shame. There is an important temporal element to shame in the sense that it threatens the narrative integrity of modern self-identity. It arises in the temporal context of a relationship between same and other, when the same notices the other's response to the same's failure to realize a given state of affairs. The same then notices that the other has registered that his/her previous views of the same were false. The result is not only a shaking of ontological security but also mistrust (1991a: 65–6).

There is then a rather one-sided ego psychology in Giddens' work, which leaves only a small place for the work of the superego and morality or for the aesthetic play of the unconscious of the French post-structuralists. Giddens pays little attention to either the Enlightenment-cognitivist or Romantic-aesthetic moral sources of the self. This is clear in that whereas Charles Taylor's idea of reflexivity involves a drawing on sources of the self, Giddens' involves an almost cybernetic-like 'monitoring' of conduct. The notion that there are sources of the self involves ideas of metaphor and of depth, and these are the opposite of reflexivity via monitoring.

The remaining sections of this chapter attempt to develop the aesthetic and expressive sources of the self, beginning with some considerations of the Maussian tradition.

BODIES AND CLASSIFICATIONS

In his recent work, Giddens has come to speak more about the role of the body. In *Modernity and Self-Identity* he writes specifically about the appearance or self-presentation of the body (1991a). He notes that, not only in modernity but also in tradition, the body presents itself in an individuated manner. The difference is that while in tradition this is a matter of social identity, in modernity it becomes more a matter of *personal* identity. In high modernity the cultivation of bodily regimes becomes a means of reflexively influencing the project of the self. Thus anorexia nervosa is a quintessentially high modern phenomenon. Unlike anorexia mirabilis of traditional social formations, in which fasting is bound up with social symbolism and may be associated with collective guilt, anorexia nervosa is personal and connected with the emotion of shame. Modern anorexia is, Giddens observes, 'a pathology of reflexive self-control' (1991a: 105). This is a useful insight. The point in the present context however is that in tradition and modernity Giddens' bodies are things to be monitored by practical consciousness constructed on the model of the ego. Giddens' body thus is 'monitored', and such monitoring is a significant component of self-reflexivity. He writes: '[T]o learn to become a competent agent – able to join with others on an equal basis in the production and reproduction of social relations – is to be able to exert a continuous and successful monitoring of face and body' (1991a: 56). It is incidentally surprising that Giddens does not go on to analyse the monitoring 'of the body' involved in sports and leisure clubs with their individually tailored fitness programmes, the monitoring involved in 'healthy eating' and 'weight watching', or the narcissistic practices of sun-bathing and the 50 or so different levels of sun-tan lotion! The cognitivist bias in Giddens' and Beck's idea of reflexivity would tend then to inform a subject-object dualism, in which the body is an object to be monitored by the ego or subject. For thinkers such as Mauss and Bourdieu, however, the body (or habitus) is neither subject nor object and reflexivity becomes hermeneutic and aesthetic.

We will mainly deal here with Mauss (see 1979a, b, as well as Durkheim and Mauss 1970). Mauss's concept of the body must be distinguished from other key concepts, in particular 'the habitus', 'practical reason', 'rites' and the 'physio-chemical'. The technical nature of the body is a sort of subset of Mauss' 'longstanding views' on the 'social nature of the habitus'. Like the social nature of the habitus the *technical* nature of the body is constituted through 'education', either public or informal, or through 'imitation'. In the latter, 'symbolic capital' plays an important role in that 'what takes place is prestigious imitation' (1979a: 99, 101). The body like the habitus for Mauss is not only socially constituted through education, but it is also 'assembled by and for social *authority*' (1979a: 120, emphasis added). The social reproduces itself and its relations of power through the education of the habitus in general and bodies in particular.

For Mauss the 'habitus' is the key component of the self or subjectivity. The habitus is a complex combination of practical reason and tradition. Mauss takes pains to dissociate the habitus from 'pure reason'. The habitus is he says neither the 'acquired ability' nor the 'faculty', nor the 'soul and its repetitive faculties' (1979a: 101). The habitus involves instead 'the techniques and work of collective and individual practical reason' (1979a: 104).

Mauss distinguishes between two types of traditional actions, 'rites' and 'techniques'. Rites include 'magic, religious and symbolic actions'. Techniques are less highly *mediated* than other 'effective traditional' 'modes of action', such as religion, symbolic or juridical action, life in common and moral action. They are more immediate in that their transmission is likely to be oral and not discursively formulated (1979a: 104). Techniques of the body, what might be called 'bodily-technical action', are also less highly mediated than rites in being very much on the 'nature' end of the nature-culture continuum. They are felt by the actor as 'actions of a mechanical, physical or physio-chemical order' (1979a: 104). They are 'physio-psycho-sociological assemblages of series of actions' (1979a: 120). Bodily-technical action is also less highly mediated (more natural and less cultural) than other sorts of technical action. Thus other forms of technical action such as production in a modern factory would be through the means of highly mediated and cultural machinery. Bodily techniques by contrast, rather like the Platonic techniques of music and of dance, do not necessarily presume an instrument. The 'body' instead 'is man's first and most natural, instrument' (1979a: 104).

But the very minimal mediation of body techniques, about as close as the social can get to the natural, is combined with the more 'cultural' component of practical reason. Mauss' techniques comprise especially the heightened goal-orientedness of Kantian practical reason. Bodily technical action is 'pursued' with a 'physio-chemical' 'end in mind'. The body is 'man's first and most natural technical object, and at the same time technical means' (1979a: 104). And body techniques are 'the constant adaptation to a physical, mechanical or technical aim (for example, when we drink) pursued in a series of assembled actions' (1979a: 104–5). Similarly on the lines of practical reason, body techniques are 'selected on the basis of determinate efficiency', 'allowing' a 'response of coordinated movements setting off in the direction of a chosen goal' (1979a: 121–2).

The main point here is that for Mauss the body is a more integral part of the self than it is in Anglo-American action theory. For Giddens, practical consciousness, the pivotal component of the self, monitors the body. For Mauss, the body techniques do comprise composure and a certain control of the unconscious by the conscious mind, but here both the conscious and the unconscious mind make up the body. Giddens' practical consciousness monitors the body. Mauss' body techniques, on the contrary, involve very important dimensions of practical reason. Giddens' self is something which masters the body, while the Maussian self involves the body. In other words, the body in Giddens is an important object, but not the subject, of reflexivity. In Mauss the body takes on important dimensions of such subjectivity. In more recent French theory the body is the primary, and sometimes exclusive, agent of reflexivity.

Overall this chapter is devoted to the consideration of the reflexivity of subjects, and in particular to changes in the latter in the process of modernization and postmodernization. Our argument is that the concept of reflexivity enables us to open up another dimension in post-organized capitalist order which runs parallel to hypercommodification, the 'flattening' effects of the society of the spectacle, the disposability of cultural objects in consumer capitalism and the like. This presumes a three-fold analysis of reflexivity – its subject, its object and its means. The subject of reflexivity in Beck is a moral-cognitive ego or 'I', while in Giddens it is a strategic-cognitive ego. French theorists such as Mauss and Bourdieu displace the subject of reflexivity in the direction of the body. The object of reflexivity for Beck is science in particular, but more generally social processes; for Giddens especially in his recent work it is the self. The means of reflexivity is the third component. The means for Beck is 'critique' in the tradition of Marxism and the Frankfurt School; for Giddens it is 'monitoring', in an ethnomethodological, though seemingly at the same time 'cybernetic', sense; for Taylor as we shall see below it makes no sense to talk of means because he speaks of 'sources' of the self. But these sources are nonetheless ways in which the self is 'mediated'.

The notion of classifications provides a route into the notion of what we understand as aesthetic reflexivity. The genealogy of this reflexivity is Durkheim and Mauss' *Primitive Classifications* which attempted to uncover the social constitution of the Kantian categories, which are the categories of Aristotelian logic (1970). In his doctrine of the body, Mauss as structuralist sees the self as constituted via the 'total social fact' and its subcategories of tribe, lineage and ancestors. He does not view the self – as Bourdieu does – as constituting through conflict the social via the medium of how agents classify. This idea of classifications that he and Durkheim purveyed can however serve as a basis for aesthetic (or hermeneutic) reflexivity. We will first consider reflexivity. Mauss' structuralism pre-cluded him dealing in such terms, while for Bourdieu reflexivity is often very much reduced to taking cognizance of one's own social position. He insufficiently understands reflexivity as being upon or through the classifi-catory categories themselves.

There is a tradition of thought on reflexivity which indeed sees the phenomenon in this sense. For example – as Nietzsche noted in *The Genealogy of Morals* – Kant already implicitly broke with the early modern Cartesian notion of the self identical ego through the complexification of the self as embodying the logical and perceptual categories (1956). The point here is that there has been a fundamental break in a number of diverse late or postmodern thinkers with notions of the self identical ego or its equivalents, the 'philosophy of consciousness' or 'identity thinking'.

It is in keeping with late modern reflexivity that its object and medium should be Mauss-like classifications. There is something, moreover, very importantly *aesthetic* about both Durkheim and Mauss' 'primitive' classifi-cations and about the classifications of Bourdieu's *Distinction* (1984). And this is due to the fact that these sorts of classificatory categories are of a very low level of mediation. For categories to be highly mediated is for them to be 'emptied out' and 'abstract'. Categories of a lower level of mediation are more concrete, more rooted in place, more rooted in the particular. To classify is to valuate and in a very important sense to judge. Kant importantly distinguished between three types of judgment. Cogni-tive and moral judgments presumed the subsumption of a particular case by a universal category. But in aesthetic judgments there was the subsumption of a particular by another particular, but with reference to a universal. What Kant has in mind for aesthetic judgment was something along the lines of the English Common Law, in which, in contradistinction to continental systems, it was not the general norm under which a particular case came, but instead under a similar previous particular case. There is subsumption of a particular by a particular, though with reference to a universal because the previous particular case functions as a general norm would.

Bourdieu in *Distinction* thinks of the classifications and classificatory struggles of socially stratified taste categories in the terms of Kant's aesthetic critique (1984). Indeed the French original version of the book is subtitled *Critique sociale du jugement* in place of Kant's *Critique of Judgment*. If Kantian aesthetic judgment is his least mediated form of judgment (that form which takes place through the very least universal of universals), then Bourdieu's is even more particularized; even closer to 'nature' in the nature-culture continuum. This is because it is not an original work of art or an 'auratic' natural phenomenon that is being judged, but only the everyday objects of consumer capitalism. Further, it is not an abstract ego that is doing the judging, but socially located individuals of everyday life.

The crucial point then about aesthetic judgment which would extend to both reception and production is that it takes place through the least mediated of universals. Like judgments, classifications have to subsume particulars under universals, except that classifications are not concerned with validity and are only indirectly concerned with value. The intention in *Primitive Classifications* of Durkheim and Mauss is to uncover such universals of the most immediate level. For the authors the history of the lineage of these classifications which eventually lead to the Kantian categories is a history of ever greater emptying out, ever greater abstraction, ever greater mediation of these categories. But in tribal societies, the aesthetic, the ethical and the cognitive are not differentiated from one another (see Habermas 1984). Hence all classifications in pre-modern societies are not uniquely aesthetic but are always partially aesthetic.

On most analyses the distinguishing character of humans is that their actions are mediated, by means of production, language or symbols. And in each case such mediation assumes some set of universals making possible the transition from 'nature to culture' and of subsuming or generating particulars. Thus classifications stand in regard to particulars which are classified. Thus *langue* as a set of universals stands in regard to the particulars of *parole*, or linguistic competence to linguistic performance. Thus rules or norms stand in regard to the particulars of individual actions. The connection of these least mediated universals becomes specifically aesthetic only in modernity. It is with modernity that a differentiated aesthetic sphere and a particular mode of assessment of the aesthetic develop.

Modernity, observes Taylor, comprises two main secular sources of the self. The later of these is aesthetic, romantic and hermeneutic, and grew out of a reaction to the first, the Enlightenment tradition of the cognitive-moral dimension. It developed as a reaction against the emptying out, the increasing abstraction of the Enlightenment tradition. What it involved was a search for the 'original' 'uncorrupted' symbols before the 'fall' into excess mediation, commodification and the like. Thus Kant's aesthetic which inspired generations of Romantics concerned not the production of art but the perception of art and natural phenomena. Kant wrote fully in the tradition of the recently constituted modern aesthetics of Baumgarten, who understood the aesthetic to be not so much art but perception. Thus Kant's high-sounding 'transcendental aesthetic' is in many ways only another name for the human perceptual apparatus. And perception like cognition must proceed through universal categories. Only these universals will tend to be of a much less highly mediated nature than will those of logical, cognitive thought.

Romanticism and later hermeneutics in the social sciences were partly a search for these unmediated universals. Thus there was the cult of the poet who could intuitively, through the prism of his/her own individuality, come into contact with the unmediated universals of an untainted pure originary language or symbol system. This sort of cult inspired those around the Stefan George circle in turn of the century Germany, including Simmel and Lukacs. The exemplar was Goethe and by implication George himself (see Lepenies 1989). The task of a hermeneutically oriented *Geisteswissenschaften* was in its own way to understand these fundamental, pre-abstraction, symbolic networks. Thus the Durkheimian *conscience collective* comprised in mechanically solidary formations these originary systems of symbols. Similarly a generation later Heidegger would hermeneutically look for the same inspiration in the poet Rilke. It was and is the task of the hermeneutic tradition in the human sciences not to legislate and explain, but to understand and interpret these most fundamental and unmediated universals (Baumann 1987). This is an aesthetic task in that it corresponds to that taken up by poets, painters and filmmakers. It is also aesthetic in its typical mode of expression.

But it is more than this. This same hermeneutic tradition of modernity provides a key foundation, a moral source for contemporary post-organized capitalist oppositional politics. This is particularly the case for Green, communitarian, environmental and localist new social movements. The Romantic reaction of these movements against Enlightenment-type rationality has been thoroughly documented by many analysts (such as Eder 1988; Weiss 1987). It is reflected in the rejection of abstract, bureaucratic centralization for the immediacy of locality; in the rejection of the abstract commodity form and of consumer capitalism in general; in the rejection of highly mediated forms of material culture for an empathy with nature; in the rejection of cold abstract logic for feeling and empathy; in the rejection of abstract politics of the public sphere for a politics of the personal. It has been understood by some analysts as an assertion of neo-tribalism (Maffesoli 1991) and to be compared with the more reactionary neo-tribalisms developing among neo-Nazi football enthusiasts in eastern Germany, and gangs of skinheads everywhere in Europe (Wieworka 1991; and see chapter 11 below).

What is not so often noticed is the extent to which this rejection of modernity is itself eminently modern. By modern we do not mean especially or even primarily the sense that the aims of the movement are rational (Weiss 1987; Beck 1992a). Rather we mean modern in the sense of involving important components of reflexivity. This involves first a reflexive creation and invention of the sort of symbol-systems that will give collective solidarity to movements. For anthropologists concerned about the (mythic) transition from nature to culture, the first symbols, the first universals, entailed the repetition and later the ritual repetition of a particular until it gained the status of a universal, until it gained in significance and could become a representation, a symbol, a classifier rather than just a classified. Eder in his study of ecological communes notes just such a process, in which things and events of everyday life in the commune became elevated, through their repetition and taking on of significance in everyday life, to the status of a universal (1988). Moreover, the process in these new social movements, as Eder describes it, is one in which the participants are very conscious, indeed discursively conscious of their creation of such symbol systems. In this sense the process is one of reflexivity. It is also reflexive in that it often takes place via the mediation of 'abstract systems'; in fact participants are commonly students or ex-students that have read some anthropology, such as Eliade or Turner, or some other discussion of 'symbols'.

This reflexivity entails the incorporation of abstract systems in several ways, and not only in the sense that these traditions are consciously 'invented'. Expert systems play a role also in the use of science and their own lay technical expertise in challenging institutional science (Beck 1987; Yearley 1991). Also the new communitarian philosophy itself, of MacIntyre and Taylor and others, which is becoming so influential in the academy, though conceived as a challenge to abstract systems, will function itself as a time-space distanciated abstract system in mediating this sort of reflexivity.

Reflexive action not only entails the mediation of such abstract systems, it also involves significantly deciding between alternatives. If ideal-typically we can distinguish between traditional and reflexive action, the latter involves a rather larger role for agency than the former. It opens up a greater choice between alternative means, ends, conditions and legitimations of action. Thus the difference between the new communities and traditional *Gemeinschaften* is not just that the symbol-systems are reflexively created in the former, but that people are not born into them. They have to decide whether to join or not. And this involves a significant identity risk, partly because movements, Greens, new religious movements, punk, radical lesbianism and their associated 'post-traditional *Gemeinschaften*' involve new forms of identification (see Berking and Neckel 1990).

Most of all, the new political culture also entails an attempted *democratization* of reflexivity (see Melucci 1989). There is democratization because, as compared with the old Leninist and social democratic social movements, no longer does the party function as an 'organic intellectual', but everyone effectively becomes an organic intellectual. That is, there is a displacement of reflexivity from the party and union onto the grass roots themselves. The potential realization of this sort of Gramscian utopia is, in comparison with the older organized capitalist social movements, not so much a transformation of political *culture* as a birth of political culture in the strict sense of the word. Why is this?

It is first because the abstract systems which serve as sources of reflexivity change from political institutions, such as the party, to cultural, media and educational institutions. Second, the constitutive basis of these political forces shifts from the organizational to the symbolic. And finally, the aims of the post-organized capitalist movements, in comparison with the old movements, are not so much political revolution and overthrowing the state, but the very transformation of culture *within* civil society (Touraine 1974).

SOURCES OF THE SELF: THE USES OF ALLEGORY

The notion of aesthetic reflexivity that we are developing here has been most insightfully elaborated by Charles Taylor. In *Sources of the Self* Taylor is engaged in an unabashedly 'foundationalist' enterprise (1989). Taylor's sources of the self are foundations. They are in his words 'constitutive goods'. As constitutive goods they serve as foundations for the 'life goods' which regulate various life spheres. Taylor here shares a concern with issues of ethics and morals with other contemporary neo-communitarian philosophers such as MacIntyre, Walzer and Sandel (see A. Gutman 1991). Thus his two central secular sources of the modern self, the 'disengaged reason' of the Cartesian and Enlightenment tradition, and the romantic-aesthetic modernist tradition, are both *moral* sources. Though the Enlightenment tradition may be primarily cognitive and the latter tradition mainly aesthetic, both figure as *moral* sources of the self. This concern with ethics leads to an understanding of regulation of life practices via a notion of 'goods'. Taylor wants – as an Hegelian – to attempt to re-establish the value of community within the modern. He thus sees the modern self as having foundations, yet sees these as being, not absolutist, but plural.

The hermeneutic-aesthetic sources of the modern self are understood by Taylor in terms of the 'voice of nature', in the sense of finding spirituality in nature and being expressivist. This is chronicled as a shift from 'theistic goods' to 'natural goods', as the 'providential order' develops towards a picture of nature as a vast network of interlocking beings. With secularization, nature becomes a moral source 'without an author'. These sources are not only in nature but also expressivist in the sense that they 'lie in the depths of nature, in the order of things, but also as [nature] is reflected within, in what wells up from my own nature, desires, sentiments, affinities' – this is a nature 'to whose principles we have access within ourselves' (Taylor 1989: 314–15). With the displacement of romanticism by modernism, focus shifts from nature to the aesthetic, but still it is a matter of 'a moral source which is *outside* the subject [which is registered] through languages which resonate *within* him or her, the grasping of an order which is inseparably indexed to a personal vision' (1989: 510).

This expressivist turn was thoroughly opposed to the radical, utilitarian and materialist Enlightenment and its instrumental view of nature. The latter's tradition was formed in the tracks of Descartes' conception of matter as inert, and God as the prime mover; a conception which Holbach radicalized, understanding nature as a locus of force in which 'all beings are driving to maintain themselves in their being'. Nature for expressivists, in opposition to Descartes, is a 'locus from which thought emerges' (Taylor 1989: 318, 348). Its critique of Enlightenment utilitarianism was based in an ethos advocating the fulfilment of one's expressive potential; the existence of meaning in the natural and built environment; and the belief in a purpose in and expressive unity of life beyond utilitarian aims (1989: 500).

There is a further aesthetic source of the modern self. If the romantic-expressivist tradition which is carried into much of high modernism can be captured under the rubric of 'symbol', this second 'lower' modernist tradition should be understood under that of 'allegory'. Goethe canonically made this distinction, counterposing 'symbol', which he identified with the modernist turn towards subjectivity, with 'allegory' of classical antiquity. The ancients, unlike the moderns, connected reason not with the subjective but with an objective order. And allegory's principle was correspondingly not expression, but mimesis of this objective order.

Modernist allegory breaks indeed both with romantic and high modernist expressivism and with classical assumptions of mimesis of an objective order. Benjamin found its roots in baroque allegory. Taylor points to the same tradition and labels it 'post-Schopenhauerian', in the sense of Schopenhauer's rejection of expressive subjectivity. Gadamer (1955), like many others, developed this distinction, again like Goethe taking the side of symbol versus allegory.

We will now set out some of the main distinctions between symbol and allegory. First, romantic expressivism and symbol presume a natural order comprising the unity of the sensual and spiritual. This partly came from the Rousseauan influence on *Sturm und Drang*, on Hölderlin, Schelling and Novalis, as well as Schiller, Goethe and Hegel. This initial romantic expressivism – continued in important currents of high modernism – saw expressive fulfilment as compatible with morality. In contrast the tradition of allegory, founded in Baudelaire and Nietzsche, repudiated nature, and called the harmony of the sensual and spiritual into question. Now the instincts were to have their revenge on the spiritual, and nature was to become a vast source of *amoral* power. Moreover, the romantic ethic of benevolence is discarded since the aesthetic life is deemed to be incompatible with the moral life (see Taylor 1989: 457).

Second, the notion of symbol is grounded in the assumption of a unity of form and content. The symbol on this count is no mere 'signifier', but always 'partakes in the reality it renders intelligible'. This is the source of the idea of the 'perfect symbol' in Kant's Third Critique, in which the 'aesthetic object manifests an order for which no adequate concept can be found'. That is, the content or matter here is not graspable by the forms of reason. It is not 'exoterically' available and only made manifest through the development of a different and non-conceptual order of language.

In contrast, allegory radically separates form and content. On the one hand, form may turn partly against content in what Habermas has identified as a Jewish tradition including Benjamin, Adorno and Derrida, in which the name of God (content) cannot be spoken but only alluded to allegorically (1987). Or it may turn against content more radically such as in Lawrence's dictum against 'the freighting of things with meanings', or surrealism's and futurism's erasure of meaning by, respectively, instinct and the will (Taylor 1989: 470–1). This privileging of the signifier, and denial of a separate order of meaning, is taken to its extreme in deconstruction's reluctance to admit the existence of an *hors du texte*.

Allegory may on the other hand turn radically against form on the side of the referent (or the reality), such as in the early Barthes' zero degree of writing. It may thus opt for iconic or figural signification as instantiated in Pound's fascination with Chinese ideograms and usage of cultural fragments to set up a sort of force field. Or it may entail the invocation of poets such as Tony Harrison to get away from any transcendental notion and approach the immediacy of things through the 'brute realism' of making words 'clang' like things (Eco 1976; Lash 1988, 1990b). This shift to things and to fragments involves at the same time a break with the notion of expressive unity and an acceptance of the subject only as de-centred.

Taylor, as a Christian and an advocate of hermeneutics, logically would reject allegory for symbol. But he is too favourably disposed towards the modern to do this, so he attempts instead to assimilate allegory to symbol (1989: 485). He argues that there is something moral, epiphanic and foundational about the allegorists (which for him would include practically all of contemporary post-structuralism and postmodernism) after all. But in this he is mistaken. There is no reason why an anti-foundational ethos cannot provide a foundation for contemporary sensibility. There is further no reason why this source which fuels an important segment of contemporary ethics must itself be moral. Why cannot it simply be an aesthetic source of contemporary morality? He is further mistaken in attempting to assimilate allegory to symbol, in that symbol and allegory offer, we think, two vastly different constitutive (aesthetic) goods for two very different dimensions of today's cultural and political sensibility.

The first, 'symbol', the expressivist and romantic tradition, with its call to nature, its non-separation of form and content, its advocacy of deep symbolisms and expressive unity, is very much the bedrock of the Green and communitarian movements in post-organized capitalist political culture. The second, 'allegorical' mode corresponds to a less well-structured force because its very impulse is anarchistic. It harkens not back to rural unity but to urban complexity. Its utopia is a 'heterotopia'. It is less local than global, but its globality is not, like the radical Enlightenment, emancipatory but instead cosmopolitan (Rorty 1992). It seeks not a rural harkening back, nor Enlightenment metanarratives, but continual change. Its spatial mode of existence is public space rather than the privacy of place underscored by symbol. Yet its public space is not that of Enlightenment discursive rationality and communication, but that of Benjamin and Baudelaire's more figural communication.

AESTHETIC REFLEXIVITY AND TIME-SPACE

We have argued that the post-organized capitalist social order is much more than just a matter of time-space compression in which the increased velocities and distances of mobility deplete and flatten economic, social and political life as well as culture and the personal sphere. There are also many positive life spaces opened up by the new social-structural arrangements, in particular space for an increasing reflexivity of subjects. Yet in this we have differed significantly from Beck and Giddens. First, the aesthetic element, whether evidenced in popular music, cinema, leisure or tourism, is quite central to this new 'condition' – what we would call the 'postmodern'. Second, we would insist on relating this condition to political-economic changes (see Lash and Urry 1987: ch 9). Our view is that it is only in late modernity (or postmodernity) that aesthetic reflexivity comes to pervade social processes. That is, although art and literature became reflexive in the sense of self-referential with the advent of modernism towards the end of the nineteenth century, aesthetic reflexivity in the sense of allegory and symbol as a source of the self in everyday life is much more of a late twentieth-century phenomenon. Such ideas bear some consistency with Featherstone's notion of the aestheticization of everyday life (1991). And they are associated with the spread of a kind of aesthetic cultural capital to wider groups of people. This generalization of the aesthetic partly involves the spread of the influence of 'expert systems' as subjects use these reflexively to regulate everyday life. Now for Giddens these expert systems are quintessentially social-scientific knowledge and techniques of self-therapy. For Beck they are the spread of lay knowledge in regard to the science and the environment. What we want to add to this is the importance of aesthetic 'expert systems', of the use of film, quality television, poetry, travel and painting as mediators in the reflexive regulation of everyday life. At the same time these point to a set of aesthetic 'life goods' in high (or post-) modernity. And they are based on a set of foundations, described above under the categories of allegory and symbol, which become moral sources of the contemporary self.

These changes can be characterized in terms of transformations of time

and space in postmodernity. They are interestingly captured in an interview with German cineaste Wim Wenders, just after the release of his film
Bis ans Ende der Welt, starring William Hurt and Solveig Dommartin
(1991). The film takes place in the future, and according to Wenders is
about 'the future of vision' in an age which makes our present rate of
'inflation of images' look vapid. That is, the film is about the future
restructuring of the gaze and our 'relationship to images' (1991: 28).
What this means, Wenders continues, is:

> that our sense of space, our sense of time has in the last ten, twenty years
> changed. We are travelling differently, we are used to seeing differently, we see
> much faster. I think that an audience today can apprehend and understand a lot
> more things at the same time than they could in the past. And also I have tried to
> make a science-fiction film (about future speeding up) because we too can
> recount (*erzählen*) very compressed, very fast and very many things at the same
> time. (1991: 29)

What Wenders is referring to is a transformation of perception, a recasting
of our spatial and temporal senses. Wenders' cinematic claim is not that the
inflation of images leads to an inability to attach meanings or 'signifieds' to
images, or even to the triumph of spectacle over narrative. It is instead that
the speed at which we attach meanings to signifiers has and will greatly
increase. Narratives themselves will retain centrality, only now we are
becoming able to follow a great number of narratives simultaneously (also
see Collins 1989). In the course of Wenders' film a blind mother is enabled
to see. She then dies at the end of an 'overdose of images'. This is similar to
the ending of David Cronenberg's *Videodrome* in which, so to speak,
images kill. Wenders and Cronenberg in their cinematic reflections on the
power of images have not made films about, but instead have exemplified,
aesthetic reflexivity.

These spatial changes can be characterized more precisely. Pre-modern
space was filled with the markers of place. It was filled with and only
recognizable by social practices. These social practices were in effect place
markers. It was space not dominated by the temporal element; that is,
space not to move through, but to live in (although Aboriginal space seems
to be very different from this). Modernity witnesses the emptying out of
place markers and the greater development of abstract space (especially in
north America). Modernity is the context of the map, of Cartesian space.
It is the era of the 'grid', both horizontal grids as in city planning and the
'vertical grids' of the skyscrapers (Sennett 1991). Modern space is objective
space, as subjectively significant symbols are emptied out. Reflexive
modernity though is accompanied by a re-subjectivization of space, only in
a reflexive form. The subjectivization of space proceeds especially through
the transformation of communications, information and transport
networks. The development of global cities disrupts the time-space
coordinates of natural space. Also re-subjectivization takes place through
the reconstitution of discursive and political public spheres.

Space can also be conceived as 'allegorical' or 'symbolic'. The former is exemplified in Berman's very public urban heterotopia. It is instantiated in the notion of 'complexity' that architects such as Venturi counterpose to the simplicity of modernist zoning. Designated here is not Habermasian discursivity, but Walter Benjamin's 'figural' public spheres. At issue is not discursive but 'figural reflexivity'. Symbol is a more private version of space. Whereas allegorical space uses place and heritage mainly as uprooted signifiers in a cosmopolitan pot-pourri of urban 'difference' and complexity, this new sort of localized space, like symbol in literature, effectively re-weights locality with the sense and affective charge of place. This is the sense of space of the new, localist social movements. This symbolically weighted place is not that of the traditional *Gemeinschaft* (see Berking and Neckel 1990). Instead the very process of symbolic weighting takes place reflexively.

Given this framework of late or post-modern reflexivity, we can examine various spheres of post-organized capitalist social life.

To the extent that Taylorist and Fordist production systems are being replaced by flexibly specialized systems there is a transformation of workplace time and space. This is essentially a shift from early modernist objective time and space to a late or post-modern subjectivization of workplace time and space. There is here a shift from the Taylorist, 'gridded', objective shopfloor space to the subjective and flexible organization of workplace space on an ongoing basis by employees. The necessity of shorter production runs for specialized consumption involves a continuing restructuration of workplace spatial layouts. Shopfloor workers are increasingly responsible for this and must subjectively restructure workplace space. The result is that workers invest personality in this 'production of space', so that workplace space can tend once again to take on the qualities of 'place', as it had in the pre-organized capitalist days of craft production. Only this time – in contrast to the more traditional craft *Gemeinschaften* – such place is created via abstract systems of discursive knowledge, and on a continual basis. This itself involves chronic reflection on the rules and resources of the work environment.

The shift from early modern objective space, rigidly fixed by hierarchies, to the more subjective, flexible space is also instantiated in the transformation of the firm in vertically disintegrated production systems. Instead of the fixing of supplier networks and outlet networks through the objective space of the hierarchical firm, production organization becomes reflexive and decided through the flexible outsourcing of supplier functions. The context of this is the more flexible and subjectively cast space of transaction-rich market networks of post-organized capitalist agglomerations. These newer inter-firm relationships also involve changes in the temporality of production systems. No longer must supplies come in the context of the objective time of vertically integrated, geographically dispersed production systems. Instead flexibility within a locality can through outsourcing make possible the 'just-in-time' delivery of intermediate goods and materials.

This change concerns more than just the degree of rigidity (objective nature) or flexibility (subjective and reflexive nature) of shopfloor and enterprise time, but also the *length of time* that a job-task entails. The very short cycle job-tasks of Fordism have been displaced by some longer cycle job-tasks. This applies not just to skilled manual workers, but also to professional jobs in services (see chapters 6 and 8). If the job-task cycle of Charlie Chaplin in *Modern Times* was 10 seconds, then that of skilled mechanics troubleshooting equipment in a contemporary factory may be two to three hours. Some technicians and engineers have job-task cycles from several days to several weeks. Advertising executives may have job-task cycles according to the length of time necessary to consolidate an account, say two to three years. This would be similar to a lecturer's task-cycle of producing his/her next book (sometimes it is much longer!). And the time-sense of a number of professionals in the advanced services is increasingly extended to the reflexive organization of their entire careers.

But post-organized capitalist economies involve not only this increase in reflexivity. At the same time there may be a decrease in reflexivity in what Sassen calls the 'downgraded services' and in 'downgraded manufacturing' (1988). Post-organized capitalist society is the two-thirds society, in which the gap between the increasingly reflexive service class and the skilled working class is increasingly separated from that of the so-called 'underclass' (see chapter 6).

In the case of the 'ghetto poor', W.J. Wilson (1991a, b) argues that there is a shift of significant cultural practices from the sphere of work to that of consumption. This is largely due to the virtual and rapid disappearance of the semi-skilled, unionized and reasonably paid manual jobs that ghetto males previously filled. And the same applies in the white underclass ghettoes of many public housing estates in north America and Europe. In this there is a displacement of reflexivity from production to consumption, in which personality is instead invested in clothing styles, sport, dance, music, recreational drugs and borderline criminal activities such as 'ram-raiding'. In fact the American ghetto poor have to a degree set the parameters for the popular-cultural lifestyle of the white middle classes.

At issue here is not so much cognitive but aesthetic reflexivity. In the sphere of work, more than cognitive reflexivity is involved. The creation of culture itself and the growing component of design in increasingly symbolically coded material goods entails an important aesthetic component in production itself. Hence in chapter 5 we analyse, not so much increasing knowledge- or information-intensivity in production, but design-intensivity and, with the decline of importance of the labour process, the growing importance of the 'design process'.

In terms of consumption, aesthetic reflexivity can be seen in several senses. First, there is the increased choice element of consumption. Inasmuch as consumption has taken on heightened significance in contemporary identity-building, choice here should not be understood in a simple utilitarian sense. Even in traditional societies there existed a plurality of say dress styles. But the latter were symbolically distributed by specific social positions. Dress styles in late modernity are much more personality-specific rather than specific to social positions. They suggest a freedom from the symbolic distribution of the latter by the social. Further as 'taste' they instantiate not just a set of invidious status and class distinctions (Bourdieu 1984), but an autonomy from such ascribed distinctions. They thus involve a very important set of identity-choices and identity-risks, especially for young people.

There is an important temporal element in such consumption, captured in the recent work of the anthropologists Miller (1987) and Silverstone et al (1990). They challenge the postmodern theses described in chapter 2, in which objects of consumption have become increasingly disposable and meaningless. They argue on the basis of research on the cultural consumption in middle-class and working-class households in London that, while the working class tend to consume televison, radio and pop music in the channel switching and 'video mode', the middle classes are much more likely to consume in a 'literary mode' (see Abercrombie 1991). There is an interesting temporal difference here. The middle-class households spend large amounts of time and concentration in various forms of culture consumption. The consumption of culture simultaneously involves the *use* of time in order to accumulate cultural capital. In the working class, households are said to consume popular culture through 'wasting time' or 'passing time'.

One further mode of consumption in which aesthetic reflexivity plays an increasing role is that of personal mobility, especially of travel and tourism. We will see in chapter 10 that an increasing part of tourism can no longer be characterized as mass tourism – there is a progressive rise in the number of 'free and independent travellers'. Further, one important element in much contemporary tourism is a concern for the environment – that in some ways the current environmental consciousness is inconceivable without large-scale personal mobility. Many visitors are becoming increasingly skilled at evaluating landscapes and townscapes, at building up their cultural capital so as to be able to form more sophisticated aesthetic and environmental judgments (see Urry 1992).

Such 'middle-class tourism' practices can be characterized in terms of the notions of 'symbol' and 'allegory'. 'Symbol' in this context would capture the sort of visitor who eschews the artificiality of mass tourism for a search for the original qualities of nature in the mountains or of peasant life in a Romanian village. This is the sort of traveller in search of a time when time, space and culture were full of affective charge and form was not yet separated from content. It is the tourist as pilgrim seeking the authentic experience. An alternative set of middle-class travellers will 'allegorically' revel in the obvious constructedness of the whole experience. Their tourist gaze might involve also a reflexive grasp of how tour operators and 'the natives' manipulate their semiotic environment in their own material interests. This is the experience of the 'post-tourist' (see Urry 1990c: ch 5).

Finally, this increased aesthetic reflexivity of subjects in the consumption of travel and of the objects of the culture industries creates a vast real economy. It produces a complex network, which Zukin begins to capture in *Loft Living*, of hotels and restaurants, of art galleries, theatres, cinemas and pop concerts, of culture producers and culture 'brokers', of architects and designers, of airports and airlines, and so on (1988; and see 1992a). It results in a French waiter serving a German business traveller in a New York restaurant advertising cuisines from around the world. The traveller will jump into a taxi driven by a Pakistani immigrant, get her shoes repaired in a shop owned by a Russian Jewish émigré, and make her way to the latest Broadway musical direct from London.

Aesthetic reflexivity is the very stuff of post-organized capitalist economies of signs and space. It produces hugely significant and paradoxical industrial, social and cultural consequences (as we will see in the following chapters).

PART 2

ECONOMIES OF SIGNS AND THE OTHER

4

REFLEXIVE ACCUMULATION: INFORMATION STRUCTURES AND PRODUCTION SYSTEMS

In this chapter we argue that substantial economic growth after organized capitalism must be based on a process of 'reflexive accumulation'. The three principal forms of such accumulation will be outlined.

We believe that the notion of reflexive accumulation provides a better account of contemporary socio-economic processes than the influential concepts of flexible specialization, flexible accumulation and post-Fordism. These otherwise useful frameworks do not sufficiently account for four important aspects of contemporary economies. First, they are not really helpful in understanding the extent to which contemporary socio-economies are based on services. Second, they do not devote sufficient attention to the extent to which knowledge and information are fundamental to contemporary economic growth. What is not captured in the notion of flexibility is the extent to which production has become increasingly grounded in discursive knowledge. Flexibility analysis does not account for the extent to which a sort of information-intensive research and development process has succeeded a material labour process, and to which there has been some democratization of knowledge-intensive production so that certain research and development functions have been devolved to the shopfloor. The opposition of materially based versus culturally based production is more useful than that between flexibility and rigidity. Third, flexibility analysis is one-sidedly 'productionist'. By contrast we argue that social and socio-cultural processes enter as importantly in the moment of consumption as they do in that of production. We shall argue that specialized consumption and flexible production entail knowledge-intensive production. And finally, flexibility theory has not grasped the extent to which culture has penetrated the economy itself, that is, the extent to which symbolic processes, including an important aesthetic component, have permeated both consumption *and* production.

'Reflexive accumulation' has a number of important characteristics. It emphasizes how knowledge and information are central to contemporary economies. Knowledge though is not just a question of increasing information intensivity as a way of coping with a complex and uncertain economic environment. Knowledge on the basis of reflexivity operates via not just a single but a double hermeneutic, in which the very norms, rules and resources of the production process are constantly put into question (Giddens 1984; Malsch 1987). Further, reflexivity is partially aesthetic and hence contemporary economies not only involve information-processing capacities but also symbol-processing activities. Symbols here include both information and aesthetic signifiers and other non-informational symbols. Hence there is an important centrality in production of the design process.

Moreover, reflexivity in reflexive accumulation comprises not only production but also reflexive consumption. We mean by this not just the proliferation of styles in the sense of niche marketing associated with notions of invidious social 'distinctions' (Bourdieu 1984). What is more important is the process of *Enttraditionalisierung*, of the decline of tradition which opens up a process of *individualization* in which structures, such as the family, corporate groups and even social class location, no longer determine consumption decisions for individuals (see Berking and Neckel 1990). Whole areas of lifestyle and consumer choice are freed up and individuals are forced to decide, to take risks, to bear responsibilities, to be actively involved in the construction of their own identities for themselves, to be enterprising consumers (see Keat and Abercrombie 1991). It is these processes which are largely responsible for the shift to extremely small batch production in goods and services; for the proliferation of advanced consumer services which provide professional help (and 'expert systems') to de-traditionalized individuals; and the semioticization of consumption whose increasingly symbolic nature is ever more involved in self-constructions of identity.

Finally, non-material products are increasingly involved in the reflexive economy, whether as services, communications or information. The reflexive economy entails a centrality of communications structures, both within the firm and in final outputs. These communication structures entail a certain closeness to markets, in which a maximized flow of communications enables quick changes in production lines. Further services as final outputs, especially the more complex services such as education, social work, law, psychology, physiotherapy and medicine, involve a co-production consisting of dialogically structured communications in order to maximize their chances of success (Offe 1985).

There has been a lengthy debate on the nature of work in Western capitalist societies. This can be seen in Braverman's famous counterposition of work as execution and the expenditure of physical energy, and of work as creativity and the expression of reason (see 1974; Ganssmann 1990). Paradigmatic for the Ancients is Aristotle's view of work as execution, as a necessary evil with respect to which society must construct hierarchies. On this view freedom is also freedom from labour. For the Moderns and the Enlightenment work becomes, not execution, but conception. That is, work becomes a medium for the realization of reason, one which will lift the human species out of a state of nature. For Kant nature 'forces man' to surmount nature 'through prescribing to him a special telos which through work will allow him' to do so (see Ganssmann 1990). Work is for Moderns a cultural learning and educational process (Ganssmann 1990: 4, 11; Jaccard 1960; Keane 1984).

Ganssmann has interestingly taken this Ancient/Modern counterposition of work and brought it up to date in a systems-theoretical understanding of contemporary information-based societies (1990: 8–9). Work in this account is defined as human activity which transforms matter and energy, and which uses information with the ultimate aim of providing means of needs satisfaction. The labour process is an 'open system' involved in material or substance exchanges with the environment. This involves the expenditure of energy by individuals and the appropriation of matter from the environment. Both human systems and the environment reproduce themselves through this material exchange.

With modernization the growing complexity of the 'social division of labour' entails the proliferation of large numbers of 'tasks of coordination, control and steering' in order to bring together many 'separate work processes'. This has the effect of making the work process reflexive. This is reflexivity in the sense that 'the work process of some becomes the object of the work process of others' (Ganssmann 1990: 9–10). Thus the development of Taylorism was part and parcel of this increase in reflexivity, as the object of the work process of Taylor and the various engineers became the work process on the shopfloor (see Lash and Urry 1987: ch 6). Ganssmann, drawing on Luhmann, notes that in Taylorism 'the work process observed itself and described itself; and thus internally differentiated used this description for steering and thus controlling itself' (1990: 11). From the point of view of workers such a reflexivity was imposed by hierarchies from above.

Ganssmann goes on to analyse the relationship of information-processing and control (1990). There is a cybernetic hierarchy of systems, in which systems that use relatively little energy and considerable information control systems that use a great deal of energy and comparatively less information. Quite high in this hierarchy would be what might be called meta information-processing systems, similar to Giddens' 'expert systems' (see chapter 3 above). These systems would be instances of meta reflexivity. If information-systems control productive systems, then these more information-intensive meta reflexive systems, such as economics, management sciences and other social sciences, monitor and steer the regulation of relations between productive systems. They also monitor exchanges between the systems of work and their environments, one of which is education. Ganssmann understands the 'total work system' as having social and natural environments, themselves being open systems involved in exchanges with each other through the production of inputs and outputs for one another (1990: 20). Each functions in the interests of the reproduction of the other. The coordination of these is mainly a matter of coordination of communications, involving each of Luhmann's (1986) moments of communication: 'information', 'notification' and 'understanding'.

Ganssmann sees modernization as leading in the direction of ever greater informationalization; of moving further steps up this cybernetic and (systems) reflexive hierarchy (1990: 10, 17). The increase in reflexivity of the social work process means that an ever larger portion of individual work processes are only indirectly linked to the basic function of the total work process, the ascertaining of the material exchange between people and nature. This means that there is an increasing cultural mediation of this material exchange over the stages of historical progression. There have been three steps: first, the direct exchange of energy for matter in agriculture, mining and forestry; second, the machine mediation as matter is means, object and output of production; and third, symbol-mediated exchange.

There is a further element here. Post-organized capitalist economic growth entails not only the increase in informationalization and thus systems reflexivity, but also a democratization of reflexivity. Ganssmann's higher levels on the information hierarchy involve not just conceptualization, but that decision-making, planning, responsibility-taking, risk-taking, information-processing, control and monitoring are devolved. The last of these is the most important. What happens with reflexive modernization is that there is heightened self-monitoring, both in the literal sense that one's own labour process is the object of one's labour process, and in a much more indirect sense through the operations and use of abstract and expert systems.

In this chapter we will address three ideal types of reflexive accumulation, the J-form (Japan), the G-form (German-speaking), and the A-form (Anglo-American) production systems (see Walker 1988; Storper and Harrison 1990).

J-form systems involve *collective* reflexivity. The strong ties of Japanese obligational contracting involve collective reflexivity in the sense of information-sharing, risk-sharing and collective decision-making. This collective reflexivity, including information and risk and decision sharing, takes place within autonomous work groups, between units of production whether in the same or different firms (*kanban*), between shareholders and the corporation, and between employees and the firm.

G-form systems are grounded in a more material sort of self-monitoring that we call, following historians of architecture, tectonic or *practical* reflexivity. Here education is less discursive and more practical. Production largely consists of machine-building of other machines. Output has a comparatively high ratio of mechanical to electronic components. G-form systems are regulated by craft and corporatist forms of administration. Yet monitoring at work is much more individualized than on the Japanese model and ties in networks tend to be weak rather than 'obligational'. The G-form system largely operates via the notion of *Beruf*, incorporating profession and trade, and resembles the idea of 'craft administration' (see Stinchcombe 1959). The professional ethos of G-form systems features an important role for institutions of higher education; it also partly erases the distinction between craftspeople and professionals in increasingly assigning professional functions to craft workers, and leaving open routes of upward mobility into technician and engineer positions.

A-form systems involve *discursive* reflexivity. It is at its most evident in highly informationalized sectors, in high technology manufacturing and advanced services. Discursive reflexivity means a greater centrality of expert systems, especially of abstract knowledge. A-form systems involve a very high professional-managerial component of the workforce. They are often characterized by a deep social division of labour, of networked small forms, connected by weak ties. A-form systems involve quite fluid labour markets in which much of the flow of information comes through moving from one firm to another, or the spinning off of new firms.

Finally here, it should be recognized that the term 'reflexive accumulation' looks like a contradiction in terms. Reflexivity is cultural, accumulation is economic. However, we use the term to enable us to capture how economic and symbolic processes are more than ever interlaced and interarticulated; that is, that the economy is increasingly culturally inflected and that culture is more and more economically inflected. Thus the boundaries between the two become more and more blurred and the economy and culture no longer function in regard to one another as system and environment.

We will see in each of these three cases that reflexivity in production is more than the freeing or autonomization of agency from structure. It will be seen that reflexive production has for its precondition the existence of a particular set of information and communication structures. Moreover, we take postmodernity to constitute an integral part of the more encompassing advent of 'reflexive modernity'. Such a modernity is only possible in the context of a tendential decline of 'society', of conventionally understood social structures. But such a decline does not entail the entire disappearance of 'structure'. Instead it entails the displacement of nationally based, organizationally and institutionally framed social structures by globally (and locally) situated, decreasingly organizationally and institutionally framed, information and communication structures.

Much of the rest of this chapter is devoted to detailed accounts of such information structures which underlie these three forms of capitalist disorganization and reflexive modernizations. We will begin with 'collective reflexivity' in Japan.

COLLECTIVE REFLEXIVITY: JAPANESE PRODUCTION SYSTEMS

Within the 'Western' economic sociology of Japan there have been three main generations of analysts. The first mainly dealt with issues of industrial relations and were importantly culturalist in their analyses (Dore 1973; Cole 1971). The second generation focussed on the nature of 'lean' and 'just-in-time' production (Monden 1983; Sayer 1986; Wood 1989a; Jürgens 1990). The third generation, especially Aoki (1988) and Coriat (1991), have focussed much more attention on the morphology of the firm itself (see also Whitley 1990). In this section we shall draw heavily on Aoki's exemplary analysis of the Japanese firm. Aoki advocates an understanding of the firm as an 'information structure'. For him the classical Fordist or organized capitalist firm would be characterized by a vertical information structure. By contrast the contemporary Japanese firm is characterized by horizontality. We shall see throughout this chapter that all three forms of reflexive accumulation involve the horizontalization of the information structures of contemporary productions systems.

Aoki juxtaposes two ideal types. The American firm corresponds to Williamson's ideal-typical 'hierarchy': vertically integrated, functionally departmentalized and bureaucratically structured, with control located in management and execution functions carried out by labour. Specialized operating units are coordinated through layers of administrative offices. These administrative offices themselves are ordered and each is assigned 'information-processing tasks . . . that will maximise savings on the market using cost' (Aoki 1988: 7). On the shopfloor, jobs are finely and functionally divided, partly due to the successes of previous generations of American job-control trade unionism. The result however is that the integration of these functions is hierarchically centralized in the information-processing jobs of engineers (Aoki 1988: 16).

By contrast the J- (for Japanese) firm is not vertically but horizontally structured, in terms of the relations within and between productive units and between shareholders/finance and the firm. Information structures feature horizontalization of information-processing activities, information flows and control. Problem solving is decentralized to the shopfloor. The flow of information is not vertically organized from management to shops but occurs horizontally between shops. And control is displaced from the verticality of hierarchical management to market demand at the end of the production chain.

Through his focus on the firm as distinct from more corporatist structures, Aoki points out the post-organized capitalist set of economic arrangements characterizing contemporary Japan. Before the oil crisis of 1973, economic governance in Japan had been fairly standardly organized capitalist in the terms we previously set out (see Lash and Urry 1987). The main features were, first, the crucial role of the *keiretsu*, groups formed across industries, often with a major firm in each important sector, and structured around a single important bank; second, the importance of employers' associations within individual sectors who figured centrally in economic governance often in corporatist articulation with MITI (Ministry of Trade and Industry); third, the central organizing role of the state, and especially MITI; fourth, bank lending to industry was the most important form of finance; fifth, the major firms had very high levels of vertical integration; sixth, fast growth was achieved through the realization of economies of scale; and seventh, major industrial sectors such as steel and shipbuilding played leading roles in post-war economic development (O'Brien 1989).

But since 1973 economic governance has become more clearly dis-organized. There have been a number of interacting changes: inter-nationalization and the increase of foreign direct and portfolio investment have meant a declining role for the state; the role of sectoral employers' associations has become less marked as has the *keiretsu*; individual firms increasingly act independently, especially in foreign markets; the role of banks has declined, as internal finance and securities finance have become increasingly central; major firms, following the strategy of 'lean produc-tion', have disintegrated production to realize external economies of scope, and at the same time they have, partly through forsaking economies of scale, achieved rapid increases in product diversification; and less traditional sectors, such as motor vehicles, consumer electronics, financial services and property development, have come to constitute the leading roles in the economy.

Thus much discussion in recent years about Japan has been misleading. Some writers have effectively argued that Japanese economic relations are and have for a long time simply been Fordist (Morgan and Sayer 1988; Coriat 1991). Others have argued that Japan has been for a long time post-Fordist (Jürgens 1990; Wood 1991). Both these arguments underestimate the transition *from* Fordism to post-Fordism, or from organized to dis-organized capitalism, in Japan. Having said this, what is distinctive in Japan has been an early horizontalization of information structures and the hegemonic role of groups rather than individuals in such information structures (Morishima 1991).

We can now examine the particular mode in which information struc-tures in the Japanese economy have become horizontal via consideration of employment relations, transactions between productive units and financial transactions. In each case, as Dore (1989) has maintained, 'relational contracting' is found instead of Western 'arms-length contract-ing'. It is this that underpins the collective nature of reflexivity in the Japanese economy.

Employment relations

These will be analysed initially via the concept of the 'information structure'. While Aoki speaks of the information structure of the firm, we will conceptualize the information structures of the 'production system' as a whole (see Walker 1988; Storper and Harrison 1990). Thus where there is a deepened social division of labour and in systems which are vertically disintegrated, the information structure would overlap firms. Further, the information structure of production systems will include flows of information in and out of institutions of education, which can more or less shift from 'environment' to 'system' in relation to a given system. Finally, it should be noted that included in the term information structure are the various modes of symbol-processing, especially of aesthetic, design and image-related symbols.

There seem to be three components to a production system's information structure: information-processing activities – including innovation, problem solving and the like; the accumulation of cultural capital; and the flows of information. These three analytically distinct processes are intimately related and occur more or less at the same time. For example, information flow encourages the accumulation of shopfloor cultural capital which is then used to advantage in information-processing activities. Cultural capital accumulation is learning. It is the 'langue' which makes possible the 'parole' of information-processing activities; the 'code' which makes possible the 'message' of innovation; the 'linguistic competence' which is the condition of the 'linguistic performance' of workplace problem-solving.

Corresponding to the three production systems are A-form, J-form and G-form information structures. Of the three component processes of information the most crucial in distinguishing between the three systems is cultural-capital accumulation or learning. Key in this context is, as Koike (1988) asserts, that in the Japanese firm the incentive structure is based on the information structure.

This is reflected in policies regarding redundancies, transfers and promotions in many Japanese companies. Although the rise of wages with age in large Japanese factories is steeper than in the West, incentives are much *less* linked to seniority. In Koike's comparisons of large Japanese and American factories, incentive structures in the latter were far more seniority based than in Japan. This is especially the case with regard to redundancy. In the US workers with the lowest seniority are normally first made redundant. Those with the most seniority are more protected. In Japan it is accumulation of cultural capital rather than seniority which regulates redundancy and transfers. Often it is older workers, especially those in their late fifties, who are the first to go (Koike 1988: 171). And because of the firm-specific nature of Japanese skill formation, it is to these workers that redundancy is most costly. Worse, in Japan this is exacerbated by the much greater prevalence of older workers in the labour force.

In 1975 before European countries fully installed early retirement policies, the labour force participation rate of males aged 65–9 was a staggering 69 per cent in Japan (Koike 1988: 175; Cheng 1991).

With the further ageing of the labour force, large firms have begun to use transfer and not dismissals as a separation strategy for older workers. Already in 1975–8 the share of intra- and inter-firm transfers among all separations in large Japanese manufacturing establishments was at 34 per cent, while the proportion of such transfers in all manufacturing establishments was 15 per cent. This transfer policy was largely made possible by the response to the 1973 oil shock of vertical disintegration and diversification. Thus a MITI survey showed that the proportion of large firms involved in diversification efforts was 48 per cent in 1979 and 60 per cent in 1982. Further, those diversifying into unrelated fields comprised 15 per cent in 1973 and 35 per cent in 1982 (Brunello 1988: 119, 130).

A study of 68 large manufacturing enterprises in 1985 examined the 1980s trend towards the spinning off of less profitable departments onto separate firms. In this, cost savings were used to diversify into more information-intensive product lines, either alone or through joint ventures. In this survey the average firm spun off 12.2 affiliated companies from 1975 to 1985. The most commonly given reason for spinning off in 75 per cent of the interviews was in order to diversify. The second most often given reason was the establishment of buffer firms for the re-employment of older workers (Koike 1988: 122). In the shift to post-organized capitalist 'lean production', large firms faced with necessary separations find themselves opposed by unions and facing loss of reputation if these are resolved through redundancy. Hence there is the turn to more acceptable transfers. Such transfers do seem to result in considerable savings (Brunello 1988: 125).

Japanese incentive (and disincentive) structures are thus not seniority-linked as they are in the US owing to the historic power of industrial unions. They are also not job-related as they are in Britain owing to the power of craft unions. They are instead connected to the amount of cultural capital a worker accumulates and in this sense much more closely resemble white collar remuneration in Western countries (Koike 1987a). In the large firm sector, Japanese personnel departments have extraordinary power in the recruitment and in the promotion of workers. Both depend upon the amount of cultural capital accumulated. Recruitment is a lengthy and carefully selective process, typically involving two-day workshops (Wood 1991: 32). Large firm recruitment exemplifies in the extreme what Thurow has understood as the transformation in labour market competition from wage competition to job competition. That is, there is strong competition for access to the very limited number of entry ports (quoted in Dore 1987: 10). Promotion too is highly competitive, tightly monitored and controlled by personnel departments.

Thus Japan, in contrast to the USA and UK, is characterized by a strong linkage between the information and incentive structures (Koike 1984).

But what sort of cultural capital, what sort of skills are at issue here? And what form of governance of such information structures is involved? A number of recent commentators have stressed the importance of tacit or empirical or practical information involved in Japanese 'learning by doing', in which informal structures, grass-roots-initiated teamworking and job rotation enable individuals to learn and help each other informally in groups to get tasks done (Wood 1989a). But this account underestimates the discursive or theoretical knowledge involved, the centrality of information-processing skills, and the 'white collarization' of blue collar workers. The Japanese smaller firm sector, including probably some two-thirds of manual workers, follows the more typically Western blue collar pattern. But the large firm sector importantly involves discursive knowledge. Partly this is because manual workers have diplomas from the more academically oriented high schools and not from trade schools. Moreover, further training involves an important discursive element. Typically large firms offer further training courses to workers approximately every five years. Access to them involves strenuous competition and promotion depends in part upon achievement in these training courses. Personnel departments closely monitor work performance to date and give written tests on for example the assembly of electrical machines (Koike 1987a: 298–9; 1987b).

Learning through job rotation also involves important discursive elements (see Koike 1987a: 305). A worker's chances of being promoted are facilitated by large amounts of job rotation. Personnel departments take job rotation importantly into account, largely because it is an indicator of accumulated cultural capital. And job rotation is common. A comparative study of integrated steel plants in the USA and Japan found that the average American worker had been through 12 jobs in his career and the average Japanese through 36 (Koike 1987a: 304). Furthermore, job rotation opens up a more horizontal promotion structure. In Koike's American steel plant, strict union-enforced seniority rules kept workers from switching from one shop to another so positions within one vertical ladder could be filled only from within that ladder (1987a: 303). In the Japanese plant multi-skilled, rotated workers could be promoted on any of a number of such ladders (see also Deutschmann 1986; Bratton 1991).

Finally, quality control circles may be as importantly based in discursive as in practical-tacit knowledge. Although practical knowledge is imparted during quality circle (QC) meetings, Koike argues that QCs can only function in plants where workers have high levels of education (1987a: 306, 324; 1988: 154). This underlies their willingness to participate in QCs; their ability verbally to articulate process and product problem-solving issues at the meetings; and the necessary background that workers must have in technological and production mechanisms in order to participate in them (Hill 1990).

The issue then becomes how these information structures are governed. The answer is that they are governed in the least corporatist manner possible. Training systems can be styled as school centred, theoretical and statist, on the one hand, and practice centred, empirical and corporatist-controlled, on the other. Japan, even more than France and Italy, is on the statist and discursive side of the continuum. The German-speaking world is situated at the corporate and practice-centred end, with Britain and the USA somewhere in between. The USA has historically been more statist and theory centred than Britain, but Britain, with the decline of apprenticeship by some 67 per cent from the mid-1970s to the mid-1980s, has been moving quickly away from the practice-centred model (Burrage 1972; Dore 1987: 20; Lutz and Veltz 1989).

State-governed normative systems tend to be more codified, more abstract and more theoretical compared with those regulated by corporate bodies. In Japan craft workers have a comprehensive state-sponsored training and skill testing system. This serves the mobile smaller firm sector. Elite firms train their lifetime employees in house. The Japanese model of 'deductivist' cultural-capital formation outdoes either its French or Italian competitors (or American) in the quality of discursive secondary education that blue collar entrants to the large firm sector possess. Further, it is much more of a dual system than elsewhere in that firm-based training is more systematic and theoretical.

How much of the Japanese model is then due to cultural difference? By 'culture' is usually meant the persistence of traditional social relationships, including many of the 'rigidities' included among Dore's 'flexible rigidities' (1986). In recent years it has become fashionable to dismiss such culturalist explanations. For example, Aoki (1988) and Koike (1988) provide a strongly rationalist explanation of employee loyalty to Japanese firms. They argue that firm-specific skills give employees a stake in the firm because of the enormous devaluation of their cultural capital should their firm go bankrupt. Further, employees' chances for promotion and further accumulation of cultural capital are proportional to the expansion of the firm and their commitment to it.

Cole by contrast provided a culturalist explanation (1971). He argued that the more modern and successful firms are more culturally traditional, that is, with lifetime employment, prominent bonus schemes, enterprise unions, teamworking, and quality circles. It is the major international Japanese firms with highly educated blue collar work forces that are more culturalist-traditionalist than are smaller firms, which operate more on a market model, without firm-specific skills and so on. In other words Dore's 'community model' of the firm applies to the modern Japanese firms, but not to the more traditional ones. The paradox here is one of increased traditionalization *with* modernization.

Ideal-typical bureaucratic and market relationships are characterized in the literature in terms of impersonality or an absence of 'ties' between individuals. Granovetter (1985) has argued that often these relationships in the West are socially embedded in networks, and instead of impersonality there exist 'weak ties' between individuals. By comparison networked social relations in the Japanese economy would be characterized by 'strong ties'. Commentators on culture and the Japanese economy speak of two types of such strong ties. First, there are the asymmetrical ties of firm and worker, which Dore in 1973 understood in terms of welfare corporatism, and which Aoki describes in terms of a 'gift relationship' between employer and employee. The other type of network consists of horizontal ties. Its prototype is the *mura*, pervasive from seventeenth-century Tokogawa Japan. The *mura* were semi-autonomous, multi-functional and informal village units which 'were constitutive', notes Murakami 'of society's substratum' (1987: 35–6). Equally, Cole argues, Tokogawa 'legal system had a principle of collective responsibility, and allocated complete authority and responsibility for performance and conduct of group members to group representatives like village headmen', though in practice this led to a great autonomy of village communities and urban neighbourhoods (1989: 9). It is significant to note that the types of collective structures in the restructuration of the Japanese economy have shifted from asymmetrical gift relationships to *mura*-type relationships. In the growth period of 1955–70, what was crucial was not the *keiretsu*, the successors of the pre-war *zaibatsu*, clustering around a bank. Key firms, such as Toyota, Nissan, Honda, Sony and Matsushita Electric, were 'independents' and not in *keiretsus*. Key instead were partly asymmetrical corporatist groupings such as that between MITI and the various trade associations, and that of the Ministry of Finance and Bank of Japan with Japanese banks (Murakami 1987: 47, 52; O'Brien 1989). In contrast post-Fordist collectivities, such as team working and quality circles, are closer to the horizontal *mura* structure. Indeed, instead of welfare corporatism (asymmetrical and gift-relationship based), analysts such as Dore have come to speak of a 'community model' of the firm. This underscores the point that collectivities and communication structures have become more horizontal. And organization has become at the same time more reflexive. What has happened is that the form of traditional culturally bound and collective relationships has been filled by a new modern content. Further, the 'expert systems' of economists and industrial relations theorists as well as cultural analysts have played their part in the growth of such reflexivity.

We have thus described reflexive accumulation in Japan in terms of the employment relation. This is reflexive in the sense that the labour process involves self-monitoring – the labour process becomes the object of the labour process. This has involved the decentralization of decision-making. Lincoln et al (1986) in their large-scale survey showed that in directly comparable cases similar decisions were taken on average one step lower in firm hierarchies in Japan than in the USA. In Japan self-monitoring becomes collective self-monitoring. This applies to problem-solving regarding both process and product. Process problem solving is monitored collectively via teamwork. Quality circles are a further process of collective reflexivity effective in both process and product problem solving.

Transactions between production units

These also involve reflexivity. Reflexivity in Japanese production systems takes place not only with regard to the labour process, but also in the relation between production units, that is, between labour processes, in which the output of one labour process becomes the input of the next. In terms of Ganssmann's information-processing hierarchy this sort of monitoring is higher on the scale of reflexivity than self-monitoring of the labour process. In conventional Fordist vertically integrated hierarchies, monitoring of relations betwen shops is quite centralized. In J-form production systems, monitoring is flattened out in a horizontal information structure. This can be seen in both just-in-time and *kanban*.

The externalization and horizontalization of information structures took place only with the shift from the dominance of mass or 'process' production to 'diversified quality production' (Abegglen and Stalk 1985: 21 ff; Sorge and Streeck 1987). In 1955 the national sales leader in Japan was a textile company, Toyobo; in 1965 it was Mitsubishi Heavy Industries, the world's largest shipbuilder; in 1975 it was Nippon Steel; and in 1983 it was Toyota. From the 1970s Japan largely shifted out of process industries, such as petrochemicals, non-ferrous metals, petrol refining and chemicals, largely because of the absence of energy and raw material sources, but also because of the environmental consequences of these industries. It was the older industries, owing to the continuous process nature of production, which lent themselves to vertically integrated plants.

More generally the Japanese firm has tended to set its main aims around not profits nor even sales growth, but around market share. This means that a company such as Casio, when it diversified into hand calculators, at the time a market growing at 200 per cent per year, fixed its prices to realize sales growth of 100 per cent per year. In doing so they effectively drove American and European firms out of the market. Casio followed the typical Japanese pattern of conquering the low end of the market with volume and price competition and then moving up through 'diversified quality competition' (Abegglen and Stalk 1985: 53–6; see also Whitley 1991).

Such diversification into higher technology areas was financed through spinning off departments to become suppliers. This 'streamlined management' strategy of quasi-disintegration has led to an increase in the number of a firm's subcontractors. Among small- and medium-size firms with under 300 employees, the proportion of subcontractors increased from 53 per cent in 1966 to 66 per cent in 1981. It was even greater in modern sectors like electronics: some 85 per cent in 1981. At the same time the ratio of investment in subsidiaries to total paid in capital increased enormously: in all manufacturing industries from 11 per cent in 1965 to 44 per cent in 1984 (Aoki 1987: 283–4). Comparison with the USA is instructive. Towards the end of the 1980s, while General Motors produced some 70 per cent of the value of its autos in-house, Toyota externalized about 70 per cent of its value-added (Hill 1989: 466).

What happened was that the shift to 'lean production' in Japan had led to the development of a chain of firms; production systems had quasi-disintegrated into a set of 'layers' or tiers of firms. In this the further down the chain a subcontractor is from the large parent firm, the smaller is the establishment. As early as 1978, MITI estimated that the average Japanese auto maker had 171 first-layer, 4,700 second-layer and 31,600 third-layer part makers. Many of the third layer are 'crowded backyard family workshops' where families turn out small stampings on floor presses 10 hours a day, 6–7 days a week, and include a substantial portion of informal work arrangements. Even quite small firms engage in considerable out-sourcing to their own subcontractors, including some 50 per cent of firms with as few as 4–9 workers (Hill 1989: 462, 466; Demes 1989).

Lean production in Japan has meant that accountability (for product and profits) has in effect been shifted to the lowest levels of the production process, in which every step is its own profit centre and subject to the market. The shift to diversified quality production explains part of this, but so too does the absence of 'mature skills' on external labour markets. Hence when there is little time to develop in-house expertise, the 'make'/ 'buy' decision will be in the direction of 'buy' (Patrick and Rohlen 1987: 349). All this has meant a new shape for the information structure of Japanese production systems. This structure is partly one of a cybernetic hierarchy, in which information-processing (and monitoring) activities are largely carried out by parent firms and first-tier subcontractors, while the energy-expenditure component becomes more prominent the lower that one moves down the chain. This is reflected in the monitoring of subcontractors by parent firms, in which the latter must take responsibility for productivity. That is, subcontractors and contractees enter into contracts; for example, in the auto industry the basic contract is often for the four-year life of a model. Within this stable framework of a longer-term supply contract, the subcontractor must innovate so as to reduce production costs (Uekusa 1987: 501–2).

Asymmetry in information and monitoring hierarchies is also shown in the fact that for many subcontractors the determination of design specification and delivery is set by the parent company, while quality and price are negotiated. For some very small firms far down the chain, the parent firm supplies not only management advice but often also machinery (Uekusa 1987: 501; Patrick and Rohlen 1987: 347). Indeed most subcontracting enterprises begin with the parent firm's patronage of a stable sales base. With good performance they can gain more autonomy from the parent firm, and where they use general purpose (non-dedicated) equipment, they can threaten to change from one parent firm to another. Yet their weak position in the cybernetic information hierarchy is clear from the relative wages paid. In the Japanese car industry only 25 per cent of workers (those in final assembly, engine and transaxle assembly and major body stamping) receive the premium rate, while the others in second- and third-layer subcontractors are paid 20 to 70 per cent less. In the USA wages for all workers are much more equally distributed (Hill 1989: 467).

Although we have noted this vertical pattern in subcontracting information structures, there now seems to be a growing trend towards horizontalization. The market position and hence terms of trade of subcontractors have been improving as the average number of firms which small and medium firms deal with increased to four by the mid-1980s, and the number dealt with by firms with 200–300 employees increased to an average of eleven. Further, in the old pre-1973 dualist Japanese system, subcontractors served mainly as a buffer, as a shock absorber against decline. The newer role of subcontractor is as a sharer of risk and of knowledge (Aoki 1987: 283; Kawasaki and McMillan 1987; Sheard 1989).

The irony is that this takes place through closer and more reliable long-term relations between subcontractor and client. Thus modernization is fostered by the growth of traditional diffuse relations. The higher the level and hence the more modern the subcontractor is, the more diffuse (not impersonal) the relations are with the client firm (Uekusa 1987: 502). The more backward and lower down the chain the sub-contractor is, the more market-like and non-collective the relation. So again, as with the employment relation, Japan shows collective reflexivity. Reflexivity in the West grows mainly with individualization while in Japanese industry it varies positively with collectivization.

Production scheduling in Fordist hierarchies is centralized and based on market forecasts. Japanese *kanban* provides a decentralized alternative to production scheduling, and is an important part of the horizontal information structure of J-form production systems. *Kanban*, originally developed by Toyota in the 1960s and 1970s, is a 'pull-led' system of production scheduling (Monden 1983: 35). It features a 'just-in-time' system of delivery that Toyota discovered while observing the stocking procedures in American supermarkets. This is led by daily orders by dealers. These orders, received a few days before, are then transmitted to computer terminals at the head of the assembly line. *Kanban* is a particularly fast way of responding to orders in rapidly fluctuating markets. It is able as a system of production scheduling to 'ensure the coordinated supply of each of thousands of parts, materials and half-products' (Aoki 1988: 21). It is further a way of reducing inventory costs, which become all the more excessive with diversified production, because one has to keep a much wider range of materials and parts in stock. It is also a way of cutting costs in managerial hierarchies with decentralized scheduling and quality control.

A *kanban* is literally a card placed in a vinyl envelope. The final assembly line, in implementing its daily production schedule, places a 'production-ordering' *kanban* 'on a post' adjacent to the relevant inventory store when it withdraws its inventory. The upstream shop supplying this inventory comes several times a day to this post and looks at the card, which specifies what was withdrawn and the time of delivery for its replenishment. When the upstream shop delivers its replenishment it returns the card along with it. In this sense the *kanban* is 'both an ordering form and a delivery notice'. The upstream shop, in its turn, dispatches its own order forms to shops immediately upstream to them. A '*kanban* system' is thus a 'chain of bilateral order-delivery links', which extends to regular external subcontractors (Aoki 1988: 22–3).

Kanban with subcontractors entails spatial contiguity. Subcontractors must make such frequent deliveries in small batches that in effect they become a 'spatial extension' of the parent firm. The sort of spatial concentration entailed by *kanban* is exemplified by the Tokaido megalo-polis, and specifically in Toyota City, as probably the world's most spatially concentrated production system. This contrasts strongly with the old Fordist car production systems in the USA, with their outlying assembly plants often in areas as distant from Detroit as Los Angeles. At these distances supply lines were easily disrupted and it was necessary to have vast buffer stocks (not just-in-time, but 'just-in-case'), so that some assembly plants were effectively 50 per cent warehouses, entailing also vast labour costs for the logging in and out of inventory. Shifts in the direction of lean production have meant the closure of these outlying plants, and relocation often within a day's lorry ride from suppliers (Hill 1989: 469–70; Mair et al 1990; Jones and North 1991).

Kanban, as Wood (1991: 9) notes, is an 'information system', comprised of two components: of just-in-time delivery, and of autonomous 'defects' or quality control. *Kanban* cannot, he argues, stand on its own. It entails the totality of Japanese production systems, including teamworking, multi-functionality and collective responsibility. *Kanban* is based upon 'the integration of production flow and information flow' (Aoki 1988: 35). All modes of reflexive accumulation feature not just horizontalization of information processing, but horizontal information flow. Such information flows proceed in two ways.

First, information flows through labour markets. In J-form production systems this largely works via internal labour markets, often through job rotation in the same shop or between adjacent shops, or between quasi-disintegrated subcontractors. Second, information flows along with parts and semi-products, the outputs of production units which serve as inputs for other units. But whereas the information which flows through labour markets is in fact information-processing capacities, that which flows along with products is like the information involved in market signals. In other words, the information which flows through labour markets has to do with problem-solving capacities, while the information that flows along with products involves the problems to be solved. The two sorts of information are further connected. Where production scheduling is run via hierarchies, through either the commands of Soviet-type hierarchies or the 'forecasts' of Fordist private sector hierarchies, then the information processing is also likely to be hierarchical. That is, where the problems are set by hierarchies, the problem solving will be hierarchical. Where the problems are set by markets, or market like *kanban*, and decentralized, then problem solving is likely to be decentralized. Finally, with the fluctuating post-Fordist market environment, only the latter decentralized-type information is likely to be accurate.

Kanban, as noted, includes decentralized quality control, and assumes that the downstream shop can refuse on the spot to accept defective parts. It further assumes multi-functionality, because the fluctuation of demand for specific parts means that at times the worker is going to be released to other tasks or adjacent shops. Now reflexive production scheduling, autonomous quality control and multi-functionality all presuppose considerable information-processing capacities on the part of workers, acquired both through learning-by-doing and through initial bouts of considerable discursive education. The horizontal communication and information structures of the J-form production system not only increase information-processing capacities, but also presuppose considerable amounts of these to start with. They also generate 'communication rents' in the form of higher sales, faster growth and ultimately higher wages, so that the information structures and incentive structures are tightly linked (Aoki 1990). And the information structures, in this ascending virtuous spiral, by generating growth become themselves incentive structures.

Financial transactions

Post-war Japanese financial networks have worked through three types of 'obligational contracting', each of which has permitted very fast growth. All three have assumed risk-sharing and a trust relationship between industrial firms and other financially relevant economic actors. The three forms of obligational contracting have been, first, between the firms and their employees, who initially have accepted relatively low proportional wage gains in comparison to firm growth; second, between firms and consumers; and third, between firms and financial institutions, banks and shareholders.

The main pattern is that consumers with very high rates of savings have 'lent' money at low interest rates to banks. The banks in turn have lent enormous sums of money to firms, so that they could follow impressive growth policies at rates of leverage almost unknown in the West. Finally, shareholders have been satisified with very low dividend payouts. In Anglo-American arm's-length contracting, employees, consumers, banks and shareholders follow their own short-term interests, and will 'opportunistically' 'exploit' industrial firms when it suits them. Japanese obligational contracting rules out such short-term opportunism. The sacrifice of short-term interests by employees, consumers, banks and shareholders leads to an optimization of long-term interests.

The extraordinary role of banks in regard to industry in Japan is not brought about by the power or dominance of financial capital, but follows from the growth strategies of Japanese firms, that is, to increase market share in rapidly growing markets. A 1980–1 poll of higher management in Japan showed that the three top priorities were first, market share, then return on investment, and third, new product development (Abegglen and Stalk 1985: 177; in the USA return on investment was placed first). Such increase in market share in rapidly growing markets presumes rapid firm sales growth which itself depends on very fast growth in the firm's asset base. The asset base consists of equity and debt, and because of the limits to growth of equity, the firm must take on mountains of debt and become highly leveraged.

In very rapidly expanding markets, such as certain micro-electronic-related markets which in the 1980s were growing at 100 per cent per year, Anglo-American firms were happy to focus on an annual growth of sales of about 20 per cent. But even with this respectable growth they lose market share. Japanese firms during this period expanded volume by more than 100 per cent in order to increase market share. The American firm will price with a specific goal regarding profits and dividends, the Japanese with an eye to increased market share. To do so, the Japanese firm will increase capacity seemingly recklessly and then 'pull the rug out from underneath prices until they can fill that capacity'. All of this requires what for Western firms is reckless levels of risk-taking, part of which is registered in the necessarily extremely high gearing ratios (debt/equity) of Japanese firms. American firms have wanted high margins, high dividends and little debt, while the Japanese price cutters are happy with lower margins, low dividends and considerable debt (Abegglen and Stalk 1985: 155–6; Florida and Kenney 1990). The Japanese company not only practises risk sharing. It takes greater (shared) risks.

The Japanese firm pays very low dividends; from 1979 to 1984 mean dividend was 1.8 per cent of average share price in Japan, and 5–6 per cent in the USA. It pays lower dividends partly because it must devote so many resources to paying back bank loans and partly because prices are set to realize smaller profit margins. A study of 21 matched large Japanese and American companies showed dividend payments to come to 11 per cent of total Japanese profits in comparison with 85 per cent of US profits. Yet this short-term sacrifice of investor interests may have enabled Japanese investors in the long run to do better when both dividends and capital gains are taken into account. They outscored US investors 175 to 39 per cent in pre-tax appreciation plus accumulated dividends as a percentage of gain over original share price. And capital gains are not taxed in Japan. Another survey of investors from 1971 to 1982 showed that when dividends and capital gains were taken into account Japanese stocks yielded a 14 per cent average compounded annual return in comparison to 11 per cent in Britain and 7 per cent in the USA and West Germany (Abegglen and Stalk 1985: 168–76).

What all this entails is that Japanese (and German) financial contracting is producer centred, while Anglo-American finance is consumer centred.

In J-form production systems, loans largely proceed from consumers; in A-form production systems, they proceed to consumers. That is, Anglo-American finance is largely centred around consumer credit, mortgages and shareholders. In Japan (and Germany) it is centred around manufacturing firms. The financial services in Japan and Germany are thus largely producer services, in the USA and UK largely consumer services. Moreover, J-form and G-form production systems are just that, production systems. Anglo-American production systems are largely consumption systems.

This difference can be seen by considering the different role of leveraged finance. In Japan as we just saw, it has been a way to achieve very rapid industrial growth. Japanese levels of leverage were only reached in the USA and UK for a very short period in the late 1980s. Here debt was used, not for growth, but for buyouts, which were only possible by very high bids which transferred resources to consumer-shareholders. And debt repayments were not managed through limiting dividends and fast asset growth, but through asset stripping with little interest in growth.

Although there are these generic contrasts with Western financial systems, Japanese financial contracting has been substantially transformed in post-organized capitalist restructuration. Perhaps the most crucial factor in this was the shift in growth objectives after the 1973–4 oil shock. The Japanese economy began to aim for 4–5 per cent growth per year instead of 8–9 per cent as previously. At the same time, firms began to rely more centrally on internally generated finance, and considerably reduced dependence on high leverage (Feldman 1986; Takagayi 1988). Firms such as Honda, when they were chasing sector leaders from far behind, were operating at 6:1 gearing ratios in the early 1950s. By 1960 when it had become the world leader in motorcycles, gearing was reduced to 1:1. Sony, as a sector follower in consumer electronics in the early 1980s, used three times as much leverage as sector leader Matsushita. Post-Fordist giants such as Toyota and Matsushita operate at notoriously low levels of debt. A survey of the 600 largest Japanese companies showed that in the 1960s an average of 80 per cent of new necessary external funding was raised through bank loans; a proportion which dropped to 56 per cent from 1978 to 1983 and 14 per cent in 1983–4 (Abegglen and Stalk 1985: 151).

With slower growth and more equity finance, demand for loans has considerably sunk. Before 1973 when industrial borrowing was voracious – exceeding the amounts of capital made available by very high consumer savings – city banks had to borrow from the Bank of Japan, who then themselves could control the level of interest rates (Cargill and Royama 1988). After the oil crisis, with demand for loans low, the supply of consumer savings was still exceedingly high. Because of high supply and low demand for loans, it no longer became either possible or desirable to keep interest rates low, so they became effectively deregulated. It was also no longer viable to keep exchange controls on (Takagayi 1988). And indeed a foreign exchange law passed in the early 1980s established a policy of non-interference in exchange rates and controls (Horne 1985; Suzuki 1987). Japanese investment flooded abroad, where demand for capital exceeded supply.

Excess savings on the part of firms have increased their role as shareholders in other firms. In fact the securitization of Japanese financial institutions in the 1980s has been largely a question of industrial firms and groups of industrial firms holding shares in other industrial firms. Orru et al go so far as to argue that the place to look for networking among Japanese capitalists is not in interlocking directorships, but interfirm shareholding (1989). In any event almost all forms of interfirm shareholding have increased since the post-1973 restructuration.

Within *keiretsu* groups, though financial dependence on a group's bank has been reduced, interfirm shareholding has grown. In *keiretsu*, individual large firms hold typically 2–7 per cent of other firms, so that the combined shareholding of one firm in a group by all of the others ranges from 20 to 30 per cent (Orru et al 1989: 556–60). More important however are the 'independent' firms which comprise almost all of the post-organized capitalist super-growth firms – Nippon Steel, Hitachi, Nissan, Toyota, Matsushita, Toshiba and so on. These mega independents do not typically invest enormous amounts in the shares of other large companies, with the exception of the large independent banks. That is, the giant industrials tend to own a lot of shares in the same independent banks that own the largest amounts of shares in them. Toyota and the Tokai Bank exemplify this sort of reciprocal shareholding, as do Nippon Steel and the Industrial Bank of Japan. The large independent industrials do, as indicated above, have considerable shareowning in their own (often spun-off) suppliers. The top ten independent industrials thus hold from 21 to 44 per cent of the shares in from 14 to 39 of their affiliated companies. Finally, the *keiretsu* own considerable equity in the large independent companies, but not vice versa (Orru et al 1989: 561–3).

What then are the implications of this pattern for the information structure of the Japanese production system? First, despite the drop in debt finance, banks are still commanding actors for firms. Despite securitization of financial contracting, banks arrange bond issues for large firms abroad as well as mediate mergers and acquisitions. Banks are legally permitted to own no more than 5 per cent of total shares in non-financial companies. Yet taken together the proportion of stock owned by banks, insurance companies, *keiretsu* groups and other corporations in firms commonly form major blocks consisting of around 70 per cent of a firm's equity. Banks effectively play a coordinating role for these shareholders with regard to a given industrial firm. But they do so mainly through their role as creditors. That is, even 'low-geared' Japanese firms can typically have debt/equity ratios of 1:1. Lending in this is typically through a consortium of banks managed by a 'main bank' (Aoki 1989: 353, 364).

The question then becomes: How do 'financial contractors' exercise their control over the firm? Or more importantly for our purposes, what are the implications for the firm's information structure of the mode of control? The answer to the second question is that the mode of control of financial contractors is exercised external to the firm's information system in the Anglo-American case, while it *is part and parcel of the information structure* in the Japanese. This is first because on the Anglo-American model there is such a rapid turnover of controlling blocks of shareholders and of debt instruments that financial contractors have little time to 'settle into' the information structure of the firm. This is also true of the mode of replacement of managers through the external managerial labour market – in contrast to Japanese internal promotion – which brings a 'discontinuity with the internal knowledge base' of the firm. Moreover, the ultimate sanction for management of the Anglo-American hierarchy – that stock-holders exercise via the board of directors – is of outside takeover. The other means of control of shareholders and the board over management is through market-oriented incentive contracts. In both cases the criterion of managerial performance is the maximization of share price (Aoki 1989: 353–4, 358).

By contrast in the J-firm, the ultimate sanction of financial contractors comes not through outside takeover, but through 'inside takeover'. That is, the main bank acts rather like Anglo-American venture capital, in that the firm effectively functions as collateral against the loan so that if performance deteriorates badly enough, the bank literally takes over the firm. For a firm to be taken over by its main bank's 'reorganization specialists' is probably the most acute and publicly humiliating experience a Japanese industrial manager can undergo. The Japanese model depends on a great deal of information sharing between main bank and firm. In good times the main bank shares control with entrepreneurs, but with sufficient deterioration of performance, full control is transferred to creditors (Aoki 1989: 355, 364). In any event the bank on the J-firm is at the top not only of the control, but also of the informational hierarchy. It is fully integral to the firm's information structure.

This sort of financial contracting is part and parcel of the 'collective reflexivity' of Japanese production systems. We have spoken of such collective reflexivity also in employment contracting and in interfirm contracting. However, this obligational contracting, in contradistinction to 'arm's-length' contracting, cannot be understood in terms of a simple counterposition of tradition and modernity. This is because the more traditional Japanese firms are the least 'obligational', and the most modern are the least 'arm's-length'. What we are talking about instead is a specific Japanese model of reflexive modernization. It is collective in its assumptions of information- and risk-sharing between the firm and its workers, suppliers and financial contractors. There is not just a horizontalization of information structures, but a set of much more inclusive and broader information structures.

If we follow Aoki and understand the firm as a 'nexus' of employment, financial and interfirm 'contracts', we see that in each case where the Japanese production system extends its information structure, Anglo-American hierarchical systems exclude contractors from the information structure (1990). That is, in Japan production system and information structures are co-extensive.

This collectivization, horizontalization and broadening of means represent the generation of considerable 'information value'. Employees 'together generate information value by utilising on-site information efficiently and coordinating their operating decisions horizontally' (Aoki 1989: 359). This leads to the generation of 'information rents', which is for Aoki the 'value of information generated' by these 'semi-autonomous, horizontal coordinating mechanisms less the cost of training and horizontal communications' (1989: 360). This is the essential link between incentives and information-structure whose ultimate implication is a firm primarily devoted to the 'accumulation' of 'information assets'. Again, to quote Aoki, 'if rents arising from information system-specific human assets are thus shareable between employees and other contracting parties in the nexus, . . . the rate of accumulation of these assets will become the central issue of corporate management decision-making, in which all parties are interested' (1989: 362).

Collective reflexivity has generated what has been an extraordinarily successful economic form in much of Japan. In the next section we will consider the G-form.

PRACTICAL REFLEXIVITY: GERMAN PRODUCTION SYSTEMS

In the German case we shall see that the production system and the information structure are co-extensive, in particular that education, finance and shopfloor functions are included within the information structures of German production systems. As with Japan a set of 'rigidities', in comparison with Anglo-American markets, encourages both information flows and the accumulation (and democratization) of information-processing capacities.

Interestingly this runs counter to the view that contrasts markets favourably with central planning in view of the informational advantages of the former. Now it may be that deregulated liberalism may bring advantages regarding information availability in labour, commodity and capital markets. But all this changes when seen from the point of view, not of markets, but of production systems as a whole. Here information flow, and the development of information-processing capacities, is minimized by market or neo-liberal (or hierarchical) governance, while sets of institutional rigidities actually enhance the information structure of production systems. It is these sorts of institutional rigidities which permit the development of expanded and inclusive information structures. Market relations themselves tend instead to yield exclusive and ineffective information structures.

The 'flexible rigidities' of German production systems, whose information structures we shall see expand to include trade unions, chambers of commerce, works councils and technical colleges of higher education, are very different from those of the Japanese. While the information structures and production systems of the latter are characterized by collective reflexivity, in Germany post-organized capitalist relations are far more individualized – in for example the relationship of worker to firm, and of client firm to its suppliers.

Furthermore, there is increased reflexivity in German production systems via substantial inputs of new information technology, the massive role of the technical colleges in production, an increasingly discursive training for workers, and finally the increasing abilities of production systems effectively to reflect on and transform themselves. But this modernization and rationalization, this qualitative development of reflexivity which has characterized Germany's successful restructuration after the oil crises, have been grafted onto the traditional basis of craft, of *Beruf* regulation which has always constituted its substrate. That is, in Germany a weakly developed introduction of Taylorist principles permitted the survival of a craft substrate onto which this new reflexivity, this new rationality, has been grafted.

Thus alongside the high technology, modernization and reflexivity notions of the German model is an alternative and obverse set of processes. These are grounded not in theoretical but in *practical* knowledge (Streeck 1989). Germans are thus, unlike the French and Anglo-Americans, a nation of hands-on 'machine builders'. This accounts for the continuing presence of a sort of guild ethos of German production with the foregrounding of apprenticeship and practical training. This also explains the more prominent role of trade unions in Germany in education and technological change as well as their other functions on enterprise councils (Mahnkopf 1992). In addition, it accounts for the centrality of the local, municipal level of social life as well as the power and role of local chambers of commerce in contemporary German production systems. And finally, there is the crucial German concept of the *Beruf* – meaning profession and/ or trade, though maintaining an element of the ethos of a 'calling' – as a basis, indeed as a virtual precondition of personal identity. Without a *Beruf*, without a trade or profession, one is almost a non-person, almost beyond the pale.

German production systems are thus contradictory. On the one hand reflexive, on the other practical; on the one hand grounded in abstract knowledge, on the other in the concrete and immediate, on the one hand rationalist-deductive, on the other hands on and empiricist. What will be shown is that there is a kind of creative unity resulting from this duality which partly at least accounts for the success of the German model in economic terms.

Re-integrating conceptualization and execution

In the 1980s German sociology was effectively recast in the direction of neo-modernization analyses. Two books played a central role in this: Kern and Schumann's *Das Ende der Arbeitsteilung?* (1984) and Beck's *Risk Society* (1992a), published in German in 1986. We discussed the latter in chapter 3. The context of the former was the Marxist analysis of the 1970s. It had there been argued that capital would rationalize the labour process, and that labour would become ever more impoverished as it became more abstract. Further, white collar workers were understood as increasingly proletarianized (Beckenbach 1991: 151). By contrast to this capital-centred paradigm, the Kern–Schumann thesis of 'new production concepts' provided a modernization paradigm. More specifically Kern and Schumann proffered a 'techno-theoretical' standpoint in which the new information and communications technologies as applied to immediate production would lead, not to 'complexity reduction', but to the 'increasing complexity of objective labour' (Beckenbach 1991: 153). What this meant was the 're-transference of *Produktionsintelligenz*' into the sphere of execution; it meant the 're-professionalization' of the sphere of production (Kern and Schumann 1984: 97–8).

There are a number of central components of this 'neo-modernization' or 'neo-industrialization' model, and here the model might be taken in a very important sense as ideal-typical both of German industrial sociology and of German production systems. First, modernization produces winners and losers. The winners include those whose skill level has been improved especially by the introduction of computer numerical control technology. Modernization losers include a large number of workers who are made unemployed by the inclusion into production of the new information and communication technologies. It includes workers in declining sectors. There is also a polarization of workers into an increasingly qualified and professionalized more footloose component and a plant-specific workforce whose life chances on external labour markets are minimal (Kern and Schumann 1984: 191–3). The losers also include craft workers who become fewer in number.

Second, there is the re-circulation of practical and empirical knowledge in the form of deductive knowledge. The introduction of the new information and communication technologies is a contradictory process. On the one hand, it potentially represents an extended 'imperialism of instrumental reason', through threatening the complexity of the lifeworld's pre-discursive communication culture. And on the other, it can represent the 'development of the reflexive dimension of societal reason' and thus erase the boundaries between 'technology and organization, between production and administration, execution and conceptualization, between system and environment' (Malsch 1987: 2–3). In this Malsch sees two possibilities, the monological and the dialogical, arising from this 'replacement of expert work by expert systems' (1987: 11). The monological option was already present in Taylorism and in centralized Anglo-American processes of informationalization. But there is an option as well for the 'dialogical relation between systems analyst and skilled worker', involving the active participation of the labour force. Only this will 'optimize the algorithmization of experiential knowlege into the expert systems' with which the skilled worker must subsequently work (Malsch 1987: 10).

Third, most of Kern and Schumann's empirical work was carried out in the automobile and machine tool sectors (1984). Such sectors are characterized by what Sorge and Streeck call 'diversified quality production' (1987). Such production is effectively 'medium batch' production (see Sorge 1991 on contrasting forms of production). The Germans and the Japanese are particularly successful in such sectors, in cars, machine building and consumer electronics. Diversified quality production as medium batch production can be characterized as 'neo-Fordist', by comparison with the 'Fordist', low diversity, high volume sectors, and the post-Fordist advanced services and high technology (Sabel 1982). The Fordist sectors are characterized by a small proportion of managers/professionals involved in long-cycle conceptualization tasks and a mass of shopfloor workers involved in short-cycle execution tasks, with a very strong boundary between the two. Diversified quality production sectors involve a blurred boundary betwen managerial/professionals and shopfloor workers, each engaged in medium-cycle job-tasks (Sorge 1991: 165-6). Post-Fordist sectors involve the participation of a mass of professional workers, each of whom engages in quite long-cycle job tasks. These constitute in most cases a majority of the labour force.

There are two points to note here. First, although these diversified quality production sectors may determine economic success at present, in the long run it may be the post-Fordist sectors which will be of greater importance, especially for economies apart from Germany and Japan. Second, those who have carried out extensive comparative work advocate a 'contingency theory', which maintains that there is no single best organizational form or training system (see also Maurice et al 1982). Indeed the latter must be seen in the context of industrial structure. Here the spreading of diversified quality production sectors in Japan and Germany would seem to lead to similar human resource training practices. But in fact the two could not be further apart, Japanese training being much closer to the school-based system of the Americans and the French (Schlegel 1991).

Finally, Kern and Schumann argue that there is an 'end of the division of labour' (*Das Ende der Arbeitsteilung*, 1984). By this they mean that there is the re-integration of conceptualization and execution in the labour process, and specifically the re-integration of production planning, maintenance functions and quality control with direct shopfloor labour (Lane 1988). Jürgens et al have researched such issues at Volkswagen (1989). They argue that these problems are differently solved within different production systems. For the same sort of problem, Germans will find a rationaliz-ation solution in terms of the modernization of human and machine technology; the Japanese will find a 'human resources solution'; while the Americans (and by implication the British and French) remain locked in a classical Fordist fix.

Some of these differences can be seen in the car industry. Enormous capital costs are entailed in its modernization, for example, in the introduction of almost fully automated welding in body shops. This has served to reinforce the minimization of downtime, whether due to changeover or to process or product defects. Hence the increasing importance of maintenance and quality control. This lends itself to two sorts of decentralized solution: either to collectivist job rotation and quality control circles, or to the upgrading of individuals in the workforce who take on the decentralized functions individually. The latter has been largely the German solution, as previously direct workers have been upgraded to the position of *Anlagenführer* (complex equipment monitor). The *Anlagenführer* takes on new set-up, maintenance and monitoring responsibilities. This stands in contrast with the situation at American-owned plants such as GM/Opel where this work is still carried out Fordist-fashion in the maintenance department (Jürgens 1991a: 19; Jürgens et al 1986: 265–6).

Part of this specific nature of German production systems is due to the intervention of the unions and works councils. Thus for example whereas Ford and GM have understood mechanization in terms of the automation of machines, the German metalworkers union (IG Mctall) has conceived of this in the ancient notion of techne or the German idea of *Technik*. This has as strong a human element as a machine element, and necessarily implies the upgrading of labour (Mahnkopf 1990; Crouch and Finegold 1991). Whereas Ford and GM were rather quick to adapt Japanese quality circles, the German *Betriebsräte* supported QCs at first but then grew sceptical, especially as unions were less than enthusiastic about the election of circle leaders. Instead much of decentralization of quality control has taken place through mechanization, that is, the development of computer-based automated measurement procedures (Jürgens et al 1986: 275–7).

Volkswagen along with Fiat – more so than American or Japanese firms – were first in their development of a systematic automation strategy. General Motors for example instead was embroiled historically in product-model change competition with Ford. The VW beetle, having even much longer product runs than the cars in the American giants, did not have to worry so much about conversion costs when shifting to new models and hence could focus on process (that is, automation) strategies (Jürgens et al 1989: 60). The higher such conversion costs were, the more a company would persist in non-automated, manual production. General Motors, earlier and more thoroughly than Ford, adopted a systematic automation strategy only from the early 1980s. Yet the initiation of robotization was somehow more organic and integral to VW's development by comparison with the seemingly more artificial evolution at GM. While GM and Fiat purchased robots from other companies, VW had them custom made in-house through its established relationship with Siemens for information and control technology (Jürgens et al 1989: 50, 65–9).

American firms such as Ford and GM understood an automation strategy as something which essentially involved equipment, without the participation of unions on the tabula rasa of new green field sites. Management strategies were not seen in terms of new production concepts, but as the replacement of men by machines. In Germany by contrast automation was understood to mean both machines and workers. Unions and assumptions of a certain degree of democracy were seen as integral to an automation project (Jürgens et al 1989: 245). Robotization at VW has thus also brought a lot more upgrading of production workers, not just to *Anlagenführer*, but to *Robotbetreuer* and *Strassenführer* grades. The new category of *Guteprüfer* and Quality Upgrade Operators has been created as well, in which production workers need qualifications in statistics, data processing, inspection planning and measuring techniques (Jürgens et al 1989: ch 13 passim).

Central to all this and to the viability of information structures in German production systems is the process of professionalization. In Germany the idea of skill is understood also as profession. The terms *Fach* and *Beruf* apply both to skilled workers and to professional specialists. The stratificational chasm separating skilled worker and engineer in the USA, the UK or France is greatly diminished in Germany. To be a skilled worker carries with it notions of 'comprehensive responsibility' and 'self-regulation' (Jürgens 1991a: 11). This notion of skill as profession means a certain self-confidence that tends to minimize the demarcation disputes, either lateral or vertical, common in the USA and UK. While wage differentials are much greater between skilled and unskilled in Germany than in the Anglo-Saxon world, confident German skilled workers are willing to carry out less skilled, routine operations. They benefit from this in the familiarity gained with the sort of work that is done on the assembly line (Jürgens et al 1989: 276–82).

Professionalization most of all means a re-integration of management and direct labour functions. Professional engineers and technicians stand in relation to skilled workers, not so much in a 'policing function', as in a 'service function', similar to a sort of consultancy relationship where workers ask the professionals for advice. Communication becomes more open and *sanktionsfrei*. Information tends to flow to different parts of the organization.

The Beruf: craft regulation and professional competence

We have so far focussed on the abstract knowledge, the informationaliz-ation and rationalization involved in the restructured German production systems. But these 'new production concepts' have been overlain upon a non-conceptual, hands-on, practical and empirical basis. Further, German restructuring has been far less drastic than that in other countries. This is emphasized in Lutz and Veltz's work on the comparative industrial structure and education in Germany and France (1989). Their characterization of Germany and France respectively as nations of *Maschinenbauer* and *Informatiker* is borne out by the pattern of public subsidy of R&D spending in the two countries. In metalworking and machine building, public expenditure accounted in 1984 for 18.5 per cent of total R&D spending in Germany and only 6.5 per cent in France. In aerospace these figures were reversed to 18 per cent in France and 6 per cent in Germany, while the public proportion of R&D spending in electronics and 'information' sectors was 28 per cent in France and 24 per cent in Germany (Lutz and Veltz 1989: 234).

Even in the same sectors, and regarding similar issues, what for the French is a theoretical problem is in Germany a practical problem. What for the French comes under R&D or the 'design process', for the Germans comes under the labour process. In French industry, computer-supported production is called *productique* and is – even in machine-building sectors – not seen as a machine-building problem but a problem of information. What in France entails an organizational revolution is understood by the Germans in terms of organizational continuity. At Renault in the 1970s for example, the initiation of informationalized production was the occasion for the creation of a Director for Scientific and Technical Affairs, the latter to be an esteemed outsider arriving with a contingent of abstract-educated top university personnel. In Germany by contrast the similar introduction of computers is instead an issue of 'branch-specific technical competence with the appropriate (branch-specific) engineering-science training development' (Lutz and Veltz 1989: 226–8).

Maurice et al (1982) have further shown that engineers, technicians, foremen and skilled workers occupy the same 'qualificational space' in Germany. This qualificational space is simultaneously a space of flows of information of agents from one category to the next. The social stratification of production systems is intimately related to their information structures. In France by contrast there could not be a greater diremption between skilled workers and engineers. The origins of this lie in the flourishing in nineteenth-century France of a very prominent technical and scientific elite, constituting a fraction of the bourgeoisie alongside the classically educated elite. In Germany the corresponding fraction comprised those with a juristic training, while engineers and technicians were much lower down the social hierarchy. If engineers received an abstract and mathematical training in the French *grandes écoles*, German engineering schools later to become today's *Fachhochschulen* were infinitely more practice oriented. The very concrete nature of training in the *Fachhochschulen* is instantiated in their departmental structure (see Brater 1991). Thus engineers occupy the middle ranks of German social stratification ladders but the upper ranks of French ones. Moreover, German skilled workers occupy the middle ranks of these ladders while French shopfloor workers occupy the lower ranks.

The concreteness, the particularism of German production systems lie in the central role of *Beruf* or craft as a mode of economic governance. Such governance resembles the practices described in MacIntyre's new communitarian political philosophy (1981, 1988). These practices for MacIntyre are modelled on the Aristotelian virtues and feature the setting of standards internal to a practice. They presuppose the pre-eminence of such 'internal goods' (that is, excellence at a given practice) as distinct from 'external goods' such as money, status and power.

There is some evidence for a greater internalist setting of standards in Germany (Streeck et al 1987a, b). This *Beruf* mentality is extended to the *Habilitation* and PhD in Germany, in which younger academics must meet criteria set by their elders until nearly the age of 40, instead of very quickly going for creativity, market niches and the commercial publishing possibilities of especially French and British, but also American, academics of a similar age. In this sense *Berufe* have norm setting powers. *Beruf* is indeed involved in a 'double function': on the one hand as an 'objective structuring principle of technical knowledge'; and on the other as 'a framework for the acquisition of technical knowledge and technical competency'. This technical competency is not a property of rules as in Taylorism or objectified in computers, but is instead a property 'of persons'. It enables the 'valorization' of these persons on the labour market (Lutz and Veltz 1989: 261).

We should not overexaggerate the significance of *Beruf* economic governance in Germany. In training, chambers of commerce, trade unions and employers, organizations play an important role in setting standards. And the best and most sought-after apprenticeship training is in the largest firms such as VW which must involve an important element of governance by hierarchies. And yet specialists from the education sector (hence closer to the actual skills of the *Beruf*) play a much more important role in standard setting in Germany than in say Britain (Green 1992). Further, on the shopfloor in the major enterprises, craft groupings themselves fulfil the greater part of the training function.

The apprenticeship is of course the lynchpin of German production systems. German apprenticeships are integral to a dual system, with enterprise and school training. This contrasts with both the school-based systems of France and Japan, and the old 'single' (workplace-based) training system of traditional apprenticeships (see Casey 1991). Training is to an important extent centrally regulated, through the setting of minimal standards, which the large firms exceed. The 1969 Vocational Training Act took some twenty years to be incrementally implemented. This proceeded via industrial branch agreements, through tripartite negotiations of employers and trade unions supported by the resources of the Federal Training Institute. In each branch one agreement was concluded for local chambers of industry and commerce and another for the artisan chambers. The very concreteness of training is reflected in the number of occupations for which exams are available, 382 in 1989. There has been increased standardization of exams across Länder, as more exams and teaching materials are purchased from the Institute for Vocational Examinations (Streeck et al 1987a; Casey 1991: 213–14). The apprenticeship period is lengthening to an average of 3.5 years.

There is a strong tendency in Germany today to follow the Japanese model and encourage 'general competences' in apprentices. In 1991 an estimated one-third of shopfloor workers use computer-aided equipment, a proportion that is expected to increase to two-thirds by 2001. This is fostered by additional rationalization prescribed in the 1987 Federal Training Law, which features the re-ordering of metal trades into only 16 trades with 17 specialisms, and the electric trades into four trades with eight specialisms, as well as a first apprenticeship year dedicated to basic general training followed by 2.5 years of specialist training. This principle is more fully developed in Volkswagen where apprentices work in teams of six, often mixed by race, gender and education level, frequently on complex trial machinery, and are encouraged to learn from one another and to develop quality consciousness. Here often electricians and mechanics work on the same teams, and individuals are rotated to different plant areas by three-month periods (Meyer-Dohm 1991: 3, 9, 13).

Technical colleges and industrial districts

We have thus described the two sides of German production systems: on the one hand, the abstract and theoretical elements of the 'new production concepts', and on the other, the concrete and praxis-oriented *Beruf* regulation of production. What the post-organized capitalist economy in Germany has therefore involved has been the grafting on of the 'superstructure' of new production concepts onto the *Beruf*-like basis of traditional German industry which had never been disrupted by a classical Fordist hiatus (Boyer 1986: 20–9). Where theory meets praxis here is above all through the informational structures of the *Fachhochschulen* and the German industrial districts, which can be usefully understood as the social embodiments of this conception of *Beruf*.

The literature on districts has increasingly come to understand them in terms of a set of exchanges regulated by the social networks in which they are embedded (Brusco 1990; Granovetter 1985, 1990). Different sorts of districts feature different sorts of network-linked exchanges. For example, the clothing industry in Emilia-Romagna is characterized by network-linked exchanges between small manufacturers and distributors. New industrial districts in high technology districts are organized around network-linked market exchanges between small producers (Scott 1988b). In the culture industries in London, as we shall see in the next chapter, labour markets are the most important network-linked exchanges (as is argued in Granovetter 1974; Shapiro et al 1992).

By contrast in the German industrial districts the paradigmatic network-linked exchange, which is at the same time the characteristic feature of German information structures, is that between the technical colleges (*Fachhochschulen*) and medium-sized firms, not simply between medium-sized firms (as argued by Sabel et al 1987). The following are the main features of the German education- and training-based industrial district. First, as stated above, the *Fachhochschulen*, technical colleges of *higher* education, play a central role. They are the principal component of the supply-side of these district information structures, with the medium-sized firms the demand-side. In some Länder such as Bavaria and Berlin, the *Fachhochschulen* are not very strongly developed by comparison with the universities. In other districts such as Mannheim, the colleges are very well developed, but the requisite demand-side is not so established. In yet others like Baden-Württemberg there is both a well-developed technical college system and the requisite demand-side of medium-sized firms (Bernschneider et al 1991; Hoffmann 1991: 95–6).

These classic German industrial districts are very much a post-organized capitalist phenomenon. They involve, as Hoffmann observes, the displacement of 'the extensive economic growth phase of the 1950s and 1960s by an intensive hi-tech-based development phase' (1991: 74). 'Extensive' and 'intensive' in this context refer importantly to spatial parameters. Thus there was a shift to what in Baden-Württemberg was called *Technologieförderung* and in Berlin an 'innovation and technology policy'. In Baden-Württemberg there had been a pre-existing cooperation between the *technische Fachhochschulen* and the Land's economy. But this took a more explicit and goal-oriented direction from the late 1960s with the establishment of the technical consultancy services. These disposed of little money or personnel and operated largely through the good will of the technical college teachers. In 1971 the Steinbeis-Stiftung was set up, as a private law umbrella organization to help coordinate such services (Hoffmann 1991: 75–6).

Second, there must be a critical mass of innovation-oriented medium-sized firms. Small firms and traditional medium-sized firms are unattractive for the college teachers to work with. Students do not want to be seconded to them. And they cannot attract good technical college graduates as engineers. Large firms can provide much of their technological consultancy in-house. The main types of interaction between the colleges and these modern medium-sized firms are through consultancy meetings, cooperation through college-based long-term research projects and via personnel exchanges. These personnel exchanges include secondment from the firms to the colleges; secondment for teachers from the colleges to the firms; and the firms' recruiting possibilities of college graduates. Recruitment is a key motivation for firm management to work with the colleges. But directly financial incentives also are a factor: to obtain R&D input from the colleges is simply cost-effective (Herrigel 1988; Hoffmann 1991: 82–4). The colleges in turn participate because the project may be interesting to students, because some of them and younger lecturers may get employed in the companies, and because the colleges may gain extra funding and student places (Hoffmann 1991: 79; Maier 1987: 5 ff). This makes for a lively circulation of information and personnel in German productive systems.

Third, in general the federal government plays only a minor role in these technology transfer initiatives. Much more important is what happens regionally and locally. Baden-Württemberg is paradigmatic of decentralized governance, in which the Land plays its role mainly in the 'aggregation and organization of regional modernization interests' (see Bernschneider et al 1991: 60). These local 'modernization interests' include the chambers of commerce and Handwerk chambers, the communes, the districts and the *Fachhochschulen*. The initial arrangements were typically corporatist. Coordination in the early 1970s of the technical consultancy offices was through the private law Steinbeis-Stiftung for Economic Assistance. The offices, though run by college teachers, were sited at local chambers of commerce. Coordination, but little finance, of consultancy in the 1970s was provided by the Land Business Office, itself created by the Land government's Economics Ministry (Hoffmann 1991: 77). From the 1980s, as the language of 'technology consultancy' was displaced by that of 'technology transfer' and 'innovation promotion', the Land government began to enter as a major factor, hugely increasing its annual funding of the Steinbeis-Stiftung. Also the chairmanship of the Steinbeis-Stiftung was taken over by the Land government's new Commissioner for Technology Transfer, who from 1984 to 1985 coordinated a set of 16 technology consultancy offices in the technical colleges, 64 technology transfer centres based in Baden-Württemberg's municipalities, and 10 other technology centres directly sponsored by the Land government (Bernschneider et al 1991: 60). Further, from 1987 the Land Credit Bank in conjunction with the refurbished Steinbeis-Stiftung were to extend their functions to responsibility for all of the Land's economic assistance programmes. Though 80 technology transfer centres were created from 1983 to 1988 in this context, this increased statism was accompanied by deregulation, as technology transfer centres were to self-finance after an initial state input, with teacher-directors bearing budget responsibility. The general concept in this was for the state to play, not a bureaucratic role, but one as 'service-entrepreneur' (Hoffmann 1991: 97).

Finally, there must be a demand constituted for the products of the medium-sized firms. This is typically exercised by very large firms in a given region which have moved from mass to diversified quality production. Mass-producing client firms – with dedicated tools – only need either to produce in-house or to buy their standardized tools from mass-producing smaller firms. The input of a range of innovating medium-sized firms is only necessary when the shift of the client firms is made to diversified quality production. Thus Herrigel (1988) describes the lack of success of the American machine tool industry – which was quite successful in the Fordist era – in moving into innovative production of a range of goods. At this point they were decisively overtaken by the German industry. The major final large producer in the Stuttgart district is Daimler-Benz, which in 1986 used more than 10,000 suppliers from Baden-Württemberg (Dankbaar 1989; Hoffmann 1991: 89).

A region where such a new industrial district significantly developed is the Ruhr. It was the classic Fordist or organized capitalist region with much in-house production, with extensive chains of vertical integration. It seems that these chains had become counter-productive to growth. However, it has made a successful transition. First, as the large individual steel producers began to move towards specialized products, the division of labour markedly deepened. An industrial infrastructure of suppliers developed, especially in machine building, but also in electronics, accounting for some 190,000 jobs by 1976. More important, the big steel firms began to move into non-steel products and processing. The mix also shifted from non- and semi-finished materials to processing. In 1970 4.2 per cent of non-steel production consisted of processing; this increased to 23.7 per cent by 1986. Perhaps the most sweeping re-orientation of these vast steel firms was into plant engineering and environmental technology. In both of these, at issue is not even diversified quality production, but highly specialized products, often one-offs. Hence the production process itself became unusually specialized with a vast division of labour, as different mixes of small firms were contracted in alliances to engineers and to build single plants and design highly customized environmental technology. By the end of the 1980s the environmental technology complex of North-Rhine Westphalia consisted of more than 600 firms accounting for around 100,000 jobs (Grabher 1990: 15, 17).

The so-called 'rigidities' of German production systems are not nearly as rigid as those of the Japanese. The strong measure of craft or *Beruf* governance of training leads to significant external occupational labour markets, rather than to the less flexible structures of the Japanese. However, when networks in German production systems have been connected by strong ties, the result has often unfortunately been 'rigidifying' rigidities. Thus Grabher (1990: 7–8) argues that the Fordist fix of the Ruhr was due partly to the too strong personal and relational contracting between firms, which led to serious problems with 'boundary-spanning functions'. At issue here are difficulties in scanning the economic environment and making external information, concerning the identification and mobilization of external resources, relevant to the firm. Some 57 per cent of the machine-building firms surveyed entered new product development in close cooperation with their main customers; 33 per cent said they cooperated with only their single most important customer; only 9 per cent would have been able to realize significant innovations without their main customer; and 35 per cent drew their innovation ideas from the main customer (see also Jürgens 1990). The result of these intense personal relations was to impede the mass of information flow through the productive sysem. The result was as Grabher notes an absence of system 'self-reflexivity' (1990: 12–13). The system here could react to the environment; it was insufficiently reflexive to question its own rules.

The way out of this Fordist fix was through the creation of looser ties, in the shifting alliances mentioned above as the big companies diversified into the production of filtration and de-contamination plants. This meant boundary-spanning functions had to be improved, so that the right partners could be known for each problem. For example, some 200 of the firms in the area's environmental technology complex are specialized component firms. And information flow from within these companics must be maximized, as 50 per cent of the orders in plant engineering are accounted for by highly complex mechanical engineering and micro-electronic control systems. Thus weak ties can be better for information flow than strong ties (Granovetter 1985, 1990). The information that flows through flexibly-linked networks is 'thicker' than that which flows through markets, and freer than that which flows through hierarchies or through stronger communitarian, relational contracting. This openness with regard to boundary-spanning functions, to R&D, to marketing, encourages 'the openness and reflectivity of the entire network' (Grabher 1990: 18).

Like Japan's collective reflexivity, German 'craft reflexivity' involves the grafting of the highly modern onto a traditional basis. Hence we have the very modern reflexive nature of Kern and Schumann's new production concepts grafted onto the pre-reflexive craft tradition. The craft tradition's pre-discursive ethos is closer to guild regulation, to convention, to habits and habitus. With the shift to policy focus on more cutting-edge technologies, in Bavaria, in public and university spending on the development of Ulm in Baden-Württemberg as a 'science city' to the tune of DM 385 million in 1988 alone, it would seem that the future may lie in the 'reflexivity' rather than 'craft' (Bernschneider 1991: 61). It would, however, be foolish to doubt the viability of the craft basis and *Beruf* mentality that is so pervasive of German culture.

The persistence of the craft tradition, in the context of peculiarly German modernization, would seem to foster the continued strength of trade unionism. Previously the German unions had been seen as favourable to modernization (Mahnkopf 1990, 1991, 1992). But in Bavaria they have been effectively excluded from technology transfer policy making. In the Ruhr – with the exception of environmental issues – they have played rather a traditional role. They have played next to no role in the planning in Baden-Württemberg. Unless the unions can reconstitute themselves as a modernizing force, the democratic ethos of German production systems will be seriously under threat.

DISCURSIVE REFLEXIVITY: INFORMATION-RICH PRODUCTION SYSTEMS

So far we have discussed Japanese and German productive systems and information structures in terms respectively of collective and practical reflexivity. We have compared post-organized capitalist Japanese and German production systems with the Fordist counterparts in the UK, USA and France. We have noted that the German and Japanese production systems are more expansive than Anglo-American Fordism. The former embrace a wider range of institutional units, subcontractors, technical colleges and chambers of commerce, than do their Anglo-American counterparts. Moreover, in Japan and Germany production systems and information structures are co-extensive. Whereas in the Anglo-American Fordist model, significant elements of production, most crucially shopfloor workers and financial contractors, are substantially excluded from information structures. Moreover, while Japanese and German information structures (and flows of finance) articulate predominantly with production systems, in the US and UK information structures (and financial flows) are largely interdependent with systems of consumption.

In this section we will consider various advanced sectors of the world economy, of high technology and of certain producer services. Such sectors are to be found in certain concentrations in the US economy and to a lesser extent in the UK and parts of western Europe. We shall consider whether these sectors can and are already constituting a kind of post-industrial core, a core based upon a 'discursive reflexivity'. These sectors typically involve small batch production and are thus post-Fordist. The production systems are to a large extent at the same time expert systems. The sectors are very specialized with short product runs. They are highly flexible with very long job-task cycles. Their basis is discursive knowledge, in which half to three-quarters of the workforce is comprised of professional-managerial employees, that is of experts themselves.

Production is characteristically not so much material as informational. While knowledge has always been central to technological change, only now 'is the raw material itself information and so is its outcome' (Castells 1989: 30). The initiation of this new informational economy was signalled by the introduction of the integrated circuit in 1957, the microprocessor in 1971, gene-splicing techniques in 1973, and the microcomputer in 1975. These developments together with the exponential growth in computer power have transformed (1) the storage of information, with drastic reductions in cost per unit of memory, (2) the retrieval of information, the processing or analysis of information, the organization of sets of instructions which handle information in order to generate new information, and (3) the transportation of information, with advances in telecommunications (Castells 1989: ch 1).

So we are concerned here with an informational economy, with how information is materially embodied in goods and services. There are some interesting contrasts with the production of material commodities. First, the inputs are different. Informational inputs are less marketized compared with inputs for material production. Information is often free and to be 'retrieved' while a machine-tool, for example, always must be paid for and purchased. The boundary-scanning abilities of individual employees as 'subjects' are more important in securing information inputs, thus contrasting with the primacy of market price which apparently inheres in 'objects' in the production of material commodities. Second, training systems in the material economy are practically oriented by comparison with the theoretically oriented abstract education necessary in the information economy. Third, the means of production in the informational economy has a qualitatively higher ratio of electronic to mechanical components than in the case of material means of production. Fourth, human capital operates on objects of production through discursive knowledge in the information economy, through practical knowledge in the material economy. Fifth, the transportation of material goods differs significantly from that of informational goods, since much of the latter comprises 'communication'. Sixth, in the informational economy, services contain a higher proportion of abstract knowledge. Moreover, with increasingly individualized consumption, especially in the new middle classes, this is often a matter of a dialogic co-production, involving the development of fine classificatory distinctions through interaction between service producers and consumers (Bourdieu 1984). Further, in that commodities in the information economy transport, transform and store information, or signs or images (televisions, telephones, home computers, compact discs, video recorders), they serve to increase the degree of self-servicing in the economy.

These distinctions partly undercut the debate about the nature of services. Walker suggests that the proliferation of services and especially producer services is associated with the rise of territorially concentrated production systems, in which economies of agglomeration enable the vertical disintegration of a number of services by manufacturing firms (1985, 1988). The new visibility of these small service firms then makes it seem as if there is an emergent service or information economy. The reality instead is only a deepening divison of labour *within* manufacturing. Thus information-processing would be just a more roundabout way of manufacturing or material processing. So for Walker the apparent proliferation of services is in fact merely an increase in the 'roundaboutness' of manufacturing material commodities. We will argue by contrast that with information and services becoming increasingly prominent, and in important senses predominant, as final and intermediate outputs of production units, it could be argued that manufacturing is becoming a more roundabout method for producing services.

Production systems as expert systems: US hi tech

In order to assess these kinds of claims we need to develop a more precise concept of the production systems of the information-rich advanced sectors. Storper and Harrison understand 'production systems' to consist of an input-output structure, of sets of linked-together units of production of different sizes; a structure of governance; and a given (dispersed or concentrated) territoriality (1990: 5). The input-output structure for Storper and Harrison varies mainly in terms of the number of production units involved in a system. Where there is vertical disintegration and a large number of units, the system is characterized by a deep division of labour. The governance structure of a system varies between the ideal type of a 'core' structure in which a given large firm dominates a system, such as GE, Sony and Westinghouse in electrical products, to a 'ring' structure in which say two semiconductor firms enter into a short-term and symmetrical alliance to bring out a specific chip. In many cases there is a combination of core and ring with a lead firm, but in which a number of suppliers with high asset and skills specificity have strong countervailing bargaining power (Storper and Harrison 1990: 15–16). Finally, systems can be more or less geographically dispersed.

What this otherwise interesting formulation ignores are four elements which we have emphasized at various points in this chapter: the significance of non-economic institutions within the economy; the crucial interconnections between different sectors, especially high technology and producer services; the importance of collegial and cultural forms of governance in the informational economy; and the proliferation of expert systems within consumption as well as production.

The importance of these can be seen by considering the model of the production system of high technology proffered by a number of American analysts. This comprises the following elements: a horizontal structure of a 'ring' type; a deep division of labour; territorially concentrated production with forwards and backwards linkages inside a given district; a horizontally disintegrated structure resulting from spin-offs of new firms from research institutes and existing firms; a transaction-rich agglomeration of market exchanges embedded in a set of networks; the generation of trust relations; a certain degree of community; and a distinct district culture (Saxenian 1985; Scott 1986, 1988a, b; Granovetter 1985; Brusco and Righi 1989).

This model has many virtues. But it fails sufficiently to recognize that knowledge-intensive advanced sector production systems have adapted information structures which are of a different order from those in classical manufacturing production. This is because production is very much a 'design process', a 'research and development process' (Lash 1991). The central production process is not dependent on research and development as in Japanese and German systems. Rather it *is* research and development. At issue is a production system that no longer operates like a production system. It is a production system that operates instead like an expert-system. Expert-systems are primarily cultural and what counts in for example the software sector is the 'creative milieu' and 'the exchange of ideas and people'. At issue here is much more than agglomerational economies (and by implication 'flexible accumulation') and 'the external economies of an informational production unit'. The micro-electronics 'innovative milieu' is closer to 'the situation of writers and artists, or stock exchange traders in New York, or to film and TV producers and actors, or financial consultants in LA' (Castells 1989: 69, 89).

It is similar to what one would find in a university research institute. Indeed in 1964 two-thirds of the Boston agglomeration's 64 semi-conductor based electronics firms originated in spin-offs, not from other large firms, but from research facilities. Twenty-four of these were located in local universities, 21 at MIT. In the Bay area, Stanford University more explicitly began to develop industrial contacts as early as the 1940s. The University opened its Industrial Park in 1951, offering low rent space to high tech companies such as Lockheed in aerospace research. Subsequently Stanford faculty and student body were responsible for the majority of the foundings of research-related enterprises in the late 1950s and early 1960s (Saxenian 1985: 83; Castells 1989: 49–51).

Thus on the original supply-side (for labour and product innovation) of these economies of agglomeration were non-economic institutions. On the final demand-side was another non-economic institution, the military. Especially Stanford, but also MIT and the fledgling computer and semi-conductor industries in California, Massachusetts, Texas, Arizona and Florida developed very strong initial links with the military (Markusen and Bloch 1985).

In this very important sense high technology districts are much more than 'economic districts', they are also 'cultural districts'. On their supply-side are cultural sectors and the university, more a matter of a 'cultural system' than a production system – or a 'unit of culture' rather than a unit of production. On the demand-side was the military, again far from a production system, instead a system of organized violence. Caught in between was the emergent high technology sector, itself taking on more the model of a cultural system, or a cultural institution, than that of a unit of production. We will now show this in detail by considering aspects of the American high technology industry and especially the production of semi-conductors. We will see the increasing importance of discursive reflexivity as production has become more knowledge-intensive.

Semi-conductor manufacturing consists of four central operations: the research and design of the circuit, the work of scientists and advanced research engineers; the engineering of the circuit that will go into the chip, including circuit reduction through lithography techniques – involved here are engineers and technicians; wafer fabrication, in which the silicon material support for the circuits is made and the wafers are then chemically treated, before being divided into individual chips – centrally employed in this are skilled manual workers; and the assembly of chips to make electronic components. These are the final products of semi-conductor production. They are either integrated circuits or discrete devices (Malecki 1985; Castells 1989: 73; Angel 1990: 212).

Mass production in semi-conductors, the work of 'merchant' or 'commodity device' firms, entails outlays of $150–200m to set up a high volume fabrication plant. The mass market here has increasingly been dominated by Japanese and Korean firms. But the lower volume, customized sector of the market has been growing disproportionately. In 1989 21 per cent of the value of total output of integrated circuits was comprised by application-specific devices. This output is largely provided for by new firms. Trends in new firm formation in semi-conductors exemplify advanced sector information structures in their proliferation, their intellectualization and their concentration. Proliferation follows demand for customized product. Data on new firm start-ups from 1957 show that there were about three times as many new firm start-ups in the 1970s as in the 1960s, and about twice as many in the 1980s as in the 1970s. This can be partly explained through increased demand for low volume product. But it is also the result of computer-aided design and manufacture. Though the costs of setting up high volume, dedicated fabrication facilities is prohibitive, the setting up of small modular fabrication facilities is less expensive. Here computer-aided design technology lowers the time and cost of new product development. It also introduces flexibility in the production of many different custom-designed proprietary circuits on the same production line, as well as cheapens product change in reducing downtime.

Of new firms founded from 1978 to 1987, the great majority were in customized markets. Thirty-three per cent manufactured application-specific integrated circuits, and 49 per cent were involved in the production of specialized linear, memory or gallium arsenide devices. Interestingly the failure rate of these new firms is low. Of 124 of such start-ups from 1978 to 1987, only 9 had stopped production by 1989 and only 8 others had been acquired by other firms (Angel 1990: 214–16; Garnsey and Roberts 1991). Locationally these new firm start-ups have been quite concentrated. Of 124 new firm foundations between 1978 and 1987, 63 per cent were in Silicon Valley, 13 were in the greater Los Angeles region, and only 2 were in the Boston agglomeration. In Silicon Valley in 1987, these new firms made up some one-third of all semi-conductor establishments in the region and employed more than 15,000 workers (Angel 1990: 218–19).

The most important point though for our argument here is that the semi-conductor sector in the First World is becoming much more knowledge based. Almost none of the new firms carry out their own assembly. At the beginning of the 1990s about 70 per cent of assembly work is outsourced to the Third World and especially to southeast Asia (Sklair 1990; Henderson 1989: 63-7). Moreover, an increasing proportion of fabrication is also being outsourced. Only about one-third of the American companies starting up between 1978 and 1987 established their own fabrication facilities. Wafer fabrication carried out by skilled workers is instead conducted partly in the larger US plants, but mainly in Scotland in Silicon Glen and in Singapore and Taiwan (Angel 1990: 218; Henderson 1989: 150, 156). Thus in the new small US companies most of the work is actually done by engineers and technicians in the research and development and engineering of circuits and in the development of prototypes. The occupational make-up of these new semi-conductor firms will approach that of the software companies, in which about three-quarters of the labour force is comprised of professional-managerial and technical staff (Malecki 1985).

There are a number of characteristics of the information structure present here. First, it is one in which the information circulating tends to be highly discursive. Second, the information circulates over an increasing proliferation of nodes, as new firms multiply. This particularly occurs through spin-offs resulting from individuals leaving research institutions and larger firms to found their own firms. Involved here is information flow and learning through the increased intensity and duration of interaction of individuals from different firms involved in supplier-client relations. This becomes increasingly intense along with the customization of products (Williamson 1985). There is an increase in transaction costs involved in this intensification and duration of the social bond between supplier and client. Angel's survey of clients in the semi-conductor industry showed that the client's propensity to purchase and use application-specific devices depended on the ability of firms to produce as quickly as possible working prototypes on demand. This involved virtually relational-contracting with clients in 'the development of circuit designs and architectures through a series of prototypes and product devices' (1990: 214). As a result one of the producers employed one application engineer for each field agent employed, while typical of mass-producing merchant firms was one engineer per 16 field agents.

Biotechnology, as an emergent sector, parallels high technology in a number of ways. In terms of the means of production, raw materials and the product are entities whose informational content is more prominent than their material support. The information processing involved is contained in 'the ability to decode and reprogram the information embodied in living organisms' (Castells 1989: 12). Genetic engineering is an information-processing activity.

Crucial events in the development of this industry were the first model of DNA in 1953 and Boyer and Cohen's gene-splicing techniques in 1973 which opened up the possibility of recombinant DNA. What this made feasible was the transformation of everyday micro-organisms into cheap and prolific facilities for manufacturing proteins characteristic of other species. The output of biotechnology is 'information inscribed in living matter', the engineering involved being the processing of such information (Barley et al 1991: 5).

In 1975 the US Patent Office granted Stanford University and the University of California rights to Boyer and Cohen's technique. With aid from venture capital Boyer himself founded Genentech in 1976. This was followed by a public stock offering in 1980, and Genentech becoming one of the most sought-after items on the New York Exchange. Venture capital flooded into the industry and between 1980 and 1982 about 155 dedicated biotechnology firms were established. By the mid-1980s some 500 free-standing biotechnology firms were engaging in genetic engineering, joined by a number of other large chemicals and additional firms who had developed their own in-house capacities (Barley et al 1991: 6–7).

Biotechnology resembles the semi-conductor sector in the way in which firms develop as spin-offs from university research facilities. Similarities can also be seen in its concentration in certain districts, the Bay Area, Boston and Washington, DC (this reflecting the enormous role played by federal government grants in the industry), as 'milieux of innovation'. Whereas the founding figures of microelectronics firms had often worked as engineers previously for large firms, the biotechnologists had almost all been pure research scientists. Unlike the microelectronic small firm capitalists, they had little knowledge of production, marketing and finance. While some microelectronic firms were established as 'milieux of secondary innovation' (to produce devices whose prototype already existed), virtually all biotechnology has been engaged in original research in the development of prototypes (Barley et al 1991: 8; Castells 1989: 68).[1]

Towards horizontal information structures: US hi tech

We will return now to the analysis of semi-conductors. The origins of the semiconductor industry can be traced back to AT&T and Western Electric's New Jersey-based Bell Laboratories, home to invention of the transistor in 1947 as well as to most of the original research and development in semi-conductors. The intention was to attempt the vertical integration of the communications industry. The consequences were however quite different, as the researchers at Bell spun off and set up independently as Fairchild and Intel in semi-conductors. Bell's liberal licensing of its discoveries was also responsible for Texas Instruments' early start in semi-conductors. The latter was a Dallas-based electronics company producing anti-submarine detectors during World War II. Keeping its navy markets in the post-war period, scientists at Texas Instruments, simultaneously with colleagues at Intel, invented the integrated circuit in 1957. Texas has been the typical vertically integrated company, connecting military markets and cheap assembly and fabrication labour in Dallas. Company policy has been to keep information structures and technical know-how of the Dallas research milieu strictly in-house (Castells 1989: 43–5; Henderson 1989: 32–5).

When the big electronics companies, Westinghouse, RCA and General Electric, began to produce semi-conductors in the late 1960s, it was through backwards integration from their own production in consumer or household electronics. They have developed into large employers. The average plant size is over 2,000 in semi-conductors and they often are dominant in a local economy. Motorola is an instructive example here. The company was founded to produce car radios, located in Phoenix in 1949, when it decided to invest heavily in its research laboratories. These

developed a precursor of the integrated circuit in the early 1950s and soon
after initiated production process innovations for transistors and semi-
conductors. As producer and standardizer of 'work-horse chips' in the
1960s, using offshore assembly, Motorola was the world's largest producer
of silicon devices. However, no 'industrial district' in Phoenix developed
since oaths restricting the circulation of employees' ideas effectively
precluded spin-offs, and backwards linkages were few with less than 5 per
cent of supplies being purchased locally (Glasmeier 1988: 291–3).

By contrast with Arizona one of the major high technology complexes
did develop in Los Angeles, in Orange County. It is interesting to note that
prior to the 1950s Los Angeles did not really possess a large industrial base
of its own. Besides the film industry and real estate, it mainly possessed a
large selection of branch plants, in a variety of economic sectors. This was
remedied in the 1950s as the region became the national centre of the
partly military-related aerospace industry, which along with communications equipment formed the original core of the region. This was highly
concentrated, serving a final demand concentrated in the military and the
large private airlines. The communications equipment manufacturers were
vertically integrated 'systems houses' such as Babcock Radio Engineering
and Hughes Ground Systems, making not standardized products, but very
expensive custom-designed special purpose output (Scott 1988b: 158;
Davis 1990).

These companies, with a high proportion of scientific and technical
personnel, began to decentralize from Los Angeles so as to avoid
congestion, high rents and expensive house prices. They moved south to
Orange County (Kanter 1984). The industry was though remarkably
concentrated. In 1959 18 per cent of Orange County manufacturing
employees worked in just four large communications equipment plants. If
the communications industry was at the core of emergent regional high
tech, perhaps the main feeder industry was the computer sector, always
more horizontally integrated than semi-conductors. The population likewise jumped from 0.70m in 1960 to 1.42m in 1970 to 1.93m in 1981. Among
employees professional-managerial grades were disproportionately represented. In 1978 the US proportion of blue collar workers in manufacturing
was 74 per cent, while in Orange County high technology firms it was only
58 per cent. Of all employees in 1980, 21.7 per cent of Americans were in
professional-managerial grades; this figure was 28.9 per cent in Orange
County (Scott 1988b: 164, 181).

By 1980 Orange County's originally integrated production and shallow
division of labour underwent transformation. Sectors which were suppliers
to the original communications and aircraft core came themselves to
constitute new poles of economic activity. The division of labour deepened
as both routine assembly and other work processes were outsourced. Local
backward linkages to smaller non-high technology 'penumbra' firms in
printed circuits, milling and lathing, and the like multiplied. Horizontal
disintegration ensued as average high technology plant size, which stood at

35 employees in 1955 and increased to 125 from 1960 to 1970, declined
back down to about 70 by 1983 (Scott 1988b: 184, 187).

So far then we have identified two sets of firms in high technology
industry in the USA. On the one hand, there are horizontally structured
networks of research and development-intensive innovating small firms,
and on the other, vertically integrated, hierarchically structured firms
consisting of massive-sized plants of 'nimble-fingered' assembly workers.
However, the bulk of employment in the sector is in neither. It is in
intermediate qualification levels: of more routine engineer and technician
jobs and of skilled manual workers. Alongside classical horizontal and
vertical structures have developed for example a number of 'secondary
milieux of innovation'. These are typically based around a set of 'technical
branch plants' that have relocated outside of primary milieux such as
Silicon Valley or Massachusetts' Route 128 (Castells 1989: 114).

Such technical branch plants are post-Fordist counterparts of the Fordist
branch plant. They are normally staffed by engineers and technicians who
tend to be white and non-unionized. They develop in bunches in smaller
university towns such as Austin, the North Carolina Research Triangle,
Santa Barbara, Colorado Springs and Santa Cruz. The relocation of
secondary innovating functions to technical branch plants outside of the
primary districts is often due to the availability of cheaper engineers.
Illustrative of this is the experience of the Rolm Corporation (subsequently
acquired by IBM), the manufacturer of computer-controlled telephone
exchange systems for offices and computers for high altitude environments.
Founded in Silicon Valley in 1969 and experiencing very rapid expansion,
rising housing costs combined with rising pay demands led Rolm to set up
sales and service and subsequently technical branch plants in Colorado
Springs and Austin. Even when in Silicon Valley, Rolm prospered through
the enhancement of off-the-shelf and custom components with software it
tailored to the needs of customers. In the Austin branch plant less basic
research has been done with the needs of being integrated into new
variations of existing Rolm products (Glasmeier 1988: 296). In Austin,
Rolm has been joined by technical branch plants of many of the microelectronics giants – IBM, Texas Instruments, Intel, Control Data, Motorola
and Hughes. Following them, and attracted to the University of Texas, a
research consortium and a semi-conductor industry trade association, with
defence department research and development funding, have also been
established (Castells 1989: 47–8).

A nationwide study of the work histories of 275 semi-conductor
engineers between 1980 and 1986 confirms the existence of a remarkably
fluid external labour market, especially in Silicon Valley but also in the
country as a whole. There were 209 job turnovers during the six-year
period; 56 per cent of them had changed jobs at least once. New job starts
peaked during the boom year of 1984 at 35 per 100 engineers. Job
separations peaked that same year at 20 per 100. Even in the slump year of
1985 virtually all separations went immediately to other jobs, as unemploy-

ment among engineers stood at under 1 per cent. The difference was that during boom years recruitment had to be largely from the universities, while during slump years firms could hire already experienced engineers (Angel 1989: 103–4).

The geography of job change provides something of a dual labour market. Whereas 72 per cent of largely primary sector engineers originally recruited by Silicon Valley firms came from Bay Area universities, only 54 per cent of the 'provincial' firms recruited from their local universities. The big non-Silicon Valley firms have set up some research and production facilities in Silicon Valley to take advantage of its labour market. Moreover, producers throughout the country recruited from the major centres, that is Dallas, Phoenix and Silicon Valley, of production. While 34 per cent of moves were interstate, 50 per cent of all job changes from 1980 to 1986 were between Silicon Valley firms. And 79 per cent of all engineers who left Silicon Valley firms took new Silicon Valley jobs. Angel concludes from this that the labour market 'serves as a conduit for the rapid dispersal of knowledge and manufacturing skills among Silicon Valley firms' and that this 'accelerated flow of information contributes to innovative capabilities and technological dynamism of production complexes' (1989: 108). Yet the same data show that this information flow, passing through the nodes of labour market exchanges, is at least nationwide and functions in the secondary as well as the primary market – in secondary milieux of innovation and production too. What in Japan develops through the job rotation of engineers in the same firm (and thus repesents an intra-firm information structure) takes place through external labour markets in the USA and constitutes almost a national and increasingly international information structure on a sectoral level.

Oakey and Cooper's (1989: 351–2) comparative study of small firms producing high technology instruments and electronics in Silicon Valley, southeast England and Scotland (which has the largest concentration of semi-conductor fabrication plants in Europe) suggests that innovation and horizontal structures characterized all three agglomerations. Despite some variation in backward and forward linkages a similar proportion in each area (about 60 per cent) of firm founders had previously worked for firms in the same area. Furthermore, the rate of product innovation was not very different in the three regions – in 1985–6, 91 per cent of Bay Area, 78 per cent of SE England, and 60 per cent of Scottish firms registered at least one new product innovation (Oakey and Cooper 1989: 352, 355).[2]

More generally there is some evidence of the considerably reduced importance of internal labour markets in these high technology companies. Kanter showed that career patterns tend to be more flexible, there is greater use of teamwork, and the labour market is less rigid and more varied (1984). More generally Savage et al argue that there is a decline in the effectiveness of organizational assets and a greater importance of 'self-directed career paths' (1992: 64). They demonstrate three points in detail: the heightened propensity for professionals and managers to move between firms; the way that organizational careers offer reduced security to managers so they are more inclined to move into self-employment; and the attempt to professionalize management (see Savage et al 1992: ch 4).

So far then we have argued that despite important tendencies towards the verticalization of information structures in microelectronics and allied sectors, there has been the overall constitution of horizontal and discursive-knowledge rich information structures in the sector. Thus innovation has spread from one or two centres to a set of secondary milieux. Despite the fact that information flow is facilitated in primary milieux like Silicon Valley via the extensive forwards and backwards product-market linkages, extensive horizontalization has taken place in secondary milieux too. This has occurred through the formation of collections of technical branch plants associated with university research institutes and training; a national network of information flow through labour markets which are increasingly externalized; considerable numbers of successful spin-offs in secondary centres; and still high levels of product innovation in these various centres. In some ways these high technology companies resemble universities, with relatively fluid external labour markets as conduits for information flow, with far-flung 'imagined communities' generated by extensive social networks, and with a kind of collegial governance inscribed in a set of non-economic symbolic competences.

High technology and the service economy

The 'advanced sectors' in especially the north American economy include not only the production of microelectronics but also various kinds of services. Although these will be discussed in detail in chapter 8, we will briefly consider services here. In particular we shall show the ways in which there are increasing interconnections between microelectronics on the one hand, and advanced producer services on the other. They are increasingly part and parcel of the same information structures (Hirschhorn 1985: 177–8). They are interlinked in part because the final demand market for microelectronics has changed from the military and defence to office work in services. The two key linkage sectors between microelectronics and the office are telecommunications and software.

This new centrality of telecommunications equipment is shown in their growing preponderance among alliances between high technology companies. The deregulation of telecommunications services, itself associated with the demise of captive markets for national telecommunications equipment companies and the new prominence of Telecommunications Network Services and Value-Added Network Services (VANS), has led to a vast increase in the number of alliances in such sectors (see Mulgan 1991). 'Triad' (European, American and Japanese) computer and communications production in 1986 totalled $228bn, and has experienced average real market growth of 8 per cent per year from 1975 to 1985. The proportion of this made up by American production declined from 52 to 46 per cent in 1984–6, while that of European production increased from 23 to 26. Among Europeans in 1986, the British were leaders accounting for 5.0 per cent of the triad total, while France was second with 4.7 per cent (Cooke and Wells 1991: 349).

The precedent for international alliances in high technology was increased by American tariffs on semi-conductor imports in 1986. Japanese firms such as Fujitsu reacted by developing equity joint ventures. This has telescoped into a set of massive Japanese–American semi-conductor joint ventures in the 1990s, which have been based on a quid pro quo of R&D product development input from the US firms for Japanese production technologies (*The Economist*, 18 July 1992: 71–2). Unlike this and unlike the similar biotechnology R&D for production alliances, computing and communications alliances have been largely marketing oriented. Of 677 alliances that Cooke and Wells documented from 1987 to 1989, the largest portion (38 per cent) was within the computing and communications sector, often opening up foreign national markets in telecommunications equipment for computer firms (1991: 350). Twenty-one per cent of alliances were with non-communications sector firms, reflecting the increased importance of users in shaping the nature of VANS provision. Eighteen per cent were with telecoms services firms, enabling smaller countries to retain partial control over their services run by the multi-national equipment giants such as Cable & Wireless. And 11 per cent were between communications equipment firms. These are usually international marketing alliances that are necessitated by the increase in development costs of for example new digital switching equipment. For a firm such as Britain's GPT, these costs can only be borne in the context of obtaining a 20 per cent world market share. This results in the need for strategic alliances (Garnham 1990).[3]

The point here is that market-oriented information structures are becoming increasingly pervasive in high technology and the advanced services (and more frequently between the two). No longer do production-side complexes such as Silicon Valley have the monopoly on high technology information structures. The latter are locating more closely to final markets in head offices and the business services, and they are more likely to be constituted by bilateral inter-firm structures.

The other conduit linking high technology and business services is software. The software sector, whose US sales were under $1bn in the late 1970s, registered an estimated $20bn sales in 1990. It is commonly viewed as part of high technology consultancy. The most important subsectors are first, consultancy and non-standardized software and second, data processing and standardized software.

In France for example the growth of these subsectors has been exponential. In 1975 employment in consulting and non-standardized software stood at 14,000; in 1986 at 68,700. For data processing and standardized software, employment increased from 14,000 in 1975 to

34,200 in 1986. This compares to annual growth during these years in France of 3.86 per cent in the professional services, 1.80 per cent in all services and −0.26 per cent in the economy as a whole (Moulaert et al 1991: 9).

Non-standardized software and consultancy are the crucial sector to note (Moulaert et al 1991: 11). IT hardware producers such as IBM and Bull have been quite active here especially in the provision of systems integration services. Indeed IBM has transformed its firm structure from product-based divisions to market-sector-based divisions (Cooke and Wells 1991: 351). Some accounting and auditing firms, such as Arthur Anderson, have also diversified into IT consulting; but leaders are often the software (systems) houses, such as France's Cap Gemini Sogatti which in 1987 was European market leader with $530m in sales (Moulaert et al 1989). Indeed 6 of the top 20 firms in western Europe at this point were French, 5 British and 5 American. Among the top 10 French firms, 65 per cent of their revenues stemmed from professional services (including specialized software), 27 per cent from data processing services, and only 8 per cent from the packaged software itself (Moulaert et al 1991: 12).

Locational questions in high technology consultancy (HTC) are very concerned with 'whom do they talk to?', and the answer is first and foremost head offices and then regional offices. There has been some decentralization of consultancy in France for example. Moulaert et al note the spread in usage to the regional headquarters of large firms and to medium-sized firms (1991: 17, 20). The inter-firm information structures between the software sector and a number of other sectors are thus reinforced. This results first through labour markets, as the software sector recruits specialized personnel to design systems from a plethora of service and manufacturing sectors; and second via product markets. On the latter Moulaert et al argue: 'HTC is not a unique product/unique allocation kind of business, but rather a lasting interactive relationship involving a multiproduct which is implemented and followed up throughout the client's organization' (1991: 20).

It should further be noted that about 80 per cent of all computing, communications and information technology equipment sold was purchased by services (Castells 1989: 137). The bulk of information technology has gone, not into material processing or manufacturing, but into information-processing itself. This suggests that Walker's dictum might perhaps be reversed – the goods involved in information technology are essentially a more roundabout way of producing services, rather than services being a more roundabout way of producing goods (1985). A number of points support this alternative formulation.

First, the implication of Walker's argument is that most growth of specialized producer services would result from the externalization of functions previously provided in-house by manufacturing firms. But most studies in fact show that they increase even without externalization and result mainly from increased demand for specialized inputs, given the increase in complexity of both the external and internal environments of organizations (see Coffey 1992).

Second, if producer services are simply part of the increased division of labour of manufacturing systems, then these services would be concentrated in agglomerations of 'disintegrated' small batch production. But research in the Netherlands suggested this has not happened. Most producer services have located close to head offices and not in the areas of small batch production. It was also noted that it was the region's big firms that were far more likely to use the services than small ones; and that three-fifths of the producer services had neither a municipal nor regional, but a national or international clientele (de Jong et al 1992).

Third, the suggestion that a healthy service sector is dependent upon manufacturing has not been proven. Cleveland is probably the USA's paradigmatic de-industrialized city (see chapter 6), and yet producer services have boomed. From 1974 to 1981 employment in the business services increased 40 per cent to 46,000, in insurance carriers by 33 per cent to 11,000, in banking by 9 per cent to 11,000, in real estate by 45 per cent to 11,000 (Goe 1990: 333; Hutton and Ley 1987).

Fourth, Walker's roundaboutness hypothesis would presume that most of the output from producer service output would consist of inputs into manufacturing. Yet in Holland in 1988 28bn guilder of producer services figured as inputs for other producer services, compared with only 18.9bn guilder of inputs into manufacturing (de Jong et al 1992: 155). In the US rustbelt, in Cleveland only 46 per cent of producer services firms had forward linkages to manufacturing while 79 per cent were linked to services (Goe 1990: 335).

Finally, a significant proportion of producer services is in fact *consumer* services. In a study of a stratified sample of 788 producer services establishments in northeast Ohio, it was found that 40 per cent of firms gained more than 50 per cent of their revenues from consumer services. This was dependent on the subsector – for example, in the securities industry, insurance, banking, other credit, real estate, and insurance and legal services (the whole of FIRE), 65 per cent or more of firms were involved predominantly in consumer services. The ratio of consumer to producer services also varied by locality. In the more post-industrial Cleveland, owing to the concentration of manufacturing firm head offices, medium-sized firm offices, regional offices and other producer services, a high proportion were inputs into production. But paradoxically in the more heavily industrial, medium-sized Ohio towns a greater proportion of services were in fact consumer services (Goe 1990: 335–9).

CONCLUSION

Our argument in this chapter has concerned production systems and information structures. It has been argued that information structures are becoming increasingly central to, indeed increasingly coextensive with, production systems. In terms of the discursive nature of the knowledge that flows through their 'arteries', production systems have become, not so much dependent or interarticulated with expert systems, but expert systems themselves.

We have taken Aoki's notion of information structures and analysed it in terms of production and consumption. These information structures are in fact economies of signs and space. In information structures cultural capital or information-processing capacities can be accumulated (in training and education) and spent as information flows are applied in problem solving. In chapters 2 and 3 we spoke of increased intensity and speed of flows, on the one hand, and increased reflexivity, on the other, as contradictory factors in contemporary social restructuring. But information structures flows do not run counter to reflexivity, but are instead a condition of it. Thus the thick interweaving of information structures and production systems in Japan and Germany, fostered by non-market modes of economic regulation, means that production itself is more reflexive than in the Anglo-American cases.

Information structures and related symbolic structures are importantly related to individualization and (reflexive) modernization. That is, the thick interweaving of information structures makes the institutionally regulated Japanese and German production systems more 'modern' than market-regulated Anglo-American production. The paradox is that institutional regulation in Germany and Japan is bound up with pre-modern social forms. Equally paradoxically, the most modern, cutting edge firms in the two countries have the most traditional (least market regulated) forms of governance. By contrast Anglo-American *consumption* is much more modern, individualized and reflexive than its Japanese and German counterparts. This has all sorts of knock-on effects for a somewhat retarded modernization of civil society in general (especially in regard to gender and ethnicity in Japan and Germany). We address this in some detail in chapters 6 and 7 below.

The increased intensity of articulation of symbol structures with production and consumption systems is linked with the development of not just utilitarian, but also expressive, individualism. Hence we spoke of aesthetic reflexivity in chapter 3. Expressive individualism is involved as we shall see in chapters 5 and 10 in decision-making in cultural consumption, in the design-intensity of the culture industries, and in the negotiated construction of place-myths by tourists.

Reflexivity as we argued in chapter 3 is dependent on the development of 'expert systems'. For example, individualized and reflexive consumption in Britain and America is dependent on the use of therapists, of personal finance officers and of other experts as effective 'reflexivity enhancers'. Sometimes these experts are conduits as it were for information flows, for example in drawing up a personal finance package (here a successful service is a co-production). But often the expert-systems are conduits for the accumulation of cultural capital – in the cases say of a golf instructor, or a foreign language instructor in an evening school. This individualization (of agency) has a structural pay-off in the creation – via this necessity of expert systems – of a massive advanced consumer services sector. What is significant is that in the USA and UK this sector as a proportion of the national workforce is about twice the size of that in countries with less individualized consumption. In fact a large majority of employment in the advanced services in Japan and Germany is in producer services, whereas in the UK and USA employment in consumer services is more prominent. We are back full circle to the consumer-centred nature of information structures in the Anglo-Saxon world, by comparison with their closer interlinkage with production systems that has characterized Japan and Germany.

Finally, here it is worth noting three important differences between *The End of Organized Capitalism* and this book. These are first, that the earlier book was consistent with the thesis of vertical disintegration, flexible specialization and post-Fordism more generally. This book instead maintains that flexibilization entails informationalization and suggests that the flexible economy is one based on information.

Second, this book suggests that there are three ways in which this information is organized, through collective, practical and discursive forms of reflexive modernization. In relation to the north Atlantic rim we have shown that its model of development is only one of three possible routes to reflexive accumulation; and that its distinctiveness lies in the complex interlinks between high technology and various advanced sectors. What we have not established is whether there is here a 'post-industrial strategy' able to compete successfully with the highly successful institutionally regulated economies of signs and space in Germany and Japan.

And third, while the earlier book attempted to understand cultural postmodernism through the mediation of the link between culture and economy via the new middle classes, this book understands the link through the ways in which economic life is itself becoming cultural and aestheticized. In the next chapter we shall address this last issue directly, through an examination of the paradoxically termed 'cultural industries'. The growth in importance of such industries, organized as they are partly around notions of the aesthetic, reflects the increasing culturization of economic life.

NOTES

1. The irony here is that in spite of these quintessentially horizontal and discursive information structures, biotechnology firms have had to enter into very *vertical* alliances with some rather large firms (see Smith et al 1990; Flecker et al 1991). Owing to the nature of the product, the only sort of firm able to handle the production end has been substantial firms. Because of the nature of markets in biotechnology, made up often of final consumers rather than other networked firms, only large firms have had the resources to market the products.

Most important, the dedicated biotechnology firms became dependent on alliances with large firms for finance. Biotech products, due to the strictness of regulatory procedures, have turned out to have a development phase of exceedingly long duration. This was not acceptable to the original financiers, the venture capitalists, who began to withdraw their resources from the early 1980s. The quid pro quo for venture capital loans was a substantial proportion of the biotech firm's equity. But venture capital firms were funded through partnerships, themselves based on advanced capital with a fixed payback date. And the development time of biotech prototypes was simply too long for this. Instead the bio-technology firms, lacking collateral for bank loans, had to turn to big diversified firms in the pharmaceutical, chemical, food and agriculture industries for alliances. The established firm funds the development of a new application in exchange for the acquisition of an exclusive licence to market the product, while the biotechnology firm retains patent rights and receives royalties (Barley et al 1991: 11–12).

2. In terms of forward linkages firms all three regions score quite low, i.e. 66 per cent of all firms surveyed disperse less than 25 per cent of output to their local district. Yet some difference was registered in amount of output directly exported – 35 per cent for southeast England, 29 per cent for Scotland, and only 9.3 per cent for Silicon Valley in 1985–6. Further, the Bay Area firms had far stronger local backward linkages – in 1985–6 some 58 per cent of these firms purchased more than 50 per cent of inputs from other local firms, the corresponding figures being 38 per cent in southeast England and 17 per cent in Scotland (see also Begg and Cameron 1988; Bassett and Harloe 1990).

3. Alliances themselves constitute inter-firm information structures (Cooke 1988). These arteries and hence structures can have greater or lesser breadth and strength. For example, product supply agreements and licensing agreements comprise some 23 per cent of alliances. Licensing agreements are concluded so that a company can achieve penetration of a previously inaccessible market, but they involve more than just transfers of blueprints and patents. They – in for example the Swedish Ericson's licensing of cellular radio base-station production to Orbital UK – also entail joint training, supervision, and product and process development. That is, they entail a developed inter-firm information structure. This stands in contrast to product supply agreements in which for example Olivetti supplies its product to a British company who supply-markets it under its own badge. Strength of inter-firm information structure also varies with equity participation arrangements and whether or not the alliance constitutes a joint venture (entailing the establishment of a new corporate entity; Cooke and Wells 1991: 352–3).

5

ACCUMULATING SIGNS:
THE CULTURE INDUSTRIES

Chapter 2 of this book addressed the ever faster and increasingly long-distance circulation of subjects and objects in postmodern political economies. In this context we emphasized the increasing emptying out of meaning, the flattening of subjects as well as objects, of goods, work, communications and symbols. Chapter 3 addressed what was identified as a counterposed tendency, that is a growing reflexivity, a growing freeing of individuals from social structures so that they could reflect upon, and in a transmogrified form once more find meaning in, the various spheres of social life. In chapter 4 we argued that these two principles of, on the one hand, flows and, on the other, reflexivity were not necessarily contradictory. We argued that given certain circumstances the flows, the economies of signs and space, are indeed conditions of reflexivity. Here we devoted special attention to particular flows of signs in space; that is, those economies of signs and space which are information structures as interlinked with production systems. Thus we spoke of information structures which facilitated information flow and the development of information-processing capacities as structural conditions of reflexive accumulation, as conditions of reflexivity in the sphere of work.

Indeed although information and communication structures (through which economies of signs and space are networked) are very often counter-reflexive, reflexivity is not possible in the absence of such sign economies. That is, reflexivity is often seen to be a matter of individualization via the decreasing importance of social structures, such as the family and class, and the concomitant freeing of social agents. This individualization however entails a lot more than just the relative retrocession of social structures. It entails the replacement of social structures by information structures. Without the presence of information and communication structures, enabling a certain flow of information and accumulation of information-processing capacities, reflexive individualization (and modernization) is impossible. Instead what takes place is the replacement of socially structured space by unstructured space, the displacement of 'tame zones' by 'wild zones', of 'live zones' by 'dead zones' (Luke 1992). When socially structured space is not replaced by information and communication structures, the result is not individualization but anomie and the sort of social disorganization evidenced in eastern Europe or in the American ghetto, as we shall discuss at length in chapter 6.

In chapter four we discussed reflexive accumulation in terms mostly of production, but also of consumption. In both cases the structural conditions of reflexivity were information structures (themselves informed by expert-systems). In the present chapter – which will deal with cultural production in the 'culture industries' – we extend this discussion of structural conditions of reflexivity to include not just information structures, but broader information and communication structures. We understand these structures as not just linked with given production systems, but with the entire flow of information and communications through networked channels – through fibre-optic cables and via satellite that we discussed at length in chapter 2. That is, we understand the production and consumption-linked information structures as only part, albeit an integral part, of the vaster global flow of information and communications.

We concentrate in this chapter on the flows of other sorts of symbols, other forms of communication through aesthetic symbols, images, sounds and narratives.[1] Production in the culture industries is design-intensive. We suggest a second, aesthetic dimension to information and communication structures, of the flow not of cognitive symbols or information but of aesthetic symbols. These structures also contain spaces for the acquisition of symbol-processing capacities, incorporating not just information-processing, but also the processing (or better the interpreting) of aesthetic symbols. What we are talking about are the structural conditions for, not cognitive, but aesthetic reflexivity. Aesthetic reflexivity has its place in production and consumption in the culture industries. Its structural conditions are the sort of symbol flow, cultural capital creation and aesthetically cast expert-systems. Reflexive modernization in this context results in an individualization which, on the one hand, is cognitive-utilitarian and, on the other, aesthetic-expressive. Some sociologists such as Beck and Giddens have overly focussed on the cognitive-utilitarian dimension of this such individualization, while others such as Bell (1979) and Martin (1981) have concentrated on the aesthetic-expressive dimension. Where certain of these analysts fail is in understanding such individualization in terms of the *disappearance* of structure or of the emergence of 'anti-structure' (following Turner 1969). Rather what we have seen in chapter 4 and will develop in this chapter is that they are dependent on the presence of a new kind of structure, that is on the pervading of information and communication structures.

This chapter breaks down into four sections. The first addresses the kind of production systems found in the culture industries, flexible production systems. We examine book publishing, cinema, the record industry and TV, and trace a process of vertical disintegration of production. We argue that flexible production is always necessarily reflexive production, that post-Fordism must always be post-industrialism.

The following section considers trends that run counter to flexibly specialized market-governed networks. Here we see that disintegration onto market governance in the culture industries has the tendency to minimize the effectiveness of information structures. We see that dis-integrated (decentralized) production tends to be tied to an ever more concentrated and globalized distribution function. And that only these concentrated distributors can provide the finance for the decentralized producers.

The third section addresses the nature of these cultural objects, under-standing them not as material objects, but as already reflexive objects, produced through an aesthetic operation. It looks at how, as these objects circulate, they undergo a juridical operation to become intellectual property. In most cases these objects then further undergo branding, another aesthetic operation carried out either by advertising agencies or by the culture industries' stars themselves.

The concluding section examines the implications of the circulation of the objects of the culture industry as branded, circulating intellectual property. In it we understand this popularization of the aesthetic, of the concomitant de-differentiation of the aesthetic and social life, not as reflexive modernization, but as postmodernization. We observe that consumption of these cultural objects can provide conditions, on the one hand, for genuine aesthetic reflexivity, for aesthetic-expressive individual-ization. And on the other hand, it can create not individualization of reflexive subjects, but individuation, in the sense of the atomization of normalized, 'niche-marketed' consumers.

FLEXIBLE PRODUCTION: DISINTEGRATED FIRMS

From Fordism to flexibility

The culture industries came particularly late to Fordist mass production – cinema being the exception to this rule, initiating Fordist regimes in the USA from the 1920s and in Britain from around World War II. Because of its large initial costs, television effectively began its existence as Fordist, with the onset of mass ownership of TV sets from the mid-1950s (Porter 1985). The record industry arguably did not take on definitive Fordist profiles until the development of a mass youth market in the 1960s (Hirsch 1990; Kealy 1990); while the publishing industry arguably did not develop Fordist structures until the integration of hardback and paperback publish-ing in the 1970s (Coser et al 1982). The American advertising industry took on Fordist size and horizontal integration from the inter-war period, while the British industry remained largely pre-Fordist until the 1970s.

It is possible to speak of Fordism in terms of process, of product and of firm morphology. In terms of product, Fordism presumes large batches of a very few formulaic models. In terms of process it presumes short-cycle job-tasks with dedicated labour and dedicated tools. In book publishing, Fordism's take-off came with the rise of paperback sales. For example, Penguin, now one of the largest publishing houses in Britain, first became a major firm with the introduction of product Fordism through the initiation of mass paperback sales from the 1930s. Unit sales of books took off on a qualitatively different scale with the production of paperbacks. The more general introduction of product Fordism in the book industry impacted on the development of process Fordism, as dedicated labour and dedicated tools (formulae) came to produce seemingly interchangeable narratives in science fiction, detective novels, romance and erotica/soft porn (Morpurgo 1979).

The vertically integrated firm began to appear in the inter-war period in British publishing, initially with functional differentiation of production departments from commissioning editors. After the Second World War functional departmentalization fully developed with separate departments of commissioning editors, finance, marketing, production, rights and contracts, sales and design. Economies of scale and scope here had their costs, according to one Rights and Contracts Director interviewed. With the development of specialized departments, he noted, the editor will 'have no idea of how a book is produced, how it's sold, . . . how a contract works; he could not argue a contract out. I think that's a pity because . . . you don't get an all-round publisher' (Abercrombie 1990).

The shift to post-Fordism via vertical disintegration is no less complex and variable a matter than the development of Fordism. In some cases, such as cinema, the flexible specialization thesis is valid. Here Storper and Christopherson (1987) have argued that the decline of mass consumption of cinema in the USA, with the introduction of television from the late 1940s, created a situation in which transaction costs were minimized through disintegration of cinematic production. That is, given that a smaller batch of films was going to be made, it became less expensive to reduce overheads and hire labour and facilities out of house rather than integrate them into hierarchies (although see Aksoy and Robins 1992).

The decline of mass movie consumption, and hence product frequency, has led to flexibility via disintegration of first, creative or 'above-the-line' (labour) costs such as stars, directors, writers and producers. This is 'upstream' disintegration and has led to the disintegration of (downstream) technical or 'below-the-line' labour costs. Otto Plaschkes, Chief Executive of the British Film and Television Producers Association, described below-the-line costs as 'real costs' and above-the-line costs as 'bullshit costs' (Plaschkes 1989). It has resulted finally in disintegration of facilities: movie theatres, studios, film libraries, camera, sound and lighting equipment, and the like.

The result is a transaction-rich nexus of markets linking small firms, often of one self-employed person, who must live in the local area. The way in which such networks may operate is illustrated in the shooting of *Batman* in 1988 at Pinewood Studios in London. *Batman* was a $40m film which Warners made in the UK partly because of the excellence of British special effects, but mostly because of what was judged as favourable dollar/sterling exchange rates at the time. Such big budget films usually entail a 'twenty week shoot'. If a given technician is employed for even half of this time, he or she can make a comfortable year's living. Warners brought along almost all of the actors, the producer and the executive producer, and screenwriter from the USA, none of whom were Warner employees. The rest of the workforce was British (Lockett 1989).

In the process of shooting such a large budget film there are effectively four steps. First, Warners had to hire a studio – in this case Pinewood, which has its own maintenance staff, post-production staff and construction staff. Some of these would be permanent employees, others would be self-employed and on contract.

The next stage is pre-production. This was a big task in *Batman*, because the set for Gotham City had to be built. First, the Americans had to hire a (British) art director. He or she was the pivotal figure in pre-production. Along with the art director, the Americans from Warners would find a production designer and assistant art director. Then technical staff, draughtsmen, and wardrobe and costume designers were brought in. Hiring here would not be a question of pure markets since they are highly networked. Information and personal contacts are at a premium. They are almost quasi-subcontracting relations in the labour market, as an art director will have one or two assistant art directors and production designers whom he/she likes to work with. These in turn will have their networks of wardrobe and costume designers. A good number, if not most, of these people are self-employed. Yet they will appear in trade listings and statistics as separate firms. Storper and Christopherson (1987), following Scott and Piore and Sabel's model of the Third Italy, have described the movie industry in terms of a 'transaction-rich network of firms'. The industry, at least in London and to a great extent in Hollywood too, should be viewed as a 'transaction-rich nexus of individuals' who also happen to be firms. Finally, for set building about fifty or so skilled workers must be hired to do the actual construction and the scaffolding. These are not technician members of the ACTT (Association of Cinematograph, Television and Allied Technicians), but are manual workers and members of BETA (Broadcasting and Entertainment Trades Alliance) (Lockett 1989).

The next stage is production. Even before set construction Warners will have concluded a deal with all the unions involved in the project: the ACTT, enrolling all technicians up to the level of director, Equity for actors, the Musicians Union, BETA for wardrobe, make-up and construction, and the FAA for extras. This will include negotiation on the length of time members are to be employed, who is to be employed, and the like. For production, Warners would have to hire facilities through the market – cameras, and for example sound equipment, usually from one of London's three major equipment hire companies. American directors will typically already have contacts in England and know who they want as director of photography and as assistant directors. A film like *Batman* needs at least two assistant directors because it will have three camera units, one with which the director works. The director of photography will have personal networks of lighting and sound people. He/she will find a special effects supervisor who brings his/her own special effects technicians. The cameras bring in their own camera operators, their follow focus and grips. All of these technicians may be self-employed, but the relationships are of usually strongly tied networks, sometimes quasi-subcontracting (Lockett 1989).

The next stage is post-production. Warners here could use the Pinewood Studios' dubbing theatre, effects theatre and hardware equipment. Most directors will have dubbing specialists whom they like to work with in Britain. For example, Steven Spielberg often works with Elstree's Bill Roe, who himself is a permanent employee of the studio as are his staff of 10–15 technicians. Finally, it would be necessary to find an editor. Editors are not normally studio employees. They might have an editing company with two or three of their own employed assistant editors, or they might employ freelance assistant editors (Lockett 1989).

Vertical disintegration: publishing, television, records

We will now consider certain cultural industries in which there is flexible disintegration, beginning with publishing. The common wisdom among publishers seems to be that the deterioration of terms of trade was the reason why overheads had to cut and functions disintegrated. The problem was that both booksellers downstream and authors upstream had gained leverage over publishers and squeezed them. The publishing economy has undergone disintegration on a considerable scale. Furthest 'downstream', warehousing and invoicing are now commonly done out of house, often with several firms sharing the same warehousing company, such as Tiptree which is owned by a group of publishers. A bit less downstream, copy-editing and design are no longer done in-house in most of the major British firms. Specialist companies do design. Much copy-editing is put out to freelances, often women with a family who work at home.

Crucially important has been the increasing power of the authors to command huge advances. In this case cause and effect have been reversed in that disintegration has led to deterioration of the firm's terms of trade. That is, only when functions previously handled by publishers have been externalized onto agents have authors been able to attain such leverage. The rise of the agent in British publishing has been a phenomenon of the 1980s and especially the late eighties. By 1990 firms of agents had developed with a number of employees, in several ranging from 20 to 40 employees. These firms are themselves functionally departmentalized, with for example rights departments (Agent interview 1989). Agents have always represented authors, finding a suitable publisher, intervening between author and publisher, and negotiating the best terms for the author. The truly modern agent however goes much further than that. On the one hand, he or she does get good deals for authors. This can work on all levels of the contract. Through agents, authors receive larger advances, better royalty terms, a larger share of rights sales by the publisher (such as for newspaper serialization), and a better slice of the paperback deal if the publisher is going to sell on rights to a paperback house. In addition, agents will attempt to influence production decisions such as the physical appearance of the book and will try to secure a good promotions budget for the author (Rights and Contract Manager interview 1989; Abercrombie 1990).

We will see below that the 'irreducible core' of each of the culture industries is the exchange of finance for rights in intellectual property. What the agent effectively does in this context is to get the author the maximum of finance for the minimum of rights. If the agent can make separate deals for paperback rights, for rights to publish in the USA, for film rights and the like, then he or she will. Hence there will be several exchanges of finance for rights. Here the rights themselves are disintegrated from the (publishing) firm onto the author and agent.

Though publishers like to complain about agents as altering the terms of trade in their disfavour, the agent in fact benefits the publisher in that he or she is in effect performing many of the tasks previously performed by the publisher. The negotiation of subsidiary rights used to be handled by the publisher dealing directly with the author (Abercrombie 1990). Editors may not like to deal with authors:

> because working so directly with an author on a commercial transaction is not very easy because the author just doesn't understand the commercial transactions, you know. And it is much easier to have a half-hour discussion with an agent than it is to spend a whole day with an author, explaining what is meant by foreign rights and the royalty you might expect to get, with the author probably thinking that he's being ripped off all the time. (Senior Contract Manager 1989)

More significant is that the agent takes over some very significant elements of creative management. First, agents effectively vet books. They:

> don't take on authors who are going to be difficult to sell because there's going to be no commission for them in that. So the fact that somebody has been agented, and especially by a good agent, means that the good agent has actually studied that person's work and thinks they can sell it. (Senior Contract Manager 1989)

Second, publishers will sometimes ask agents to find them a book on a certain topic – a straightforward farming out of the commissioning function (Abercrombie 1990). Third, and even more fundamental, the agent has taken on the nurturing role, giving encouragement and advice and suggesting rewrites. As one very senior editor said:

> The agent is trying to supplant in one function the editor, which is being guide, philosopher and friend to the author. By definition lonely people leading isolated lives who need guides, philosophers and friends. And at the same time getting her 10 per cent by getting the most money they possibly can. (Family Firm Editor 1990)

A number of respondents attributed the changing functions of the agent to the rapid changes within publishing companies which resulted in editors moving around frequently:

> And what the agents are having to do is be you know the solid enduring part of
> the whole thing because there's so much movement and disturbance in
> publishing houses . . . [which] no longer enables [editors] to have the clout or be
> able to do what they set out to do. (Interview with a publishing journalist,
> London, October 1989)

Whatever the causes of the shift, there is little doubt that agents are
performing some of the vital creative management tasks undertaken until
recently by editors in-house. The result is a diminution in the editorial role:

> editors in these big groups take on a much more production-line sort of attitude,
> and things are forced through systems and done without a great deal of
> participation with authors who are treated simply like manufacturers of raw
> material. (Marketing Director 1989)

Thus in publishing the rise of the concentrated sellers, though it may have
some economizing effects for the firms, have made publishers more cost
conscious and so they have outsourced below-the-line tasks. The publishers perceive that the rise of author power has had a similar effect. But
this rise of the author has partly been an effect of the previous disintegration of very much less routine, in some sense 'above-the-line'
functions from the firms onto agents. Most agents interviewed had
previously been publishers. The disintegration of these functions onto
agents was not an economizing decision taken by firms. It was instead the
agents themselves who decided to leave the firms (Abercrombie 1990).
These now externalised agents then had to in effect usurp these functions
previously handled by the large firm as well as to acquire themselves
bundles of intellectual property rights which had previously been possessed
by the firms. In any event, in contrast to the conventional model, cause
becomes effect and effect cause, and agency (in this case literary agents)
displaces structure (the firm) as effective motor of change in economic
organization.

We will now turn to consider flexibility in television. In Britain (as
elsewhere in Europe) television is so unlike any economic sector that it is not
treated by the state as an economic sector and hence under the Department of Trade and Industry, but instead comes under the Home Office.
Correspondingly the economic governance of the BBC in the first decade
of British television was a sort of hyper-Fordist combination of vertically
and horizontally integrated hierarchies overlain by external control
through such quasi-state bodies as the BBC governors. Competition from
independent television established in 1955 catalysed initial change as the
BBC recruited new creative talent, the so-called 'mercenaries' of the
'ratings war'. This entailed a few tentative steps in the direction of
flexibility internal to the corporation, in a slackening of central control,
resulting in a burst of innovative programming in news magazines, satire,
drama and comedy. Further change in the direction of flexibilization was
introduced with the award to the BBC of a second channel in 1964, to
produce largely for the 'high culture' audience (Shapiro et al 1992).

The best example of outsourcing in British television, now serving as a model for further developments in Britain and Europe, is Channel 4 (C4). C4 itself came onto the broadcasting agenda partly in the wake of the 'expressive revolution' of the late 1960s and early 1970s. In the initial discussions a number of figures in British broadcasting wanted a second ITV station to be awarded. The existing ITV firms very much wanted an ITV2. Other more creative-oriented and left forces in British public cultural life wanted a station catering to minority audiences, to blacks, Asians, women, gays, lesbians. C4, launched in 1982, was emphatically not an ITV2. Its shows were largely critical. They did cater to a minority audience. C4 did not sell advertising. Its finance was guaranteed by advertising revenue from the (Channel 3) ITV stations. However, the crucial point for the purposes of this chapter is that C4 did not have its own studios. It followed what was called a 'publishing model', and outsourced all of its programming (Shapiro et al 1992).

The upshot of this has been some first-class and imaginative televison. Some of the externalized production for Channel 4 has been taken on by the big ITV companies. Much of the rest has been by very small independent producers. The monopsony position of C4 vis-à-vis these producers has altered the terms of trade against the latter. Thus it has been estimated that the cost per hour of television for the independents is £30,000, while it is £60,000 for the BBC and £150,000 for ITV (S. Harvey 1989). Few of these independent producers currently survive for more than a year or two. Some have claimed that these reduced costs reveal – as they were intended to do – the inefficiencies of the established duopoly producers and restrictive labour practices operative in the industry. Indeed the 'demonstration effect' has caused, so far, Tyne-Tees, LWT (London Weekend Television), TV-AM and Thames to force flexible deals on their workforces (Robins 1989b: 153). Its logic is also reflected in the cost-cutting measures by the BBC, reducing its number of employees from 24,000 to 20,000 between 1986 and 1989 (Lockett 1989).

Similarly in the record industry, the turning point regarding dis-integration was the onset of the 'group' phenomenon, when in the middle 1960s pop bands began to write and produce and even sometimes record their own music. Prior to this, major British record companies carried out most functions in-house. Musicians were hired as wage workers. The songwriter worked in close association with the company. Producers worked in-house as did the A&R man. A&R stands for artist and repertoire, and in the early, pre-Fordist days of the industry, the A&R man inter alia signed up the artists and found them songs to sing (Morten 1989). The old A&R man was like the multivalent publisher prior to the specialized modern firm. He was the producer as well. The music had to be arranged and the songs assembled; this too was the A&R man's job. Functional departmentalization serially took these jobs away from A&R. Today's A&R man will 'primarily find and develop the acts'. He will work with the band's chosen producer in order to maximize production values.

He will maintain relations with the major acts, and even sometimes work with marketing specialists on LP covers (Stubbs 1989). But the old centrality and indispensability have now substantially gone.

In the past two to three decades these Fordist arrangements have been transformed. The musicians are now part of the group itself. Now on royalties, they are no longer wage workers. Writers, previously working for the company, now not only work for the group – they are the group. Producers have moved out of house, where they can increase their income when paid royalties. Perhaps the symbolic turning point for the producer was when George Martin, the EMI in-house A&R man who famously produced the Beatles, left the company in 1968. There are now about twenty top rank producers in Britain, all independent. Their relationship with the record companies is more a market than a subcontracting one. The company, though more often the artist, chooses the producer – a given top producer will work with say half-a-dozen bands. Often the very successful ones will only need to make about three LPs per year, while others will make six to ten per year. A producer will want an advance for an LP of some £20,000 to £50,000 on royalties of as high as 3 per cent, which will come – depending on the terms of trade – out of the band's royalty (Laing 1989; S. Smith 1989).

Studios have also been largely externalized from firms. To be sure some studios like EMI's Abbey Road, almost part of Britain's national heritage, are of the highest level of technical advancement and still in demand. Further, companies have made use of their own studios in for example their African subsidiaries in order to develop world music acts. But a band like Deacon Blue, located in Scotland, will typically not use their company's London studio. There are a dozen or so quite reasonable studios in Glasgow and Edinburgh which can be rented out for a few hundred pounds a day. Other groups have invested tens of thousands of pounds to buy, or more commonly build, their own studios. Small independent companies do not typically own facilities, but prices have dropped so low that for £2,000 independent groups can have a studio in their cellar. 'Entry' has thus become so much easier on the production end of the business. And this is true not just for studios. There are, according to Laing (1989), about one hundred records released per week in the UK. It is said that 'if you can find £2,000 you can put out a single, make a couple of thousand copies and form your own little label'. In a number of cases now, after contract, the artist appropriates all the functions of the production process, and just presents the final tape which he/she brings and, so to speak, 'leases' to the record company (Laing 1989).

From flexibility to reflexivity

Let us digress for a moment and cast a brief glance at some features of the car industry. Few companies today are still more classically Fordist than General Motors (GM). In 1990 GM employed some 775,000 people worldwide, compared with the more flexible Japanese producers where the three largest carmakers together employed only 280,000. GM sells 10 cars annually per employee, Toyota 45. GM has still some 100,000 white collar staff, more than Toyota's entire worldwide blue and white collar payroll. In Japan the design-time per model averages 47 months, in America 60. The average replacement period per model in Japan is 4.2 years, in the US industry 9.2 years. Average annual production per model in Japan is 120,000, in Detroit it is 230,000. Finally, the Japanese motor industry has 72 models in production, the American 36 models (*The Economist* 14 April 1990: 15, 100).

Thus in Japan more specialized product (quicker product turnover, more models available at any one time) necessitates more flexible (flattened hierarchies) process. One valid indicator of the degree of specialization of product would seem to be, not how many of a given model are produced, but how much revenue is made by the company per model. Assume an average new Japanese car sells for say $12,000 and an average new American car for $15,000. Taking average annual sales and average life per model into account, then revenue per model in Detroit is about $3.5bn per year and about $32bn over the lifetime of a model. In the more flexible Japanese industry it would be about $6bn for the lifetime of a model. The success of Japanese car companies in this context, with smaller batch production (some 500,000 per model in comparison with 2.1 million cars per model in the US), is dependent not just on more flexible production. They must also innovate a lot more quickly than do American companies. To attain the same level of income as their American counterparts they have to innovate about five times as quickly.

Now consider the culture industries, such as a record company. If the Japanese motor industry has 72 models in production at any one time, and the American 36, then one British record company, EMI, has about one thousand models in production. This is the number of LPs that were pressed in 1989 by the company (Stubbs 1989). Further, for a record company to bring in revenues comparable to those which one American car model brings in, it must innovate some 1,500 (platinum) LPs or 'models'. In fact the world record industry has sales of about $20bn per year for which it must innovate many thousands of models.

If flexible production is innovation intensive, it is also knowledge-intensive production. Specialized product requires flexible process, requires innovatory process, requires knowledge-intensive process. Now Bell in *The Coming of Post-Industrial Society* (1973) defines post-industrialism from the standpoint of knowledge-intensive production and in particular the primacy of theoretical knowledge (of engineers and technical specialists) in the production process. Thus from the point of view of production inputs – where flexibility is, for all intents and purposes, knowledge intensity – post-Fordism must at the same time be post-industrialism.

But flexible production is more than just knowledge intensive. It is at the same time *reflexive* production. This is partly encapsulated in Sabel's (1990) invocation of the 'reintegration of conceptualization and execution'. It is reflexive production in the sense that shorter product runs mean that employees must make decisions more often on the best process suited for new products. It is reflexive in the sense that much work must go into the design of new products; these are typically long-cycle job-tasks entailing a whole series of judgments and decisions between alternatives in regard to product quality and process optimality. It is reflexive in regard to individualization. Employees as agents must take more individual responsibility with the 'slimming' of the firm's management structures. This increase in reflexivity is registered in the notion of 'shopfloor epistemology' or Lipietz's (1992) discussions of an increasingly 'reflexive habitus' in economic life. This sort of reflexive economic actor is no longer to such a great extent circumscribed by the constraints of 'structure', subject to the rules and resources of the shopfloor. Instead he/she operates at some distance from these rules and resources; he/she makes decisions as to alternative rules and resources; and he/she finally is responsible for the continuous transformation of both shopfloor rules and (in process and product) resources.

Post-Fordist production is thus reflexive production. There are two ways that this can take place. One is via the devolution of innovation to the shopfloor. The other is that the shopfloor plays a less important role altogether, as the paradigmatic component of value-added labour is displaced onto the tasks of professional-managerial workers (see Hill 1990; Lash 1991). This latter scenario is increasingly the case in a number of advanced areas (high technology, the advanced producer and consumer services) that are largely 'conceptualization sectors', in which much 'execution' has been done away with altogether.

Let us return to the Japanese car industry. For it to be so much more innovative than the American industry, considerably more work ceteris paribus would need to take place in Japanese research and development. That is, the ratio of value-added from R&D compared to direct labour is much higher in the Japanese than the American industry. More work is proportionally going on in developing models, and less work in producing them. But consider the 'model' in a culture industry, say music or publishing. Here the far greater proportion of work goes on in 'developing' the model – by the pop band or book author. And much less goes on in the 'production' of the model once it is developed, the printing of the book or the pressing of large numbers of CDs, tapes and vinyl albums. That is, in the culture industries R&D is the main activity, while production is secondary (see Garnham 1990).

What we want to point to in this context is what we see as two perhaps misplaced conceptions in the vast literature on the culture industries. The first is the conventional idea that what the author does is production, while the process of duplication is 'reproduction'. In this, analysts often take their point of departure from Walter Benjamin (1973), in which the 'author' produces the 'auratic' work of art, which then loses its aura in the 'age of mechanical (or electronic) reproduction'. If we begin however not from the metaphor of the cultural economy, but from the real economy, then what is commonly called reproduction is in reality production. And what is called production is in fact design, product development or R&D.

The second misplaced conception lies in a literature which is concerned with the growing commodification of culture. Here it is argued that culture, which once in a golden past was part of a 'sacred', is becoming more and more like manufacturing industry. Our point is rather the opposite. Even in the heyday of Fordism, the culture industries were irretrievably more innovation intensive, more design intensive than other industries. The culture industries, in other words, were post-Fordist avant la lettre. We are arguing, pace many Marxists, against any notion that culture production is becoming more like commodity production in manufacturing industry. Our claim is that ordinary manufacturing industry is becoming more and more like the production of culture. It is not that commodity manufacture provides the template, and culture follows, but that the culture industries themselves have provided the template.

Let us stress here that when we say design intensive, we mean literally design and not knowledge intensive. We mean that production has become not just more knowledge infused, but more generally cultural; that it has become, not just a question of a new primacy of information-processing, but of more generic symbol-processing capacities. In the culture industries the input is aesthetic rather than cognitive in quality. Closest to the culture industries in being highly R&D intensive is the manufacture of software. But whereas the software sector entails abstract, codified knowledge, what the culture sector entails among its artists who are so important in creating the value-added is not cognitive knowledge but a hermeneutic sensibility (although video games of course entail such an aesthetic sensibility). It is to be able hermeneutically to sense, or to intuit, the semantic needs of their public. In this too the culture industries are in advance of manufacturing. Whereas the aesthetic component in manufactured products (and services) has in particular come to the fore in recent times, the culture industries have always operated through this aesthetic sensibility. Whereas 'sign-value' has only challenged the use and exchange value dimensions of manufactured goods more recently, in the culture industries, both use-value and exchange-value have always been sign-values.

LIMITS OF FLEXIBILITY: TRAINING, FINANCE, DISTRIBUTION

In this section we examine the limits of flexibility in the culture industries. We shall consider first how disintegrated market-connected networks are often the least favourable 'shell' for reflexive production. Second, we shall show that there are tendencies for power to remain or even gain in concentration, as disintegrated production is counteracted by centralized finance and distribution.

We spoke above of flexibility in the television industry, which has in fact been in large part an exercise in multi-tasking, labour shedding and general cost cutting. It takes another sort of flexibility often to produce creative television. For major drama and investigative programmes, Roy Lockett, Deputy General Secretary of ACTT, argues that 'you need large internal staffs' (1989). And only 'institutional TV' can provide this, not the small independent company 'which is hustling from job to job' and needs the 'immediate cash return'. This sort of programming entails considerable training. It is not 'disintegrated' but institutional TV which has the resources to allow young people to mature and learn in-house. One reason for deficiencies in training of all skilled workers in Britain is the absence of an institutional base since the decline of the technical schools from the 1960s. As Streeck et al (1987a) have noted, it is irrational for any one capitalist to provide training for workers likely to leave his/her firm. But it is very rational for capitalists as a class to have trained workers. This training must then be done institutionally. It is precisely because the BBC and ITV diverge from the market form of economic governance that has made it possible for them to provide such training.

Further, Lockett (1989) argues, quality TV needs 'continuity' and long-run experience. For good investigative journalism such as *World in Action*, 'you sometimes need a nine-month lead-up research period, plus the staff for this. This is very hard for a small independent company to handle' (Lockett 1989). The independent company cannot compete with such a 'major programme production team' or a 'drama department inside the BBC which has continuity, experience, can train people and has autonomy and strength in depth that an independent cannot have'. There is 'no fat at all in systems' like C4. Independent producers 'are always dependent on money from the next job to keep in business and then on to the next job and so on'. Surely the old form 'was elitist, mandarin'. The 'Reithian tradition' did have 'scholar princes' who were key producers in each area. But these salaried producers were 'left by and large to take risks, to move, they had the autonomy'. The question before was of making quality TV. Now 'the questions are what is the pre-production money? Who is going to buy this? What is the audience? Where do the Americans come in? Who can we pre-sell it to?' (Lockett 1989).

There are important parallels here with publishing. In this industry flexibilization has meant not only vertical disintegration but also new flexible work arrangements for executives inside the firm. In the Fordist past, with stricter segmentation of functional departments, editorial meetings were often meetings of commissioning editors. From the late 1960s the post-Fordist norm has become for these meetings to include representatives from several departments, most commonly marketing and finance. This has led to less space for creative work by commissioning editors, as marketing executives and cost-conscious production managers began to decide what will and what will not be published. It is significant that Penguin, the one British company which has continued to stick to Fordist principles (even copy editing and jacket design are done in-house), at the same time grants the largest creative space to the commissioning editors (Abercrombie 1990). Strict functional departmentalization allows commissioning editors to make decisons on what to publish without permission from marketing and production managers. Thus Penguin employees referred to the 'company culture' as an 'editorially driven company' (see *The Times Higher Education Supplement* 9 March 1990). Ironically the flexible post-Fordist mix has enabled people with, not product and process expertise, but finance and marketing backgrounds to move into positions as senior executive directors.

Centralized distribution

In the second part of this section we will consider how the decentralization of production can co-exist with centralization of distribution. Consider for example the deregulation and globalization of British television. Here the result has not necessarily been a new hegemony of transaction-rich networks of small firms. In the case of Channel 4, as much original production has been bought from the big five ITV-integrated production/ transmission companies as is outsourced to independent British producers. The same sort of outcome seems to be the case as a result of the 1990 Broadcasting Act's stipulation that BBC and ITV outsource 25 per cent of their programme production. Further, the opening up of British satellite and terrestrial broadcasting has brought bigger (than the BBC and the original ITV companies) global players onto the scene. These are the diversified culture companies such as Newscorp, Bertelsmann and the two biggest of them all, Time-Warner and Sony-CBS-Columbia.

This central role of distribution has increasingly been recognized in local government strategies. In the mid-1980s, a number of local councils initiated de facto flexible specialization strategies for their culture industries, attempting to help create local networks of small firms through provision of training, post-production facilities and local information-sharing forums, and even through the planning of cultural enterprise zones such as the Sheffield Culture Industries Quarter (Cornford and Robins 1992). This local council support seems to have produced an increase in the number of local independent producers, especially in the 'franchised workshops', whose roots lay in radical and alternative filmmaking. But the vast majority of independent production units still remain in London and the Southeast (over 85 per cent).

Moreover, councils have come to understand the extent to which the transactions of these small firms are not with one another, but with the giant, centralized distributors. Hence policy has evolved towards promoting access to the latter. Central in this has been an effort to attract programme makers to film on location in provincial cities. Here efforts have involved the cultural heritage rehabilitation of city centres – such as Glasgow and Dublin which have been European Cities of Culture. They have included the establishment of 'screen commissions' to promote given regions as locations. Hence the establishment of corporatist entities such as the Northern Media Forum embracing, on the one hand, private sector bodies – Tyne-Tees and Border TV, Channel 4, Zenith (Britain's largest non-ITV production firm) and bigger independents such as Trade Films – and, on the other, public sector bodies such as British Screen, BBC Northeast, the British Film Institute, Northern Arts and various northern city councils. One aim has been to raise funds for film producers. More important perhaps has been forming a screen commission to promote the region, offering outside film makers a 'one-stop shop' for all facilities and personnel, as well as subsidies for films in which a majority of direct production costs are spent in the region (Cornford and Robins 1992: 432).

So far however these efforts have met with little success. Of the culture industries it is TV and cinema which seem most prone to neo-Fordist domination by distributors because of the very high entry costs involved. In cinema an international film will cost on average $20–$25m. TV is even more conducive to distributor power. Cost per unit (averaging $200,000 to $300,000) may be marginally less than even that of a book by a best-selling author or an LP by a pop star. But whereas say EMI must turn out 1,000 models or units in a year, a TV station must turn out 1,000 hours of programming in a couple of months. As Vincent Porter (1989) says, cinema is a matter of one-offs but TV is a 'machine', a programming machine, that must like a factory run two and one half shifts per day. And this 'machine' 'must be fed'. Hence the extraordinary pressures for constant and on the spot innovation in television, and the necessity of mass production in series and serials in programming. In this even the design stage of TV involves (neo-Fordist) short-cycle work and long product runs.

Distributor dominance in cinema has yielded the phenomenon of the 'captive' production company, where exorbitant costs of making single films hand terms-of-trade power to the major studios. In some cases the phenomenon of the 'tied producer' is a voluntary one. For example, Don Simpson, producer of *Flash Dance*, *Top Gun* and other films, was previously a Paramount executive and now even has his 'independent' production offices on the Paramount lot. Others among even the very most successful production companies such as Lansing/Jaffe, who made *Fatal Attraction*, *The Accused* and *Black Rain*, will normally engage only a handful of permanent employees. Lansing/Jaffe regularly make films for Paramount. Despite the eminence and success of these producers, the studio still has considerable power in vetting their films. Patently the majors cannot fully tie very successful producers to them because other majors will quickly pick them up. But very long-term working relationships do materialize in the industry. The fact that some of the most successful producers have become company executives at the biggest studios and vice versa (for example Sherry Lansing, David Puttnam, Don Simpson) attests to this.

Distributor power is due to their capacities as financiers, which is exacerbated by the temporality of big-budget filmmaking. The majors set up the intake of revenues for a film so that they recoup all of their advance (and more) before the producer touches a penny. For say a $25m film, the studio will often split profits 50–50 with the production company. The major will typically put up 70–75 per cent of the advance, say $19m of $25m, most of which is spent during the (20-week) shooting. The producer must get the other 25 per cent from elsewhere (Brabourne 1989; Porter 1989). Majors only provide this sort of finance when they are also the distributors of a film. The distributor is paid by the exhibitor a certain fee for renting the film. The distribution company first pays itself about 30 per cent of these rental revenues for distributing the film. The studio/distributor pay themselves back the principal of their advance to the producer plus interest on this loan as well as the studio's printing, advertising and marketing costs. After this point the film is into de facto profits, a percentage of which the studio/distributor pays itself as the 'end money guarantor'. Now, and only now, can the producer receive 50 per cent of remaining profits. But before s/he can touch a cent of these s/he must pay back the principal and interest on the loan taken to finance the other 25 per cent of the advance (Porter 1985).

Only rarely will a movie reap sufficient revenues in theatres to enable the producer to glean any income at all. Most often a film is in release for two years, and on its way from video through pay TV, before a producer can be in the black. Well before this point the studio has recouped its advance and more, and is on its way to financing several other films. From the mid-1980s films tended to make one-third of their revenues at the box office, one-third through video and one-third through pay and free television. But by 1990 though, despite a continuing boom in British theatre receipts, video rental revenues were about 60 per cent higher for distributors than theatre rentals (*The Economist* April 1990). The problem is of course that producers have major cash flow problems. Hence the necessity of making programmes to feed the TV machine in between films and thus of captivity to the majors.

Beyond Hollywood: a European public sphere?

Is there a way out of this domination of the global distributors which to a large extent is simultaneously domination of the USA in world culture? Is it possible to find the financial backing for international films which are British and European? In a film such as *Fatal Attraction*:

> there were large-scale scenes in it, it was a piece of cinema . . . below-the-line costs must be in the region of £6m, almost all shot on location. But the expense is in its shooting in so many places. Always very expensive. For a £2m British film you are locked into two locations (and a 6 to 7-week shoot), or you film in

London . . . all you can do for a £2m film is a film which doesn't travel internationally because they must be 'naturalistic', 'realistic' films; they are not fantasy films, and they don't use special effects. It is not a vision, it is realist. We used to call this sort of thing 'location dramas'. (Plaschkes 1989)

What is needed is not just $20–30m to make one international film but a rolling fund of over $100m to make several. This was the strategy that lay behind David Puttnam's initiative with the unfortunate Goldcrest. Some steps in the direction of a genuinely post-Fordist and European film industry may be in the making, via the financial consortia put together by the British producers, Puttnam and Jeremy Thomas. The precedent was *The Last Emperor*, the big budget box office success produced by Thomas and directed by Bernardo Bertolucci. It was mainly Bertolucci who found the mostly European financiers for the movie. The 'real nightmare' in this was that they 'didn't pre-sell the major territories'. This was intentional. They 'kept the major territories free in the hope that a sort of killing could be made'. That is, so that they could control the terms of trade with distributors. And the risk paid off. In any event *The Last Emperor* would have never appealed to the US major distributors: 'A homosexual story about this Chinese idiot?!' (Plaschkes 1989). In the end it did not have the greatest commercial success in the US, being blocked by the major studios.

Whereas Puttnam's Enigma Productions does take part of its finance from Warners, Thomas' Recorded Picture Company is 'financed entirely independently' and 'he sells off each film territory by territory, without a major American distributor being attached' (Plaschkes 1989). Most of Thomas' money is Japanese, whereas Puttnam's $50m of finance is through a joint venture in which Warners, BSB (British Satellite Broadcasting), a Japanese company and National County of Westminster Bank are advancing the cash. This consortium of interests has provided Puttnam with a revolving fund that re-invests profits back into more films and guarantees against loss for four years. According to Puttnam:

the important thing as far as my present set-up is concerned is not that I'm back in Britain and what nationality some picture is – which is the kind of concept that's hopelessly out-of-date now – but where does the money return to and will that money make it possible for more films to be made? (*Weekend Guardian* 5–6 May 1990: 12)

And his Enigma Productions has been making European films, in the medium budget $7–9m range (between the typical $3m European film and $23m average now for Hollywood), and especially central European films with directors Istvan Szabo (Hungary) and Jiri Menzel (Czechoslovakia). If post-Fordism means, as we argued above, an increase in the design, hence the cognitive or reflexive component on the production side, it should mean the same thing on the consumption side. It should mean a set of cultural institutions aimed at constituting public opinion, not in a Hollywood or populist sense of *das Publikum* but as a more European *Öffentlichkeit*, a public sphere.

Again to quote Puttnam:

These are not your orthodox commercial projects, I know. But I have a theory, which I can illustrate best by making the analogy with classical music. Every single research report indicates that there is a massive market out there for classical music. But the problem is that the audience is nervous. They know what they like and they are not sure what they might like. This is what the record companies and so forth are beginning to address. Now the cinema finds it hard to do that. It hasn't found its way around that. And until it does, we're in trouble. (*Weekend Guardian* 5–6 May 1990: 13)

Might this be the way? Hollywood's big success secret has been the diversification of its risks. That is, they make a large number of $20m films, knowing that most will be failures and needing the blockbusters to pay for the former. But the Hollywood majors are companies whose assets vary between 2–3 and 7–8 billion dollars. These European producers have but $50–100 million and can scarcely afford anything like the normal Hollywood failure rate. Part of the answer for Europe, though on a lesser scale for Britain, has been finance by television stations. Channel 4 is the main source in the UK, spending about $17m per year on film finance in exchange for exclusive TV rights. Virgin and Zenith (owned by Carleton Industries) provide finance in exchange for video rights. At the moment the ITV stations and C4 are squeezed for film cash because of deregulation and the necessity of keeping liquid in order to bid for franchises. But in the medium term, when this is done and satellite is a major presence, considerable amounts of TV finance could be available (Brabourne 1989). This must not however be overestimated, as even the major British ITV stations have incomes (of about $400 million) per year which are tiny by comparison with the Hollywood majors.

Another important financing element must come through subsidies. That is, European governments have to regard culture as more than an industry. Culture must also be seen as a source of identity, as telling Europeans who they are; as being about the transmission and critique of values. Again continental Europeans and especially France, under the regime of Minister of Culture Jack Lang, have far outpaced Britain. There have been two main types of subsidy in Britain (as elsewhere in Europe), both of which the Thatcher administration's deregulation have destroyed. The first were 'capital allowances', tax write-offs on substantial items of spending, which were annulled by legislation in 1987. The second was the Eady Levy which was in force from 1948 to 1985. The Eady Levy was intended to preserve the UK film industry as a part of 'national culture'. In Eady 12 per cent of each theatre ticket sale for American films in British cinemas was paid into a fund to subsidize British pictures. In 1989 dollars the levy brought to British films subsidies of $35–45m per year. The successor to Eady is the paltry (£3.5m) fund adminstered by British Screen (Department of Trade and Industry official 1989).

But even from a purely economic point of view, British and European culture industries may in the long term benefit from globalization, precisely because of their increasing design-intensivity. Globalization in this context can be more precisely defined as international horizontal integration. There are a number of forms this can take, depending on the intensity of integration. Most intense is first, direct or outward investment, in which a firm sets up production facilities in another country, such as in the Japanese auto and consumer electronics industries from the 1980s. Next and in descending degrees of intensity are, second, the acquisition of production facilities in another country, which can be more (through functional departmentalization) or less (as a division) integrated into the parent firm; third, production alliance of firm A with firm B in country B; fourth, firm A's setting up of distribution facilities in country B; fifth, an alliance in distribution with firm B; and sixth, the licensing of distribution to another firm in country B.

It is not unlikely that Europe and Britain will indeed benefit from the long-term growing intensity of integration. Publishing for instance has always been a major export industry for Britain. Some 40 per cent of publishers' sales come from exports. Britain is indeed the world's number one exporter. In contrast, of retail book sales in the UK in this same year, only 10.5 per cent of revenues came from imported books. Commissioning, as noted above, is a publishing company's most design-intensive function. Its export is at the same time the export of design.

In the culture industries the battle for predominance may thus be decided by where the 'design skills' are located. In the record industry and the advertising industry, UK firms have made major advances on a world scale owing to their growing comparative advantage on the creative side. In the record industry this is instantiated in the substantial movement of the big US companies to set up facilities in Britain almost equal in size to their US operations. Warners, BMG (RCA/Arista), MCA and CBS have UK branches on the scale of more than 1,000 employees. The reason for this, according to music trade association executive Peter Scaping (1989), is 'because the talent is here'. The above-named companies set up in the 1970s and the 1980s in the UK 'because they wanted to record UK groups. [The] Americans realized they could make a lot more money if they set up production, marketing and distribution here in the UK. They saw Britain as an important source of repertoire' (Scaping 1989).

One important source of this design-intensivity is the British independent record sector. The British 'indie' sector, proportionately dwarfing its American counterpart, provides groups for the majors, while continuing itself to thrive. All this has had very positive effects for Britain's balance of payments figures. British consumers account for some 6–8 per cent of total world retail sales value of records. But British producers have a hand in some 20–25 per cent of all sales around the world. Total sales of the UK record industry is about $4.5 bn; some three-quarters of British records are produced for export.

Typically these 'British' exports are by an American company which has been taken over by a European or Japanese firm in another sector (such as

Sony-CBS, Phillips, Bertelsmann Music Group). How are they, then, 'British'? When say CBS-UK develops 'an act', then the 'income from that act first accrues to the UK company', and this includes the income from foreign sales, through licensing to record companies abroad. Here CBS-Germany would have first refusal for German licensing, and if they refused, then CBS-UK would find another major in Germany who would press and distribute the record. The parallel case in other industries might seem to be say Japanese outward investment in auto or consumer electronics. But the cases are different in that, in the case of Nissan-UK, the economic activity is being initiated in Japan, whereas when CBS-UK develops an act the economic creativity is coming from the UK. The key variable again here is who is doing the design. In the case of Nissan, product and process design comes from Japan. In the record industry, design is purely domestic. In fact export to the big market countries like the USA and Germany takes place entirely through licensing. That is, manufacturing, production and distribution take place abroad. What is exported from the UK is purely design.

REFLEXIVE OBJECTS

From popular music to popular culture

A music trade magazine editor spoke of how Barry Manilow was marketed through his manager. Manilow, he noted, is a 'Radio 2 artist', and 'record shops won't stock him' because he 'lowers their esteem in the eyes of youth'. Manilow's 'buyers' in any event 'don't come into [record] stores to browse. They know what they want when they come into a store.' Manilow's manager in this context had to find ways to reach his target audience. He used 'women's magazines, TV adverts, posters on railway stations. People who watch soaps buy Barry.' His 'marketing manager', upset by record shops who wouldn't stock Manilow records, 'made lists of all those shops which did stock him and published it in the Manilow fanzine' and further 'persuaded supermarkets to stock the stuff'. The point for us is, as this respondent continued, 'Barry Manilow's more part of popular culture than of popular music' (Laing 1989).

A marketing manager from a major record company insisted that the record industry was not big business until the 1960s. He noted that his company EMI was originally one of the two majors in Britain. EMI and Decca dominated the market until the early 1970s: 'The US companies pretty much had to license their records to one of us; we paid them so many cents per disk, then we got on with making and marketing it.' But despite EMI's effective oligopoly position 'the industry was a fairly low-keyed industry in those days'. The industry and the company only really 'boomed when we signed the Beatles', after which 'we more or less got all the Liverpool acts'. This boom, he continued, was only possible, when music became 'a part of teenage lifestyle, you know, you had to have it and you had to listen to it'. Previously young people not only did not have walkmans and tape players, 'they didn't have record players' (Stubbs 1989).

What these record industry insiders are noting is that cultural artefacts are no longer transcendent as representations, but that they have become immanent as objects amongst others circulating in information and communication structures; and that these become the reality of everyday life. Thus 'popular music' becomes 'popular culture', that 'music' becomes 'part of the teenage lifestyle'. In less differentiated, pre-modern tribal societies, culture functioned only as symbol; only with modernization and the autonomization, hence differentiation, of the cultural, does culture become primarily representation. But more recently we have seen representations taking up the functional position of objects, objects which only differ from other objects of everyday life in their immaterial form and aesthetic character. Madonna as a star is not just an image, a representation. She is a cultural object in the anthropological sense of culture. As a cultural artefact, young people wear her on their T-shirts; they dress like her. Such artefacts structure the way young people classify things and tell them who they are.

It should be noted that we are not claiming that the cultural becomes de-differentiated into the social or that society becomes aestheticized. We are suggesting instead that it is only with the declining significance of (society as) social structures and their partial displacement by information and communication structures that the aestheticization of everyday life is possible (Featherstone 1991). Analysts such as Martin (1981) have argued that the mass audience for rock music depends on the development of a certain liminal life-space, on a retreat or destabilization of social structures, in particular the class structure. According to one music industry source:

> [The] class structure had just wobbled sufficiently you know for the working classes to have access to the pleasures of the aristocracy, and you see it in the kids coming over Battersea Bridge from south London into Chelsea, you know with their sharp suits on and going to the dance halls. It was fashionable to be a working-class boy in the sixties and have designs upon an aristocratic girl you know, and it was fashionable for aristocratic girls to have designs upon working-class boys. [Think of] all of the films, sixties films such as *Room at the Top*. (Scaping 1989)

If postmodern liminality does on the one hand entail the relative declining significance of social structure, it is not just a matter as Victor Turner would have it of 'anti-structure'. Urban sociologists such as Shields (1991a) have used Bakhtin's notion of 'carnival' as a spatio-temporal liminal zone. Carnival is more than just an unstructured time-space. It is a zone in which revellers wear masks; in which they are free to try on a set of masks or identities. And the range and variety of masks provide an incipient communications structure in this socially unstructured zone. In the framework of today's highly developed information and communication structures, the masks of carnival have now become the ubiquitous, ever circulating aesthetic objects of popular culture. The paradox is that in Bakhtinian carnival people try the masks on. In the circulating information and communication networks of contemporary popular culture, the masks may largely be trying people on. The condition thus of a mass audience for popular music is the space opened up for reflexivity by the relative weakening of social structure. In regard to popular culture this takes the form largely of aesthetic reflexivity. As we noted in chapter 3 above, reflexivity entails judgments and all judgments involve the subsumption of a particular by a universal. But whereas such universals are highly abstract, highly mediated in cognitive and ethical judgments, in aesthetic judgment the universals are relatively unmediated or relatively concrete.

This notion of judgment through unmediated or concrete universals is an implicit theme of Bourdieu's *Distinction* (1984). His source in this is Durkheim and Mauss for whom these universals are symbols which are constitutive of identity in pre-modern societies. Now the pop culture figures which help form the identities of contemporary young people are those which become the universals through which they classify. Hence thrash fans and Madonna wannabees will classify and therefore judge a great number of objects and events through the prism of the symbolic cosmology of their respective heroes. The negative consequences of this are that the ubiquity and centrality of such popular-culture objects to youth lifestyle can swamp the moral-practical categories available to young people. And entities and events which would otherwise be classified and judged by moral-political universals are judged instead through these aesthetic, taste categories (though see Lamont 1992).

There are two very meaningful ways in which this phenomenon is properly postmodern. First, in the sense in which the postmodern is already pregnant in aesthetic modernity, which itself is constituted as a critique of the rationalist/utilitarian ethos of the Enlightenment. Further, a number of writers, Bell, Martin and even Lyotard, observe that post-modernism is in effect the generalization of aesthetic modernism to, not just an elite, but the whole of the population.

The second way points to, not the extension of, but a radical break with aesthetic modernism. Aesthetic modernism presumes an autonomous subject, possessed with an expressive depth, with an *Innerlichkeit*, for aesthetic reflection. It assumes an aesthetic-expressive subject, a reflexive subject. But the circulation of images in contemporary information and communication structures entails not aesthetic subjects, but objects; not reflexive subjects, but reflexive objects. As the objects – the aesthetic images – become reflexive as already mediated, the subjects can tend to become flattened and unmediated. Thus the ubiquitous information and communication structures lead doubly to postmodernization, first through their very ubiquity, their popularization, and second through a tendency towards displacement of reflexivity from subject to object.

This is indeed Baudrillard's dystopia. Here it is not the agents who decide, reflexively among the symbolic objects, but the objects which choose the agents. This system of objects is different than the Durkheim–Mauss symbol systems of tribal societies in that they are largely depleted of meaning; they are 'flat' and depleted of affective charge. Baudrillard's hyper-reality, in which these immaterial objects are doing the communicating and passing of information, through a largely lifeless set of agents, who figure mostly only as switch-points between nodes of these networks of communicating objects, may well have increasing descriptive purchase on contemporary culture. Thus as the EMI executive said, for the industry to be really big business the music had to 'become a part of teenage lifestyle'. That is, for true mass culture, more traditional social, and especially class and family, structures must partly subside, and atomizing, niche market- and lifestyle creating communication networks must take their place. Atomization and massification through reflexive objects thus are the condition of the creation of Fordism on the consumption side.

The irony is that these reflexive objects, in a twist of the tail of the dialectic of aesthetic enlightenment, can cut two ways. Increasingly and differently reflexive subjects can engage in another more hermeneutic relationship with these cultural entities. This sort of hermeneutic reflexivity would seem tendentially to increasingly inscribe innovation, positive meaning-making and creativity on the production side, and more or less encourage flexibility and post-Fordism on the production side. Thus in a sort of 'contradiction of cultural Fordism' the pervasive flow of popular cultural objects through the information and communication structures can be simultaneously a condition of Fordist consumption and post-Fordist cultural production.

Symbolic exchange: finance for intellectual property

The immediate output of the culture industries, as we have suggested, consists of 'reflexive objects'. But these objects are not yet ready for market. First, they must become intellectual property. That is firms can only exploit or make money from cultural objects, when they have been juridically converted into intellectual property. Only when firms are able to exclude other entrepreneurs and consumers from rights to the use of cultural objects can the culture industries survive.

We traced in the opening section of this chapter how flexibilization occurs through vertical disintegration, a process in which not just down-stream distribution functions but also 'midstream' (lateral) technical functions were disintegrated. And finally often also the creative process was outsourced from the firm, the upstream 'above-the-line' costs. This would seem to be the 'core' of the culture industries. But when even creative production is disintegrated, what then remains?

What remains as the irreducible core is the exchange of finance by a given culture firm for a bundle of intellectual property rights. We say, not rights in intellectual property, but a bundle of such rights, because often a number of culture firms will share these rights. These bundles of rights in intellectual property often come under the heading of 'copyright'. Rights in any kind of property (Hohfeld 1914) are rights to use that property in a way specifically characteristic of a particular type of property. They are always rights in some sense to 'exploit' a given form of property, even if that exploitation will not yield monetary reward. The typical kind of use of intellectual property rights in the culture industries is to copy intellectual property, through copying it and selling it. The main production process then is the copying of already acquired intellectual property. Culture companies are thus in the business of exploiting rights in intellectual property by copying it and selling it. Through this culture companies obtain the finance which furnishes the advances that they exchange against new bundles of intellectual rights. Further, commonly the exchange of finance for rights is not between the firm and the producer, but between two culture firms, for already existing intellectual property or, in the case of 'pre-selling', of intellectual property produced in exchange for the finance of one firm to be split with the finance of another.

We have above already begun to discuss the issue of rights in the publishing industry. Every economic sector, as Traxler and Unger (1989) have noted, can be distinguished by its attempt to solve a specific set of problems. And there is no economic sector for which rights are more important than the music industry. In 1990 in the UK and the US about two-thirds of LPs sold were on audiotape. And it was estimated that for each audiotape sold there were four illegal copies made. It was the widespread phenomenon of tape piracy which led to the incorporation of the British record industry's trade association, the BPI (British Phonographic Industries Association), in 1973. The piracy problem is likely to be exacerbated with the spread of digital audiotape (DAT) which enables the making of perfect sound recordings.

The BPI and its international counterpart the IFPI exist largely for, according to BPI Research Director Peter Scaping, 'the protection of intellectual property rights'. That is, for copyright exploitation, or with the aim 'that copyright ownership is established incontrovertibly as belonging to the people who are responsible for putting all the resources together for producing the music which is consumed by the broad public' (Scaping 1989).

The issue of whose rights is an important one. And the creative producer is in a particularly complex situation. For example, the author of a book does have a copyright on the manuscript but not on the rights to publication. Yet the royalties in the contract give the author a parcel of rights in the published material too. The question of whose rights is also the question of who does not have rights in a bit of intellectual property.

That is, rights are always exclusive rights to the exploitation of intellectual property. Exclusivity means that competitors cannot copy a firm's intellectual property in a given territory. It means that a firm's potential customers cannot themselves (now possible with audiotaping, photocopying, videotaping) copy this intellectual property. Because if competitors and customers are not so excluded, the firm cannot adequately exploit the copyright it has paid for. What we are talking about is really the exploitation of capital rather than of labour, in that intellectual property like other forms of capital is not living, but dead or embodied labour.

Intellectual rights are the main form of capital in the culture industries. That is, they add the greatest amount of value to the product. In material production sectors the outcome of R&D is a material object with a patent. Most of the value added to the product would come from skilled labour, production management and capital-intensive equipment. In the culture industries and in computer software the equivalent of R&D yields an intellectual object which comes under copyright and only becomes intellectual property when that copyright is owned (Lury 1993).

Both patent law and copyright law refer to rights in a prototype that can be reproduced. In patent law that prototype is a material object; in copyright it is an intellectual object or an idea. In patent law the assumption is that the material object is copied. In copyright the idea is copied onto a material substrate – like a software disc or a compact disc or a video cassette. The higher that rates of innovation become and the more that information technology figures in innovation even in sectors in which the material components of objects produced outweighs the informational component (see chapter 4 above), the more widely copyright law becomes appropriate. In the culture industries it is this intellectual property as a main element of constant (fixed) capital – in Marx's sense – which transfers value to the product.

In the music industry there are two main sorts of intellectual property. There are copyrights both on the the record (the 'sound recording') and on the (published) music. The main royalties paid by the record companies, which usually have world rights in the sound recordings, go to the band, from 10 to 20 per cent, and to the music publisher. It is not possible under law to make a sound recording unless there is payment for rights to use the published music (Stubbs 1989). Copyright on the sound recording and the published music also provides royalties from live or broadcast performances of the song. From 20 to 33 per cent of UK-generated income by the British record companies comes from such performance rights. These are collected for major and independent companies by two other trade associations. Live performances alone generate $170m per year, of which 15 per cent is taken by the companies if they also have rights in the published music (Scaping 1989). And an increasing number of them do, paralleling publishing's neo-Fordist move towards diversification into paperbacks, the industry's second main area of intellectual property acquisition. When culture companies 'license' other firms or subsidiaries of their own companies to press and sell an LP in Germany, they are effectively selling intellectual property rights to the licensee.

Repetition and intellectual property: 'the brand'

But the core exchange of finance for rights is more complicated than this. In the most important cases finance, in the form of an advance, is exchanged for the signing of a contract to produce more than one unit of intellectual property. Pop group contracts with major companies are thus typically for three records. Authors sign contracts for several books. What we are referring to is not intellectual property as a one-off. Rather what we are pointing to is iterated intellectual property. Repeated or iterated successful productions of intellectual property place the emphasis no longer on the object produced but on the artist. Thus what a record company is selling is not so much the record, but the artist. It is indeed, Scaping continues, 'selling the artist as a brand' (1989). Thus record companies do not sell themselves as brands, as say Audi and BMW do: 'No one cares if they're buying a Warners record or not. No. The brand isn't Warners. They are buying the "Michael Jackson brand" '(Scaping 1989). Similarly publishers buy and then sell the Salman Rushdie brand while film majors buy and market the Steven Spielberg brand.

This phenomenon of culture companies paying advances in order to exploit brands is significant in several ways. First, it means buying not one set of, but iterated intellectual rights. Second, it takes the focus off the cultural object produced and puts it onto the artist/author. Third, it entails that value added to the product from the intellectual property, or from the artist as producer, comes not only from the artist's creative abilities. The notion of brand connotes image. And value-added also stems from the artist's image. In the otherwise closely related software industry, value-added stems from the author's semiotic skills and abilities. In the culture industries, value-added results from semiotic skills as well as from image. In software, value is transferred to the product according to the semiotic achievement of the creator. In the culture industries it is transferred according to semiotic achievement and semiotic ascription. Fourth, Scaping argues that the recording process itself – where the group works with producer, sound engineer and the like – is a matter of relative indifference (1989). The record company's role comes more in 'packaging' the group. The record company buys the intellectual property, packages the artist and then sells the artist as a brand. In this sense the record company plays a role similar to that of the advertising firm. It sells not itself as a brand, but another product as a brand. Just as J. Walter Thompson advertises (that is, packages) and sells Ford cars, Warners sells Michael Jackson records.

This confounds the orthodox Marxist commodification theory of culture, in which the culture industries become more similar to other industries in that what they produce becomes increasingly like any other commodity. This may well have been the case at one (Fordist) point in time. But it is not so now. What (all) the culture industries produce becomes increasingly, not like commodities but advertisements. As with advertising firms, the culture industries sell not themselves but something else and they achieve this through 'packaging'. Also like advertising firms, they sell 'brands' of something else. And they do this through the transfer of value through images. The culture industries are becoming not more like industrial commodity producing firms but increasingly like post-industrial firms such as producer services. In their loss of a manufacturing function, in their advertising function, in their taking on of mainly a financial function, the culture industries are becoming increasingly like business services. This branding activity can be undertaken by advertisers, by the managerial hierarchies of culture industry firms, by self-branding stars, or by creative culture industry *auteurs* such as cinema directors.

Advertising: new paradigm for the culture industries

The importance of advertising to the culture industries in Britain can be seen in the wave of British commercial filmmaking in Hollywood itself in the 1980s. The filmmakers concerned all had their roots in the advertising industry (Adrian Lyne, Ridley Scott, Hugh Hudson, David Puttnam, Alan Parker). For perhaps the first time British filmmakers were able to achieve better production values than the Americans. These were the 1980s directors with backgrounds in advertising. According to one informant:

> Shooting commercials gives you a real ability to work with telling images that work very effectively on screen. [That's why] they're good . . . popular . . . directors. They organize their material well [as they must do in an advert which lasts only 30 seconds]. It's all there. It's all visual in a sense. It's all there on the screen. [Shooting commercials affects] not only the skills [these British directors] bring to feature films, but also the assumptions they bring. (Lockett 1989; Porter 1989; and see Brabourne 1989)

There is no place where that money has to be put on the screen more quickly, more forcefully and more tellingly, with the quickest cutting and the biggest close-ups, than in adverts. They are supremely visual. British directors were unable to realize these values in the pre-war cinema, even in expensive films, since they were hampered by their narrative and literary traditions in theatre and their overdependence on the spoken word. Cinema always has to be much more a spectacular form than theatre. Hence playwright Alan Sillitoe said after scripting his first cinema screenplay that he'd just 'written a 600-act play'. Hollywood directors have always put on a much more spectacular cinema that was less literary. It achieved its effects with images, with the visual. And adverts involve even less narrative and much more spectacle than standard Hollywood cinema. Abercrombie (1991) has contrasted an audience trained in a 'literary mode' with one whose reception is more via a 'video mode'. The British filmmakers trained in adverts were perfectly suited to the contemporary cinema audience whose sensibility is decidedly that of the video mode.

As other culture sector firms become increasingly like advertising, advertising is itself becoming more like a culture industry. Advertising firms typically have two functions, to make and place ads. That is, they have a 'creative' side, and a more purely business side which is their function as 'media space brokers'. The brothers Saatchi (1987) describe their (advertising) business as 'commercial communications', and indeed this – in that the term commercial connotes 'industry' and the term communications connotes 'culture' – describes the story of its evolution. Advertising in effect evolves from a free-professional type business service to, in Fordism, an industry and, in post-Fordism, to a fully fledged 'culture' 'industry'.

Firms shifted in the early years of the twentieth century to working in contiguity with their clients in the 'manufacturing system', and began to Fordize in the USA at about the same time as Henry Ford. The joint-stock company began to be known during the inter-war years, though firms boasted that they remained essentially 'free professionals' in that there was little control by shareholders. Firms functionally departmentalized, and integrated horizontally through acquisitions and the opening of branch offices. Concentration ensued as the top five firms garnered a progressively greater proportion of the nation's billings. Firms such as Ogilvy and J. Walter Thompson developed 'philosophies' which regularized and Taylorized so to speak the labour process of advertising services, and competitive advantage became 'philosophy advantage' (see Lury 1990).

Global horizontal integration was the next step for the US industry as firms expanded abroad, usually at the behest of their manufacturing clients – Fordist ad firms advertising Fordist products – through acquisition and through direct investment, as 'networks' (the term is used by the advertisers) of international offices of groups formed at a rapid pace. Thus, for example, Interpublic's two largest networks, McCanns and Lintas, operated in 1989 in 70 and 62 countries respectively (*Campaign* 3 March 1989).

The US firms came also to dominate British advertising. Before World War II, the American agencies operated in Britain through a series of alliances, called 'associations' in the trade, in which each would handle the other's accounts in their own country. Post-war saw a series of again client-driven acquisitions of British firms and the establishment of branch offices. Between 1957 and 1967 US firms purchased 32 British agencies. In 1970 the Americans accounted for 42 per cent of declared billings of ad firms in Britain, and in 1972 for 86 per cent of declared billings of the top 20 UK agencies (Lury 1990).

The turn around of national dominance in the ensuing two decades has been just as rapid. From the late 1970s the British industry launched into take-off and became simultaneously Fordist and neo-Fordist. After a strong rise in British advert billings during the consumer boom from the mid-1950s to the mid-1960s, the industry slumped from 1966 to 1976 – perhaps partly because the monopoly of ITV on advertising squeezed the firms – so that the employment of IPA (Institute of Practitioners in Advertising) members declined by some 33 per cent. The upswing from 1980 to 1989 was awesome, as the income of the top 50 British agencies rose by four-fifths, pre-tax profits by 85 per cent, and shareholders' funds by 72 per cent. Between 1980 and 1987 advertising expenditure in the UK grew by 126 per cent, twice as fast as officially recorded tangible or 'real investment', and market research expenditure grew by 100 per cent (Lury 1990).

Two British firms, Saatchi & Saatchi and WPP, have risen to world dominance on the crest of this wave, to which they have responded with some adept financial manoeuvring. The Saatchi brothers have led the British industry belatedly into the era of Fordism. There was, first, the pervasion of the Saatchi characteristic 'philosophy'; second, the supplanting of the principles of the 'professional partnership' with that of 'business' principles (King 1988); and third, a programme of acquisitions. Saatchi & Saatchi, founded in 1970, had already purchased three British firms, when they made their major move in 1974, merging with the publicly quoted Garland Compton. Now they could expand further through acquisitions in Britain funded by rights issues. The 1980s were years of overseas expansion and major acquisitions of US companies, including Ted Bates. The latter, bought through a $700m rights issue, gave the Saatchis the basis for a second global network – Backer Spielvogel Bates (Warren 1989).

This late British transition to Fordism was at the same time a shift to neo-Fordism, in that several advertising companies through acquisition were put under the roof of the same disaggregated firm. In general Saatchi's tendency is horizontally to integrate these under more or less the Saatchi philosophy or Saatchi 'brand', while WPP's tendency is to leave them with their separate philosophies, their separate identities in a more disaggregated form, keeping WPP only as a 'financial brand' (*Campaign* 23 February 1990). It is also neo-Fordist in terms of intersectoral diversification, WPP initially through its base of marketing companies, and Saatchi through its development of the full range of marketing services – including design consultancy, public relations, market research, direct marketing – and outside of marketing services into general business consulting firms, as part of an even broader 'commercial communications' package. The outcome of this has been disaster, and plunging share prices have opened up the company to takeover (Lury 1990).

The upswing in demand for advertising in Britain from the late 1970s was an economic condition of these sea changes in the advertising industry. But the cultural conditions were as important, and especially in what is known in the trade as the 'second wave' of British advertising. This second wave was based on pathbreaking innovations both in product and in process. In the case of product a new type of advert was created from the late 1960s, a characteristically 'British' advert that was not over the top or bombastic or literal as the American adverts were, but based on a sort of humorous, self-deprecating, ironic, more subtle style. This style subsequently came to pervade even American adverts. The British style began in the same decade, the 1960s, in which the peculiarly British version of the expressive revolution came to world notice in music, fashion, TV, cinema and literature. Adverts were not immune to this new creative ethos. It not only opposed the rather bombastic and literal nature of the American style, but also counterposed an ethos of creativity to the latter's market-research-diluted blandness (Boase 1989).

Innovators in this in the later 1960s, especially Backer Spielvogel Bates and Stephen King at the British J. Walter Thompson branch, systematized this departure in product innovation through a new direction in process innovation. They developed what is known as 'account planning'. What account planning does is to reconcile the creative and marketing research approaches to advertising. That is, an advert is 'planned' for an account by testing it out on small samples of consumers, through focus groups. These small groups of consumers view the advert collectively while the latter is in a design stage, and by way of group discussions play a crucial role in the final form an advert will take (Fletcher 1989).

Account planning is emblematic of the implosion of the economic, advertising as a business service, into the cultural, advertising as a 'communications' or a 'culture' industry. One respondent noted that the consumers who participate in account planning act in effect as 'creative judges'. They look at adverts not in terms of business or economics so much as in terms of 'entertainment'. Adverts here are not economic objects functioning as means to sell goods but are, he noted, 'artefacts', 'abstract things' (Fletcher 1989).

Firms then initiated account planning departments as the second wave became institutionalized in the mid-1970s, led by firms such as Collett, Dickenson & Pearce. Part and parcel of this whole movement were the Saatchis, who integrated both second-wave product and process innovation into company culture and married a broad (British) Fordist philosophy to their aggressive business expansionism (Warren 1989).

As in the record industry, in British advertising the cultural condition of mass consumption also catalysed the disintegration of the production side. Thus in advertising new small 'media-buying shops' have disintegrated from the major companies. Further, there is growing use of outsourcing of design and video production. Finally, there is a proliferation of very small companies in what is called the 'third' wave of the late 1980s in British advertising. Concentration has fallen from a peak in the mid-1960s in which the top 10 per cent of British firms accounted for 85 per cent of advertising expenditure in the press and commercial television. The ethos of creativity has played a role in this 'third' wave. It stands in contradiction to the standardization of creative philosophy in a firm like Saatchi. Hence the cultural condition of Fordism in British advertising is also the condition of Fordism's demise.

CONCLUSION

A number of analysts have berated Baudrillard for saying nothing more – in terms of the media and mass society – than Adorno and Horkheimer said decades ago. Perhaps this judgment should be turned around and it should be realized that it was they who were uncommonly prescient. In *Dialectic of Enlightenment*, mistaking class struggle for class structure and some fifty years ahead of their time, Adorno and Horkheimer speculated about social-structural decline as a condition of possibility for the atomizing and individuating powers of the aestheticized National Socialist state as well as its banalized counterpart in America's culture industries (1972). Our argument in this chapter indeed has underscored the baleful implications of globalization and informationalization, in the increasingly concentrated culture companies, which through their stranglehold on finance and distribution have become increasingly concentrated and powerful.

We have suggested that the information and communication structures which displace the more traditional social structures are at the same time knowledge/power structures and underpin what Foucault called normaliz-ation and 'individuation'. Isolated from the bedrock of social networks, the 'specialized consumption' of cultural and other commodities is not so much a matter of 'difference' or 'pluralized life worlds' or even 'neo-tribes', but instead a matter of niche marketing and disembedded lifestyle enclaves (Bellah et al 1985). Such are the consequences of the culture industries, which are not, we noted, coming more closely to resemble straightforward commodity production. They are becoming, not more of a business, but instead a business *service*, as production is increasingly outsourced to leave a core of finance and distribution functions, and whose branding activities and content are more and more coming to resemble that of another business service, advertising.

Adorno has often been castigated in the culture studies literature for a one-sided cultural pessimism. But in his aesthetic theory he foreshadowed the opening of space for another set of developments (1970). This departed in two radical senses from the Marxist tradition. First, with the marginal-ization of class struggle, Adorno claimed that the moment of critique had passed from the working class to the aesthetic realm. And second, he held that the construction of a new 'totality', the positive moment of the dialectic, was to be abandoned for a more limited 'determinate negation', a critique which finds its utopian moment, not in any kind of totality or identity, but in the 'non-identical', in that which eludes any sort of subsumption by the Same.

Adorno's aesthetic was crucially a very 'hands-on' aesthetic, featuring not abstract aesthetic reason, but the concrete working through of the possibilities in the aesthetic material. Moving onto the end of this century, these aesthetic materials are to be largely found among the circulating signs of the information and communication structures. Thus the flows of signs of the various culture industries also provide the materials for aesthetic critique. On the reception-side this is conducive not just to niche-marketed individuation, but simultaneously to authentic aesthetic-reflexive individualization. On the production side this opens up and helps reproduce a space disintegrated from the culture-industry behemoths from which meaningful aesthetic critique can be launched. In this same context globalization must not be seen necessarily as equivalent to global domination of a small number of American and Japanese diversified multinationals. Globalization also makes possible a growing 'cosmopolitanism', a chance hermeneutically to extend reflexive critique beyond the 'neo-tribes', a chance for translation between speech communities (Bauman 1987; and see chapter 10 below). We pointed to such possibilities in a conceivable future development of a European film industry, of interpretation to the other of the different European nations, of the creation of European public spheres.

Critique today must be launched primarily from the cultural precisely because social life today is increasingly culture laden; because the society of a not yet completed modernity is in the process of being replaced by a 'culture-society' (Schwengel 1990). This is more than an aestheticization of everyday life. It is a *Vergesellschaftung* (societalization) of culture, rather similar to an earlier societalization of the industrial principle. The societalization of culture is the principle even of an ever more information-intensive industrial production. That is, though manufacturing decidedly matters, it itself is increasingly information- (hence culture-) intensive.

One obvious problem of this *Kulturgesellschaft* is that there are many losers. What can reflexive production and consumption mean to a single mother in the Chicago ghetto? In terms of any global division of labour, what proportion of workers actually engage in this sort of design-intensive production? How great is the density in most geographical locales of the information and communication networks? Does not post-industrial production entail the creation of more downgraded labour, more 'junk jobs' – to think of the 25 million new jobs created under the Reagan and Bush administrations in the USA – than existed under earlier industrial capitalism? What sort of reflexivity for those effectively excluded from access to the globalized, yet spatially concentrated information and communication structures? Chapters 3, 4 and 5 of this book have dealt with the 'reflexivity winners', the cultural-capitalist benefactors of today's 'two-thirds societies'. Chapters 6 and 7 will now take a closer look at the 'reflexivity losers', in the wilder zones of the disorganized capitalist socioscape. These chapters will turn to the underclass and the migrants for whom the subsiding social structures are not yet adequately displaced by information and communication structures; and for whom this deficit of regulation results inter alia in literal disorganization.

NOTE

1. This chapter is based on an interview study of the London culture industries carried out by Nick Abercrombie, Celia Lury, Dan Shapiro and Scott Lash, based in the Department of Sociology, Lancaster University. Each industry was written up in a draft report by the researcher who had carried out the original research. An extensive overall report on the project was written by Scott Lash and revised on several occasions. That report has been reworked by Lash and Urry in the context of this book to form the bulk of this present chapter. For further material from this research see Abercrombie 1990; Lury 1990; Shapiro, Abercrombie, Lash and Lury 1992.

6

UNGOVERNABLE SPACES: THE UNDERCLASS AND IMPACTED GHETTOES

We have now discussed the nature of 'reflexive accumulation', of how post-organized capitalist economic arrangements require the development of reflexivity in economic organization. We have examined increasing reflexivity among both the professional-managerial classes and the skilled working class in divergent modes of contemporary growth in the more traditional yet thriving sectors.

But what about the other side of recent economic development? How should we understand the recent and sharp growth of an ever more 'impacted' ghetto in the inner cities of the USA and the UK? What about the recent qualitative increase in streams of migrants working legally or illegally in the sweatshops of the clothing industries of various global cities? What about the 'nimble-fingered' immigrant (and native) women peopling routine assembly in the electronics industry from Orange County to Scotland's Silicon Glen? How is it that there are increasing numbers of homeless people filling the streets of London, New York and Paris? What about the development of an alternative crack economy in Los Angeles and New York? What of the massive and seemingly sudden growth of an apparent underclass in minority ghettoes in America's Northeast? And what are we to make of the whites in Europe, who lit up the autumn of 1991 with races between stolen 'hot-hatch' cars along many council house estates in Britain, or in eastern Germany's Hoyerswerda where skinheads have turned their rage and fire in Klan-like burnings of the rooming houses of non-white asylum seekers?

In this and the following chapter we shall argue that the same process of reflexive accumulation that gives rise to an extensive service class also gives rise to what is becoming the bottom and excluded third of the 'two-thirds society'. But in arguing for and describing the 'making' of this new lower class, we are not suggesting, as many American social scientists have, that the working class no longer exists. Rather the new lower class represents a sort of structural downward mobility for substantial sections of the organized-capitalist working class, as well as a set of structural social places into which large numbers of immigrants flow. The new lower class then is filled with, initially, social and then geographical flows of social agents. The new lower class takes its place at the bottom of a restructured stratificational ladder in which the hierarchy of capital and labour is replaced by a three-tiered ordering – a mass class of professional-managerials (alongside a very small capitalist class), a smaller and comparatively under-resourced working class, and this new lower class. Paradoxically, this new quasi-Weberian pattern of social stratification is brought about by the eminently Marxian processes of capital accumulation and effective positioning of new lower-class agents by the dominant classes themselves.

The chapter divides into four sections. The first addresses the emergence of a pronounced American underclass and demonstrates its relationship to the particular form of disorganized capitalism in the USA. Particular attention is directed to the flows of people and investments within the USA which have brought about increasing social and spatial inequalities. The next section addresses more briefly some European correlates of these developments, particularly addressing the British and French cases. In the third section we will consider how such an impacted ghetto is directly brought about by the dominant classes themselves, how the two-thirds society produces the impoverished one-third. The final section will examine the politics of space and the more specific mechanisms by which upper income groups generate an impacted underclass.

In the following chapter we will analyse the *international* migrational flows which lead to the development of a new downgraded manufacturing sector in the advanced economies, which – while offering the possibility of substantial upward mobility for male migrants – functionally brings the export-processing zones of the Third World right back into the heartlands of advanced capitalism. It also argues that these kinds of structural change do not necessarily lead to the development of an underclass or even the creation on a large scale of a new lower class. Instead the extent of underclass and new lower-class formation depends on a deficit of institutional regulation in economy and society. By contrast in societies such as Sweden and Germany, different institutional set-ups lead to a different outcome, that is to a preservation of quite a large working class and a much more limited development of a new lower class. However, the price of institutions preventing underclass formation is an overregulated society in which minorities and women are more effectively excluded from the occupational system.

THE AMERICAN UNDERCLASS

The underclass thesis

William Julius Wilson has brought ethnicity and race once again to a central position on the social science and policy agenda (see 1978 and 1987 in particular). Questions of race had become progressively more marginal to sociological discourse from the early 1970s until the late 1980s. By the early seventies debates in Europe and especially Britain in race relations had stagnated as a stand-off between Marxists and Weberians. The former claimed that ethnic minorities were part of the working class, but that capital had divided this class against itself through the creation of white skin privilege at work and the marginalization of non-whites in unskilled jobs and as constituting a reserve army of labour (see Castles and Kosack 1973). Weberians by contrast pointed to the importance of housing market conditions, and a more complex competition of black and white social actors in a plurality of markets (see Rex and Moore 1967).

The problem was that neither group of writers had brought in the element of social change. Wilson does just this by arguing that the Marxist model is more or less valid until the beginning of the 1970s, that is roughly during the period of organized capitalism, with blacks making up a significant fraction of the working class. But with the decline of industry and the rise of services, with the disappearance of jobs for ghetto blacks in recent decades, and with the concomitant shift of lifestyle from job-related to non-job-related practices, the Weberian model is now more applicable. Thus according to Wilson, the validity of the Marxist perspective has been displaced by that of the Weberian view, but this has come about for the eminently Marxist processes of structural socio-economic change.

In north America sociological debates on race had also become some-what sterile. In the USA the left's advocacy of structural factors were arrayed against the more anthropological explanations taken up by conservatives. The latter were given policy-oriented consecration in 1965 in the Moynihan Report, whose theoretical forebear was Oscar Lewis' assumptions of a 'culture of poverty', the adaptation or reaction of the poor to their position in an individualistic society (1961). On this account young people were not geared to take advantage of increased economic opportunity, but instead reverted to the values of their peers in local subcultures in an increasingly vicious circle. The effect of the Moynihan Report was to buttress a conservative public policy in which welfare spending could be cut, because the real need was to change the values and the behaviour of the minority poor (see W.J. Wilson 1987: 13).

Subsequently there were two reactions to Moynihan and the culture of poverty argument. Either left-oriented sociologists tried to prove that this sort of 'underclass' was not really developing, that things had stayed pretty much as they were. Or like Gutman they examined black culture to find that it contained all sorts of richness and positive values and strengths (1976). Wilson again turns the tables on both sides by incorporating a social change argument. He accepts the conservatives' culture of poverty argument, but again for eminently Marxist reasons. That is, it is structural change (in our terms the demise of organized capitalism) which he maintains creates the conditions of existence for these cultures of poverty (Wacquant 1989).

But most of all, from the early to middle 1970s the social scientific left ignored race, poverty and urban inequality altogether, being much more concerned with issues of growth and accumulation. Very recently however attention has been dramatically called to the fact that it is this headlong rush into accumulation, and the growth coalitions that may make such accumulation possible that themselves have led to the creation of an apparent underclass.

Wilson's portrayal of the underclass in *The Truly Disadvantaged* is stunning. The level of male unemployment and proportion of female-headed families to which he directed attention, for example some 90 per cent of families with children in Chicago's Cabrini-Green homes, is astonishing (W.J. Wilson 1987: 30–2). He defines the underclass in terms of six central characteristics: residence in a space isolated from other social classes; long-term joblessness; consequentially, female-headed households; absence of training and skills; long spells of poverty and welfare dependency; and a tendency to engage in street crime (1987: 8).

Furthermore, his understanding of the underclass is fundamentally spatial. It is grounded in his initial insight into the development of a black middle class in *The Declining Significance of Race*. This middle class, as well as the black working class, partly because of the lifting of restrictive covenants by a 1948 US Supreme Court decision, have both moved out of inner city neighbourhoods on a massive scale beginning in the 1970s. It had been this middle class that had kept the churches and community organizations going, and also served as role models for lower-class blacks. The development of a culture of poverty has then largely been due to the 'social isolation' subsequent to their departure, which also has deprived inner city ghetto residents 'of the kind of cultural learning from main-stream social networks that facilitate social and economic advancement in modern industrial society' (W.J. Wilson 1991a: 463).

This ghetto flight of black middle and working classes took place concomitantly with the awesome de-industrialization of urban USA, itself accompanied by the mass movement of remaining industrial, but also retail, jobs to the far suburbs and to the West and South. Inner-city males without cars cannot get to these jobs. And the normative vacuum is combined with an economic vacuum. The two taken together are the condition then of the disintegration of the black family, or what one might call the 'end of the organized city'.

More poverty, more education

We will now consider certain aspects of this in more detail. The most obvious point is that there has been an increase in the proportion of the US population under the poverty line from the early 1970s to the late 1980s, this poverty line being established in 1965 at a 1963 income level that roughly divided the poorest fifth of Americans from the other four-fifths (Peterson 1991: 5). Astonishingly this increase in poverty has occurred during a period in which national income per capita rose by about one-third (between 1974 and 1988; Jencks 1991: 33). Racially the breakdown of the poor has not significantly changed, the proportion of blacks below the line remaining steady at about one-third in 1970 and 1987, and of whites remaining steady at about one-eighth at both of these dates (Peterson 1991: 5).

Poverty has though been redistributed, most significantly according to age. The proportion of Americans over 65 years of age with incomes below the poverty line declined from about 33 per cent in 1960 to 25 per cent in 1970 and to about 12 per cent in 1987. The proportion of under 18s in poverty rose from 15 per cent in 1970 to 20 per cent in 1987. And in terms of child poverty the USA, while 6 points higher than Britain, was some 10 points higher than the average of a range of other advanced societies (Peterson 1991: 8).

Why this shift of poverty to the young? The most significant cause was the Great Socicty legislation implemented under the Johnson and Nixon administrations. This legislation inaugurated a major shift in American welfare spending towards universalism. In the 1960s in the USA there was much controversy generated by the famous War on Poverty, a set of means-tested social assistance programmes. However, these were insubstantial in comparison to the resources devoted to the universalist benefits, mainly pensions, medicare and cash payments to the disabled, of the Great Society. The consequence of these programmes was, as Skocpol (1991) notes, to skew welfare benefits away from the 'undeserving poor' and towards the 'deserving poor'.

Liberal welfare-state (means-tested social) assistance aimed at the 'undeserving poor' included the relaxation of eligibility restrictions on ADC (Aid to Dependent Children), the distribution of food stamps, and an increase in housing subsidies as well as medicaid to poor families. But ADC, administered by the individual states only, was cut in line with the federal government's food stamp programme. Moreover, means-tested medicaid for under 65s may have fostered greater child poverty by its functioning as a disincentive to labour market participation in relatively low paying jobs typically not providing medical insurance (Skocpol 1991: 432).

This skewed age redistribution of poverty was exacerbated by the deterioration of the labour-market position of young men of all ethnicities. And this took on really awesome proportions because of the explosion of female-headed families. It is true that whites have had the same proportional increase in female-headed families, 8–13 per cent, as blacks, 28–42 per cent, over the period 1970–87 (Holloway 1990: 331–2, 336–7; Peterson 1991: 7), and that black women have cut their fertility levels in half in the last two decades (Jencks 1991: 84). Nonetheless the rise of female-headed families has led to large increases in levels of youth poverty. Thus in 1960 only 25 per cent of all poor Americans lived in female-headed families, while in 1980 this figure had risen to 35 per cent and in 1987 to an estimated 40 per cent (Peterson 1991: 7).

More important, the proportion of poor families accounted for by those headed by women increased from 28 per cent in 1959 to 63.7 per cent in 1988 (Jencks 1991: 33). In terms of long-term poverty, during the 1970s about one-third of the poor families in any given year were not poor in the next year. Yet the proportion of black women with children whose mean money income fell below the poverty line for a six-year period rose from 16.5 per cent in 1967–72 to 24 per cent in 1980–85 (Jencks 1991: 35).

The family is an absolutely essential component of the institutional cluster defining the shape of the new underclass. This can be examined by the use of Esping-Andersen's typology of different welfare states (1990: 122–5, 133–5). Christian and *corporatist* welfare states such as Germany and Austria protect the family, but not necessarily the interests of women, through the assumption of a family-wage paid to male workers, plus generous transfer payments to the jobless. *Liberal* welfare states such as the USA and the UK, based on a universalist minimum and means-tested public assistance, do not pay the same level of family wage, and hence it has been increasingly assumed that women will work at least part-time. The 'family' is not protected and a good number of female-headed families are destined for poverty. While *universalist* Scandinavian welfare states also do not assume the family wage and there are high levels of labour force feminization, the generous universalist welfare net has up to now largely kept single parent families out of poverty.

Sociologists have tended to see social inequality and class as factors operating as independent variables in the explanation of families, welfare states, trade unions and the like. What we want to do is understand all these institutions as independent variables and class itself, the formation of the new lower class, as the dependent variable. It should also be noted that the effects of keeping children and young people out of poverty through more corporatist regimes also have their downside, the effective exclusion of women and, we shall see, minorities from the labour market. The price of certain, though limited levels of, class equality which corporatist regimes can produce is bought only at major cost in gender and racial equality.

We will now turn from issues of income and poverty to those of education and training. In the USA tertiary education is widespread. Of all 25–9 year olds, about 23 per cent of whites and 11–12 per cent of blacks have college degrees (see Jencks 1991: 67–70, for the following). At the same time the proportion of black non-high school graduates aged 16–24 who are not in school has declined from 27.9 per cent to 14.9 per cent between 1970 and 1988. The level for blacks in 1988 is pretty much what the white level was in 1970, while Hispanic non-studying non-graduates in this age group increased from 29 per cent to 36 per cent between 1975 and 1988. For blacks then there has been an extraordinary improvement in intergenerational educational mobility, as in 1940–9 some 64 per cent of blacks with high school dropout parents also failed to finish school, while from 1970 to 1982 this figure had fallen to only 25 per cent. Moreover, this improvement in staying in school actually reflected an improvement in skills, not just on mathematical tests, but in literacy. The basic literacy rate among black high school students improved from 82 per cent in 1971 to approximately the same as the white rate of 97.1 per cent in 1988.

However, none of this is reflected in an increased success in obtaining regular full-time employment. Joblessness comprises both unemployment and non-participation in the labour market, which in the USA is defined as not having looked for a job in the past four weeks. And whereas unemployment varies more or less with the economic cycle, labour-market non-participation is a more secular and serious matter. The number of American men who are non-participants rose from 3 per cent in 1958 to 6 per cent in 1988. There is also a secular rise of the long-term jobless from 4 per cent in the early 1960s to 8 per cent in the later 1970s. This increase took place among all educational groups but especially among high school dropouts. Thus the proportion of American male high school graduates with steady all year round jobs (over 48 weeks) declined from 85 per cent in 1967 to 74 per cent in 1967; among high school dropouts the fall was from 77 to 59 per cent. Black males were especially hard hit. By 1979–80 8 per cent of whites but 16 per cent of blacks were jobless. Similarly the rate of long-term jobless was three times higher for blacks as for whites (Jencks 1991: 41–6, 54).

At the same time there has been a degradation in the earnings of young men aged 25–9 over the period from 1973 to 1986. Overall this was 20 per cent, but among blacks it was 28 per cent and among high school dropouts 36 per cent (Peterson 1991). The deterioration of the labour market position of young males is explained by the decrease of well-paid industrial jobs, in which older, protected workers have a monopoly; by the decline in trade union regulated jobs; by the slower start of male earnings in entry level white collar jobs; and by female competition for males in a growing number of jobs, especially as their educational qualifications have risen markedly.

De-industrialized spaces: the impacted ghetto

There are three further factors involved in this seeming paradox of better education yet more joblessness among black American males (and to some extent females). The first is the declining proportion of manufacturing jobs in the economy as a whole; the second is the shift of remaining manufacturing employment from central city to suburban and ex-urban locations (Moore and Laramore 1990: 643); and the third is the redistribution of employment among different types of metropolitan areas. The last of these is less well-known and requires examination of a typology of three different kinds of city (it should also be noted that we are concentrating here upon black ghettoes).

The first are de-industrialized cities, which started from a large industrial base, have lost most of it, and have not made a successful post-industrial transition. These are the typical 'rustbelt' cities – Cleveland, St Louis, Detroit, Philadelphia, Buffalo and possibly Baltimore; in the UK Stoke and Newcastle; in France the area circumscribed by Roubaix and Tourcoing; and in the next half decade just about everywhere in eastern Europe. The second are restructured cities that have effected a successful transition to a post-industrial economy. These include a great number of global, or quasi-global, cities such as New York, Chicago, London, Manchester, Paris and Düsseldorf, but also distinctly non-global locations such as Pittsburgh and Leeds (Koritz 1991). The third are post-industrial cities, which never had more than 27–8 per cent of their labour force in manufacturing, and which have grown much more recently. These include most 'sunbelt' cities such as Houston, Phoenix, Denver and Atlanta but also Los Angeles, though it has a growing industrial sector; and in Europe cities such as Bristol, Munich and Grenoble. Some older cities which never had high levels of manufacturing such as Boston, San Francisco and Edinburgh fall in between the second and third categories.

Noyelle and Stanback have shown that income inequality tended to be greater in the restructured cities, especially when they were global cities, than in de-industrialized or post-industrial cities (1985). Kasarda's work would suggest that inequality is at its lowest in the USA in the post-industrial cities (1990). This is because post-industrial cities have very few areas of extreme poverty, that is census tracts in which the poor comprise over 40 per cent. And at the same time they have the smallest proportion of jobs requiring the highest number of years of education.

The very comparative growth of population in the post-industrial cities has been astonishing. While a de-industrialized (central) city like Detroit lost 21 per cent of its population during the 1970s, the post-industrial cities such as Los Angeles and Phoenix gained respectively 5.4 per cent and 35 per cent (Knox 1990: 215–16). De-industrializing cities experienced disastrous losses in total central city employment, that in St Louis for example falling from 431,000 to 273,000 between 1953 and 1986. Central city employment in restructuring cities held rather steadier, in Boston rising from 402,000 to 497,000 during this same period. Post-industrial cities though experienced a veritable employment explosion, Atlanta and Denver for example more than doubling total employment from respectively 204,000 to 487,000 and 160,000 to 347,000 between 1953 and 1986. Over this same period total employment in Houston quadrupled from 313,000 to 1.20m (Kasarda 1990: 242–3).

De-industrialized cities also tend not to have very highly developed service sectors, and to have started from very high percentages of manufacturing workers. For example, in 1953 the proportion of manufacturing in total employment in Philadelphia was 45.5 per cent, in St Louis 44.9 per cent. Restructuring cities fall somewhere in between, always having a base of rather highly educated service employees; thus New York's manufacturing made up 35.9 per cent of total 1953 employment and Baltimore's 38.1 per cent. Post-industrial cities however started from low bases of manufacturing employment, Atlanta, Houston and Denver registering between 24 and 28 per cent in 1953 (Kasarda 1990). It should also be noted that all three types of cities kept their distinctive profiles over the past three decades.

What are the effects of these economic and spatial transformations on the restructuring of social and racial inequality? First, many manufacturing, retail/wholesale and blue collar service jobs that have left the older cities for their suburban and ex-urban areas have remained in the cities in the post-industrial sunbelt. Another major difference between the rustbelt and sunbelt metropolises was that the overall level of industrial jobs in rustbelt SMSAs (metropolises) remained massively higher than those in the sunbelt. For example, in 1977 metropolitan Chicago had 568,000 manufacturing jobs (equally divided between city and suburbs). Metropolitan Los Angeles, with a population some 3.5 million higher than Chicago's, had a similar number of 550,000 manufacturing jobs (Scott 1988a: 13, 16).

Owing to the persistence of manufacturing, retail and blue collar services in post-industrial central cities and suburbs, young men with relatively low levels of education can find employment not too distant from their residences. But this is not so in the 'rustbelt'. And it is important to stress that not only have manufacturing jobs disappeared from the central cities, but so have other jobs often filled by young black men (and women). First, in the ghetto itself, as the major black areas in the inner cities have changed from fairly poor to very poor, so many shops have either closed down or moved out. Though not typically owned by blacks, these commercial establishments were significant sources of employment for young black men and women (as stereotyped in the person of Mookie, the pizza delivery man working for small Italian-American entrepreneurs in Spike Lee's *Do the Right Thing*). Second, whites previously living in central, though not inner, city locations have moved to the suburbs, taking with them a number of consumer services jobs that were well inside the 'commuting shed' of inner city black males, but are no longer. Finally, the displacement of retail and entertainment centres from inner cities and for the most part from central cities has destroyed another whole range of black-occupied service sector jobs (Scott 1988a: 123–30; Kasarda 1990: 238).

It is also important to note that the blacks are increasingly found within the de-industrialized cities, and are less found within post-industrial cities. Thus de-industrializing Detroit, while losing 21 per cent of its population between 1970 and 1980, actually increased its number of black households by 88,000. While post-industrial Phoenix, which experienced a 586,000 increase in population during this decade, added only 9,000 black households. Los Angeles, while increasing in population by 5.4 per cent in the decade, actually experienced an absolute loss of black households (Scott 1988a: 13; Knox 1990: 215–16). Furthermore, a full three-quarters of the increase in extreme poverty tracts between 1970 and 1980 was accounted for by three rustbelt cities, Chicago, Philadelphia and Detroit. Of these 527 new extreme poverty tracts only 35 were in post-industrial sunbelt cities (Jargowsky and Bane 1991; Kasarda 1990: 235).

Hughes has called these extreme poverty tracts the 'impacted ghetto', and has used a more complex set of social indicators to identify them.

These indicators are numbers of male jobless, female-headed households, high school dropouts and welfare (means-tested social assistance) recipients. For him metropolitan statistical areas must register numbers above twice the national median on all four of these indicators to qualify as 'impacted ghettoes'. With these indicators Hughes finds the largest ghetto growth in de-industrialized Philadelphia and Detroit. Philadelphia experienced an increase from 7 to 42 impacted ghetto census tracts from 1970 to 1980, and an increase of the ghetto tracts' population from 29,000 to 191,000. Detroit correspondingly skyrocketed from 10 to 40 tracts, housing populations respectively of 31,000 and 123,000. Cities such as Chicago and Baltimore, which share characteristics of restructured and de-industrialized ideal types, experienced a somewhat less dramatic increase, Chicago from 15 to 35 tracts, Baltimore from 9 to 21 tracts. However, restructured New York added only one impacted ghetto tract to increase from 5 to 6, while post-industrial Los Angeles actually decreased its number of tracts from 13 to 2 (Hughes 1990: 276, passim).

Thus while the underclass, in terms of de-industrialized and concentrated poverty, in Europe and in parts of eastern Germany is pervasive also among whites, in the United States it is overwhelmingly a racial and black phenomenon. There are more poor whites than poor blacks in America, yet these whites almost never live in very highly concentrated areas of poverty. Hispanic and white males in the sunbelt commonly have lower levels of education than black people in major city centres, yet they do not experience the same inflated rates of joblessness. Young black males, though much better educated than they previously were, do not live in areas in which jobs for their levels of education are readily available. The areas in which they do live offer reasonably paying jobs only for those who are very highly educated. And relatively few blacks are very highly educated.

Thus in America's largest 98 central cities the fastest growing areas of service employment are producer services and social (that is, medical, educational amd government) services. The mean level of education in the producer services in 1986 was 14.3 years; in social services 15.1 years (Moore and Laramore 1990: 643). But these educational requirements are wildly skewed between sunbelt and rustbelt cities. Between 1959 and 1986 de-industrializing (central city) Philadelphia and Baltimore lost respectively 222,000 and 101,000 jobs requiring fewer than 12 years of education. In this same period sunbelt Houston and San Francisco added respectively 378,000 and 49,000 of such jobs (Kasarda 1990: 247). Many of these jobs, it is true, in Philadelphia and Baltimore migrated to the suburban ring, where they are just as inaccessible to black males as they are in Houston or San Francisco. These jobs in the suburban ring are inaccessible because most inner city black males do not have cars. Even given this, blacks have longer mean commuting times than whites, and fully 80 per cent of black males with high school education or less are dependent on private vehicles for commuting (Hughes 1989; Kasarda 1990: 254; O'Reagan and Quigley 1991: 289). These jobs of suitable education level are further inaccessible for blacks owing to the fact that they are excluded from significant information networks to which many white males have access (O'Reagan and Quigley 1991: 285-6). Finally, even where blacks do live outside of the inner and central city in suburban areas, the areas of significant suburban job growth tend still to be at a great spatial distance from them (Schneider and Phelan 1990: 308).

Finally, jobs requiring high school diplomas only also declined in areas of large black concentration, some 11 per cent in Philadelphia and 29 per cent in Detroit's central areas between 1970 and 1980. New York during this decade lost 600,000 jobs requiring a high school diploma or less while it added some 500,000 requiring at least some college education. Central city jobholders in Chicago in 1980 divided quite evenly into quartiles of 25 per cent each of high school dropouts, high school only, some college and college graduates. Yet black males were overrepresented among dropouts (45 per cent) and underrepresented among college graduates (3 per cent).

What then are the spatial parameters of these bleak developments? First, poverty has shifted from rural areas to the central city. In 1960 28.2 per cent of America's rural population was poor; in 1987 only 13.8 per cent. The proportion of those in central cities who were poor increases over this nearly three-decade period, despite a virtual doubling of gross domestic product, from 13.7 to 15.4 per cent (Peterson 1991: 5; W.J. Wilson 1991b). This shift of poverty concentration to the central (even inner) city rustbelt meant that the number of ghetto-poor among black people in southern cities and Hispanics in Texas has in fact been decreasing (W.J. Wilson 1991a: 464).

Second, although there are more than twice as many poor whites as poor blacks in America, these whites are unlikely to live in areas of concentrated poverty (Kasarda 1990: 254). Fewer whites lived in impacted ghettoes in 1980 than in 1970. The total ghetto-poor population increased by 66 per cent over the decade, while the number of blacks doubled and Hispanics tripled in this population (W.J. Wilson 1991a: 463). The whites mostly took flight. Between 1970 and 1980 the white population of New York decreased by 1.4 million, of Chicago by 700,000 and of Detroit by 400,000.

Third, among blacks there were a number of interrelated developments: a move from there being islands of impacted ghettoes to the development of quite large 'continents' of contiguous census tracts (Hughes 1989: 196–7; 1990: 278, 280); a substantial decline in the number of non-poor black neighbourhoods, as wealthier black people and their institutions moved out of the ghettoes, turning 20 per cent poverty areas into 40 per cent poverty areas (W.J. Wilson 1991a: 470–1); and a substantially larger proportion of the newcomers to the central city was already poor (and black) than was the case in previous decades (Jargowsky and Bane 1991).

How then theoretically are we to understand these massively important developments? W.J. Wilson has impressively captured the social and spatial change aspects, yet his overly action-theoretic outlook seems to understress important structural parameters of such change. He understands culture in terms of 'the extent to which people follow their own inclinations as they have been developed by learning from other members of the community' (1991a: 469). Hughes' notion of the 'impacted ghetto' is useful, but we would eschew his understanding of it as apparently the spatial coincidence of individuals bearing a set of shared social characteristics. Wacquant has attempted to understand the phenomena in a less methodologically individualist vein (1989). He looks at older definitions of the classical ghetto as a space in which all of the institutions of the dominant society were reproduced in parallel, and in which individuals excluded from the institutions of the host society were active in this parallel set of institutions. The difference between the classical ghetto and the contemporary 'impacted' ghetto (Wacquant calls it, we think unhelpfully, the 'hyper-ghetto') is that such institutions have largely disappeared.

What we are addressing however is a matter of both structure and agency. It is as if American blacks, acting as agents, followed certain rules in order to take their successful place in US society, and then somebody moved the very structures to which they were moving. The issue above all is not that blacks do not want to work. After all in the past they migrated in great numbers from the American South to work in the manufacturing cities of the Northeast. For a period of a quarter of a century or so they successfully filled these jobs. But then the jobs moved (see Kasarda 1990: 252–3). However, not only did black people move, but they have also become, as we saw above, massively better educated. But then the education levels attached to central city jobs were transformed. Bourgois has captured this well in his study of crack dealers in Manhattan (1991). In today's New York, when black kids grow up 'learning to labour', there are no jobs for them to labour in. The result is often joblessness or labour in the political economy of crack.

The point is that racism, and the creation of an underclass, is something that resides in institutions. Further, the institutions in which such racism resides vary from country to country. In each case they function as institutions of exclusion. In a densely institutionally governed society such as Germany these mechanisms lie in corporatist institutions interlinked with the family. In the wholly uncorporatist USA, homeland of institutional governance by Williamson's famous 'markets' and 'hierarchies', the mechanisms of exclusion reside in markets themselves, in mainly labour markets (which themselves are largely controlled by large firm hierarchies controlling the movements of branch plants) and housing markets as institutions. In Germany, as we shall see, these institutions operate in the main functionally; in the US mainly spatially (Schmitter 1982).

We will now rather more briefly consider aspects of underclass formation and ethnicity in Europe.

THE UNDERCLASS IN EUROPE

The counterpart of an underclass on the model of American blacks is best found amongst Afro-Caribbeans in Britain. The similarities of condition are striking (see Cross and Johnson 1988 on the following): first, the initial place of migration for both was from west Africa; second, both were transported as unfree labour to plantations in the New World; third, in both cases racism has been shaped by an original encounter in the context of slavery; fourth, both Afro-Caribbeans and American blacks voluntarily migrated to white Protestant-dominated centres of industrial activity; fifth, in neither case, unlike most of today's ethnic minority contexts, has there been an issue of citizenship – indeed blacks have been in the USA for a longer period than have most white communities, while Afro-Caribbeans came to Britain as citizens of the Commonwealth; sixth, in both cases the spatially targeted nature of social spending has hindered mobility outwards to areas where more jobs would be available; and seventh, de-industrialization has led to the economic marginality of blacks, at which point the state has largely shifted its functions from that of welfare to that of policing (Fainstein and Fainstein 1989).

The outcome is similar since the main areas of settlement have been, as in the USA, in areas of the highest population and employment decline, that is central city areas. British non-whites, of whom about 40 per cent are Afro-Caribbeans, make up some 4 per cent of the national labour force. Although ghetto neighbourhoods are not nearly as racially exclusive as in the USA, regional concentration is considerable. Thus 58 per cent of non-whites live in the Southeast of England and another 14 per cent in the West Midlands, in which areas they comprise about 7 per cent of the labour force. They make up approximately 3–4 per cent of the labour force in Yorkshire and Humberside, the East Midlands and the Northwest (Ward and Cross 1991: 118). Judging from central city concentrations the proportions of the labour force in places such as West Yorkshire would be about 7–8 per cent, Manchester about 6–7 per cent, while in London and Birmingham about 12 per cent.

In the above areas unemployment rates among ethnic minorities are 2–3 times as high as they are for whites, though this is indeed skewed in that West Indians and Pakistanis have much higher rates of unemployment than do those whose families came originally from India. At the same time there are extremely high rates of labour force participation for Afro-Caribbean women, 68.5 per cent in 1983 in comparison to an overall British female participation rate of 47.5 per cent (Cross and Johnson 1988: 78). Also Afro-Caribbean males have been concentrated in manual manufacturing jobs to a much greater extent than have American blacks, or other ethnic minorities in Britain. In 1984–6 77 per cent of West Indian males were either in craft or in non-skilled manual jobs, compared with 65 per cent of Pakistanis, 54 per cent of whites and 45 per cent of Indians (Ward and Cross 1991: 120, 123).

Most extraordinary, given the structural social mobility in Britain which through the 1970s and 1980s produced one of the world's largest professional-managerial classes (proportionately), is the blocked mobility of Afro-Caribbean males. In 1986 34 per cent of whites had experienced upward mobility and 17 per cent downward mobility from their last job to their present job. The figures for West Indians were 26 per cent upward mobility and 33 per cent downward. Intergenerational mobility patterns are even more striking. Twenty-five per cent of Afro-Caribbeans with professional-managerial fathers were downwardly mobile to non-skilled manual jobs, and 55 per cent of those whose fathers were office or service workers had non-skilled manual jobs. Upward mobility was slight. Whereas 22 per cent of the last generation's white manual worker fathers produced sons now in professional-managerial jobs, this figure was only 2 per cent amongst Afro-Caribbeans (Ward and Cross 1991).

In the 1950s and 1960s Afro-Caribbeans faced loose labour markets but tight housing markets. They thus found themselves forced into the shrinking private rental sector. Just after World War II over 50 per cent of all Britons lived in this sector. By 1971 only 9 per cent of all Britons lived in the private rental sector, yet 43 per cent of Afro-Caribbeans did, of which one-half lived in furnished housing (Rex and Moore 1967; Ratcliffe 1988: 133). By 1981 however some 45 per cent of black Britons were in local authority housing, in part because their places of residence – particularly pronounced in areas like Hackney and Lambeth – were its greatest concentrations. Here though, in comparison to the whites that had not yet left for the private ownership sector, conditions for Afro-Caribbeans have been poor, partly owing to the fear of local authorities with regard to white demands for segregation. Particularly striking is the comparatively negative position of West Indians among owner-occupiers. In a 1979 survey of owner-occupiers in London, 16 per cent of black-owned units in comparison with 6 per cent for whites were deemed unfit for habitation, while 36 per cent of black-owned units in comparison with 16 per cent of white units were in serious disrepair (Ratcliffe 1988: 138). Finally, there are remarkable similarities with American blacks in terms of those neighbourhoods which are accessible to the middle classes. That is, middle-class blacks are more likely to live in poorer neighbourhoods. Thus among owner-occupiers in 1979, 60 per cent of Afro-Caribbeans lived in terraced housing built before 1919 compared with 16 per cent of whites, while one-half of Afro-Caribbean privately owned houses were in 'poor residential areas' as compared with only one-tenth of whites. How is this housing-market racism regulated? Not through the legal system of restrictive covenants, but via opportunism in markets through estate agents who mark sales cards not to be shown to blacks and building societies which will only lend to blacks on certain properties (Ratcliffe 1988: 140, 142; on markets and moral universalism see Boltanski and Thevenot 1988).

France may have a corporatist welfare state, as Esping-Andersen has argued, but unlike say Germany and Austria, institutional racism is mediated, as in the Anglo-Saxon world, mainly through regulation by the market. A key difference between the Anglo-Saxon countries and France is that residence of immigrants is not so much in inner or even central cities, but in the suburbs. In the case of Paris this breakneck suburban-ization – which took place on the same scale, but slightly earlier, for the native French working class – seems to be governed as much by 'pull' factors of industrial relocation and the creation of more favourable housing as by the push factor of gentrification on a scale unknown in even New York or London.

Thus after decades of relative demographic stability, industry emigrated, partly owing to government incentives, on a massive scale from Paris and the *proche-banlieue* to the outer suburbs and the lower Seine Valley. These were the famous movements of Renault to Flins, of Simca-Chrysler to Poissy, of Citroën from the 15th arrondissement to Aulnay-sous-Bois. The immigrants, whose largest group by far has been Algerians, proved willing and somehow able to commute the long distances to work. For example, at the beginning of the 1970s a survey showed that 84 per cent of the workforce in the Massy industrial district in the Essonne were not resident in the département. At the same point in time some 25 per cent of foreign workers were active in the building industry in Paris's central city, clearing the old units, renovating others and building the new units that would displace them from the city by western Paris's growing central business district and the upper- and middle-class French people who were taking up residence in the city to staff the latter (Minces 1973; Barou 1982: 138–9; Sayad 1977).

This residential migration has taken immigrants and manual workers out of Paris's geographical core, the 1st to 4th arrondissements, to the central city's outlying arrondissements and then to the suburbs. In this geographi-cal core of four arrondissements, from 1955 to 1975 total population declined by 38 per cent, the number of lodging units by 10 per cent, and the number of units deemed overcrowded by fully 60 per cent. There were also important changes in age, class and ethnic composition. The proportion of children under age 15 declined by almost 50 per cent, those over 65 increased by 45 per cent. Native French declined in the geographical core by 44 per cent, while the numbers of immigrants increased by 79 per cent. All of this increase of foreign population came from 1954 to 1968, as afterwards the numbers of foreigners actually decreased. Finally, the numbers of people with working-class jobs decreased by 43 per cent from 1955 to 1975, while the professional-managerial classes increased by 36 per cent in the short period from 1968 to 1975 (Barou 1982: 142).

This demographic change is sharply visible on the more microscopic level of Quartier St Gervais in the 4th arrondissement's Marais district. Here from 1954 to 1968 the number of immigrants increased to 3,200 or 16 per cent of the total population. Native French manual workers began their exodus at the same time as the immigrants flowed in, the numbers of the former dropping by 66 per cent from 1954 to 1968, and further dropping though, as the immigrants themselves started to flow out, by 49 per cent in 1968–75 (Barou 1982: 143). The overall pattern has been one in which single male immigrants have been located in the outlying central city popular arrondissements and the nearby suburbs, alongside the increasing proportion of immigrant families in the far suburbs. There were a large number of publicly commissioned 'foyers-hotels' in the former areas, housing about half of the entire Parisian region's single immigrant workers in 1978. This number of bachelors has decreased quite sharply since then as more and more families join the immigrants. For families residence in the central city is rare. Even in 1975 only 15 per cent of ethnic minority children under age 17 lived in the central city, the remainder equally split between the near and the far suburbs (Barou 1982: 145).

The process of gentrification in Paris is somewhat like that in New York's SoHo (see Zukin 1988). It began with idealistic intellectuals, artists and teachers who wanted to live side by side with the poor and where accommodation was cheap. The unintended consequences of their inflow was a rise in rents, increase in renovations and increase in prices in local shops which starts to force the outflow of immigrants and workers as well as prepare the way for the inflow of the really well off.

In the following section we shall consider these complex relations between the poor and the wealthy directly, seeing how the growth of the latter in some senses causes ghettoization and an ethnic underclass in today's disorganized cities. We have seen that there has been a spatial emptying of institutions – of labour markets, commodity markets, welfare state institutions, trade unions, the family – out of the ghetto that leaves a terrible vacuum, the deficit of economic and social regulation which has given rise to the underclass. We will now consider the motive force behind the movement of these individual and collective subjects and institutions that have produced such an outcome.

POLARIZATION: POVERTY AND PROFESSIONALS

The new lower class suffers not only from deficits of regulation and casualization but also from increasing poverty. At the same time the wealthy have got richer. In the USA, Britain and elsewhere, middle income groups are becoming scarcer as income distribution increasingly assumes a bimodal pattern.

In the United States, for example, median family income had risen steadily from 1945 to 1973. After this point one could make no such assumption. In durable goods manufacturing the average real wage in 1973 was $10.73 per hour; in 1986 it was $10.33 per hour. In 1973 the average wage for non-supervisory workers in the private sector was $8.55 (1982 dollars) per hour; in 1990 it was $7.46, a 13 per cent drop. Low incomes became more widespread, as the increase in proportion of the full-time and all-year-round labour force earning less than \$11,103 increased from 12 per cent in 1970 to 17 per cent in 1986 (Harrison and Bluestone 1988: 113; *The Economist* 4 November 1991).

Income differentials have increased enormously. In 1990 the top quintile of families received 44.3 per cent of total family income, this being 3.2 per cent more than it had received in 1975. The average male college graduate with 6–10 years' work experience in 1987 earned 70 per cent more than the average male high school graduate with comparable experience. At the same time the share of the lowest quintile declined to 4.6 per cent, being 0.8 per cent less than in 1975. Moreover, 33.6 million Americans were below the official poverty line in the 1990 census, some 13.5 per cent of the population. The increase in poverty at the lower end was registered as well in the doubling of federal transfer payments from 1979 to 1986, and the increase in state and local government social assistance payments by 9 per cent (see Harrison and Bluestone 1988: 123; *Die Zeit* 8 November 1991: 41). Similarly a 1990 survey in Los Angeles gives evidence that incomes over \$50,000 per year tripled during the 1980s from 9 to 27 per cent of the city's population, while Angelinos with low incomes, that is under \$15,000, increased from 30 to 40 per cent. This left a 'middle' which had shrunk from 61 per cent to only 32 per cent over the course of the decade (Davis 1990: 7). This famous 'disappearing middle' can also be seen in the processes of job creation. While in 1963–73 9 of 10 new jobs were created in the middle income range of \$11,000 to \$44,000 per year, this proportion declined to one of two new jobs in the period 1979–86.

The United States stands in sharp contrast to European countries (although see Brown and Scase 1991: 13 on the UK). Real wages have increased in Europe, but have fallen in the USA. Job creation has been minimal in Europe, about 3–5 per cent over the 1980s, while in the USA it has been about 30 per cent. From 1977 to 1987 while national income growth in the USA was only about 20 per cent, total employment increased from 65 million to 85.5 million jobs (Sassen 1991: 141). A large proportion of these new US jobs was filled by married female labour-force entrants, another very sizeable amount by immigrants (as we will discuss in chapter 7). This increase in population through immigration means that US national income per capita has grown more slowly than the European average, exacerbated by the fact that growth of total American national income has been substantially slower than average European growth.

In this process of polarization, the relative position of American blacks has worsened. From 1970 to 1986 the proportion of white families in the population with incomes of less than \$10,000 stayed constant at about 10 per cent, while the proportion of black families who were this poor increased from 26.8 to 30.2 per cent. Further, there was a greater percentage point increase in the number of whites with incomes of \$50,000 or more. In 1970 4.7 per cent of black families and 14.8 per cent of whites were in this upper income category. By 1986 8.8 per cent of blacks and 22.0 per cent of whites were in this top income category. This racial disparity is heightened when wealth is considered. Thus upper income blacks had assets worth only 46 per cent of whites' assets, a disparity that was much larger in the lower income groups (Fainstein and Fainstein 1989: 192–4).

What are the reasons for these increases in income (and wealth) inequality? In the USA some one-fifth of the increase in wage inequality from 1965 to 1986 can be explained by the structural shifts in employment from manufacturing to services (Harrison and Bluestone 1988: 120; and see chapter 8 below). In producer services, which are the most favourable of growth sectors, about one-half of employment in finance, insurance and real estate (FIRE) in New York is made up of clerical workers. And clerical employees in non-manufacturing are considerably worse off than those in manufacturing (Sassen 1991: 225). On the other hand, the salaries of professionals and managers in the producer services are substantially higher than in manufacturing (Sassen 1988).

But the extent to which the shift to services will further accentuate income inequality will only increase in the future according to US Bureau of Labor Statistics projections, in which from 1986 to 2000 there should be an increase of 64,000 positions for paralegal personnel, of 56,000 for data processing equipment repair posts, of 24,000 posts for peripheral data equipment operators, and of 250,000 computer systems analysts. Yet these same projections will see increases of 2.5 million jobs in restaurants, bars and fast food, just under a half million in hotel and motel employee positions, and just under 400,000 as department store employees (Harrison and Bluestone 1988: 71–2).

The other reasons for increased income polarization are not structural and systemic, but derive from social relations and entrepreneurial strategies. Harrison and Bluestone estimate that one-third of the increase in pay inequality in the US is due to increasing inequality in the number of hours worked (1988: 49 ff). Yet to look only at wages here is to underestimate inequality. These non-standard workers for instance are much more likely to be among the unemployed; in Britain one of eight unemployed people in 1987 had been just previously working in a temporary job. When out of work they are additionally disadvantaged if benefits are not fully inflation-linked. Further, one way that Western governments have been able to tamper with unemployment figures is to disqualify progressively more non-standard workers. This makes the figures look better and saves unemployment benefit payments to these workers. Finally, when public sector services are contracted out, so generally are public sector workers, with the immediately attendant deterioration in their position as they often become non-standard employees (Fevre 1991: 67).

In the USA the number of temporary employees grew at twice the rate of gross national product from 1970 to 1984. In Britain the number of temporary workers increased from 1984 to 1988 by 7 per cent among men and 5 per cent among women. Women still comprise 88 per cent of all part-time workers in Britain, whose numbers increased by 61 per cent among men and 17 per cent among women from 1981 to 1988 (Fevre 1991: 58). Much of this though can be accounted for by system change, that is the continued expansion of services at the expense of manufacturing. In 1987 in Britain, of service workers 12 per cent of men and 47 per cent of women were part-time, while in heavy manufacturing only 1 per cent of men and 17 per cent of women were part-time (Fevre 1991: 60).

A further major reason for wage polarization in many Western countries was systematic and successful anti-trade union strategies pursued by governments and employers. Hence Reagan's revamped National Labor Relations Board in 1984 set a precedent by allowing firms to relocate production from unionized to non-unionized sites. Unions further lost membership as companies outsourced more of production to non-union firms; Chrysler for example by the mid-1980s was outsourcing some 70 per cent of the value of its final product to suppliers. But the unionized sector itself failed to keep pace with middle-class salaries. After consistent steady wage rises up until 1980 in unionized workplaces, the unions – in the face of the threat of Japanese competition – were forced into 'concession bargaining'. This comprised wage freezes across the board, and the decline of the long struggled for COLA (cost of living adjustments) (Coriat 1985). In 1983 one-half of union contracts had COLA provisons; in 1985 less than one-third did. At the same time conditions inside the unionized workforce were polarized, as sector after sector was forced into fragmented plant bargaining, and as unions were forced to accept a 'two-tier wage' system, in which entry level workers were paid as little as 60 per cent of base rate for as much as 5–10 years. By 1987 two-tier contracts covered more than a third of the unionized workforce (Kochan 1985; Harrison and Bluestone 1988: 40–2).

We will now consider in a little more detail just who the new wealthy are; and how the growth of various kinds of services has served to bring about a new polarization of rich and poor. For the moment we should note that what we might call 'advanced services' seem to play a centrally important role in this polarization process. These include software, personal finance, education and health, business services, the culture industries and parts of hotel, catering and retail services. The advanced services on this view involve specialized products, constant innovation, products whose content is primarily symbolic and which are protected by copyright rather than by patents. Innovation-intensive and very short-production-run industries like film, recording, TV and publishing are governed by copyright law, which is literally the exclusive right to make copies, copies of an idea. Copyright thus deals with intellectual property in a sense that patent law does not. Further, the advanced services have a content which is highly symbolic. Whereas we may buy a washing machine partly for its sign-value, its use value is to wash clothes. The very use-value of the advanced services lies in their symbolic character – they are symbol-intensive (see chapter 5 above, as well as Lury 1993). The advanced services are very much involved in what we have called 'reflexive accumulation', in that they comprise reflexive producers selling things and producing services for reflexive consumers.

There are a number of points to note about these new services: first, the multiplication of class fractions creates very many niches for highly variegated advanced services (see Bourdieu 1984; Lash and Urry 1987); second, they are consumed because of a growing reflexivity of consumption patterns, which are de-traditionalized and individualized; third, such services are often very specialized, small batch, even one-offs and entail co-production between the service provider and recipient; fourth, they entail quite high levels of cultural capital on the part of the service provider, of information, symbolic skills and the like; and fifth, they produce symbols, which contain cognitive, moral, affective, aesthetic, narrative and meaning dimensions. Thus we live in an increasingly individuated and symbol-saturated society, in which the advanced-services middle class plays an increasing role in the accumulation process. This class fraction assumes a critical mass in the present restructuration. As symbol-processing producers and as consumers of processed symbols they are crucially implicated in the contemporary accumulation process.

There are thus two sides of the new advanced services middle class, as high value-added individuated symbol processors and as consumers of individuated and high value-added symbols. Bell briefly analysed the role of the aesthetic 'fraction' whom he labelled as the 'culturati', those active in the media, as opinion makers and as the most powerful voices in the universities (1979). Brint more recently has analysed such a core which he labels the 'high command of commerce, culture and civic regulation' (1988). This core of upper professionals possesses highly valued intellectual resources, is employed in powerful organizations, and gets involved in the cosmopolitan side of economic and cultural life in the city. Brint goes on to identify four institutional complexes which employ these professionals: the corporation headquarters complex; the culture and communications complex; the 'civic complex', including the powerful foundations in cities; and the human capital services complex (1988).

Central to this core is a fundamental change of significant portions of urban space away from a space of collective consumption to one of individualized consumption (Sassen 1991). This is partly instantiated in the move away from organized-capitalist planning to contemporary notions of urban complexity. This in turn is responsible for new lower-class creation in the sense of providing a consumer base for downgraded goods and service production. This is because, while suburbanization assumes a capital-intensive infrastructure of consumption, gentrification's assumptions are labour intensive. Instead of suburban, capital-intensive construction of new tract housing, gentrification by those working in the new advanced services brings labour-intensive renovation of townhouses and storefronts (as represented in Penelope Lively's *City of the Mind* 1991). While suburbanization involves the capital-intensive self-service society dependent upon household appliances, advanced services gentrifiers employ people in services, in restaurants, bars, taxis, cinemas, theatres, hotels, service-intensive boutiques. The new advanced-services middle classes then provide a market not only for one another, but also for the casualized labour of the new lower class.

THE POLITICS OF SPACE AND THE MAKING OF THE UNDERCLASS

In the preceding section we have seen how the emergence of a new lower class is associated with the growth of upper income groups. We have also looked at some of the economic mechanisms by which upper income groups as it were cause the growth of the new lower class. We have considered two of such causes on the production-side, that is anti-union and outsourcing strategies. And in chapter 7 we will briefly consider how new consumption-side practices of upper income groups foster new lower-class formation. In this section we shall consider the political mechanisms by which upper income groups produce an underclass, especially through what Wolch calls the 'politics of turf' or 'turf wars' (1991). We will concentrate upon Los Angeles and Mike Davis' stunning analysis in his *City of Quartz* (1990).

What has been taking place in many towns and cities has been the replacement of Keynesian demand-side politics by the supply-side politics of post-Fordist growth coalitions. This has been at the same time a shift from an organized-capitalist politics of 'legitimation' to a politics of coercion. A whole section of the industrial working class has been economically marginalized by such politics. And what has developed has been not a politics of industrial growth, but a whole series of struggles around real estate, around land and property development. This we will now show in the case of Los Angeles.

These post-Fordist turf wars have been played out in struggles in the city around culture, policing, housing, property and the central business district. Culture in the form of 'place-myth' (Shields 1991a; Urry 1990c) was the basis of the original power of Los Angeles 'real-estate capitalism'. If organized-capitalist growth in Chicago and Detroit was grounded in industry, LA was post-Fordist avant la lettre, as its turn-of-the-century growth was grounded in real estate. And culture in the form of place-myth was the basis of the original power of LA real estate. If meat packing in Chicago and cars in Detroit moved the goods to the people, the secret of real estate capitalist growth was to move the people to the goods. And LA's founding fathers did this through the creation of the 'Mission myth'. The Mission myth – embodied in southern California architecture, in *LA Times* founding publisher Harrison Gray Otis' Los Angeles Fiestas, in countless Hollywood films and in the pioneering role of the missions themselves as theme parks – is a tasteless melange of ersatz Spanish kitsch and White Anglo-Saxon Protestant racial superiority. It 'inserted a

Mediterraneanized idyll of New England life into the perfumed ruins of an innocent but inferior "Spanish" culture' Davis 1990: 20). The semiotic strategy was that the southern California sun and the Mission myth would be an elixir reviving the Anglo-Saxon race. And indeed it worked. LA was transformed from its place in 1880 as America's 187th largest town, as San Francisco's barely noticed southern shadow with little water, no coal and no port. All at once it became the home of hundreds of thousands of Middle-Western middle-class WASPs, who streamed into the city in the first two decades of the new century.

This *avant la lettre* postmodern, Latin American Beaux-Arts, emptied-out maze of signs was the cultural counterpart of a metropolitan space that was already a maze of suburbs before it ever became a city. Thus for the German exiles – Brecht, Adorno, Horkheimer – Los Angeles embodied the destruction of civitas, of public space, in both in its aesthetic and political senses. For Adorno amd Horkheimer the vacuum of LA space as 'anti-city', as a 'Gobi of suburbs' was at the same time reproduced in the equally empty kitsch of its culture industries as described in *Dialectic of Enlightenment* (1972). This organized-capitalist destruction of civitas was a quarter-century afterwards to be inverted and celebrated by postmodernist commentators beginning with Banham (1971) and featuring later Jameson (1984). Thus Banham, with roots in British Pop Art, and then today's generation of British and American Angelinos have helped give to Los Angeles a new sort of place myth, grounded in a decentralist aesthetic of 'vernacular', of 'promiscuity', 'of movement, not of monument' (Davis 1990: 48, 84; Ghirardo 1988; Soja 1989; Zukin 1992b).

But Davis notes that small islands of at least a cultural civitas have been forming and then dissolving within Los Angeles. There are a number of examples: the implicit debunking of LA as myth and spatial reality by the film noir scriptwriters, by Ray Bradbury for whom Mars was LA's 'metaphysical double', as it was arguably in Ridley Scott's *Blade Runner*; the commentary on hot-rod and candy-coloured culture in the group of painters formed around Ed Kienholz (Lash 1990b); the work of Kenneth Anger in cinema and the early novels of Joan Didion and Thomas Pynchon; most of all the public discourse in black Los Angeles of the free jazz of Ornette Coleman, Eric Dolphy, Charles Mingus and Don Cherry in the early and mid-1960s; as well as today's homegrown south LA rap culture and east LA's Latin American poets.

Elite response to these developments has been both cultural and political-economic. Cultural incorporation has taken the form of the reproduction of the black, hot, homegrown civitas in a register that is white, cool, downtown and emptied out. This was the context of free jazz's counterpart in the white cool jazz of Gerry Mulligan and Dave Brubeck. As such it is paralleled in the invocation of LA in terms of 'cool memories' by white postmodern culture commentators such as Umberto Eco and Jean Baudrillard. The more political response has been the incorporation of rap into the record industry and graffiti art into downtown and West Side museums subsidized by public money in the face of substantial reductions of support for local arts in the minority neighbourhoods. As Davis notes, 'the inner city has been culturally hollowed out in lockstep with the pyramiding of public and private arts capital in Westwood and Bunker Hill' (1990: 78).

The collective downward mobility of the LA ghetto from working class to underclass began even before the Watts riots. In the six years before 1965 black median income declined by 10 per cent, while black unemployment rose from 12 to 20 per cent in the city as a whole and to 30 per cent in Watts. Analyses of court records showed those arrested mostly were not the unemployed, but those employed in manual worker jobs (Fogelson 1971). But the subsequent shift from institutionally dense ghetto to an emptied-out hyper-ghetto was the result of three interrelated processes. First, 'urban renewal' ate away at neighbourhood ties. Watts was just too uncomfortably close to downtown LA and to the University of Southern California. Renewal initially cleared most of the poor out of the Bunker Hill area close to the downtown Central Business District (CBD). The building of the Century Freeway had a similar effect and cleared the area which became in the early 1970s the staging ground for the rise of the streetgangs of the 1990s.

Second, there were waves of branch plant factory closures which hit just the areas where black males were most heavily employed (and not the predominantly white aerospace areas). From 1978 to 1982 10 of southern California's 12 largest non-aerospace plants were closed down, displacing about 75,000 manual workers. Other plants moved to ex-urban areas in the South Bay and north Orange County, inaccessible to central city blacks. Thus from 1971 to 1982 unemployment increased by 50 per cent in the Southcentral black area, while purchasing power declined by one-third (Soja et al 1983; Davis 1990: 296–8, 304). Third, many publicly funded institutions folded, such as the Neighborhood Youth Corps, the Job Corps and facilities developed through the Comprehensive Employment and Training Act. Recreational facilities deteriorated as total equipment funding for 150 ghetto centres in 1987 was a tiny $30,000. Further in the face of the telescoping crack-cocaine problem, nothing was spent on rehabilitation in Downtown's Nickle district, where there was California's heaviest concentration of addicts. This was partly because the resource base of city spending had been eaten away, and partly because the small amount of public funding available went into a $2bn scheme to subsidize the corporate renaissance of the downtown CBD (Davis 1990: 304–8).

The resultant vacuum from this institutional emptying out (and the parallel with the East German 'skins' is transparent) has been filled through gang-bonding. The formal economy has been replaced, not by an informal economy, but by the crack economy, as Los Angeles took over from Miami as the principal distribution centre for the drug. From 1985 to 1987 the volume of estimated crack cocaine dollars in LA stood at $3.8bn. This volume has been generated by hundreds of independent 'rock house franchises' operating in the ghetto, according to police estimates typically reaping turnover of $5,000 per day (Davis 1990: 312–13).

Running parallel to and in partial response to this has been the policing solution sought by LA's growth coalition. On the one hand, this has contributed to the gutting of the ghetto's institutional base. From the 1950s onwards the LA Police Department's new anti-corruption regime shut down the interracial night scene in Southcentral LA, and later repression wreaked on the Black Panthers destroyed political movements with which young blacks could identify. And on the other hand, police repression created another place-myth for Angelinos of a 'vast criminal reservoir' in South LA 'held in check by the blue line' of the LAPD. Repression became even more the rule as the growth coalition replaced the social coalition in the mid-1970s, and white (and black) Democrats sought to outdo Republicans on law and order. Thus the overblown enforcement of curfews in non-Anglo neighbourhoods, in which two out of every three black youths have now experienced arrest. There has even been the degrading spectacle of a Democratic City Attorney filing a civil lawsuit against Southcentral's leading street gang (Davis 1990: 273, 283, 290 ff).

How is it though that these institutions of economic, social and cultural governance have moved out of the ghetto? It has been the rich and middle income whites that have played the key role here. Their movement to ex-urban areas has acted as a magnet, removing labour markets and retail markets from the city centres. It is they who subsequently have successfully prevented black people from moving into these ex-urban areas. And at the same time they managed to decimate the tax base of the central city. White homeowners organized early in LA, establishing in the early decades of this century national precedents in zoning districts, not just to keep industry, offices and shops out, but to keep blacks, the poor and even sometimes non-Christians out. This took place via restrictive covenant, through 'deed restrictions' which included specifying minimum construction costs for a land deed as well as racial restrictions on occupancy. Penny-pinching builders or blacks violating such restrictions could be found to be in contempt of court and forced to give up their house. These were extended to include whole 'block restrictions' in the 1920s (Davis 1990: 161).

Post-organized capitalist homeowners' movements have included three components. The first is separate incorporation which allows residents to hoard their own lucrative tax base. Counties will often allow such separately incorporated towns to contract out vital services at cut-rate prices due to realized economies of scale. The basis of separate incorporation is invariably a sharp gradient between the home values of adjacent communities intended for inclusion and exclusion (Weir 1991). The second are movements to put legal ceilings on property tax such as Howard Jarvis' Proposition 13. Jarvis' late 1970s California Taxpayers League collected 1.5m signatures on behalf of tax limitation. The third is the 'slow-growth' movement which supported downzoning legislation limiting the density of

commercial and residential development. Although some environmental-
ists joined forces with the downzoners, their main impetuses were the
interests of property values and low taxes (Davis 1990: 165–7, 182 ff).

Behind these middle income politics were the dominant elites. In fact
central to all of this was the shift of the Democratic Party from the social
and Keynesian assumptions of the New Deal coalition to the new politics of
homeowners and pro-growth lobbies. Here the similarities with Berlin are
striking. As with Berlin in the Weimar Republic, LA elite politics from the
1920s comprised a struggle between two central business districts, one in
the centre and a newer one on the west side of the city. Also as in Berlin,
Protestant elites supporting the older central city district played an
important role in local conservative politics, while Jewish elites involved in
the newer western district were key figures in liberal politics (Koehler
1987: 815 ff).

Turn-of-the-century Los Angeles politics saw finance-based Jewish and
Catholic elites, originally from San Francisco, locked in conflict with newer
Protestant elites from the East Coast who controlled the LA Times and the
local Merchants and Manufacturers Association. Each side had allies in the
railroads, who themselves had acquired enormous amounts of real estate.
Turn-of-the-century struggles between these groups issued into the breakneck development of LA – instantiated in the world's number one
manmade port and an impressively modern inter-urban railroad system, as
well as the subdivision for development of Hollywood, the San Fernando
Valley and northeast LA.

The inter-war period saw WASP domination and one-sided Republican
Party government, as massive migrations of middle American small-
towners reinforced the power of the LA Times elite. The latter succeeded
in expanding their downtown base through the building of the Biltmore
Hotel, the Subway Terminal Building, the improvement of the LA
Coliseum, and the building of Union Station and the Civic Center. This
same group brought in the branch plants of middle western heavy industry.
Anti-semitism ruled as the old families of upper-class German Jews found
themselves excluded from corporate boards, clubs and law firms, while
simultaneously their vulgar arriviste eastern European co-religionists were
taking the film industry into its mass production stage (Storper and
Christopherson 1987). Further, the inter-war period saw the establishment
of the 'Miracle Mile' on Wilshire Boulevard, while homeowners in their
masses began to move west towards the ocean.

The Westside Democrats made their comeback with a vengeance after
World War II, with their bases in the entertainment industry, newly in real
estate, savings and loans, and construction (via Federal Housing Authority
'Keynesian suburbanization'), and in the emergent sportswear industry.
These largely Jewish elites still identified with the social-liberal organized
capitalist politics and were a major force behind powerful California post-
war liberals Earl Warren, Pat Brown and Jesse Unruh. Yet this liberal and
Keynesian era was coming to a close. This was signified by a certain coming

together of elites, as the *LA Times* moved steadily to the left, while Jewish real estate money was instrumental in the finance of downtown development, adding to the complex of the University of Southern California, the Museum of Contemporary Art and the Music Center, Dodger Stadium, the LA Public Library and now Frank Gehry's Disney Concert Hall (Davis 1990: 73, 124).

The Protestant–Jewish rapprochement was also a rapprochement of Democrats and Republicans, as the Democrats shifted to the supply-side and policing politics that the Republicans had always advocated. The shift of elite Democrats to the right and the marginalization of blacks have yielded a new politics whose main contradiction is between slow-growth homeowners and the developers. Democrats, then the 1960s-elected mayor Sam Yorty, and now Jewish leaders have aligned themselves with the Westside and San Fernando Valley homeowners led by their upper-class counterparts in Santa Monica and Sherman Oaks. Favoured policies here include support for property tax limits, to oppose bussing, to support law and order, and to advocate downzoning. The problem is that every government elected on an anti-growth platform winds up finally supporting the developers. But all the while new, foreign players are making important inroads on both of these two fractions of what is quickly taking on the colours of a 'comprador bourgeoisie'. Japanese capital is moving in with a vengeance, acquiring vast sections of the culture industries, establishing branch banks with assets estimated at $50bn at the end of the 1980s, and buying up as much real estate as they can. Now as always land has been LA's 'most valuable and liquidifiable asset'. In 1988 alone as Japanese investors bought up over $3bn of real estate, the region's leading 'foreign export by volume was simply empty space' (Davis 1990: 126–32).

The next chapter will deal with the issue of migration, to consider the variety of international processes which have also served to produce impacted ghettoes and an underclass in especially the USA and Britain. We will consider whether ghettoes and an underclass are inevitable features of disorganized capitalism and suggest that they are not. However, the society that seems to have avoided them, Germany, has alternative social and economic characteristics of a depressingly unattractive sort.

7

MOBILE SUBJECTS: MIGRATION IN COMPARATIVE PERSPECTIVE

So far we have examined those processes internal to particular societies which have helped to generate an underclass, concentrating mainly on the USA. In this chapter we will consider international movements of people and workers which also formed this new class. More generally we shall suggest that class formation has always to be seen as partly dependent upon international migration flows, and that such flows have altered significantly in disorganized capitalism.

We will contrast the American and German cases, the neo-liberal and the corporatist. The first section will be mainly concerned with the American case. Following this we will examine the case-study of the clothing industry. The third section will be a lengthy examination of Germany, to consider the exact opposite of the neo-liberal model. It will be seen that the institutional complex in Germany is one which precludes the development of large ghettoes, but only at the cost of significant exclusions of minorities and women from the wider society. Germany and the USA in some ways represent extreme cases of modes of disorganized capitalism (as discussed in chapter 4).

We will introduce this chapter by noting the following extraordinary divergence between the USA and Europe. Between 1973 and 1986 the United States created 26 million new jobs while western Europe created almost none (Harrison and Bluestone 1988: ch 5). This was partly due to large numbers of American women coming onto the labour market to fill jobs at all levels. But it was also due to the massive wave of immigration into the USA which began in 1965. As western Europe, from 1965 to 1973, began to shut the gates to the masses of foreign workers who had been flowing in from the early 1950s, the USA opened theirs up and many workers arrived. This chapter is concerned with the causes and consequences of such contrasting developments in the USA and Europe.

MIGRATION AFTER ORGANIZED CAPITALISM

There have been two main waves of organized-capitalist migrations to the cities of contemporary advanced societies. The first was from the turn of the twentieth century until the 1940s. During this period western Europe was drawing on native rural hinterlands to fill their industrial jobs, while the United States drew both on rural America and on southern and eastern Europe to fill theirs (Bernstein 1960; Erbe 1987: 727–9). The second began around World War II and continued through the 1960s and early 1970s. Here the United States, which had cut immigration to a trickle following legislation in 1924, drew on its native black population to work on the northern assembly lines, while western European countries sought to attract various categories of immigrants.

However, with the secular crisis of organized-capitalist expansion, western Europe cut off its immigration, while the new American immigration is connected with the development of a post-organized capitalist occupational system. Thus while only some 100,000 immigrants per year came to the USA during the 1940s (the equivalent of 25,000 per year for a western European country which would be seen as virtually nil immigration), the average was 600,000 between 1980 and 1989. And a new immigration law passed in 1990 has set a quota of 700,000 new immigrants per year from 1992 until 1994, and 675,000 annually thereafter. This law was passed in the expectation that more than 140,000 illegal immigrants per year would also flow into the country (Tenbrock 1991b).

The original moment of change in this context was the Hart-Cellar Act passed in 1965. This Act abolished previously set country-of-origin quotas; it foregrounded family connections as a principal basis for admission; and it raised the total quotas for numbers of immigrants. From 1940 to 1950 some two-thirds of immigrants were Canadians and Europeans. The intention of these loosened restrictions was to bring on a new immigration from Europe. In the event the new law's family reunification provision had scant applicability to Europeans, because the preceding immigration entry from Europe was so long in the past that few had family still to bring over. However, this was not the case for political refugees from Vietnam and Cuba. Also other West Coast Asians and Latins took advantage of the family reunification provisions. In the 1980s only 7 per cent of inmigrants were Europeans, while 44 per cent or 2.6 million people came from Asia (Tenbrock 1991a, b). The total proportion of foreign-born in the American population has risen from under 2 per cent at the beginning of the 1960s to 7 per cent in 1991 (Portes and Jensen 1989: 929; Tenbrock 1991a).

In the heyday of organized-capitalist heavy industry, migrants (Europeans and American blacks) flowed to specialized product rustbelt cities as well as to northern cities with a better balance of manufacturing and service industries. In the information-based post-organized capitalist economy, native white Americans and medium-paid jobs – from lower managerial, through retail, through heavy manufacturing – flowed to the far suburbs of the manufacturing and mixed cities, and just as much to post-industrial sunbelt cities, lower in the urban hierarchy. But the new immigrants from abroad have by contrast mainly gravitated to the new world cities, and not to the vastly expanding sunbelt cities.

The occupational distribution of the new immigrants has been complex. On the demand side, through the Hart-Cellar Law's occupational preference provisions, large numbers of professional-managerial workers have been admitted, for example 63,000 in 1986. This proportion will increase as the 1990 legislation raises the quota for highly qualified immigrants to 140,000 or 20 per cent, and provides 10,000 places per year for immigrants with more than one million dollars to invest, with the intention that this investment will create 10 or more jobs. Also many of the children of Asian immigrants are moving into the the the ranks of high value-added professional-managerials. The numbers at elite universities such as Stanford, Harvard, Berkeley and Yale are approaching 30 per cent. Silicon Valley at the outset of the 1990s employed an estimated 10,000 Chinese and 5,000 Korean engineers as well as 270 Chinese-owned enterprises (Tenbrock 1991a, b). Further, some groups of political refugees, such as Cubans in 1959–62 and Vietnamese in the mid-1970s, have also taken up high status jobs. However, in general, immigrants do not work in information-processing jobs and are concentrated in manufacturing, retail and low value-added consumer services in the information and control economies of the global cities (Portes and Jensen 1989: 929).

The post-1965 immigrants have flowed into these global cities. Fifty-six per cent of the immigrants reside in America's top 10 SMSAs (Standard Metropolitan Statistical Areas) with 31 per cent in New York and LA. Los Angeles, when undocumented immigrants are estimated and included, has more immigrants than New York: of 1965–80 incomers Los Angeles had 1.84 million accounting for nearly 24.8 per cent of its population; New York's comprised 1.27 million and 13.8 per cent of its population. Of other cities Miami and San Francisco boast the highest proportions of immigrants, with whites in the latter becoming a minority group. Some of these cities have rather homogenous immigrant inflows – Miami's is 59 per cent Cuban and Los Angeles 47 per cent Mexican. New York's is the most balanced with a roughly equal weighting of Latinos, West Indians, Asians and Europeans (Razin 1988: 288; Waldinger 1989: 214–15).

There seems to be a very common pattern of ethnic transformation: whites flow out, the immigrants flow in and black people stay put. In terms of labour markets, many services and manufacturing sectors, including the most unionizable sections of the working class, become whiter. Disintegrated manufacturing and retail sectors become taken up by migrants, while many black people suffer further economic marginalization.

There are three explanations of this migrant phenomenon: first, that the immigrants themselves create the new occupational positions; second, that there is a process of ethnic succession and replacement; and third, that the consumption needs of the dominant classes create the new positions for the immigrants. The third thesis will be addressed later.

The first, a sort of supply-side job creation thesis, is a favourite among American conservatives in government and among policy-oriented intellectuals. These analysts point to the observations of entrepreneurs that many jobs, especially in poorly paid manufacturing, would indeed have been exported to the less developed countries (LDCs), if immigrants had not come to do them cheaply in the advanced countries. This then begins a 'virtuous circle' in which immigrants create demands for products in the local economic sector. Kasarda (1990) thus cites evidence of dollars changing hands five to six times before they leave American Chinese communities. Subsequently information and hiring networks develop among immigrants, who then open recruitment channels and reduce migration costs for newcomers (see Portes and Bach 1985; Waldinger 1989).

Often, however, this supply-side job creation is not necessarily connected to the 'enclave economy' of the migrants. For example, highly educated and wealthy self-employed Iranians on the West Coast are represented in businesses – construction, transportation and communication, wholesale trade, financial services and entertainment – quite apart from the enclave economy and employing large numbers of non-Iranians (Razin 1988: 291). Moreover, increasingly immigrants are represented in large primary sector firms involved in the international economy. In some cases their entrepreneurship created these positions, for example the large number of Cubans employed in top positions in the Miami international headquarters of big American corporations. These Cubans have opened up sales for these corporations to the whole of Latin America. Indeed these Cuban migrants have transformed Miami from a sleepy town for New York tourists and pensioners – showing signs of decline at the end of the 1950s – into a booming international trade and holiday centre (see Rose 1980: 478). Also large numbers of high earning Japanese immigrants are found in managerial jobs in primary labour markets in San Francisco and Los Angeles (1980 average salary $19,600), as are large numbers of Europeans found in such jobs both on the West Coast and in New York (Razin 1988: 293). An increasing number of these have been working for head offices of firms in the USA, or for American firms involved in Japanese and European markets.

The second explanation of this migrant phenomenon is that of ethnic succession. Thus New York's labour force effectively emptied out of whites from 1970 to 1980, as nearly one-quarter exited from the central city labour force. They were replaced by about 75,000 each of Hispanic and Asian immigrants, and some 115,000 West Indian black immigrants. Ethnic succession was particularly striking in manufacturing, retail and the public sector, in all three of which white outflow of jobs was over twice as high as that predictable from overall white outflow. In the public sector it was mainly blacks who comprised the ethnic successors. Of 75,000 public sector jobs vacated by whites, some 18,000 were accounted for by native black succession. But the immigrants in their largest numbers flowed into private sector jobs. In manufacturing, white outflow was 115,000. Increases of foreign-born Latinos into manufacturing was 26,500, of immigrant Asians some 19,000. In retail, white outflow was 72,000, while inflow of foreign-born Latinos and Asians as 10,000 and 17,000 respectively (Waldinger 1986–7: tables 4, 5, 7 and 8).

Not only whites but also American blacks were displaced from these sectors, losing 8,000 jobs in manufacturing, 10,000 in retail, 13,000 in transport and communications, and 21,000 in personal services over the decade. The difference of course was that while the whites fled the city usually for better jobs, many black people had to stay and wound up unemployed.

The structural, succession thesis also accounts for the divergent outcomes among the same inmigrating ethnic groups in different cities. In San Francisco 34 per cent of Chinese entrepreneurs were in the eating and drinking sector, but in Los Angeles this figure was only 16 per cent. The explanation is that there was a much wider range of structural places open for Chinese immigrants to flow into in LA than in San Francisco (Razin 1988: tables 3 and 4).

Waldinger has creatively understood ethnic succession and black economic marginalization in terms of black people having been in the unfortunate circumstance of standing in the wrong hiring queues (1986–7: table 6). Yet this explanation does not sufficiently account for black competition for jobs with the newcomers, who subsequently bid down wages to the point where black people would not take the jobs. Further, immigrant employers will commonly hire among their own rather than among blacks. Finally, Anglo employers are often reluctant to hire American black males, and will prefer Hispanic, Asian or even black immigrants. This was the case in Miami, in which Cuban immigrants put up a labour market challenge to blacks already employed in secondary sector hotel and restaurant jobs. The Cubans, emerging victorious, subsequently found themselves in positions on the labour market demand side, and they proved even more insensitive to Miami's blacks than had the Anglos. Cuban policy of effective black economic marginalization was reinforced by the heavily racist ideologies the former had inherited from pre-Castro Cuba, as well as by their extreme anti-communist conservatism. The outcome was frighteningly summarized by an Anglo Miami observer quoted by Rose who remarked that 'the Cubans wonder what these black people are doing in this second Havana' (1980: 480).

CASE-STUDY: CLOTHING AND FASHION

The processes of migration can be very effectively seen in the microcosm of the fashion industry. In 1900 the industry in advanced capitalism's world cities was almost entirely comprised of recent migrant Jews from eastern Europe. The first step of rationalization of this always comparatively disintegrated sector came with the initial functional cleavage of the industry into 'manufacturers' and 'contractors' (Kochan 1985; Kochan et al 1986). This functional cleavage provided a structure for the industry that thrives even today. Here the manufacturer would typically take on responsibility for design, the purchase of cloth and merchandising, while the real production was carried out by the contractor (Dubofsky 1968). Almost nowhere else in the economy was entry easier. All that was necessary were skills – and the Jewish immigrants often had been tailors in their old country – and access to a supply of cheap labour. And this was supplied in plenty by their male and especially by their female immigrants. The men often did the cutting while the women did the sewing. Other costs were minimal. Machines could be rented, and premises were often shops and factories in the same tenements where the Jews lived (Morokvasic et al 1990).

But this was still the dying world of liberal capitalism. With the growth of mass consumption, and in the USA and UK a concentrated retail sector, the industry started to take on a characteristically organized capitalist form. However, it should be noted that the clothing industry could never be as Fordist, as concentrated, and as Taylorized as most other sectors because it entails a much higher turnover of styles. Hence it always has relatively short production runs and relative design intensity. However, clothing moved towards Fordism in several ways and in two stages. The first stage entailed a change in labour process to much shorter-cycle production and away from full garment work to section work. This can entail the reduction of job-task cycle from 15–20 minutes to as short as 1 minute (Morokvasic et al 1990: 160). At the same time there was a move in production to much larger factories, often away from the world cities, such as from New York to the American South. In some cases this was partly sparked by strategies of trade union avoidance. At the same time plant size became considerably larger (Dubofsky 1968). And in large concerns with the long production runs there was often considerable functional integration of retailing, manufacturing and contracting.

The second Fordist phase saw the shift of this version of mass production into the Third World. This took several forms. Retailers in advanced countries could purchase long production-run items from firms based in south Asia. In the USA for example in 1959 6.9 per cent of apparel consumption consisted of imports; by 1981 it was half (Morokvasic et al 1990: 162). Alternatively manufacturers in the advanced countries could build factories in the export processing zones of these countries in the search for cheap labour (Sklair 1990). Usually the manufacturers from the advanced countries would be involved here, but often retailers would commission from agents who themselves would deal with native manufacturers, or these first world retailers would directly invest in Third World manufacturing. In all cases the result was the employment of cheap labour, or the famous 'nimble-fingered young women' who, previously taught by their mothers, required only about six weeks' training to work as machinists for £80–100 per month (Phizacklea 1990: 41, ch 3). British manufacturers have then for example been able to obtain 'retail mark-up' on 'ex-factory costs' of 200–300 per cent on Thai-made garments in comparison with only 70 per cent on British-made ones. Phizacklea observed cases of 12-year-old rural-born girls working as sewing machinists in the Bangkok industry, sleeping eight to a room, sewing seven days a week from 8am to 11pm (1990: 44, 46).

While many long production runs continue to be carried out in LDCs, there has been a tendential move towards shorter runs and an emergent downgraded variety of flexible specialization. Even of garments imported from abroad, an increasing number are now comprised of, not low value-added, price-competitive Third World goods, but high value-added quality-competitive goods from other European countries. Thus of UK clothing imports in 1987, 10.5 per cent came from Italy and 6.5 per cent from West Germany (Phizacklea 1990: 40). The shift to more flexible production has been both demand and supply led. In the case of women's fashion, women's outerwear, lingerie and infants' wear, frequent style changes entail short production runs and relocation back into the small workshops of major cities in the advanced societies. Even men's clothing is produced for 'niche' markets, and the shift to flexible production is brought about on the demand side both by the proliferation of niches and by the rapid turnover of styles within any given niche. In Britain only one-quarter of these fashion goods was made abroad by the mid-1980s.

This tendency towards short production runs of women's fashion was accentuated after the depression of the industry at the end of the 1970s with the growing importance of 'lifestyle retailing' for women above the age of 25. From 1983 clothing expenditure of British women outstripped the telescoping growth in consumer expenditure as a whole. Leaving Fordist retailing and much of mass-produced men's clothes to Marks & Spencer, other large British retailers shifted into women's fashionwear on a vast scale (Phizacklea 1990: 9–12).

At the same time the firm structure began to transform. Retailers such as Burton and Next moved out of manufacturing, and the most concentrated British manufacturers lost in market share. While Courtaulds, Tootals and Coats Viyella continued to control 40–50 per cent of the market in men's shirts and underwear, they account for only 16 per cent of the women's fashionwear market, 72 per cent of which is produced in units of 10 or less employees (Phizacklea 1990: 12 ff). Among Europe's concentrated distributors this move towards disintegration has best perhaps been exemplified by Benetton. Benetton is so disintegrated that not even the outlets are owned by the firm. The full costs of setting up shop must be borne by the operator although s/he must operate within the rules of Benetton's shop organization, that is no backroom stockholding, a particular interior design and selling only Benetton products. Benetton itself is basically a manufacturer and an information system whose central Ponzano headquarters exercises control over outsourced production and retailing. As manufacturers the firm is involved in design, size grading, cutting, dyeing, quality control, warehousing and delivery. Like their high value-added German counterpart, Boss, they subcontract labour-intensive sewing. Also like Boss, sales are high and there is high value-added production (Phizacklea 1990: ch 1; Hirst and Zeitlin 1990).

This has in turn given rise to smaller firms. Thus in France 10 per cent output in the clothing sector was accounted for by contractors or 'jobbers' in 1979, while this rose to 21 per cent in 1984. In that year too some 60 per cent of all French manufacturing firms were doing some outsourcing. Finally, in 1984 the proportion of French firms with fewer than 19 employees stood at 90 per cent, the majority of which had fewer than 9 employees, while almost half of all garment employees worked in firms with fewer than 19 workers. Instead of shifting production to outward processing in the Third World, the Third World has moved to Paris. The advantage is quicker response to ever faster changing styles. It is, additionally, cheap labour that is available. Thus in March 1990, of Parisian clothing firms with fewer than 10 employees, less than half were French owned, while 22 per cent were Turkish owned, and 8 per cent and 3 per cent respectively were owned by Yugoslavs and Chinese (Morokvasic 1991: 271–2). For the manufacturers, other incentives for this outsourcing to immigrant jobbers have been to offlay risks, reduce corporation taxes, lower national insurance payments and circumvent labour legislation. The subcontractors themselves outsource work to others in a 'chain of subcontractors' in order further to offlay risks. Like the Jews in the twilight of liberal capitalism, Turkish entrepreneurs in Paris need only access to sewing machines and to the cheap labour of their (mostly female) compatriots.

Another aspect of this accentuated vertical disintegration is the further extension of the subcontracting chain so that even the sewing machine operators are labelled self-employed. Contractors can thus offlay enormous costs on to operators. Thus 'self-employed' machinists commonly purchase their own machines at average costs of £300. And British contractors often pay neither national insurance contributions nor PAYE (pay as you earn). Contractors further in these instances are not required to pay any wages at all during slack seasons, and operators may work a 60-hour week in the peak September to January season, a 20-hour week from January to April, and not at all from May through August. In the case of some of these homeworkers described by Phizacklea, the driver delivers cloth at 8am and collects the product at 6pm, paying the homeworker in cash; in several of these cases the homeworker does not even know who the contractor is (1990: 96–9). Savings are also made on pay. Thus average rate of pay for West Midlands clothing workers in 1984 was £1.08 per hour, while the statutory minimum was £1.50.

There is, as we have maintained, a complex cluster of institutions involved in the governance of migration, which is at the same time essentially the regulation of labour markets. The main institutional actors here are the family, the state and corporatist bodies. The immigrant entrepreneurs – whether Chinese, Pakistani, Indian, Turkish, Cuban or Vietnamese – are surrounded by extraordinarily tight family structures. This has even been the case for middle-class immigrants. For example,

Portes and Jensen (1989) report on how middle-class Vietnamese and Cuban housewives will take on quite menial jobs with the aim at all costs of preserving the family unit. If anything could have less in common with the individualization and differentiation involved in reflexive modernization, it is these pre-eminently traditional family structures which take upon themselves welfare, pension, unemployment insurance and health care functions normally offloaded onto bodies operating in the public sphere of modern societies. Perhaps most important is the implosion of economic functions into the family itself. Thus Yugoslav and other entrepreneurs in the Paris garment industry with no old country training as tailors are dependent on their wives' sewing skills to set up firms, although the husbands act as the employer (Morokvasic 1991: 266). Further, employment as mentioned above is often of the wives of either relatives or immigrants whom the ethnic employers have assisted in the immigration process. One major reason that American blacks have not followed this immigrant model and become clothing sector entrepreneurs is that their family structures are simply too modern. The high labour-force participation rates of black females, like the low level of intact families, are indicators not only of deprivation but also of modernization. As with most native American whites subject to the same processes of individuation, there is just no way that the sort of *économies de famille* of the immigrant entrepreneurs can be realized.

But the tight, integrally traditional family structure of the immigrants does not provide sufficient conditions to allow for entrepreneurial 'success'. It has to be combined with a liberal state and a low level of corporatization, that is the state and corporate bodies cannot act as powerful means of exclusion of immigrants from certain labour market positions. Morokvasic illustrates this in her comparison of Turkish clothing sector entrepreneurs in Paris and Berlin (1991: 273–4). In 1989 31 new firms were started up by Turkish industrialists, while only 44 were started by French manufacturers. In Berlin Turkish-owned firms were only a handful, despite a much greater Turkish population presence. In fact the entire small shop (*Handwerk*) sector in clothing, at the same time that it was expanding elsewhere, was declining in Berlin. On the other hand Berlin's Turks were very active as entrepreneurial tailors, making up the great majority of these in the city over the past two decades. And this majority was of a greatly increasing number of alteration tailor shops: from 12 in 1965 to 532 in 1990. Turkish immigrants have not been able to enter manufacturing. Once Turkish would-be manufacturing capitalists get past various state-set barriers of residence permit and special work permit, they must hurdle various corporatist barriers. This is so even if they had acquired extensive training and qualifications in Turkey.

Thus the clothing and fashion industry demonstrates that migrant patterns after organized capitalism are characterized, not by convergence, but by divergence. We can distinguish liberal regimes such as the USA, and to a lesser degree the UK and France; corporatist regimes such as

Germany and Austria; and welfare-statist regimes such as those in Scandinavia. In liberal regimes a significant sector of the new lower-class is accounted for by immigrant labour in the shops of small immigrant entrepreneurs. It is true that a number of the immigrant new lower-class labourers do become employers. It is true that a number of their children enter primary sector professional jobs. And it is true that even hyper-exploited new immigrant employees often see their exploiters as having done them a favour by bringing them to the West. Yet these employees undoubtedly do comprise a new lower class beneath the working class because the secondary labour market that they constitute is one that on most indicators is structurally downwardly mobile from the organized-capitalist secondary labour market. They are a part of the new lower class, and virtually all of the even more exploited women in their midst will never themselves become entrepreneurs. Indeed few will finally even be legalized into the formal labour market. They are eventually part of the new lower class because hopes for a future generation cannot fully compensate for degraded conditions of work and residence in the present that were unimaginable in the organized-capitalist heyday of the Keynesian welfare state.

CORPORATIST EXCLUSION IN A REUNITED GERMANY

Germany: the corporatist welfare state

A central theme of this book is the contrast between routes of moderniz-ation after organized capitalism. In particular we have focussed on the Anglo-American neo-liberal model versus the much more institutionally regulated corporatist and statist model of Germany. We will show in this section that Germany's corporatist institutions, though perhaps providing an exemplary growth model, also provide a model for an alternative regime of new lower-class formation based on a particular mode of exclusion of women and especially minorities from labour markets and from public life. These institutions include the state, unions, chambers of commerce, employers' associations, the craft training system, the welfare state, the family and a fundamentally national economy based in industrial sectors. Each of these institutions reinforces the other in a complex network of effectivities constituting the 'German model'.

This corporatist model can be contrasted with the two other worlds of welfare capitalism (see Esping-Andersen, 1990; and chapter 8). The *neo-liberal* variant is based primarily on a principle of means-tested social assistance. It has evolved non-means-tested pensions, health and un-employment benefits, whether funded through social insurance payments or financed through general taxation. But the levels of these transfer payments are low and are often supplemented by private (or union-bargained) supplementary pensions and private health insurance, themselves subsidized by tax allowances granted to private firms. The *social-democratic* regime is universalistic in that all citizens are covered by the same programme. It incorporates the principle of Marshallian rights of social citizenship. It is the democratic flat-rate and general-revenue financed model. Welfare resources claimed as a right on the social-democratic model are not minimal but substantial, and do not need topping up by private insurance schemes.

The *corporatist* model is complex. Whereas liberal regimes were introduced by liberal governments, and the universalist regimes by social-democratic parties, the corporatist regimes were introduced by conservative governments. The principles here were laid down by Bismarck in the 1880s, and developed on a massive scale after World War II by conservative governments in West Germany, France and Italy (Mommsen 1981; Flora and Heidenheimer 1981). Further, while liberal and social democratic regimes are secular and 'modern' in inspiration, conservative and corporatist regimes have Christian (Catholic) and traditionalist sources. There are two in particular. The first of these is the Church's pro-family principle of 'subsidiarity', in which the state is only to intervene 'when the family's capacity to service its members is exhausted' (Esping-Andersen 1990: 27). This means that welfare service functions offloaded onto the market in liberal regimes and to the state in social-democratic regimes are carried out in the family itself in corporatist regimes. The Christian principle is to support the intact family. The result however is a pre-modern state of affairs in which functions are not yet differentiated out from the family, and women are mainly confined to the private sphere.

The second principle is that of hierarchy. This system is based on the consolidation of earners into ordered status groups with different regimes of social insurance, for example the white collar employees as opposed to manual workers in Germany (Kocka 1969). Particularly privileged in these regimes are civil servants. Their privilege results from a heavily statist-corporatism which is based on tying the loyalties of civil servants to the central state authority (see Offe 1981). This is therefore a conservative and corporatist regime, in which schemes are stratified and occupationally distinct, participation is compulsory and each scheme involves a representational monopoly (Schmitter 1981). Bismarck himself favoured a more statist solution, but rural Protestant and Catholic conservative allies forced the corporatist guild and familial character into the scheme. The intention of the Bismarck 1880s coalitions as well as later papal encyclicals, especially that of 1931, was not just to preserve the family, but patriarchally to harmonize relations between the social classes and incorporate all into the patriarchal community of the state (Esping-Andersen 1990: 58–68; Lash 1990a).

Countries with conservative-corporatist regimes, such as Austria, Italy and France as well as Germany, stand midway between Sweden and the USA on most of the indicators of social welfare. But they score much higher on the degree to which there were stratified pension schemes and high pensions to government employees. Thus these four corporatist regimes devote between 2.2 and 3.8 per cent of national income to government employee pensions, while the UK, USA, Netherlands, Sweden and Japan cluster around the 1.5 per cent mark.

There are a number of implications of the German model, that is the conservative-corporatist welfare state based on the assumption of the intact family with the single wage earner and the wife performing a high proportion of welfare services in the home. First, it results in low female labour market participation rates. In Germany these are less than 39 per cent, compared with over 50 per cent in the USA, and over 75 per cent of non-student females aged 16–64 in the Scandinavian countries. Women in Germany were moreover overrepresented in low paid, non-professional service jobs (Esping-Andersen 1990: 209).

Second, there is a markedly high productivity of those in the labour force combined with a small proportion of the total population actually being in the labour force. Thus the labour force participation rate of all men and women aged 16–65 increased in the USA from 1960 to 1985 from 66 to 75 per cent and in Sweden from 74 to 81 per cent, while it actually fell in Germany from 70 to 66 per cent. Labour force limitation in Germany took place partly through early retirement, as the proportion of men aged 55–64 who were in Germany's labour force declined between 1960 and 1985 from 83 to 58 per cent, while decline in Sweden was limited from 90 to 76 per cent, and in the USA from 83 to 69 per cent (Esping-Andersen 1990: 151). The total labour force in the USA more than doubled between 1960 and 1985; in Sweden it increased by a fifth, while in Germany it declined (Esping-Andersen 1990: 197–8).

Third, mainly because many welfare and consumer services are in effect produced in the home by women, Germany is still a surprisingly industrial rather than a post-industrial society. Elsewhere in north Atlantic rim countries the increase in female labour force participation rates is directly and closely linked to the growth in post-industrial jobs (see chapter 8 below). But this growth has not happened in Germany to the same degree. In the early 1980s over two-fifths of the German labour force was employed in manufacturing industry, compared with only 25.1 per cent in the USA (Esping-Andersen 1990: 204; Sassen 1991: 209, 216).

Finally, Germany cannot afford to employ a large number of people in social services owing to its very high level of transfer payments and income maintenance, these being needed to stabilize living standards in single income families. Conversely, because Sweden pays out so much to employ people in the social services, it cannot afford to have a high proportion of its population dependent on transfer payments. The assumption is that everybody works. The result is that 60 per cent of the entire Swedish population is in the labour force compared with 49 per cent in Germany. Furthermore, one-quarter of Swedes work in health, education and welfare in comparison with a mere 11 per cent in Germany (Esping-Andersen 1990: table 6.3). The share of all employed women working in the public sector was over one-half in Sweden but only one-fifth in Germany (Esping-Andersen 1990: tables 8.3, 8.5).

Institutional stratification of immigration

This statist-corporatist institutional complex in Germany is responsible for its particular response to immigration. We will briefly describe the main features of such immigration. In 1961 there were only 686,000 foreigners living in West Germany (Cross 1987: 9). Up until 1961 and the construction of the Berlin Wall, excess labour demand in West Germany was filled mostly by East German *Übersiedler*. But there was also some foreign immigration, mainly from EC countries, and most of all from Italy. The proportion from EC countries declined from over half in the late 1960s to about one-quarter in 1989 (Hoenekopp 1991: 132). And the construction of the Berlin Wall was the immediate reason for the conclusion of state-to-state agreements on the immigration of guest workers with Turkey and several other countries.

This ushered in the second phase of German post-war immigration. The immigration was of massive proportions as the average net annual figure from 1961 to 1973 was about 270,000. By 1973 the foreign population had reached 3.97 million (Hoenekopp 1991: 130). And the main reason for this is that West Germany did not have any immigration laws (and Germany still does not). The huge inmigrations of this period were not regulated by the state, but corporatistically through recruitment by employers. The proportion of Turks and Yugoslavs among *Ausländer* in this second phase increased massively (Hoenekopp 1991: 131).

The third phase of German post-war immigration occurred between 1973 and 1988, when the number of immigrants increased by only about one-quarter of a million. The oil crisis of 1973 combined with incipient post-industrialization led to chronically loose labour markets. The Federal government issued a recruitment ban on foreign labour in 1973, and stipulated that those who returned to their native lands could not reasonably expect to find employment at a later date in Germany (Gans 1990: 29). Net migration figures had always masked the huge numbers of foreigners remigrating to their country of origin. For example, in 1989 net inmigration of *Ausländer* of 332,464 was accounted for by an absolute number of 770,897 inmigrants and 438,433 outmigrants (Hoenekopp 1991: 117). The immediate result of the recruitment ban plus economic crisis was a number of years of net remigration in this period.

The fourth phase of German post-war migration dates from 1988 and should continue for the next decade or so. This new massive migration is the result of international politics. At the end of 1991 Germany had about 5.6 to 5.7 million foreigners. This represents a higher proportion of the population than France and a much higher proportion than Britain.

In addition, the implications of the breakup of the eastern bloc in this context are profound. First of all, there has been a substantial shift in the main source of immigration. By the end of the 1980s the ratio of immigrants was 3–4 to 1 in favour of East Europeans as opposed to the Turks (Hoenekopp 1991: 128). This trend will intensify in the future owing to the imminent opening-up of the former USSR. East Europe migrants are the new *Gastarbeiter*, though often *Gastarbeiter* without jobs. Between two-thirds and three-quarters of this east European migration comes from Poland: an estimated 250,000 in 1990 (*Der Spiegel*, 30 September 1991: 32). Germany and Poland have a 'special relationship'. Further, favourable conditions for Polish workers in Germany have facilitated the movement of *Aussiedler*, immigrants of German origin who lived in Poland for generations, who have now returned to Germany. Net migration of Polish-based *Aussiedler* from 1977 through 1989 was 589,000. At the same time Poland (along with the former Czechoslovakia and Hungary) is increasingly being seen as a buffer zone against the really huge numbers of migrants expected from the USSR, Romania and Bulgaria.[1] Apart from Poles the other main category of *Aussiedler*, ethnic Germans who have lived abroad for generations, are Soviet-Germans. Figures here hovered around 7,000 annually from 1977 to 1980, collapsed almost completely between 1982 and 1986, and qualitatively took off at the end of the 1980s with 41,000 immigrants in 1988 and 88,200 in 1989 (Hoenekopp 1991: tables 4 and 5). When Soviet border controls are fully removed in 1993, it is expected that the entire *Sovjetdeutsch* community of 2m people will migrate to Germany (*Der Spiegel* 21 October 1991).

A further important category is those moving from 'east' to 'west' Germany. Migration of all ethnic Germans into the Federal Republic from 1951 to 1986 averaged 73,000 per year (Wilpert 1991: 50). The most important category of these were the *Übersiedler* from 1951 to 1961. Between 1961 and 1974 inmigration of ethnic Germans was at a low level. But with the *Gastarbeiter* recruitment stop of 1973, systematic attempts were made to attract *Aussiedler*. The total between October 1989 through to May 1991 is estimated at 700,000. But from July 1990 the flow significantly slowed owing to the removal of economic incentives – Easterners moving into the *alten Bundesländer* no longer automatically receive social benefits on a par with previous residents and no longer can recoup moving expenses and receive one-off payments. Nevertheless in April 1991 it was estimated that 150,000 Easterners were working in West Berlin alone, more than half illegally (Ganssmann 1991: 4; Wilpert 1991: 54–5; Butterwegge and Isola 1990).

Finally, there are the *Asylanten*. Germany has been the most liberal among European nations in the immigration of asylum seekers. In 1990 Germany took in 193,000 asylum seekers in comparison to France's 56,000 and Britain's risible 25,000 (*Der Spiegel* 30 September 1991: 33). A certain proportion of these *Asylanten* consists of Asians and Africans. Net Asian inmigration averaged 20–5 thousand per year from 1977 to 1981 and 35–40 thousand per year from 1985 to 1989. Of net migrants from 1977 the leading group is Poles with 421,000, while Asians have accounted for

335,000 and Africans 74,000. In comparison during this period Turkish net migration was only 38,000, and EC and Yugoslav net migration was a negative 375,000 and a negative 122,000 respectively (Hoenekopp 1991: tables 1 and 9).

We have spent considerable time outlining the main contours of migration in Germany, because it represents the alternative route to contemporary restructuring in counterposition to the neo-liberal model. It is also because Germany is on the way to becoming once again a major power. Further Germany is the closest Western country to the tumultuous *de*structuring of eastern Europe. Also it is because, although capital, images, communications, money and investment are flowing in their most advanced form in and out of the USA, Japan and the UK, the flow of people is at the moment and for the foreseeable future most significantly taking place into Germany (of migrants that is, not tourists). Finally, it is more than likely that Germany will provide the model for post-communist development to the countries in what commentators call the German *Hinterhof* (back courtyard).

Germany is also the place where the most contradictory forces with respect to internationalization are located. Partly in reaction to the Third Reich experience, in terms of values Germany is the least nationalistic, the least militaristic of nations. A good number of these very universalist values are institutionalized – in the constitution, in the limited role prescribed for the military, in the systematically universalist content of the media and especially televison. But these liberal values and institutions stand in contrast with the national and corporatistic familial-conservative institutional complex at issue in this chapter. In the context of the state and immigration both sides of this contradiction come into play. Here it makes sense to distinguish between the external and internal functions of the state. In terms of the external functions the German state is relatively universalist. In terms of its internal functions, and here it articulates with the various corporatisms, it is nationalist and particularist.

As we mentioned, the 1961–73 migration was statist and corporatist. It was statist in the sense that the agreements between the Bundesregierung and governments of outmigration were quite different from the way immigration was managed in other Western countries. These *Gastarbeiter* agreements were much closer to those made in the communist world (Hoenekopp 1991: 122–3). These included bilateral agreements in the 1960s with the governments of Spain, Greece, Turkey, Portugal and Yugoslavia (Mehrlaender 1984: 375). These agreements were corporatist in comparison to eastern Europe recruitment because West German employers and employers' federations had much greater autonomy from the state. The new migration is not one of *Gastarbeiter* and its regulation is not corporatist. Yet it still contradictorily counterposes the national principles connected to incoming *Aussiedler* to the universalist principles concerning the asylum seekers. Hence the mainstream right is more

enthusiastic than the left in promoting *Aussiedlung*, while left-liberal forces
have been much more positive towards the *Asylanten*. And a large measure
of German immigration politics is universalistic. Further, policies towards
Asylanten are more generous than elsewhere, as shown in 1992 in
relationship to asylum seekers from the former Yugoslavia.

Jus sanguinis and exclusion from citizenship

There are four main modes of the public regulation of immigration, and
they can be ranked in order of 'distanciation' of host country from
incoming migrants. Least distanciated is the sort of Commonwealth or
colonial situation that applies to West Indians incoming to Britain. More
distanciated is the ex-colonial relationship of say Algerians to France. Still
more distanciated is the non-colonial relationship of the USA to its main
sources of immigration. And most distanciated is the sort of *Gastarbeiter*
situation of Germany between 1961 and 1973. Equally perhaps distanciated is the situation of asylum seekers who are admitted under the
universalist orders of international law, in comparison with immigrants
admitted under the conditions of a country's specifically designated immigration law. We should again emphasize the very impersonal nature of the
relationship between Germany and its two main categories of migrant,
Gastarbeiter and *Asylanten*. Even in the non-colonial relationship as found
in the USA, immigration usually occurs along channels set up through
military presence, or more likely, foreign direct investment (Sassen 1988).
By contrast the main countries from which the *Gastarbeiter* and the
Asylanten come pertain to neither of these closely networked situations.

Generally, the more distanciated this relationship, the less favourable
the conditions of citizenship for incomers. In the colonial and ex-colonial
situation of West Indians in Britain, their stay was never regarded as
temporary. The original idea was assimilationist and they were from the
start British passport holders (Cross and Etzinger 1988: 13). In contrast the
situation of *Gastarbeiter* was regarded as temporary. And the highly
unfavourable conditions for inclusion into German citizenship that exist
today are in large part a legacy from the days of the *Gastarbeiter*. In
Germany citizenship is regulated by a mixture of voluntarism and unfortunately, *jus sanguinis*. There was some movement towards greater
universalism under the Social Democratic–Liberal coalition of the late
1970s and early 1980s. The Federal government-commissioned Kuehn
memorandum for the integration of workers countered the long held (and
still held) counterfactual position that Germany is not a 'country of
immigration'. The memorandum recognized a de facto immigration situation; it advocated voting rights attached to extended residence as well as
naturalization rights for adolescents. Finally, it guaranteed greater legal
security. The memorandum was brought into the guidelines of the coalition
government and presented in December 1981, but it was never enacted.
Tighter labour market conditions were at the root of the Social–Liberal

retreat. Instead the government, itself brought down for a decade in autumn 1982, issued anti-family completion legislation, forbidding the entry of children of non-EC migrants over 15 years of age (Mehrlaender 1987: 87–8).

The move towards greater national particularism and greater exclusion from all sorts of citizenship was accelerated by the Christian Democratic– Liberal coalition from 1982. They first unsuccessfully attempted to reduce child entry age to 6 and then to 12. They further initiated discussion to limit spouse entry to marriages of three years or more duration. They then put into effect financial remigration incentives in November 1983, including payments of DM 10,500 and recouping of the employee side of pension contributions. And a 1985 Bundestag-passed act guaranteed provisons for housing assistance to encourage remigration (Mehrlaender 1987: 90, 93; Gans 1990: 25).

The boundary between voluntarism and *jus sanguinis* can be a hazy one. The strict stratification of migrants into *Aussiedler* and *Ausländer* is also consistent with *jus sanguinis*. The point is, as Wilpert (1991: 54) argues, that accumulation of citizenship rights in this is not based on time lived in Germany, nor contribution to the commonweal as an earner and taxpayer, but is instead based on ethnicity. Ethnic-German migrants, an estimated 80 per cent of whose linguistic base is so weak that they have needed language training, are eligible for all social insurance benefits without ever having paid into social insurance funds. The irony is that non-German migrants, because of their age structure, have paid infinitely more in than they have received as benefits. In effect the *Gastarbeiter* have been paying for the unearned pensions and health insurance of the *Aussiedler*. Subsidies have been paid to *Aussiedler* in not just pensions, health insurance and unemployment benefits, but in moving expenses, language courses, one-off payments, vocational retraining and housing subsidies to the tune of approximately DM 6–7bn in 1989 alone. The constitution of Germany is ambivalent as to the rights of non-German ethnics to citizenship, but it is quite clear in including as citizens refugees or deportees with German *Volkszugehörigkeit*, including ethnic Germans who settled in Romania in the twelfth century!

If citizenship for non-ethnic Germans is made difficult enough to acquire, then voluntarism indeed begins to slide over into *jus sanguinis*. And the rate of acquisition of citizenship by *Ausländer* is minuscule, some 14,000 per year indicating that less than 10 per cent of all foreign residents are citizens. And by 'foreign' this includes third generation Turks. The 1990 Christian Democratic legislation, putatively intended to enable integration, has been risible. This has relaxed somewhat the conditions under which foreigners who have been legally residents for 15 years can apply for citizenship. Further, second- and third-generation German-born 'foreigners' can apply for citizenship between the ages of 16 and 23, if they have no criminal record, have attended German school for six years or more, and give up their previous citizenship. Finally, German-born foreigners are normally not citizens but in addition they have no rights of residence, and children must apply even for residence permits upon reaching the age of 16 (Huber and Unger 1982: 152–9; Wilpert 1991: 60; Mehrlaender 1987: 91).[2] German corporatism then with its notable absence of pluralism and strong articulation with the state has produced patterns of racial exclusion. It has neither individual-based anti-discrimination legislation nor positive collective provision for minorities.

The work society

This statist corporatism plays itself out in the very core of the 'German model' as identified by analysts such as Streeck et al (1987a) and Mahnkopf (1989), namely the worker training system discussed in chapter 4. In Germany it is a scandal if there are 700,000 school leavers in a given year and only 690,000 apprenticeship places. It is a political failure for a given Landesregierung not to be able to assure that all schoolleavers can find apprenticeship places. In a 'work society' like Germany not to have either studied in higher education or had a work *Ausbildung* is to be a pariah, to be beyond the pale. It is virtually tantamount to being excluded from citizenship and civil society. Social rights are, together with the very strong social insurance, rather than the general taxation principle, intrinsically connected with work.

Now Turks and other *Ausländer* have been ubiquitous in German industry. In 1979 some two-thirds of foreigners in the labour force were in manufacturing (Cross 1987: 12; Mehrlaender 1983: 45–9). But mainly they were not in skilled jobs. This is because foreigners have been largely excluded from apprenticeships (Schoeneberg 1982: 463–5, 469–71). For example in a 1980 study of 430 Turkish adolescents in 22 West German cities, not a single Turkish respondent who had arrived in Germany as an adolescent had a skilled job. Of those who had attended school in the Bundesrepublik 30 per cent had skilled jobs on entry into the labour market; of those who finished their school exam only 40 per cent did. This was by comparison with more than 80 per cent of German youths who began work in skilled manual positions. Further no matter how qualified a Turkish teenager's father was, nor no matter how prestigious the school he attended, it did not improve his chances of obtaining a skilled first job (Mehrlaender 1984: 376). In a longitudinal study of 50 Turkish and 28 German youths carried out in Düsseldorf in 1984, every single German respondent had a promise of a training place in a plant or had decided to go into higher education, while only one out of 50 Turkish respondents had such a promise (Koenig et al 1988: 57).

This pattern results from both demand- and supply-side causes. On the demand side, employers stated that they could not employ more foreigners because of the anticipated hostility among the native German workforce and of the hostility of customers to minority workers, and that the foreign applicants just did not have the 'German virtues' of the work ethic, and so on (cited in Mehrlaender 1987: 92). And on the supply side there is considerable uncertainty as to whether potential trainees will remain in Germany. Insecurity of residence as we mentioned contributes greatly to this. In 1981 some 40 per cent of Turkish workers had been in the labour force for more than eight years, the prerequisite length of stay necessary for application for a residence permit, yet only 0.3 per cent had acquired the right to stay in Germany. German anti-foreigner sentiment and this insecure legal situation are also the basis of certain anti-German sentiments among Turkish youth and their unwillingness to proceed to vocational training (Mehrlaender 1984: 378; 1987: 92). The 1984 Düsseldorf study also revealed that the Turkish family was more authoritarian than the German families in regard to job choice of youth. For Turkish youths the choice of job was often seen as a part of future plans for the whole family. These plans were based around the return to Turkey and opening up of a craft shop. Thus when Turkish youths at the beginning of the longitudinal study were asked what sort of career they wanted, most chose ones in which they could set up small artisanal shops – in TV and radio repair, as a barber and so on. German respondents wanted jobs in more high tech areas, and thus sought training positions which would be in the larger, more prestigious plants (Koenig et al 1988: 34–5, 39, 44–5). German youths were also by most objective standards better qualified candidates. Moreover, German youths had had the chance with parents, relatives and/ or friends to 'muck about' in home workshops and to experiment with different ways of doing things than what was taught in the *Berufschulen* (trades schools). For Turkish youths the schools were the only place where they had access to tools and workshops. Finally, the Germans had the cultural, linguistic and 'ethnic' capital which gave them confidence to apply for training places direct to plants even where they had no contacts. The Turks did not, and instead had to apply through the career training and information services of the Düsseldorf employment office.

Connecting the supply and demand side of training places are networks. Through these networks flow information about training places. In information networks parents play a crucial role. And parents of Turkish youth – some who had only five or less years of elementary school education in Turkey – often had little idea of how training related to labour market chances or of the available range of occupational training alternatives (Mehrlaender 1984: 377). Influence also flows through networks and the Turks had little. Whereas German fathers could help their sons secure training places in the plants where they worked, Turkish fathers were mostly semi- and unskilled workers and were active in areas in plants where there were no apprenticeship places (Koenig et al 1988: 45). Through such information and contact networks German youths were able to secure training places a full year before the places were registered at the employment office, and hence became available to Turkish youths. Thus the demand side had often been fixed in advance, and Turkish youths were excluded from even competing on the training market.

In 1991 the training market situation vastly altered. Because of demographic slump among West Germans and the inclination of Western youths to pursue higher education rather than apprenticeships, there were substantially more training places available than there were West German youths to fill them. But again the Turks were being passed over for East Germans and *Aussiedler* in spite of the fact that the latter group do not have useful information and influence networks (Funke 1991: 68–73; Wilpert 1991: 55). This seems especially to be the case in large factories. And as Streeck et al (1987a) have shown, substantially more training goes on in large firm apprenticeships than in small firms. It is indeed rational for large firms to invest in training because they can reasonably expect to continue to employ trainees after apprenticeships. Small firms can usually not expect this, so the cost of training is often wasted money. Hence small firms tend to use training places rather more as de facto sources of cheap labour.

CONCLUSION

We have in this and the last chapters analysed in some detail new lower-class formation in the wake of organized capitalism. We have discussed the underclass, the migrants, the new polarization and how in an important sense the making of the new lower class is the work of the dominant social strata. This discussion has necessarily been as much about ethnicity and race as about class because the new lower-class in the advanced countries increasingly consists of ethnic minorities. We have then discussed race and new lower-class formation in a number of countries, especially focussing on the USA and Germany. We have so focussed partly because, with the collapse of the eastern bloc, the global order seems increasingly to be defined by, on the one hand, the USA and, on the other, a Europe whose substantially greatest power is Germany. But this is also because neo-liberal America and corporatist Germany come closest to representing the two polar ideal-types of post-organized capitalist social structure.

Both neo-liberalism and corporatism are viable models of restructuration. Japan, the third pole defining the shape of the new international field, embodies important elements of both. Much of the global social change literature, such as D. Harvey (1989), Castells (1989) and Sassen (1991), presumes the existence of the neo-liberal model. There is not as much analysis devoted to the alternative corporatist trajectory as found in Germany. We will recapitulate its features to conclude this chapter.

Crucial here is that the German model uses traditionalist, corporatist structures in a successful process of high modernization. That is, the German model makes use of a number of fortunate rigidities to bring about successful growth in an age of increasing fluidities. This is then a very unmodern route of modernization (which belies German theorists, such as Habermas, Luhmann and Beck, of modernization as *Lernprozess*). It is extraordinarily undifferentiated, unindividualized and unreflexive, since corporations and the family do much of the deciding for individuals.

First, then, Germany is principally a national, and not an internationalized, economy. Corporatism has always depended on substantial levels of national integration (Lipietz 1984; Lash and Urry 1987). Germany has far lower levels of foreign direct and portfolio investment, both inwards and outwards, than do Japan and the United States. It is in this sense much more a national economy. Second, there is a high proportion of manufacturing workers and a low proportion of service workers. That is, about 40 per cent are in manufacturing in Germany compared with 20–5 per cent in the USA, Japan, UK and Sweden. Third, the service sector is small because of a strong family unit and a low female labour force participation rate, in which services that are carried out by the state in, say, Sweden or through the market in the USA have to be carried out in the family by women in Germany.

Fourth, the German economy is one in which few people work, while those who do are involved in high value-added labour based on good qualifications. These people support the rest of the population. In such an economy jobs are scarce goods to be competed for. Very often women and most often minorities come out worst in this competition. Fifth, here is an economy with a low proportion of advanced services. This is due first to its low level of internationalization, so fewer are active in producer services. It is due also to the slow development of individualistic lifestyles – which presume homeowning, divorce, urban labour-intensive consumption styles – that necessitate the development of advanced consumer services. Finally, Germany is a national economy where ethnicity-based membership criteria exclude minorities from citizenship in the state. Its corporatist structures, equally ethnically inscribed, exclude minorities from labour markets and civil society more generally. The lack of impacted ghettoes as produced by the neo-liberal model is thus bought at a heavy price.

We have therefore noted just how oddly and extraordinarily *industrial* Germany still is. In the next chapter we will examine the notion of *post*-industrialism more systematically, noting both its importance in many societies, apart from Germany, and its effects upon particular towns and cities across many societies in the north Atlantic rim.

NOTES

1. This explains the agreements of the Federal government with Hungary of December 1989 and with Poland of June 1990 on migration for training purposes, on border crossing for commuters, and on recruitment of hospital personnel (Hoenekopp 1991: 121). The quid pro quo is special privileges for Poles on German labour markets in return for Germany being allowed to send illegal Soviet and Romanian immigrants back to Poland. In any event eastern Europeans, partly also for cold war political reasons, were treated as politically persecuted even when they (as virtually all did) migrated for economic reasons. They have always had for example access to labour markets without the five-year wait necessary for asylum seekers. More recently with the deluge of *Aussiedler*, whose German-language ability and skills have

declined to match that of ethnic Poles, western Germans are having more and more difficulty in telling the Poles from the *Aussiedler*.

2. On the face of it Holland would seem to be close to the corporatist, German model. But compared to Germany, Austria and Scandinavia Dutch corporatism has been highly confessional, based on the principle of 'pillarization', in which the pillars are the religious groups, each with its own schools, hospitals, housing corporations, trade unions, social work agencies, sports clubs and even broadcasting associations. The pillar metaphor extended to the elites who were to meet at the top and so to speak hold the roof up. Though pillarization largely broke down through secularization and individuation in the 1960s, enough of its pluralistic assumptions remained and could be extended to the consideration of the migrants to Holland as pretty much just another cultural bloc (de Jong 1989: 267–72). In addition, the deeply held religious morality serving as substrate to the Dutch welfare state fostered an understanding of migration as a welfare, rather than a policing problem. Whereas in say Britain, individualistic assumptions have prevented the law in race relations from being applied to collectivities, in Holland residual corporatism allowed enabling and targeting welfare legislation to help minorities (Cross and Etzinger 1988).

PART 3

ECONOMIES OF SPACE AND TIME

8

POST-INDUSTRIAL SPACES

In previous chapters we have examined some of the ways that production has been transformed over the past couple of decades. In particular we have examined two features, the exceptional degree of design-intensity of contemporary production, and the way in which there has been the proliferation of 'post-industrial' commodities, commodities which are heavily semiotic. Either they are commodities which are literally signs (such as those produced by the cultural industries or advertising), or they are semiotically embedded (such as food or travel). In both cases design is crucial and long-term.

In this chapter we are going to examine what the implications are of the development of a post-industrial society, of the growth of an economy based upon the delivery of various kinds of services to individual consumers and to organizations, services which are increasingly design-intensive and/or semiotic. Contrary to popular conception there are countless new service products, products which often pass through a conventional product cycle (see Shelp 1982; as well as chapter 10 on product innovations within the travel industry). And these design-intensive products are purchased both by final consumers and by producers. In the latter case, these specialist producer service firms add further to the design-intensity of both manufactured and service commodities.

We shall go on to examine the social and spatial consequences of such developments: namely, is there an emerging post-industrial social structure; and, if there is, does this significantly vary within different places? Are there some particularly distinctive post-industrial spaces emerging, just as once there were some very evident 'industrial spaces'? What are likely to be some of the social and political features of such post-industrial spaces?

We shall suggest that there are indeed some localities, regions and countries which are dominated by service industry and employment. In most places, not including Germany, manufacturing employment has not merely shrunk to a small percentage of the total, but it is certain kinds of service industry which constitute the economic base upon which manufacturing employment appears to be based. Mainly our interest will be 'local/regional spaces', so we will not be concerned with the more macroeconomic arguments about why 'manufacturing matters' (see Cohen and Zysman 1987; Williams et al 1989). There is no doubt that for some countries, such as the USA and UK, international trade is crucial and that services are overall less tradeable than are manufactured goods. However, there is considerable evidence that conventional measures under-estimate the value of such trade in services and that the sums represent at least 20 per cent of world trade (Noyelle and Dutka 1988: ch 2). However, at present intra-EC trade largely consists of manufactured goods. Also interestingly, in the British case, service firms have been no more successful in trading in recent years than have manufacturing companies.

Nevertheless by the year 2000 the single largest item in world trade will be international tourism. And it is certainly the case that a country can gain international competitive advantage from trade in services. Examples include Spanish tourism, Swiss banking, producer services in the USA, transportation in Singapore, financial services in Hong Kong, and so on (see Riddle 1986; Giarini 1987; Noyelle and Dutka 1988). And in terms of output, manufacturing industry in the EC only accounts for between 15 per cent of GDP (in Greece) and 30 per cent (in Germany), with most European countries coming out at around 20 per cent (see Commission of the European Communities 1990: 19; Clairmonte and Cavanagh, 1984: 219).

It might be argued though that such services are generated by the relevant manufacturing base. For example, international tourism mainly involves people from the leading *industrial* countries travelling either to other industrialized countries or to less-industrialized countries. But there are two points to note. First, there are some countries whose whole development strategy is premised on services such as tourism (for example the Mediterranean rim, this being *the* most successful tourist area in the world) and which have a weak industrial base of their own. And second, where tourism has developed in the industrialized countries this has not generally been found in areas of industry apart from a few 'world cities'. Instead specialized service centres have developed, Blackpool and Atlantic City, Alton Towers and Orlando, and it is only as industry has departed from manufacturing towns that the tourists have come flooding in, as in Wigan in Lancashire or Lowell in Massachusetts. Obviously many other towns and cities have developed as specialized centres for the provision of other service industries.

This relative *independence* of manufacturing and services can be shown by briefly considering Britain during its supposed heyday of manufacturing in the nineteenth century, when it was the 'workshop of the world'. In the first half of the century the urban centres which showed the fastest rates of population growth were not the newly emerging manufacturing towns of Lancashire and Yorkshire but rather seaside resorts, which developed as specialized centres of consumption services (see Urry 1990c: ch 2). Moreover, in the second half of the century, although the manufacturing labour force increased between 1851 and 1901, so too did both the absolute and relative size of the workforce in services (from 35.4 per cent to 45 per cent of the total, 1851–1901; see Urry 1987). Lee states that the 'service industries thus comprised a large and increasing sector of the British economy during the Victorian period' (1984: 139, although this has been disputed). Furthermore, this growth in service employment was not directly dependent upon manufacturing industry. Different regions specialized upon services *or* upon manufacturing production. Those regions with the highest ratios of service production were those which had the highest levels of income and wealth, but were without a vigorous manufacturing base. Lee concludes that:

> the economies of southern England were to generate and sustain economic growth and high incomes without depending on transfers or spill-over effects from industries like cotton, woollens, heavy engineering, shipbuilding and coal. Significantly this growth extends in time well before such industries became large-scale producers in the nineteenth century. (1984: 151)

Four main arguments have been employed in social science to suggest that service industry and occupations are unimportant, that there are not and could not be important post-industrial spaces. First, services are said to have been insignificant in the historical development of most major societies. However, the example of the UK in the nineteenth century, or the recent development pattern of Greece, Yugoslavia, Spain, Switzerland or Italy, suggests this is simply incorrect historically. Second, the pattern of services is said to be simple to explain since it derives from the logic of manufacturing industry. This is partly countered by the examples just given. But it is also doubtful because of the likely spatial non-coincidence of the two, both within a country and between countries via internationalization. Different areas come to specialize either on manufacturing or on certain services and there is no particular reason why these will coincide within *national* boundaries. Particularly with the Europeanization of many economies, different regions are likely to become even more specialized within Europe as a whole, and the balance of economic activity *within* given national boundaries will become much less significant. Third, it is maintained that the investigation of services can be pursued simply by taking over modes of analysis developed to investigate manufacturing industry. This will be considered and criticized in the next two sections. And finally, service activities do not appear to produce important economic, social or political outcomes and therefore do not require much analysis. This viewpoint will be criticized in the section on services and the restructuring of place.

For the present though we will return to Esping-Andersen's argument that there are in fact three rather different post-industrial trajectories identifiable at the level of national economies. We will summarize this analysis here as a way of drawing to a conclusion the discussion in the previous two chapters.

Esping-Andersen particularly concentrates on the distribution of 'post-industrial' services, that is producer services, social services and personal services (1990: 196). Many other forms of service employment, retailing, administration and transportation, he conceptualizes (possibly incorrectly) as traditional or timeless. Table 8.1 sets out the main empirical trends over a 25-year period for West Germany, Sweden and the USA, the three countries which exemplify the three post-industrial trajectories.

Table 8.1   *Employment growth in 'post-industrial' industries (annual average % growth)*

	West Germany 1961–84	Sweden 1964–84	USA 1960–84
Producer services	4.2	5.0	7.9
Health/education/welfare	4.8	8.6	6.2
'Fun' services	1.1	1.6	7.2

Source: Esping-Andersen 1990: 199

The table shows that all three countries experienced considerable post-industrial employment growth between the 1960s and 1980s. This was most marked in the case of the USA, and least marked in the case of West Germany, which as we discussed in previous chapters remains much more stubbornly 'industrial'. The pattern in the USA is not one in which only 'junk' jobs (the McDonaldization of the labour market) have developed, but there is also strong growth in producer and social services. The US pattern suggests a dualist pattern of employment change, of the growth of professional-managerial jobs on the one hand, and of a large McDonaldized workforce on the other. The former in part produces the latter, although it is important to note that many people do not stay in such junk jobs all their life. Significantly women have apparently benefited from these changes, being now less under-represented in professional-managerial jobs than they were in the 1960s.

West Germany by contrast represents 'stagnation and sluggish service-evolution' – its employment remained resolutely industrial (Esping-Andersen 1990: 200). The failure to develop higher level service jobs has at the same time meant that there has been little growth in 'junk' jobs since much of that work has been kept within the household and carried out by women. There is not much evidence of a dualistic employment structure. And the job distribution remains significantly gender-segregated. The future scenario even before reunification was of the growth of an underemployed surplus population – an economically inactive population of 60 per cent – and of significant social conflict between insiders and outsiders (Esping-Andersen 1990: 227).

Sweden's development is overwhelmingly biassed towards highly professionalized social-welfare employment. The public sector has accounted for a stunning 80 per cent of new jobs, 75 per cent of which went to women (Esping-Andersen 1990: 215). The outcome is a highly professionalized economy with very few junk jobs, partly, Esping-Andersen says, because Swedes go abroad to be tourists. Women have taken a large proportion of these professional jobs, capitalizing upon a paradoxically high degree of occupational segregation by gender.

In much of the rest of this chapter we will examine some ways in which these national patterns can be seen in various localities within the same society. It will be shown that the particular economic and social structure of a locality is the product of much more diverse and complex processes than Esping-Andersen suggests. However, we will find that his three worlds of welfare capitalism provide a useful basis of classification of different post-industrial spaces.

RESTRUCTURING SERVICES

We will begin here with one of the most systematic efforts made to understand the relationship between industrial development and local/regional employment patterns, Storper and Walker's *The Capitalist Imperative* (1989). However, in their otherwise illuminating efforts to understand the interconnections of territory, technology and growth, there is no appreciation of the importance of services. Storper and Walker analyse 'territorial production complexes' and argue that these complexes may take a variety of spatial forms. And yet all the examples that they provide are when a specific urbanization pattern follows from a particular *manufacturing* industry. In each case discussed there are massive agglomeration economies and this supports their claim that there should be a 'requiem for the geography of the corporation' (1989: 141–3). The authors provide no examples of services-based urbanization. However, examples that could have been discussed include financial and business services in New York or London; culture industries in Los Angeles; consumer services in Las Vegas or Blackpool; educational services in Greater Boston or Cambridge, UK; government services in Washington, DC or around Paris; or transport services in Newark or Gatwick.

For Storper and Walker services function 'to serve capitalist industrialization by raising labour productivity, multiplying the number of products, circulating commodities faster and more effectively, circulating money and providing credit, and administering an increasingly complex system' (1989: 195). But this is a classically functionalist argument, which provides no explanation either of the particular pattern of service-delivery developing within these different spheres, or more significantly of the specific spatial distribution *worldwide* of such services.

The difficulty here is that Storper and Walker view services as office-based systems of information-handling. There are two problems with thinking of services in this manner. First, there is no examination of the *range* of so-called services, of transport and communication, of retailing and tourism, of education and science, of government and administration, as well as the various business and financial services. In the UK there are 5m employed in manufacturing and nearly 16m in services. Among the latter total there are almost 4.5m in 'distribution, hotels, catering and repairs', almost as many as in the whole of manufacturing. There are nearly 3m employed in banking, finance and insurance, while there are more employed in government, education, medical and welfare than in the whole of manufacturing industry (all figures from *Employment Gazette* March 1991: table 1.2).

Second, they suggest that much office activity has had the effect of intensifying the development of *existing* cities. But this fails to note the exceptional relocations of employment and population in recent years. Thus they do not consider whether the location of services has its own logic, separate from the agglomeration economies of industrialization (see for details of this Illeris 1989a, b). Indeed some such services are exerting their revenge and playing an important role in the location and relocation of manufacturing industry itself, as we shall examine later.

If then there are major deficiencies of the kind of manufacturing-led model of Storper and Walker, how should we proceed? Is it possible to take over the *form of explanation* found useful in manufacturing industry to explain the location of service industry? In the classic restructuring theses of Massey (1984) and Massey and Meegan (1982), it is the differential availability, price and organization of 'labour' which are central to explaining the character of the restructuring found within a given industrial sector. Can this thesis be applied to the location of service employment within a given economy (for more detail see Bagguley et al 1990: ch 3)?

First, it does seem difficult to argue that the relative *organizational* strength of labour in different plants and places is a likely determinant of the emerging spatial structure of service employment. Industrial disputes, and hence the threat of such disputes, reflecting the strength of labour are fairly rare in most service industries, at least in the private sector. In Britain in the 1980s there were only two service industries where industrial disputes were common: transport and public administration. Elsewhere in services industrial disputes were uncommon and this is true even where fairly large employers are to be found (as in the case of hotels, see Johnson and Mignot 1982; *Employment Gazette* July 1990: tables 4.1 and 4.2).

An interesting example of the industrial relations practices of a service industry is Marshall's analysis of the workplace culture of a large licensed restaurant (1986; and see the classic Whyte 1948). Marshall had expected that the combination of 'paternalism' and the opportunities for fiddles and pilferage would be sufficient to explain why most staff did not appear to resent either the long and demanding hours of work or the considerable wealth of the owner (on fiddles in waiting see Mars, 1984). However, Marshall argued that in fact such resentment failed to develop because most staff did not experience their work *as* work. Much of what they did consisted of activities that elsewhere would be classified as leisure. There was an erosion of the symbolic boundaries between what was work and what was play, what was work time and what was non-work time. This was reinforced by the fact that work rhythms were more like those outside paid work. Even poorly paid staff were 'free' to organize their activities according to their own designs. Indeed much of the 'work' of the staff consisted of socializing with customers who were often friends from outside. The staff did not even use phrases such as 'going to work'. For most of them it was a 'way of life' resulting from the physical proximity of employee and consumer, of work and leisure.

To the extent to which other service establishments take on similar characteristics then this is likely to prevent the emergence of widespread labour organization, even where the companies themselves are large, as in the case of multinational hotel groups. Nor, since most service plants are fairly small, will the availability of large pools of labour be a likely factor that could generate widespread labour organization.

There are however some other important respects in which the analysis of 'labour' is indeed central to explaining the character of the social relations found within different service industries. First, in many service enterprises labour costs represent a very high proportion of total costs, often between two-thirds and three-quarters, and so employers will certainly seek to monitor and where possible minimize such costs. Current examples would be in British universities where staff costs are around 75 per cent of the total. However, most service establishments will not be able to lower costs in the manner achieved by McDonalds – to an extraordinary 15 per cent of the value of sales (Percy and Lamb 1987; and more generally see Ritzer 1992). Some of the techniques used to lower costs include the relocation of 'back offices' or sometimes the whole office (as in parts of the British insurance industry), or the early retirement programmes in British banks or universities.

Second, since much service work is design-intensive, adequate supplies of highly qualified labour will be crucial to geographical location. For example, the availability of particular kinds of skilled labour has been central to the development of the M4 corridor and to other parts of the Southeast of England. In such cases, the provision of adequate supplies of appropriate houses (right price, size, style and location especially in rural areas) is important in ensuring an adequate pool of qualified labour (see Bassett et al 1989 on how much of the Swindon service class lives outside the town). In the USA Noyelle notes how most of the large insurance companies have reorganized their systems divisions so that they are located in university towns or technology centres where there are adequate supplies of college graduates. He sees this as illustrating a general trend, that 'spatial reorganization is driven by the need for skilled labour' (1986:

20). There has been a shift from 'vertical mobility' within a firm (often over a lifetime), to 'lateral mobility' within a profession/occupation and hence the need for *places* to provide the appropriate range of attractions and services.

Third, labour is to varying degrees implicated in the service-delivery. This occurs as the intended outcome of a necessarily social process in which some interaction occurs between one or more producers and one or more consumers, and in which the quality of the interaction is itself part of the service being offered. This is particularly important in the case of high-contact systems, where there is considerable involvement of the consumer in the production of the service (see Pine 1987). The producers whom the consumers come most into contact with may or may not be those primarily responsible for the production of the service in question (lecturer on the one hand, waiter/waitress on the other). Nevertheless because the production of most services is social there has to be some spatial proximity between one or more of the producers (but not necessarily all) and of the consumers. This is one important constraint upon location. Important exceptions to this occur where where the service can be 'materialized', such as a distance learning package rather than a directly given lecture, or the securitization of loans which can then be traded on secondary markets (see chapter 11 below; and Sassen 1991: 92, 111). Indeed many of the culture industries we discussed in chapter 5 are services which take a tradeable, storable and exportable form, but which are protected by copyright and not patent law (see Lury 1993).

Fourth, the social composition of the producers, or at least those who are in the first line, is often part of what is 'sold' to customers. In other words, the 'service' consists in part of a process of production which is infused with particular social characteristics, of gender, age, race, educational background and so on. When the individual buys a given service, what is purchased is a certain social composition of the service-producers (see Hochschild 1983 on how this applies in the case of flight attendants; but see Wouters 1989). This is particularly the case where the service is wholly or in part semiotic. In addition, it should be noted that what is also sometimes bought is a particular social composition of the other service consumers. Examples of this are to be found in tourism/travel services where differences of social tone between places develop on the basis of the social characteristics of the other visitors with whom people travel (see Urry 1990c).

Finally, since labour is in many cases part of the service product, this poses particular difficulties for management. These difficulties are more significant, the longer, the more intimate and the greater the importance of 'quality' for the consumer of the particular service. It means that employees' speech, appearance and personality may all be treated as legitimate areas of employer intervention and control, where part of the product is the person. Indeed many services require 'emotional labour', particularly to smile in a pleasant, friendly and involved way to the consumers (Hochschild 1983). In the case of flight attendants Hochschild however notes that this emotional work has been made much more difficult with the intensification of work on the airlines since the mid-1970s: 'The workers respond to the speed-up with a slow-down: they smile less broadly, with a quick release and no sparkle in the eyes, thus dimming the company's message to the people. It is a war of smiles' (1983: 127).

Such a decline in quality is exceptionally hard for management to monitor and control, even if they are well aware that the attendants are no longer providing the service that the consumers expect and which supports the 'image' of the enterprise desired by senior management. It should also be noted that the nature of this emotional labour has probably changed in recent years as air travel has become more common, more democratized. Wouters suggests that the emotional labour has become more flexible and less standardized: 'Behaviour in contacts between flight attendants and passengers correspondingly had to become less uniform or standardized and more varied and flexible . . . in each contact there is a need to attune one's behaviour to the style of emotion management of the individual passenger' (1989: 113). Such modification of behaviour necessitates employees being reflexive cultural analysts, who in a more or less self-conscious way are able to interpret and modify their interactions with customers.

The paradox of this is of course that the actual delivery of many services is in fact provided by relatively poorly paid employees, who may have little involvement or engagement with the overall enterprise, and who may be subject to 'functional flexibility'. They are often female except in older forms of transport or in societies where occupations such as 'waiting' have high status. Overlaying the interaction, the 'service', are particular assumptions and notions of gender-specific forms of behaviour, often in part involving a dominant 'male gaze' of both the customers and other staff. And yet for many consumers what is actually consumed as a service *is* the particular moment of delivery or interaction by the relatively low level and often temporary or part-time service-deliverers: the smile on the flight attendant's face, the pleasantness of the manner of the waiter, the sympathy in the eyes of the nurse, and so on. The problem for management is how to ensure that these moments do work out appropriately, while minimizing the cost and an undesirably intrusive (and hence resented) system of management/supervision, as well as minimizing friction with other more highly paid workers backstage (see Whyte 1948).

Jan Carlzon, the President of the Scandinavian airline SAS, terms these 'moments of truth' (1987). There are for SAS something like 50m moments of truth each year, each of which lasts perhaps 15 seconds, when a customer comes into contact with an employee. It is, he says, these moments of truth that determine whether or not SAS will succeed or fail.

The importance of such moments means that organizations may have to be reorganized, towards service to the customer as the primary objective. As a consequence, the actual service-deliverers, the company's 'foot soldiers' who know most about the 'front line' operations, have to be given much more responsibility to respond more effectively, quickly and courteously to the particular needs of the customer.

Recent research on a 'fun' 'southern style' restaurant in Cambridge suggests some further elaboration of this argument (see Crang 1993). What is shown is that the work of waiting in such a restaurant does not simply involve low skill and all-embracing managerial control. Intervening between the two are the geographies of skilled display to customers. Such service encounters are shown to have a performative character and thus one can think of this kind of workplace as a stage, as a dramatic setting for certain kinds of performance, involving a mix of mental, manual *and* emotional labour.

Crang considers what the implications of this kind of work are for the self. First, the staff themselves 'buy into' the restaurant and its location in the local cultural hierarchy. It is a fashionable place to work because of its image. Second, staff are chosen in terms of their possession of the right sort of cultural capital – they have to be informal, young, friendly, with the appropriate skills of emotional control, and with the right sort of body and skills in presenting it in their performances. Third, staff have to make cultural judgments when interacting with customers. They have to socially locate their customers in terms of a range of cultural categories and then to adjust their performances accordingly, even in those cases where the whole imaginary geography of such a 'southern style' restaurant is rejected. Fourth, the self is crucial to the restaurant because in many ways the staff have become the product. And the product involved being oneself, assuming that one's self is fun-loving, informal and sociable. Such selves are the product. And the place is one of emotions. Staff talk of the need to 'get in the mood' at the beginning of the evening, to allow the emotions to flow. Finally, such 'work' is very different for waiters as opposed to waitresses. In waiting work women predominate, as opposed to kitchen and bar work where men are statistically much more common. And since the work of waiting in this restaurant is intrinsically emotional, emotional work is central. Thus there is a sense in which the job of waiting is different for men and women, and this is because different selves are involved, engaged in contrasting social encounters.

Broadly speaking, there are then two kinds of design-intensive service organizations. First, there are many services similar to fast food operations. The design is embodied into the management of each outlet. As an executive in the industry said of fast food: it is 'not a chef system, but a food management system' (quoted in Gabriel 1988: 92). Such developments have dissolved the tyranny of fixed meal-times and the rigid timetabling of each day. In order to provide fresh hot cheap food at any moment, complex systems have been designed to manage the service-delivery. Such outlets typically employ young very cheap staff, so much so in Britain that working in fast food is now the commonest first job (Gabriel 1988; Urry 1990c: ch 4). The design even extends to the programming of the conversation between customers and the staff, whose script may be printed on the back of the menu.

And second, there are those service organizations, such as SAS, in which design has been pushed downwards to the 'foot-soldiers'. It is argued by Hirschhorn for example that this becomes ever more necessary as markets become 'post-industrial', that is segmented or targeted, strategy making is decentralized, information is local or subjective, and there is direct feedback via communication rather than indirectly simply through services that may or may not be purchased (1985). Many service organizations, especially in the USA, extensively use self-administered questionnaires/ surveys (including of course 'deliverers of higher education services'). As markets become more complex so organizations can no longer plan for the 'average' case, but must allow their staff to respond much more variably, flexibly and responsibly than under a mass consumption pattern (see Reynolds 1989 on some of the resulting changes occurring in British Airways, as well as Crang 1993 above).

There has been a recent discussion of the implications of this for the internal organization of firms, especially how this affects the governance of tourist-related services (see chapter 4 above on the concept of 'governance'). It is important to note that such services generate very considerable problems of information exchange and quality control spread over very considerable distances and across national boundaries. With regard to the international hotel industry, Dunning and McQueen make a very useful distinction between the two types of knowledge involved (1981). On the one hand, there is the expertise necessary to manage a hotel from day-to-day, and on the other, there is the expertise involved in the development of property. The first kind of knowledge would lead to the internalizing of ownership so as to take full advantage of a universally known brand-name (such as Hilton or Forte), an international reservation system and the ensuring of stable and uniform service standards necessary for the hotel business market. The latter form of knowledge though leads to the local ownership of firms since they will have much better information about local property markets and are less likely to generate a hostile response from indigenous governments. Tremblay suggests that the outcome of this conflict of alternative modes of governance is to result in the recent tendency for the firms based in the tourist originating countries 'to control the exchange of specialist organisational, operational and marketing know-how . . . without taking the ownership of hotels, which is a high-risk venture better left to owners of local knowledge' (1990: 11). This compromise can be seen in the growth of hotel franchising (such as Holiday Inns) and hotel consortia (such as Best Western).

It has also been suggested that because of the information-intensive nature of especially international tourism, there are two kinds of product typically involved, the actual service *and* the information, and that the governance structure will be different with regard to these different 'products' (see Tremblay 1990). In chapter 10 we will see how Thomas

Cook came to dominate the governance of the latter and rarely got involved in extensive ownership of the enterprises actually providing tourist-related services.

* * *

It should be noted that since most people in Western societies are now service producers, many will have intermittently at least to provide some kind of 'emotional work'. Moreover, the huge increase in the range and quantity of services and the fact that everyone is now the service-receiver of a diversity of services mean that the quality of services has become of greater importance to people and is on occasions intensely contested. This is for two reasons. First, it is because services meet an increasingly wide range of people's needs and wants, although we have noted that this varies and is for example more marked in the USA than in Germany. Second, their consumption often involves the spending of large amounts of time while consuming goods may take almost no time at all. The consumption of services has to occur serially and not simultaneously. So for the middle class professional, the restaurant meal is followed by the late night film which is followed by the taxi ride.

In addition, the mass consumption of services has seen some consumers constituted as socio-political groupings with considerable influence – a reflection of how politics is being in part restructured towards so-called consumption issues as a result of the widespread growth of service production. Even radical student politics can now be seen as mainly concerned with issues of service-delivery.

It is also worth noting that the production of many services is even more design-intensive than we have so far suggested. This is because their delivery is context-dependent, they depend for their successful production on aspects of the social and physical setting within which they occur. Examples include the style of furnishings in a travel agency reflecting an appropriate corporate image, the apparently safe interior of an aeroplane, the antique furniture in a country house hotel, and so on. In many cases, especially with post-industrial services, their delivery cannot be received in an incongruous physical and social context. Part of the service, part of what is consumed, is the physical and semiotic context. And this is not something that is left to chance, but has to be heavily designed.

We will now consider the main ways in which service employment is socially and spatially reorganized or restructured. There are four consider-ations relevant to determining the restructuring pattern found in a particular industry or sector: the possibilities that technical change can occur, the degree to which production can be significantly reorganized, the possibilities of spatial relocation, and the possibilities of product trans-formation. These considerations yield a number of different forms of service sector restructuring which are summarized in table 8.2 (see Blackburn et al 1985 for a much more restricted classification; Gershuny and Miles 1983; Daniels 1985).

Table 8.2   *Forms of service sector restructuring*

Technical change?
1 *Investment and technical change*: heavy capital investment within new means of
   production and considerable job losses often unequally distributed (out-of-town
   hypermarkets)

Production reorganization?
2 *Intensification*: increases in labour productivity through managerial or organizational
   change with little or no new investment or loss of capacity (effects of deregulation on
   American airlines)
3 *Rationalization*: closure of capacity with little or no new investment or new technology
   (closure of cinemas)
4 *Commodification* of a service product through market encirclement, budget centre
   fragmentation or privatization (such as the NHS in Britain)
5 *Replacement* of existing labour input with cheaper female/young/non-white labour (fast
   food industry)
6 *Flexibilization* of labour input (the part-time nature of women's domestic work in
   hospitals)

Spatial relocation?
7 *Decentralization* to areas of cheaper labour/land ('back offices' removed from city
   centre sites)
8 *Concentration*: spatial centralization of services in larger units and the closure/
   rundown of the number or scale of smaller units (closure of small 'cottage' hospitals in
   Britain)

Product transformation?
9 *Partial self-provisioning* of the function (self-service in retail distribution and
   restaurants)
10 *Domestication*: the relocation of some service work once done in large institutions to
   women's labour within households ('community care' programmes in the NHS in
   Britain)
11 *Subcontracting* or externalizing elements of the service functions to firms providing
   specialized services (growth of private specialist producer service firms)
12 *Enhancement* of quality through improved labour input, that is more skilled and/or
   better trained (development of school teaching in Britain as a graduate occupation)
13 *Materialization* or part-materialization of the labour function in the form of a material
   object which can be bought, sold, transported, stored and so on (take-out food)

Source: adapted from Bagguley et al 1990: 63–7

The table shows there are many different forms of restructuring that
characterize different service sectors; that what happens in any particular
sector will be the result of a number of overlapping forms of restructuring;
and that the combination of such forms within particular places will have
immense consequences for both the employment and the more general
social structure of given places. This means that it is extremely difficult to
predict the likely employment and social consequences which will occur
within particular localities. For example, it is unclear what will be the
effects of new technology. First, Wood notes that 'new technology is
perhaps having a greater effect than in manufacturing. In many services,
for example, keying in by customers, sales representatives and others may
well totally do away with vast numbers of intermediate workers' (1989b: 17).

And yet, second, he says that 'it is also in the service sector where we have seen the most dramatic growth of new types of monotonous and routinized labour, as well as labour intensification' (1989b: 17).

We will now consider one area of service employment in detail, namely that of so-called producer services. These are extremely important in the Anglo-American countries. By the most generous definition, 38 per cent of all employment in New York City and 33 per cent in London is in producer services (in 1987). The largest category within producer services is finance, insurance and real estate (FIRE). FIRE alone accounted for 17.3 per cent of New York employment and 18.2 per cent of London employment in 1985. More specifically the labour force in New York in legal services, business services and banking increased by 62, 42 and 23 per cent respectively between 1977 and 1985 (Sassen 1991: 199, 202; and see Noyelle and Dutka 1988).

Producer services have been disproportionately located in the global cities. In 1985 New York had roughly twice the national average of employees in FIRE, other business services and education. But recent growth has been more extensive elsewhere. Thus from 1977 to 1985, while employment increased in New York in FIRE by 21 per cent the total US increase was 31 per cent. Likewise in business and legal services New York's gains of 42 and 62 per cent respectively were outpaced by huge total US gains of 85 and 75 per cent (Sassen 1991: 130–1). Similar patterns were to be found in Britain, although this was within the context of lower employment growth overall. At the same time there has been extensive growth abroad of producer service firms. This has been particularly marked in the case of accountants, advertising, management consultants, banks and (to a lesser extent) legal services (see Noyelle and Dutka 1988: ch 3). Producer service firms have diversified and internationalized.

There are two important factors which explain the growth in producer services. The first is that of vertical disintegration, that is the degree to which there is outsourcing of producer services away from in-house production. The second is that of the absolute increase in demand for producer service inputs.

Both can be explained by the fact that the production of a more diversified range of specialized goods and services entails a much greater complexity in the structure of the firm. It entails more specialized inputs, whether these be goods or services. And in particular it entails a much greater range and number of service inputs at quite high levels of information- or design-intensity. This necessitates greater numbers employed in personnel, finance, accounting, engineering, research and development, legal, marketing and other functions, whether they are employed inside or outside the firm. And as an increasing number of the services demanded from these specialists assume the nature of one-offs, that is very low 'frequency' in Williamson's terms, it makes increasing sense to outsource them (Kanter 1984; Sassen 1991: 95–9).

Second, though, many of these companies have increasing demands not only from producers but also from 'consumers', for advice on personal finance, property, travel, architecture, accountancy, computing, insurance, the law and so on. These are all sectors which are conventionally classified as producer services, but where there is a rapidly increasing demand from the affluent middle classes (as discussed in chapter 6). This is why it is more useful to talk of these as advanced services. They involve not just information, but are symbol-intensive and specialized. The advanced services are very much involved in what we have called 'reflexive accumulation' in that they comprise reflexive producers producing services for reflexive consumers.

So far we have mainly considered 'private' services in any detail. And yet we know that many services are wholly or partly publicly owned. In the next section restructuring in publicly provided services will be considered.

RESTRUCTURING AND THE PUBLIC SECTOR

There are a number of reasons for thinking that publicly provided services have some rather distinctive features (see Pinch 1989; Ackroyd et al 1989; Esping-Andersen 1990). First, most of them are not provided under conditions of profit maximization, although of course there have been many recent attempts to develop internal markets (most strikingly at present in the British NHS). However, it should not be presumed that private sector firms are necessarily 'restructured' in the economically most 'rational' fashion; much evidence suggests that in many cases this has not happened (see Pinch 1989: 918).

Second there is an obligation on much of the public sector to provide roughly equal, or at least minimum, levels of provision, supplied to consumers roughly in the areas in which they live (acute health care, education for school-age students). In this sense public services are Fordist services. Also for a particular service to be provided publicly (whether or not there is a charge) requires that there have been social and political pressures to ensure that alternative means of service-delivery (by households, markets, informal neighbourhood networks, charity) have been deemed inappropriate or unfair or grossly inefficient (see Mark Lawson et al 1985; Pinch 1989: 907). The nature of the service, including the politics of its provision, is such that potential users have come not to trust non-state agencies to provide a fair and efficient service.

In addition, it is more difficult for certain private sector strategies to be pursued in the public sector. In particular, spatial relocation, when the service has to be delivered to the residents of a particular locality or indeed a given nation-state, is not widely available. Also there are many professional groupings involved in the delivery of public services, and they are likely to be able to sustain a greater uniformity of service than would be the case if it were delivered in the private sector. It is often part of the professional ethic that the organization of the service should be uniform across different areas or authorities. The service-provider is the final arbiter of the needs of the recipient of the service – hence this has been characterized as a 'custodial' form of management (see Ackroyd et al 1989: 613). Finally, many such services are 'experience' goods which cannot be tried out first in advance. The users of the service, such as schoolchildren or the recipients of acute health care, have to take the service 'on trust'.

How should this set of services be understood? Is there a distinct set of restructuring strategies that is employed within the state? We will examine the nature of these state activities (that is, those which are not directly marketed) in terms of the four considerations outlined in table 8.2 (see Bagguley et al 1990: ch 3 for more detail on these; Curtis 1989; and Pinch 1989, who applies more or less the same classification of restructuring strategies).

First, there are possibilities of technical change. Cost savings here are however limited. In health care, for example, technical change generally involves increased cost, either because the new technique means that the patient is kept alive for longer, or because the new technique involves increased nursing requirements, or both. The work in these sectors is highly labour-intensive since there have to be moments of social interaction between producers and 'consumers' (see Blackburn et al 1985: 184–91).

Second, the possibilities for reorganization of the production process are again rather limited. Partly this is because the lack of a market for pricing services means that calculations cannot be easily made as to the likely productivity consequences of schemes of reorganization, although the differences between this and large multinational private corporations should not be over-emphasized. Reorganization may be unlikely because such services are normally organized by relatively highly paid groups of professionals, who are responsible both for the definition of need and for assessing the level of appropriate demand (see Cousins 1986: 93; 1987). Some professionals, such as doctors, may be able to prevent substantial changes (particularly involving 'intensification') from being fully imple- mented, although at lower levels the intensification of work has been extensively applied (see Pinch 1989). Attempts may then be made to mimic a market through the introduction from 'above' of various performance indicators (see Cousins 1986); or alternatively by inserting an extra level of non-professional managers (such as 'general managers' in the British NHS).

Third, the possibilities of spatial relocation are again rather limited, this being possible in certain rather particular cases. There are two very considerable constraints on spatial relocation. First, it would be impossible to shift much of the delivery of state-provided consumer services outside a country's national territory. Hence one of the favoured restructuring strategies pursued in parts of the private sector is not viable for the state. And second, since much of the state's activities consists of the provision of services to the population at large, these have to be organized on a widely dispersed basis – although there will be considerable contestation over the degree of dispersal that is really necessary for appropriate service-delivery (such as whether it has to be 'local' or merely 'regional').

Finally, the possibilities of product transformation are likewise limited. Almost by definition the state is concerned with providing services for 'general/mass' consumption, either for almost all of a given population (school children), or for many of the least affluent (as with public housing). The state is rarely involved in producing 'specialized/niche' products, except in some aspects of higher education and in the procurement of specialized weapon systems. The product market is also one which is unlikely to change very much. State service producers cannot simply move out of unprofitable product lines (such as geriatric health care) and develop new products. They have to provide service product(s) on a mass scale and this is normally legally specified. The main possibilities of cost-saving arise from reductions in the quality of the service-product, as the 'unit of resource' has over a long period been cut in British higher education. By contrast the Metropolitan Police in London are currently intending to upgrade their product and to characterize their organization in the future not as a 'force' but as a 'service'.

Given these characteristics of state services, what are the likely forms of restructuring which will be found? Rationalization and spatial relocation will be relatively uncommon; enhancement of quality will only be found where professional groups are powerfully placed (as in the British welfare state in the 1960s and early 1970s); and flexibilization, replacement of labour input, materialization, partial self-provisioning and subcontracting will be found around the margins of the service in question (see Pinch 1989 for partly similar conclusions). The four centrally important strategies of restructuring of state services will be intensification, commodification, concentration and domestication. Intensification will result from the 'managers' in the organization being given clearer and specific objectives and being expected to meet them by managing their unit, and especially professional workers, more intensively; commodification will entail a variety of attempts to mimic markets including the centralized specification of financial targets; concentration may well involve the relevant minister and/or outsiders to that service being much more powerfully placed to 'manage' it; and domestication involves reducing the quality and hence labour input provided by the state while increasing that supplied by unpaid workers, especially women in for example care in the 'community'.

It is also worth noting that there are complex issues of information and trust involved in certain public services. There are some services where neither the producer nor the user can be fully aware of whether a good service is being received (such as social work) and hence whether its quality is or could be improved. In such cases the producers and the users have to trust the other that appropriate forms of service-delivery are taking place.

If it is not, then it is unclear who is to blame and to whom any grievances should be directed.

In other services the producers may know about what kind of service is being provided but the users do not. Such users have to take on trust the service and may therefore be unwilling to pay for such a service. Examples would include various forms of health and dental care, especially of the preventative sort.

Sometimes the opposite pattern is found. Producers do not know what the service is like but the users do, such as the care provided in homes for elderly people. The users are well aware of the deficiencies of the service-delivery, but they may have no idea of who is to blame. Indeed the various agencies responsible for the service may themselves not know who is ultimately responsible for the overall quality of the service provided (such as a late running train, which can be the result of numerous processes in a complex system).

The implication of this brief analysis is that the delivery of public services is problematic because of the problems of inadequate information, inappropriate trust and the difficulties of flexibilizing national services set up on Fordist lines. Restructuring such services to improve services is not something that can be easily achieved, certainly not by the simple adoption of methodologies from the private sector, even from private services. This can be briefly illustrated by reference to the British health service established by the 1945–50 Labour Government as a classically Fordist service.

Now however there are massive changes taking place in the health service of a post-Fordist sort. Yet this will not simply produce a post-Fordist transformation (see Walby et al 1994 for the following). There are three reasons. First, it is not at all clear who the consumers are of health care and hence how management could in fact be brought closer to the market. The distinction now implemented in the NHS between the providers and the purchasers of health care does not mean that health service managers will respond to what individual patients/consumers are wanting, only to what the often very large purchasing bureaucracies demand. Second, in order to run the information and contracting structures needed to make such a quasi-market work, Fordist structures of bureaucratic hierarchies have had to be further developed, especially following the widespread implementation of 'general management' since 1986. And third, changes taking place in the position of hospital doctors indicate that their work is becoming more Fordist, especially with new contracts for consultants following the 1989 White Paper and the development of medical audits.

In the next section we will examine the implications of various kinds of service sector development for different places. It will be necessary to remember that in many places it is these complex forms of public services that are most significant for employment and for the future trajectories of occupational and social change.

SERVICES AND THE RESTRUCTURING OF PLACE

We will now consider the impact that these patterns of service growth and restructuring are having on various towns and cities. At the same time of course the characteristics of different places importantly relate to the patterns of growth and restructuring.

It might initially be thought that the internationalization of service industries, of producer service companies, hotel groups, international airlines, huge banking conglomerates and the like, will simply eliminate differences between places and effectively make them all the same. We shall analyse this in detail in chapter 11 when we consider the intersection of global *and* local processes. For the moment three points should be noted: that the history of internationalization is uneven and does not involve the internationalizing of all services in all countries; that increased internationalization often entails *increased* sensitivity to local features, of labour and property markets and place-myths; and that the way that internationalized industries intersect in particular places will result in locally specific combinations, or what Massey calls 'a global sense of place' (1991: 29; this is shown in the case of seven British cities in Cooke 1989).

It is well known that very many places in Europe and north America have suffered enormous losses of manufacturing employment in recent years. And this has characterized apparently prosperous as well apparently depressed areas (on the USA see Bluestone and Harrison 1982). Thus in the UK this pattern is found not only in the former industrial heartlands but also in areas with new manufacturing industries. Thus in the Southeast of the UK·there are 13 per cent more employees in financial and business services than there are in the whole of manufacturing. It is predicted that the manufacturing figure will soon have fallen below 15 per cent of total employment (Donovan 1990a). Half the manufacturing jobs in the Southeast have disappeared in the last 15 years. Particularly severe job losses have been experienced in London where 100 firms a week were closing down in the late 1980s. A study by Cambridge Econometrics concluded: 'Virtually all new jobs [in the UK] are expected to appear in the service sectors' (quoted in Donovan 1990a). A further report on London argues that it was the very success of London's service growth, especially in and around the City, that generated the astronomic rents which made manufacturing uneconomic in the 1980s. Donovan summarizes:

> Spurred on by the seemingly unlimited opportunities of 'Big Bang' the whole service industry has grown at such a rate that manufacturing industry has been pushed far out into the provinces. (1990b)

We shall consider the growth of global financial cities further in chapter 11. For the moment it should be noted that the consolidation of financial services into international networks dominated by European, Japanese and American financial institutions has had the effect of concentrating employment in a small number of 'global cities' such as London, New York and Tokyo (see King 1990; Budd and Whimster 1992). Daniels summarizes:

> Financial services, two-thirds from overseas, are responsible for a large proportion of the demand for offices but accountants, solicitors, architects, advertising and public relations agencies have also been leasing more space in the City . . . reinforcing the way in which internationalization is inducing more selective agglomeration, uneven development of producer services, and the revitalization of metropolitan economies such as that of New York. (1987: 437)

In western Europe there appears to have been some decentralization of service employment out of the big cities in the 1970s and 1980s, although this was less marked in the case of producer services (Illeris 1989b: 130 f). It should also be noted that in the USA it is the urban centres of consumption-services, including tourist-cities, which have had the fastest rates of population and labour force growth (Stanback 1985).

Not *all* local economies are experiencing the same pattern. In Britain Rochdale is far from becoming post-industrial and service-dominated. Penn summarizes the 1980s experience:

> Rochdale is rather a classic modern industrial city, with well over a third of its working population employed directly in manufacturing industry and many others indirectly in the transporting, wholesaling and retailing of those goods. (1990: 23)

Likewise in the heart of the M4 corridor Swindon experienced increases in *both* service and manufacturing employment (and in population) during the 1980s (Bassett et al 1989). There were many new employers, with new forms of economic activity and work. However, these enterprises are very much integrated with national and international organizations and are dependent on the place that Swindon occupies in complex and extended spatial divisions of labour. Hence, although Swindon is in the M4 corridor, 'the locality bears little resemblance to the revitalised, spatially integrated "new industrial districts" based on subcontracting relations and the need to respond to rapidly changing markets' (Bassett et al 1989: 82; and see Scott 1988b). For example, of larger private sector establishments only 14 per cent used local suppliers as their main sources, compared with 39 per cent using international sources. Similarly it seems that the other putative industrial district in Britain, namely Cambridge, is also not characterized by strong, mutually supporting linkages between the 400 or so high technology firms. Saxenian argues that Cambridge entrepreneurs 'have failed to create commercially viable firms or to construct a regional environment which facilitates the development of successful technology-based enterprise' (1989: 454). Despite the proliferation of new firms, the overwhelming majority will not develop into successful large firms via the relations of trust and reciprocity supposedly found in industrial districts. Of course it may be, as Hirst and Zeitlin argue, that it is this absence of 'industrial districts' in British manufacturing industry which partly explains the enduring weakness of the national economy (1989).

So far then we have seen that service employment in much of Europe and north America is of great importance, accounting for two-thirds or more of total employment, and often 85 per cent or so of female employment. We have also noted that there can be distinct diseconomies of agglomeration as in the case of London, where the very growth of *services* prohibitively raised costs for manufacturing. Finally, even where manufacturing is important there are not necessarily strong local linkages of the sort projected in the industrial districts literature. Indeed in the following we shall suggest that it is the character and strength of the service economy which is often now the dynamic base from which manufacturing developments may derive. This point is well demonstrated by the Cambridge example and the central role played in the growth of its high tech industry by the extensive provision of educational, scientific and consumer services. Moreover, we shall see how the growth of services has also led to some striking changes in the culture, politics and policies of many places (see Harloe et al 1990).

The importance of services can also be seen clearly if we consider one set of recent developments which supposedly demonstrates the importance of manufacturing-led growth, the development in the 1980s of a marked divergence of the 'north–south' divide in Britain. However, it appears that this divide was in fact the consequence of relative *service* sector growth in the South compared with the North (see Lewis and Townshend 1989). Martin notes that between 1979 and 1987 three-quarters of the 1.25m jobs created in the service industries in Britain were located in the four southern regions (Southeast, Southwest, East Anglia, East Midlands; Martin 1989: 34). Moreover, much of this occurred in various free-standing towns and cities, particularly along the M4 corridor between London and Bristol. As a result the much heralded development of high tech manufacturing in this corridor has actually been of less significance in employment terms than has been the growth of services (Allen 1988: 128–9). It is services, both public and private, which are of particular employment importance in the M4 corridor. Moreover, many of these services have been located in the corridor because the area is attractive to the relatively mobile professional and managerial staff who play such a key role within them. And they tend to be attracted to those places which have a good environment and consumer facilities. Allen notes that the service class and its professional and managerial workers, especially in the private sector, have:

> the ability to choose where they live and work, and this has generally favoured areas around or in the Southern towns and cities. Locations which are attractive to key staff precisely because . . . they are relatively unscathed by previous manufacturing employment. (1988: 133)

Thus there are good reasons why new employment will often follow the provision of good services, especially where the service class is to be recruited in considerable numbers.

A number of changes have thus undermined older models of local

economies in which it was thought that manufacturing activities constituted
the base from which other forms of employment derived. The first change
is, as we have seen, the striking decline in the size and hence in the impact
of manufacturing employment in most localities. Although the proportion
of service employment in many German towns is not much over 50 per
cent, elsewhere among the leading economies the proportion is normally
between 55 per cent and 75 per cent (see Illeris 1989b for extensive detail).

Second, the changes in telecommunications and transport mean that
producer services can now be located in very many different places. As
Illeris argues:

> Services which consist of information can increasingly be sold over long
> distances. This means of course that they can be located independently of the
> local number of customers or buying power. They may become part of the
> economic base of a local area and bring money into it. (1989a: 272)

Examples of this would include accountancy firms, law companies, estate
agencies, investment bankers, data processing and computing firms,
property developers, advertisers, media companies, management consultants and so on (see Thrift and Leyshon 1992, especially on accountancy
firms). The attraction of such partially footloose companies is of paramount locational significance.

Third, the attraction of such producer service firms into a locality
significantly depends upon the provision of high quality consumer services
which appeal to skilled labour, especially to young service class workers
(see Savage et al 1992). The availability of appropriate local services has
become a crucial part of the employment strategies of many localities (see
Harloe et al 1990, especially the chapters on Cheltenham and Lancaster).
An interesting example where this is being attempted in a former industrial
city is Wigan, in the Northwest of England. The city's Economic Development Office has published a booklet concerned to publicize their area to
potential inward investors. It is called *I've never been to Wigan but I know
what it's like* (Economic Development, Wigan: undated). The first five
pictures in black and white are of back-to-back terrace housing, mines and
elderly residents walking along narrow alleyways. But we are then asked as
to whether we are sure that is really what Wigan is *now* like. The following
12 photos, all in colour, demonstrate the contemporary Wigan, which is
revealed as possessing countless high quality services, of the Wigan Pier
Heritage Centre, a colourful market and elegant shops, excellent sports
facilities, attractive pubs and restaurants, and delightful canalside walk-
ways. All the attractions presented are essentially consumer services
designed to appeal to incoming members of the service class, as well as to
potential tourists.

Finally, the increased mobility of people means that the ability of a
locality to attract temporary visitors may play a crucial role in its economic
development. Indeed there are considerable interconnections between

tourism, services and economic development strategies. In Britain there is scarcely a free-standing town or city that does not have the encouragement of tourism, that is tourist-related services, as one of the central planks of its economic development strategy. It has been estimated that the cost of creating one new job in tourism is £4,000, compared with £23,000 in manufacturing industry and £300,000 in mechanical industry (Lumley 1988: 22). Furthermore, many commentators are fully convinced that tourist services are important in attracting and satisfying prospective employees and employers. This seems to have happened in Wigan following the establishment of the Wigan Pier Heritage Centre. The Chairman of the North West Tourist Board argues as follows:

> The growth of the tourism industry has a great deal to do with the growth of every other industry or business: the opening up of the regions as fine places to visit means they're better places to live in – and thus better places to work . . . a higher quality of life benefits employees. (Quoted in Reynolds 1988)

Many of these tourist-related developments are mixed schemes located on or near a waterfront. They began in the USA with Baltimore's Harborplace which now attracts 29m visitors a year. Other examples world-wide include Boston's Marketplace and associated Harborwalk, South Street Seaport in New York, and Sydney's Darling Harbour (see Frieden and Sagalyn 1989 on the American experience). In Britain current projects are to be found in the Albert Dock in Liverpool, Hull, Walsall, Bristol, Cardiff, Birmingham Canal, Gloucester Docks and Salford Quays (see Department of the Environment 1990 on the first three of these).

The growth of these schemes which involve the development of extensive new consumer services is part of the place- or city-marketing that has become a marked feature of the recent period. The supply of services has become absolutely central to improving the relative market position of places and hence to their ability to attract footloose companies and in particular their managerial and professional staff. Since most areas do not contain the conditions for flexibly specialized industrially based growth, there are far greater chances of sustaining employment via developing or attracting novel sets of producer and consumer services.

There are a number of different kinds of place-marketing: to maintain or to adapt existing consumers of a place; or to expand and diversify into new categories of consumer (see Ashworth and Voogd 1990). Place-marketing entails the auditing of the resources of a locality and this includes both its physical artefacts and the possible place-images. It is then presumed that when visitors consume the various tangible products (such as visiting an industrial museum, buying a souvenir) they also acquire the core product of a place (such as its unique history, its cosmopolitanism or its mystery). So although there are very specific services sold, what is mostly important is how their consumption supposedly leads to the acquisition of the core product of a locality, the place-image (see Shields 1991a on the latter).

One British city that has been successful at transforming its place-image has been Glasgow and its remarkable emergence as a centre of cultural tourism. It was the 'European City of Culture' in 1990: 'Glasgow's regeneration has been largely arts-led, with the Mayfest and the opening of the Burrell collection all helping to change the city's image from a decaying industrial backwater to a dynamic growth area (quoted in Urry 1990c: 341; and see Urry 1990b). Two-thirds of visitors to Glasgow consider that there is a wide variety of interesting museums and art galleries to visit in the city. At least one-third of visitors think there are so many cultural activities available that they wish that they were able to stay longer. Fewer than one-fifth consider that Glasgow is the rough and depressing place to visit that once would have been the case (Myerscough 1988: 88–9). Mysteriously but dramatically, a services-transformation has produced in Glasgow the kind of place that people now want to be seen in and to see, and for companies like BP to invest in. A brochure produced by the Greater Glasgow Tourist Board for the 1990 celebrations declared that 'Glasgow doesn't feel like a British city . . . Glasgow looks like a European city. And feels like one' (see Bianchini 1991: 37).

In other words, many towns and cities are being reconstructed not primarily as centres of production but consumption. It has been particularly important for former industrial towns and cities 'to repackage and reposition themselves according to the global economy, often by "normalising" their public image' (Bianchini 1991: 37). Increasingly what distinguishes one place from another are the complexes of services which are available and their connections with particular place-images. The development of these is not something that just happens to occur but depends upon a number of economic, social and political determinants (see Bagguley et al 1990; ch 5, and Urry 1990b on the example of Lancaster; more generally, see Ashworth and Voogd 1990).

First, there is the social composition of the local population and of the ways in which different divisions of class, gender, race and generation overlay each other and may result in particularly powerful or distinctive social groups able to impose their habitus on their town or city. The second determinant consists of the patterns of movement into and out of the place and the different projects that groups of residents and visitors seek to realize in any particular place. Third, there are the existing and potential images of a place and the degree to which there are or are not conflicting images in the surrounding area or region. Fourth, there is the legacy of the built environment, especially whether there are available derelict buildings in particular architectural styles which can be appropriately converted into new service-based uses. The fifth determinant consists of the sets of aesthetic interests that different social groups possess – as well as their resources and capacities for effecting conservation of an area's buildings or for transforming them. Sixth, the existence or non-existence of local traditions of entrepreneurship or of patterns of mobility of potential entrepreneurs into the area will affect the nature and transformation of a locality. Likewise, the strategies of major leisure-related companies and whether the place in question meets their criteria for future investment will also influence how a place is or is not remade. The demands from manufacturing industry for various kinds of services for themselves, for their employees and for their visitors will also affect a place. The ninth determinant consists of the degree to which there is a hegemonic project sustained locally, and organized through local government, and which may entail a particular services-led transformation of the local economy in accordance with a transformed place-image. And finally, there are more general shifts in consumption and culture which change the way that different service activities are valued, such as the recent growth in fast food, in dining out in ethnically diverse settings, in the 'heritage industry', in niche shopping, in cultural tourism, and in themed parks and environments. Such cultural shifts affect the possibilities of transforming a place and its image (see Department of the Environment 1990 on the wide variety of impacts of tourist-related projects in British inner cities).

The parameters of social division and conflict are thus being transformed. In many localities there has been a remaking of the character of place, in which services and consumption differences have become primary. This has moreover come about because of the structural shifts in many local economies which have meant that they are assessed, in terms of both the supply of service-sector jobs (especially for women who are most unlikely ever to find employment in manufacturing), and the supply of services available locally, including retailing, business, cultural, educational, sporting, 'visitor attractions' and so on, which may entice manufacturing industries to relocate. The significance of services within many local economies means that there has thus been a transformation in the stakes available locally.

Furthermore, to the extent that cities become significantly 'consumer-service' oriented then this will bring about significant demographic, occupational and cultural transformations in such places. The changes produced will include some or all of the following: faster population growth; expanded numbers of low level and seasonal jobs; the increased use of flexible forms of work organization; an expansion in the numbers of self-employed and of owners of small businesses; relatively high levels of female employment; weak levels of unionization; the transformation of the built environment so that it comes to symbolize pleasure and fun; shifts towards a boosterist and interventionist political strategy; and the development of social movements concerned to protect or to conserve aspects of the physical and/or built environment – a politicization of place. These developments have been well shown by Mullins in the case of the Australian Gold Coast (1991). Many places therefore are taking on some at least of the characteristics of the neo-liberal or American model of post-industrial space as elaborated by Esping-Andersen.

* * *

Finally, we will consider in a little more detail what kinds of politics we can expect to find in these 'post-industrial spaces'. There is certainly no simple relationship between industrial restructuring (towards services) and political processes within localities (see Bagguley et al 1990: ch 6 for the following). Previous authors who have developed and used the 'restructuring thesis' have considered the effects of industrial change on spatial variation in political action, and have attempted to account for the relative strength of labour movements in different places (see Massey 1984: 234–96; Harloe et al 1990).

In order to describe the effects of the growth of services on politics, and to shift debate away from static notions such as 'political tradition' or 'political culture', we will use the concept of a 'local political environment', the sum of the structural preconditions of action of potential collective actors within a local area. Those preconditions amount to a local configuration of constraints: the economic, such as factory regimes, occupational structure and labour market characteristics (including forms of segmentation); the political, such as the embodied material consequences of previous political action (for example, council housing and the built environment), the vitality of local political associations (measured by party strength and activity), local political ritual and political socialization (including distinctive political histories); and the social/cultural, such as the symbolic boundaries between different 'imagined communities'.

While the occupational and labour process effects of recent economic change are relatively well understood, there are few satisfactory accounts of the effects of the expansion of *service* industries on political behaviour. Most accounts of the impact of services have tended to concentrate on the implications of service employment for class relations, and these have frequently been oversimplified.

One mistake is to talk of services as if they were homogeneous. There are significant differences in the socio-economic position of for instance state employees vis-à-vis private sector workers, and the new welfare professionals vis-à-vis the old professional class and the petit bourgeoisie. Within the private sector there are important differences between the experiences of employees of multinational companies and those of smaller ones. The paradox of employment in services can be illustrated by looking at the fastest-growing service industries in recent years: banking and finance, which employs a high proportion of professionals, and leisure and tourism, which employs a high proportion of lower level employees. Technological change in service industries creates a polarization between hybrid professional-managerial staff on the one hand, and lower level employees on the other. This is especially marked in the USA. Such service employees will almost certainly hold different political positions.

Moreover, the political environment does not simply reflect the current occupational structure of a locality. The politics of different kinds of service workers are spatially variable precisely because changes in the occupational structure of local labour markets occur within, and are constrained by, the previous political environment. This previous environment provides the bases, the language and the relations of local political life. Workers in some service industries are strongly influenced by the character of the local environment into which they are inserted: in the heartlands of the Labour movement in Britain, public sector professionals, the petit bourgeois and white collar workers are more favourable to the Labour Party in elections than is the case, for instance, in the Southeast and Southwest. The critical difference can be related back to the historic form of the local political environment as well as new patterns of local class formation.

This can be briefly illustrated by reference to one city in Britain, which has been investigated in some detail (see Bagguley et al 1990: ch 6). In Lancaster the political effects of service sector growth have been most unexpected. In the period between 1923 and 1987 the constituency only once returned a Labour MP. In a study conducted in 1955 the Conservatives took 11 per cent more of the vote than would have been predicted on the basis of the class composition of the city, at the time making it the most deviant pro-Conservative constituency in Britain. Lancaster was 'conservative' in other respects: there were very weak Labour movement institutions, there was virtually no industrial conflict, and there was a strong tradition of the voluntary, charitable provision of welfare. The constituency experienced dramatic and rapid de-industrialization from the 1960s onwards and there was extensive service sector growth, especially in the public sector. This duly transformed class alignments. From having been an anomalously pro-Conservative town, Lancaster became unexpectedly pro-Labour by the 1980s and 1990s, with no Conservative city wards in the 1991 local elections. As the occupational structure shifted from predominantly manual working class to professional middle class, the Labour Party has gained support. It has now much firmer support from professional and routine service workers, especially in the health and education sectors, than it ever obtained from the process workers in the manufacturing sectors of linoleum and artificial fibres industries.

But at the same time the Party has changed. It has become strongly influenced by Green and environmental issues, and has gained particular support because of its opposition to an extensive shopping centre development. A further major political division is over the degree and forms of support to be provided to the local tourism industry. Thus issues of local service provision are transforming local political environments, but these are not to be understood in any simple or reductionist manner (for further examples see the cases reported in Harloe et al 1990). In Lancaster the growth of services, within a weak labourist political environment, meant that there was something of a vacuum for radical politics; and the form this then took was of a heavily social movements-influenced labourism.

CONCLUSION

Towns and cities are thus undergoing some striking transformations as the result of the massive employment in services. One might think of towns and cities as increasingly centres for the switching of information, knowledge, images and symbols (see Mulgan 1989 for a related argument). This can be seen, both in the importance of 'smart' communication infrastructures in towns and cities (it is calculated that 30 per cent of the cost of new office building in Tokyo is accounted for by electronic installations), and in the softer infrastructures, of the knowledge, leisure and cultural activities found within the urban context, of the culture-society we discussed in chapter 5.

   Mulgan argues that education has come to play the role once attributed to the 'manufacturing base' and cites the importance of the degree of 'liveability' of different towns and cities. He notes that many pretend not to be cities at all but present themselves as 'semi-rural' (1989: 270). An enormous range of contemporary political issues is essentially concerned with questions of the 'liveability' of different places and in particular therefore *with* the size and nature of service provision, by both the private and public sector. Much contemporary social and political conflict is thus concerned with the forms of service provision; their financing; the buildings they are 'housed' in; their relationship to images of place; and their consequences for other aspects of the built and physical environment and more generally for local social experiences in multiple post-industrial spaces.

   Further ideas along these lines have recently been developed by Castells. He argues, we have noted, that contemporary capitalism has been recast into an 'informational mode of development', in which information processing has become the pivotal productive activity (1989). Knowledge has always figured centrally, in technical change, but only now 'is the raw material itself information and so is its outcome' (1989: 38). For Castells the key consideration is technological change or 'objectified' human capital. In this the development of the integrated circuit in 1957 speeded up the processing of information, the accuracy of outcome and the ability to deal with complexity. Subsequent benchmark steps were the development of the micro-processor in 1971; the exponential increase in the processing power of computers accompanied by increasing cheapness of storing information in cost per unit of memory; and the connection of units into systems made possible by advances in telecommunications. Hence he emphasizes the importance of fibre-optic networks, 'smart buildings' as well as computer-aided design, and manufacturing in flexible integrated manufacturing.

   Castells' restructured economy is very much an economy of signs, whose central axis is information-processing, the organization of sets of instructions for the handling of information. Even in biotechnology this development is governed by our enhanced ability to store, retrieve and analyse information. On this view, where machines take second place to information, the output itself is information embodied in goods, services and decisions.

Castells' reincorporation of information-processing into the framework of capitalist development has the virtue of shifting attention away from flexibility and towards the reflexivity involved in the process. Castells' information is in most cases embodied or objectified reflexivity. Such reflexivity is objectified in the increased ability of machines to retrieve, store and analyse information. Further, the information which is the output of this process is embodied in goods, services and decisions.

However, in the light of our discussion goods and services should be viewed not as *either* informational or material, but as to varying degrees 'information soaked'. Ceteris paribus the shorter-product-run goods and services will be more information soaked while large-batch runs will be less so. That is, the very short batch services and goods consumed by progressively more individuated consumers will themselves increasingly consist of objectified reflexivity.

One objection to Castells' attempt to incorporate Touraine's post-industrial theory into a neo-Marxist framework very much focusses on the hardware/software side of post-industrialism. Yet ever greater numbers of the labour force are involved in human information-processing, in the retrieval, storage and analysis of information about people. Clearly machine-objectified reflexivity has often played a very positive role as a complement to the information-processing powers of human capital. Yet the more individuated the product is, the more likely that human cultural capital plays the relatively greater role.

Sassen also attempts to bring post-industrialism into the neo-Marxist framework. Only she is less concerned with reflexivity as objectified in machines than with subjectified cultural capital. Thus Sassen cites Bell's concept of a hierarchy in the growth of services, whose initial development, linked to industry, especially to transport and distribution, is superseded by services set in the context of improved quality of life (Sassen 1991: 247). The services that the middle-class professional may consume, physiotherapy, psychotherapy, windsurfing lessons, jazz, symphony and rock concerts, 'exotic restaurants', exotic tourism and art museums, are all linked to a higher 'quality' of life. What is important here is not so much the quality-of-life notion, but the increased symbolic content of the services towards the top of the hierarchy. An example would be the replacement of material or 'sand, sun and sex' tourism by the more symbol-laden or 'place-myth' or cultural tourisms of recent years (Urry 1990c).

And contra Castells it is indeed symbols and not only information that is crucial here. The professional middle class is centrally involved in the processing and circulation of symbols. All information is so to speak carried in symbols, yet the notion of information captures only a tiny part of the multi-dimensionality of symbol. Information is too one-sidedly cognitive. The symbol also contains moral, affective, aesthetic, narrative and meaning dimensions.

We thus live in increasingly individuated and symbol-saturated societies, in which the advanced-services middle class plays an increasing role in the accumulation process. This class assumes a critical mass in the present restructuration: as symbol-processing producers *and* as consumers of processed symbols working and living in certain towns and cities. To talk of services is to talk of information and symbol and of the increasing importance of both within many diverse kinds of post-industrial space.

9
TIME AND MEMORY

We have shown in earlier chapters the importance which many seminal writers now attach to the analysis of time and space. Indeed it is a presumption of this book that the social relations of disorganized capitalism are both temporally and spatially distinct. This was to be seen in the analysis of 'mobile objects', and especially in Harvey's thesis of time-space compression, and of Giddens' dissection of time-space distanciation. Giddens for example says that 'the fundamental question of social theory – the "problem of order" . . . – is to explicate how the limitations of individual "presence" are transcended by the "stretching" of social relations across time and space' (1984: 35). This 'stretching' of social relations means that there has to be a profound redrawing of conventional academic boundaries, particularly between sociology, geography and history. Conventionally sociology has been taken to be the study of social structures merely operating *within* the environments of time and space. Time was only considered in so far as societies were thought to be undergoing change. By contrast Giddens argues that time-space is not a contentless form within which social relations exist but that it expresses the very nature of such social objects – time-space relations are constitutive features of social systems.

In previous chapters we have developed a number of analyses of the ways in which space constitutes social relations. In this chapter we intend to develop similar analyses of time. There are two major difficulties in such an exercise: that there is little content to the sociology of time and so the analysis will be fairly speculative; and that the developments in twentieth-century physics have rendered implausible the idea that time and space can be separated off from each other and analysed independently anyway.

This chapter will be divided into four sections: the sociology of modern time, considering in particular nineteenth- and early-twentieth-century writings on modernity; Giddens' analysis of time, which draws especially on Heidegger and 'time-geography'; recent sociology of time which draws upon new developments in biology and physics; and an analysis of the transformations of time in disorganized capitalism – as time becomes both instantaneous *and* evolutionary in scale. We will argue that it is the mix of instantaneous and evolutionary time that characterizes contemporary disorganized 'Western' societies.

SOCIOLOGY OF TIME

There are various senses of time analysed by different commentators. The word time designates disparate concepts. Adam says:

> It is hard to believe that these theorists have made the same 'phenomenon' central to their work. Between them they associate time with death, ageing, growth, and history, with order, structure, synchronisation, and control. They view time as a sense, a measure, a category, a parameter, and an idea. (1990: 15)

Most sociological accounts of time have nevertheless presumed that it is in some sense social. They have adopted a version of the 'French' school's approach, following Durkheim. He argues in *Elementary Forms* that only humans have a concept of time and that time in human societies is abstract and impersonal and not simply individual (1947). Moreover, this impersonality is socially organized – it is what Durkheim refers to as 'social time'. Hence, time is a 'social institution' and the category of time is not natural but social. Time is an objectively given social category of thought produced within societies and which therefore varies as between societies.

A similar emphasis upon the qualitative nature of social time is to be found in Sorokin and Merton (1937). They distinguish between societies as to whether or not there is a separate category of clock-time, over and above social time. The Nuer for example do not have any sense of time as a resource. Time is not viewed as something that passes, that can be wasted, that can be saved (Evans-Pritchard 1940). To the extent to which there are expressions of time, these take place by reference to social activities based on cyclical ecological changes. Those periods devoid of significant social activity are passed over without reference to time. A further social sense of time is that of 'structural time', the ways that apparently divergent forms of household, lineage and village organization are linked through a common developmental cycle (see Heald 1991: 132–3, and more generally).

Sorokin also notes that while most societies have some form of 'week' this may consist of anything from three to sixteen days (1937; see also Colson 1926). In many societies such divisions reflect some particular social pattern. The Khasi, for example, have an eight-day week since they hold a market every eight days (Hassard 1990). Bourdieu observes that the Kabyle of Algeria have constructed a social-time system which is hostile to clock-time (1990). The clock they refer to as 'the devil's mill' although Bourdieu notes how it introduces an element of greater calculation into social life. They are scornful of haste in social affairs, lack any notion of precise meeting points, and have no set times for eating. However, such rejections of clock-time are not only found in pre-modern societies. Roy famously shows in a study of a machine room the importance of a variety of times, 'peach-time', banana-time', 'window-time' and so on – times that had no particular connection with the clock except that some occur in the 'morning', some in the 'afternoon' (1990).

Nevertheless, there is little doubt that time in modern societies is much more based on clock-time than is the case in many pre-modern societies. Time in modern societies is not predominantly structured in terms of social activities. Clock-time is central to the organization of modern societies and of their constitutive social activities. Such societies are centred around the emptying out of time (and space) and the development of an abstract, divisible and universally measurable calculation of time. It is clear that the first characteristic of modern machine civilization was temporal regularity organized via the clock, an invention that was in many ways more important even than the steam engine. Thompson argues that an orientation to time becomes *the* crucial characteristic of industrial capitalist societies (1967). People shifted from having an orientation to task to having an orientation to time (although his account may well be somewhat overstated).

This argument depends upon the classical writings of Marx and Weber. Marx shows that the regulation and exploitation of labour time is the central characteristic of capitalism. The exchange of commodities is in effect the exchange of labour times. Capitalism entails the attempts by the bourgeoisie either to extend the working day or to work labour more intensively. Marx says that 'man is nothing; he is, at most, the carcase of time' (Marx and Engels 1976: 127). If the working class is not able to resist such pressures, competition will compel capitalists to extend the work period beyond its social and physical limits. There will be 'over-consumption' of labour-power and it will be in the interests of the bourgeois class as a whole to introduce limits on continuous extensions of the working day. However, this collective need does not ensure that reductions on the length of the working day will in fact be realized. Capitalist competition has to be constrained in its own interests (and of those of the workforce). And hence during the history of the first industrial power, Britain, factory hour legislation involving the intervention of the state was particularly important in preventing continuous extensions of the working day and heralded the shift from the production of absolute surplus-value to relative surplus-value production. And it is this form of production, with what Marx calls 'denser' forms of work as compared with the more 'porous' longer day, that led to the staggering increases in productivity that have characterized capitalist industry since the mid-nineteenth century. As the British Factory Inspectorate noted:

> The great improvements made in machines of every kind have raised their productive power very much. Without any doubt, the shortening of the hours of labour . . . gave the impulse to these improvements. The latter, combined with the more intense strain on the workman, have had the effect that at least as much is produced in the shortened working day . . . as was previously produced during the longer one. (Quoted in Marx 1976: 540)

Many later writers have noted more generally how much social conflict in industrial capitalism is focussed around time, around capital's right to organize and extend the hours of work and labour's attempt to limit those hours and to extend various forms of leisure time (see Thompson 1967; Adam 1990: 110 f). Disputes have focussed on duration ('10-hour day', '35-hour week'), intervals ('tea breaks'), sequencing ('flexible rostering'), synchronization ('wakes' weeks') and pace ('time and motion studies'). All these elements focus around the standardized units of clock-time. Such units of time separate work from context as time itself becomes commodified and the measure of work. Adam summarizes:

> In industrial societies time has become the measure of work where work was the measure of time in earlier historical periods . . . The calculation of 'man-hours' . . . like the clock-time on which it is based, is an invariable, standardised measure that can be applied universally regardless of context. (1990: 112)

However, what Marx did not pursue further is how this dominance of clock-time ('man . . . [as] the carcase of time') actually transforms people's subjectivities. Various processes in modern societies constitute people as temporal subjects, as both having an orientation *to* time, and being disciplined *by* time. Weber provided the first sociological analysis of such processes. He said of the Protestant ethic:

> Waste of time is thus the first and in principle the deadliest of sins. The span of human life is infinitely short and precious to make sure of one's own election. Loss of time through sociability, idle talk, luxury, even more sleep than is necessary to health . . . is worthy of absolute moral condemnation. (1930: 158)

And the spirit of capitalism adds a further twist to this: as Benjamin Franklin maintained, 'time is money' – to waste time is to waste money (Weber 1930: 48). People therefore have taken on the notion that it is their duty to be frugal with time, not to waste it, to use it to the full, and to manage the time of oneself and that of others with the utmost diligence (Adam 1990: 113). Not only work but also leisure is often organized in a similar fashion. It is planned, calculative, subdivided and worthwhile, 'rational recreation' in other words.

However, for all the importance of Weber's argument, time is not exactly like money. Time can be shared to a limited degree (in a baby-sitting circle, for example), time can be stored up and exchanged (in time-share holiday accommodation, for example), and people vary enormously in their capacity to use time effectively (hence the importance of 'time-management'). But these are very limited opportunities. Mostly time, unlike money, cannot be stored up and saved. Time constrains human activity more firmly than does money since it inevitably passes and subjects everyone to its passage.

Adam in fact suggests that rather than time being money, money is time. In many cases having a lot of time is of little value to people without money, such as the poor, the unemployed and inmates of total institutions (see Goffman 1968). What is important is access to money which enables time to be put to good use (even if it still inevitably passes). Time therefore varies as to the differential possession of money, as well as to differentials of status and power: 'The wealthy can buy the labour, service and skills of others as time, while agents of state and persons in positions of authority have the right to time-structure the lives of those under their control' (Adam 1990: 114). It is only if one has very little time that time is particularly highly valued. Also if one has plenty of money it may then be possible to ensure so-called 'quality time' through the purchase of the services of others.

So far in analysing the constitution of temporal subjects we have followed the framework established by Weber. We have considered how people develop the appropriate self-discipline so as to harbour the resource of time as effectively as possible. However, there are three further elements of modern time which we should note here, elements which connect the analysis to that of reflexivity discussed in chapter 3. First, people increasingly come to understand that there are many times and many spaces and not just their *own* society and its rhythms and history. To be reflexive is to have some sense of the diverse paths and patterns travelled by different societies in different periods. Second, people come to understand that all human existence is a movement towards death but that there are ways of prolonging or hastening that movement and that they can evaluate and implement different options. In the most extreme cases almost every item eaten is evaluated in relationship to the reflexive project of life-prolongation. And third, it is in a cultural sense possible now to 'travel in time', to move into the future or back into various pasts, and to simulate such periods through complex and sophisticated encounters with the cultural products, images and displays of different times.

Finally, in this section we will briefly summarize Thrift's exemplary account of the 'making of a capitalist time consciousness' in Britain, of the gradual diffusion of calculative clock-time between about 1300 and 1900. Up to the sixteenth century daily activity was predominantly task-oriented (Thrift 1990a: 106–9). The main device for telling the 'time' was the sundial and although many market towns had begun to acquire a clock these do not seem to have affected most people's lives. Moreover, the week was not a common unit of time – more important was the rhythm of the year, and particularly the seasons and related fairs and markets, the church calendar and various ritual observances. Medieval life was thus organized around 'islands of time' within seas of timelessness. There were of course some institutions, such as monasteries, which by contrast did work upon exact and planned time-keeping.

Between the sixteenth and eighteenth centuries a number of develop-ments occurred: some growth in the ownership of domestic clocks especially after 1650; the increasing use of public clocks and bells which were rung at fixed times; the growth of schools for the upper and middle classes which involved the timetabling of daily activities; the increasing attempts by the Puritans to organize work on a weekly basis, of six days followed by rest on the Sabbath; the burgeoning cash economy and its resultant need to calculate days of work and rates of pay; and the introduction of a new word, punctuality, into popular vocabulary (Thrift 1990a: 109–12; Rifkin 1987: ch 6).

And by the late eighteenth or early nineteenth century time had begun to become more fully 'disembedded' from the social activities which had previously structured it. Clocks and watches suddenly became common, partly because the clock and watch-making workshops and factories themselves became organized on the basis of time. Probably the first factory employing industrial mass production was established in France in 1772; the first watches that were entirely machine-made were produced in the USA in the 1830s; and symptomatically it was Henry Ford who first devised a mass production system for the manufacture of clocks in the 1880s (Nguyen 1992: 36–7).

It was amongst the English upper class that time consciousness was particularly marked:

> Old customs based on temporal inexactitude . . . gave way to the most rigid social timetabling and a fixed social calendar of an almost Byzantine complexity. Clock-time was fetishised, meal-times, work-times, dressing-times, visiting-times; all activities were made temporally exact and exacting. (Thrift 1990a: 112)

Indicators of such changes included the use of gongs and house bells, the dressing for formal dinner, the leaving of cards and an increasingly elaborate social timetable based on precisely what sorts of calls could be made at particular times of the day (Davidoff 1973). Amongst the new industrial workforce many temporal innovations came to be introduced: the curtailment of feasts or wakes' holidays; the increasing use of deterrents, incentives and a transformed work ethos to establish a new time discipline – a schedule of the sort that had previously been confined to monasteries; the use, and an increased consciousness, of the clock and the hooter as the basis of monitoring and control; the development of the Sunday School to inculcate a heightened consciousness of time; the regularization of the week into work time and leisure time; and an increased orientation to the future, to planning ahead through savings and credit institutions (Thompson 1967; Rifkin 1987: ch 6; Thrift 1990a: 112–20).

Thrift also provides an account of a particularly emblematic develop-ment in the nineteenth century, Greenwich Mean Time, which was in part brought about because of the problems involved in coordinating travel, a topic to be considered further in chapter 10 (1990a: 120–8). Simmel noted that much greater planning and coordination is necessary in the metropolis in order that social contact between people can be organized (1950: 412–13). However, as important as this necessity to timetable meetings within the metropolis, there is also the need to timetable arrangements for those travelling longer distances between various towns and cities within a country.

Such travel developed in England in the late eighteenth century as regular stagecoach services were established from 1784 onwards. The main problem was that most towns kept their own time zones and the coach guard had to adjust his timepiece to cope with these different zones. This problem grew much more acute with the development of railways and especially with the carrying of mail. For example, the GWR timetable of 1841 contained the following: 'London time is kept at all the stations on the railway, which is about 4 minutes earlier than Reading time; 5 minutes before Cirencester time; 8 minutes before Chippenham time; and 14 minutes before Bridgewater time' (quoted in Thrift 1990a: 122). But by 1847 or so all the rail companies decided to keep to Greenwich Mean Time, as did the Post Office and many towns and cities. However, not all towns changed – at Exeter for example the clock had two minute hands, one showing local time, the other railway or GMT (Thrift 1990a: 126). The situation only changed in 1852 when the Dean of the Cathedral gave way to a locally organized campaign for the 'conformity of time', following the introduction of the telegraph.

The second half of the nineteenth century saw increasing coordination between European countries, and between Europe and north America with regard to the standardization of time measurement (see Nguyen 1992: 32–3). Important developments included: cross-Channel and then cross-Atlantic telegraph services; the establishment of a system of national time covering the extensive distances travelled by the US railway; and the 1884 International Meridian Conference which adopted Greenwich time. Nguyen summarizes the profound consequences:

> gradually all other countries began to adopt the time zone system based on the prime meridian of Greenwich, the specifically western temporal regime which had emerged with the invention of the clock in medieval Europe became the universal standard of time measurement. Indeed its hegemonic development signified the irreversible destruction of all other temporal regimes in the world, the last vestiges of which remain only in the form of historical and anthropological curiosities. (1992: 33)

Greenwich time is thus a mathematical fiction signalling the attempted emasculation of the human experience of time (and space).

In conclusion here, we have seen how the development of clock-time separate from social time contains a number of different elements: the disembedding of time from social activities as it becomes scientifically stripped of meaning; the breaking down of time into a larger number of small units; the emergence of the disciplinary power of time; the increasing timetabling and hence mathematization of social life; and the emergence of a synchronized measure of life first across national territories and later across the globe with the development of Greenwich and 'world time' (see Adam 1990: 116; Nowotny 1975; Luhmann 1982; Rifkin 1987). Simplifying somewhat we can summarize modern (or clockwork) time as being comprised of two elements. First, there is 'clock-time' with the elements listed above. And second, there is time as the mastery of nature, as all sorts of phenomena, practices and places become subjected to the disembedding, centralizing and universalizing march of time.

In the next section we will return to Giddens and consider his effort to construct a systematic sociology of time drawing upon many of the themes considered in this section.

TIME AND THE DUALITY OF STRUCTURE

In this section it will be shown that Giddens has placed the analysis of time (and space) at the very heart of contemporary social theory (for further detail see Urry 1991, as well as Adam 1990). There is now a sense in which any such theory cannot be oblivious to the ways in which social activities are temporally and spatially organized. Giddens' various writings have authorized such a concern and provided some of the terms in which the debates are now cast. But his formulations are highly frustrating, in that they index some important issues but do not provide the basis for developing a really worked-out solution. In particular, Giddens does not interrogate the concepts sufficiently. Time and space paradoxically remain for him as 'structural' concepts demonstrating not the duality of agency and structure but their dualism. No real account is provided as to how human agency is chronically implicated in the very structuring of time (and space).

Giddens' starting point is Heidegger who is employed to demonstrate the irreducibly temporal character of human existence (Giddens 1981: 3 f). Heidegger (1978) repeatedly stresses in *Being and Time* that philosophy must return to the question of 'Being', something that had been obscured by the Western preoccupation with epistemology. Central to Heidegger's ontology of Being is that of time, which expresses the nature of what subjects are. Human beings are fundamentally temporal; they find their meaning in the temporal character of human existence. Being necessarily involves movement between or the 'mutual reaching out and opening up of future, past and present' (quoted in Giddens 1981: 32). However, the nature of time (and space) should not be confused with the ways in which it is conventionally measured, such as intervals or instants. Giddens goes on to set out five ways in which, because of their temporal character, human subjects are different from material objects.

First, only humans live their lives in awareness of their own finitude, something reinforced by seeing the death of others and of how the dead make their influence felt upon the practices of the living. Second, the human agent is able to transcend the immediacy of sensory experience through both individual and collective forms of memory; through an immensely complex interpenetration of presence and absence. Third, human beings do not merely live in time but have an awareness of the passing of time, which is embodied within social institutions. Furthermore, some societies, as we have seen, develop an abstract concept of rational, measurable time, radically separable from the social activities that it appears to order. Fourth, the time-experience of humans can be grasped not only at the level of intentional consciousness but also within each person's unconscious in which past and present are indissolubly linked. And fifth, the movement of individuals through time (and space) is to be grasped via the interpenetration of presence and absence, which results from the location of the human body and the changing means of its interchange with the wider society. This particularly involves new communication and transportation technologies, such as writing, printing, telegraphs, telephones, railways, cars, jet planes, electronically transmitted information and so on. Each of these transforms the intermingling of presence and absence, the forms by which memories are stored and weigh upon the present, and of the ways in which the long-term *durée* of major social institutions are drawn upon within contingent social acts. In order to investigate particularly these latter processes more fully, Giddens draws upon the work of 'time-geography'.

The starting point here is the routinized character of much daily life. There are various sources of constraint over human activity given by the nature of the body and of the physical contexts in which human action occurs (see Giddens 1984: 111 f): the indivisibility and corporeality of the body; the movement of the life span towards death; time as a scarce resource; the limited capability of human beings to participate in more than one task at once; the fact that movement in space is also movement in time; and the limited packing-capacity of time-space so that no two individuals can occupy the same point in space. These factors condition the webs of interaction formed by the trajectories of the daily, weekly, monthly and overall life paths of individuals in their interactions with each other. Individuals moving through time-space meet at 'stations' and comprise 'bundles'. Individuals pursue 'projects' that have to use the inherently limited resources of time and space. There are 'capability constraints', such as the need for regular sleep or food, and 'coupling constraints', which constrain activities that are undertaken with others at least for part of the time.

The result of these constraints is that daily conduct is not simply bounded by physical or geographical boundaries but by 'time-space walls on all sides' (Giddens 1984: 114). There have been major changes in the character of such walls, particularly as a result of 'time-space convergence', namely the shrinking of distance in terms of the time taken to move from one location to another. The journey from the East Coast to the West Coast of the USA took two years by foot, four months by stagecoach, four days by rail (in 1910), and five hours by air. Thus, at least for some people, the constraints on mobility and communication are much reduced.

Giddens' reservations about time-geography, that it has a defective conception of the individual, that it overly emphasizes constraint as opposed to enablement, and that it presents no developed theory of power, leads him to develop a partly alternative set of concepts by which to think through just how the life processes of individuals, including their daily, weekly and monthly paths, are linked to the *longue durée* of social institutions (see Giddens 1984: 116–19; Gregory 1985).

First, there is regionalization, the zoning of time-space in relationship to routinized social practices. Rooms in a house are for example zoned both spatially and temporally. There are huge variations in such zoning between societies and over time. In the latter case, Giddens gives two examples: the development of powerful forms of artificial lighting that has dramatically expanded the potentialities of interaction settings within the 'night'-time; and the changing zoning of social activities as more 'specialized' rooms have developed in the houses occupied by the mass of the population (see Giddens 1984: 119–22).

Second, there is the concept of presence-availability, the degree to which, and the forms through which, people are co-present within an individual's social milieu. Communities of high presence-availability include almost all societies up to a few hundred years ago. Necessary co-presence resulted from the corporeality of the agent, the limitations upon daily mobility because of existing transportation technology and the physical properties of space (see Giddens 1984: 122–4). Presence-availability has been transformed in the past century or two through the development of new transportation technologies and especially the separation of the media of communication from the media of transportation. The invention of the electromagnetic telegraph was particularly important since it meant that communication did not have to involve the literal mobility of the human body. The development of money and its power to bridge distances has also brought about forms of interchange between people who are spatially distant.

Third, there is Giddens' concept of time-space distanciation: the processes by which societies are 'stretched' over shorter or longer spans of time and space. Such stretching reflects the fact that social activity increasingly depends upon interactions with those who are absent in time-space. The structuring of time and space depends upon: the changing control of information, via the invention of writing, then of printing and, recently, of electronic information, which separates presence in time from presence in space; the development of the city as a religious, ceremonial and commercial centre and power container; the development of the more modern urban form, as a created space through the commodification of land and the disruption of the ties of the city with nature; changes in transportation and communication technologies; the development of the territorially bounded nation-state with its expanded powers of documentation and surveillance; and the commodification of time so that it becomes separated from lived experience and actual social activities and appears like money as a universal and public measure (see Giddens 1981: chs 4, 6).

Fourth, there are time-space edges, the forms of contact or encounter between types of society organized according to different structural principles. This notion is part of a battery of concepts and arguments used by Giddens to emphasize the inadequacy of evolutionary theories based upon an endogenous or unfolding model of social change. Rather, it is essential to investigate *inter*-societal systems, of the time-space edges by which for example a tribal society is confronted by a class-divided society. Episodes of social change also depend upon the emerging structures of world-time, that is the particular conjunctural phase of world development (see Giddens 1981: ch 7; 1984: ch 5).

The fifth concept here is that of power-containers, what Giddens calls the storage capacity of different societies, particularly storage across time and space. In oral cultures human memory is virtually the sole repository of information storage. In class-divided societies the city, especially with the development of writing, becomes the primary crucible or container of power (see Giddens 1981: ch 5; 1984: ch 6; Mumford 1960). Particularly significant is how religious, military and administrative power is combined within the walls of the city to give physical shape to this crucible of power. By contrast, in capitalist societies it is the territorially bounded nation-state that is the dominant time-space container of power. The city loses its distinctiveness as such (the walls come tumbling down!). A number of conditions have consolidated the unified administrative power of the nation-state: the mechanization of transportation and its separation from communication; the invention of printing and later of electronically recorded information, which expands the spatial power of the state; the enormous expansion of the documentary activities of the state, beginning with the keeping of official statistics; and the development of much more effective 'internal' pacification including in part the 'disciplinary power' of various total institutions (see Giddens 1985: ch 7).

Finally, there is the disembedding of time and space from social activities, the development of an 'empty' dimension of time, the separation of space from place, and the emergence of disembedding mechanisms, of symbolic tokens and of expert systems which lift social relations out of local involvements. Expert systems bracket time and space through deploying modes of technical knowledge which are valued independent of the practitioners and clients who make use of them. Such systems depend on *trust*, on a qualitative leap or commitment related to absence in time and/or space. Trust in disembedding mechanisms is vested not in individuals but in abstract systems or capacities and is specifically related to absence in time and space (Giddens 1990, 1991a, b).

There is little doubt that Giddens' work represents an important contribution to the sociology of time. However, it is worth noting that he does not consider the time-space organization of particular places, nor does he provide much analysis of the varying organization of time within different societies, treating all traditional and all industrial societies as more or less the same. He does not examine and explain how and why a different structuring of time is found in some industrial countries rather than others (for extensive discussion of such changes at the turn of the century see Kern 1983). Thus, as a case in point, the weekend is a time-zone implying also a particular organization of space (such as in the family home, at church or at sports events), which is more important in some countries than others. For example, until recently in New Zealand, shops did not open on Saturday or Sunday, much of the industrial labour force worked a set five-day week, and the weekend was mainly spent within the family in the space of one's home. Two key features of the pattern of institutional governance that sustained the time-myth of the weekend were the considerable strength of the labour movement in preventing the temporal flexibilization of the labour force; and the power of the churches to protect the sanctity of the weekend and especially the family from commercialization. One should also note the importance of the Judaic tradition and the myth of creation in the artificial construction of the 'week' in the first place. This is the only important time-zone that is not in some way derived from 'nature' (see Colson 1926).

Giddens seems to regard the organization of time as given, somehow embedded within the structuring of rules and resources that characterize modern societies in general. The organization of time is not seen to vary greatly between modern societies or to stem from the particular powers of social forces concerned to 'produce' different ways in which time may be either saved or zoned. In Britain the attempt in 1987 to transform the traditional Sunday by allowing all shops to open was met by furious opposition that successfully sustained Sunday as a distinct time-zone. The production and reproduction of zones of time, as with the production and reproduction of spaces or places, is unanalysed in Giddens' work. There is in effect the dualism rather than the duality of structure.

This is in turn related to Adam's criticism that Giddens does not conceptualize time as a resource (Adam 1990: 119–20). Time is seen by him as a measure of chronological distance and stacked information. Time, as in time-space distanciation, is viewed as a measure of stretching across societies. But time in modern societies should be seen as more than this since it also functions as a centrally important resource. Indeed Adam argues that time is only conceptualized as a resource in societies like ours; societies which not only have created clock-time, but also relate to that creation as *being* time and organize their social life by it (1990: 120). Or as Lefebvre suggests, with modernity lived time disappears, it is no longer visible and is replaced by measuring instruments, clocks, which are separate from social space. Time has become a resource, separate from social space and consumed, deployed and exhausted (1991: 95–6).

Moreover, this is a resource directly tied to power in modern societies:

> social time needs to be conceptualised in terms of relations of power to the extent that clock time *as* time has become an independent, context-free value, a social and economic reality that structures, controls, disciplines, and provides norms for our social life. (Adam 1990: 120)

Once therefore time has become independent it can then be used, it is a resource or a capacity to be allocated, wielded, spent and filled. For example, Frankenberg has shown in his analysis of the inequalities of waiting relations within medicine, that time and power become inextricably intertwined (1988). Giddens' account therefore does not sufficiently address a further characteristic of modern societies. It is not merely that time (and space) are disembedded from social life, but that time (and space) have developed as independent resources which can be manipulated and exploited by dominant social forces (and resisted of course). The emergence of time and space as independent resources is one of the defining characteristics of modern society.

This in turn relates to a further gap in Giddens' account, namely the importance of the use of time and space for travel. He provides no analysis of why people travel and hence why saving 'time', or covering more 'space', might be of 'interest'. One obvious reason for travel is for pleasure – it enables people to visit other environments, places and people. Giddens' conception of human activity is too routinized, too concerned with ontological security, and it is difficult in his framework to conceptualize pleasure-producing activities such as leisure, holiday-making, sightseeing, shopping, playing sport, visiting friends, time-travelling and travelling just for its own sake (although see 1991a).

Further, the key aspect of many kinds of travel is to enter a kind of liminal zone where some of the rules and restrictions of routine life are relaxed and replaced by different norms of behaviour, those appropriate to being in the company of strangers. This may entail new and exciting forms of sociability, as well as various kinds of playfulness, including what one might call 'temporal play' as on holiday. Much social activity involves semi-routines in which travel is an important element. What are involved are disruptions to everyday patterns that are nevertheless socially patterned and recognizable.

Thus in travel and related activities, the maximizing of time-space distanciation may often be irrelevant. People find it pleasurable to travel particular distances via specific forms of transportation which are not necessarily the fastest. And often there are well-established connections between certain forms of travel and resulting social activities (travelling by train to English seaside resorts, by air to European holiday destinations, by car to theme parks and so on). Travel is an irreducibly social phenomenon rather than merely a means of transcending distance (this issue will be explored further in chapter 10).

The effects then of particular means of overcoming the 'friction of distance' are complex and by no means reducible to the *extension* of time-space distanciation. Giddens does not examine how time-space changes will often have the consequence, not merely of heightening distanciation, but also of helping to encourage resistance, opposition, pleasure, autonomy or a sense of deprivation. Giddens views many of these developments in a one-dimensional fashion, as in effect 'modernization' through distanciation. This he sees as becoming more and more extensive: first, it makes people more oriented to the future and to the further progressive extension of such distanciation; and second, it gradually dissolves the significance of specific spaces or places as people are able to move through time and space in increasingly rapid fashion. But in chapter 11 we will examine how the temporal and spatial construction of place is an important component of the transformed relations of both globalization *and* localization (although see Giddens 1990). Giddens views the contemporary period as that of 'high modernity'. We by contrast view these as elements of the *post*-modern, in which the 'past' and the 'local' are crucially significant elements.

In the next section we will consider some further criticisms of Giddens (and of most other commentators) which derive from fundamentally rethinking the concept of time itself.

TIME, POWERS AND NATURE

There has been a longstanding philosophical dispute as to whether time (and space) are to be viewed as absolute entities, possessing their own natures or particularities. Is time something which is itself productive? It is to be distinguished from matter since it possesses its own properties (the 'arrow of time') – or is it merely relative, a way of characterizing the relations between the constituents of the physical world? The latter view was particularly expressed by Leibniz who argued that space is 'an order of co-existences as time is an *order* of successions' (quoted in Körner 1955: 33). According to this relational view the universe simply consists of pieces of matter, composed of various substances, and these pieces of matter exhibit temporal relationships between each other and between their own constitutive parts. Generally relationists argue that if any statements do appear to assign properties to time it will be logically possible to reduce these properties to the temporal relations between the objects concerned. Absolutists argue by contrast that time does designate particulars, such as the view that time 'flows' and that there are effects as a consequence of its passage – that there is an arrow of time (Smart 1963: ch 7).

Neither position can be simply adopted. Elsewhere we argued that it is natural and social entities which possess powers to produce outcomes, but that such outcomes will only be realized if such entities are placed in appropriate spatial and temporal relations with each other (see Urry 1985). It is now clear though that this formulation is too simplistic. Temporal relations are so varied that no simple or predictable outcomes can be said to follow from the identification of 'temporal relations' between two or more social entities. It depends on what notion of time is being employed. Nevertheless there are some irreducible aspects of time that do need elaboration for the social sciences even if one would doubt that time 'on its own' does anything or possesses clear powers. It should also be noted that time unlike some aspects of space is invisible to the senses (Elias 1992: 1).

One problem here is that the conventional understanding of time is rooted in outdated and inappropriate notions. When Durkheim, Sorokin, Merton and the like insisted on the radical distinction between natural and social time, this was based on an inadequate understanding of time in nature. It is necessary, Adam argues, to undertake a thorough re-examination of time, incorporating the insights and arguments from contemporary physical and biological sciences (1990).

She argues that we should dissolve the distinction betwen natural time and social time (and also the distinctions between subject and object and nature and culture). Most of what social scientists have seen as specifically human is in fact generalized throughout nature. The one aspect which is not, clock-time, is paradoxically the characteristic which social science has thought to be the defining feature of natural time, as that came to be historically separated from social time (see Elias 1992). Adam summarizes:

> Past, present, and future, historical time, the qualitative experience of time, the structuring of 'undifferentiated change' into episodes, all are established as integral time aspects of the subject matter of the natural sciences and clock time, the invariant measure, the closed circle, the perfect symmetry, and reversible time as our creations. (1990: 150)

Thus social science has operated with an inappropriate conception of time in the natural sciences, an almost non-temporal time, which can be described as Newtonian and Cartesian. It is Newtonian because it is based on the notion of absolute time, that from 'its own nature, [it] flows equably without relation to anything eternal...the flowing of absolute time is not liable to change' (quoted in Adam 1990: 50). Such absolute time is invariant, infinitely divisible into space-like units, measurable in length, expressible as a number and crucially reversible. It is time seen essentially as space, as invariant measurable lengths which can be moved along, forwards *and* backwards. And it is Cartesian space because it is premised upon the dualisms of mind and body, repetition and process, quantity and quality, form and content, subject and object and so on. Coveney and Highfield note that the 'great edifices of science would all appear to work equally well with time running in reverse' (1991: 23).

However, the notion of time in nature has now been transformed. It is no longer viewed as Newtonian and Cartesian. The social sciences have failed to see this change. This causes two problems: the reinforcing of the natural time/social time dichotomy, and a failure to incorporate into social science some of the extraordinary insights of twentieth-century science (see Adam 1990; and Elias, who argues that reflection upon time shows how 'nature, society and individuals are embedded in each other and are interdependent', 1992: 16).

Four such major scientific 'discoveries' of the twentieth century have transformed the understanding of time in nature. First, Einstein demonstrated that there is no fixed time which is independent of the system to which it is refers – time is a local, internal feature of the system of observation. Second, again Einstein showed that time and space are fused into four-dimensional space-time entities and that such a fused space-time is curved under the influence of mass. Third, chronobiologists have demonstrated that rhythmicity is the crucial principle of nature, and in particular that humans are not just affected by clock-time but are themselves clocks. Living things are composed of myriad internal clocks entrained to work in coordination with the rhythms of the external physical world (circadian, lunar, circannual and life-cycle). Fourth, evolutionary writers have emphasized that the time of one's body should be extended to include the entire evolutionary history of humans – that 'the time of our body is not exhausted by our finitude but arrives within it our entire evolutionary history' (Adam 1990: 166, as well as chs 2, 3, 7; Rifkin 1987: ch 2; Hawking 1988).

The implication of all of this is that nature is intrinsically temporal; and that there are many different times in nature. Especially important is the way that physical time is now conceptualized as irreversible and directional – as Eddington says: 'The great thing about time is that it goes on' (quoted in Coveney and Highfield 1991: 83). The clearest example of this can be seen in the process by which the universe has expanded – through the cosmological arrow of time following the extraordinary singularity of a 'big bang' (see Coveney and Highfield 1991). Laws of nature should thus be viewed as historical and hence it is incorrect to construct a simple dichotomy between nature as time-free or time-less or having a reversible concept of time, and society as being fundamentally temporal. Moreover, biologists have shown that it is false to assert that only human beings experience time or organize their lives through time. Biological time is not confined to ageing but expresses the nature of biological beings as temporal, dynamic and cyclical – humans as having a life-cycle. And of course, even 'dead things' like machines, buildings or physical landscapes are not merely 'natural' and time-free but are both of particular times and constructed through temporal processes of change, order and decay.

We have thus summarized a notion of time which is non-spatialized, non-reversible, multi-faceted, and where no strong distinction is drawn between the times of nature and those of humans. What we will now consider is how some of these considerations relate to one of the most intractable issues in social science; that is, how does the past, a previous 'time', impact upon the present? How does a society incorporate the past? How do societies remember?

This is not an issue that many social scientists have really developed (although see Game 1991: ch 5; Middleton and Edwards 1990; Elias 1992; as well as much work within anthropology). Often, they have relied on the contributions of Marx on the role of 'past generations' or of Freud on the significance of 'the unconscious'. In each case the account does not provide detailed analysis of the social *mechanisms* by which the past is repressed or is remembered in the present. This will be discussed further in the next section when we analyse the development of collective memory through heritage. For the moment we will briefly consider how memories are in part biological or bodily and are not entirely social.

Bergson called into question the spatialized conception of time and maintained that time or 'duration' must be seen as temporal (1950; Game

1991: ch 5). People should be viewed as temporal rather than time being thought of as some discrete element or presence. Time and body are inextricably intertwined – people do not think real time but they live it. This viewpoint is neatly captured by Irigaray who says: 'Your body is not the same today as yesterday. Your body remembers. There's no need for *you* to remember' (1985: 215). She goes on to argue for a philosophy of the 'colourful show of the sensuous here-and-now' (quoted in Game 1991: 100). There is a strong distinction to be drawn between the present and the here-and-now – it is the movement of time in the latter which makes the present impossible to conceptualize as some discrete and separate entity. And in that here-and-now there are countless memories which are preserved as traces.

Bergson goes on to argue that memory should not be seen as a drawer or a store since such notions derive from incorrectly conceptualising time in a spatial fashion. He criticizes such a notion of time, abstract, static and homogeneous, and advocates instead time as lived, as permeated, qualitative and sensuous. On this account memory, he says, should be viewed temporally and not spatially, as the 'piling up of the past upon the past' (Bergson 1913: 5–6). And such memories are wholly distinct from their representation. Game says that 'any representation consists in a spatialisation, a cutting out, an immobilisation. Representation of past, present and future is a denial of time' (1991: 97–8). It should however be noted that Bergson seems here to operate with a notion of abstract space, rather than to see how space can itself be qualitative and central to memory, that memories are overwhelmingly of spaces and contextualized by space, involving what Shields terms social spatialization (1990). So when we say that memories should not be conceptualized 'spatially' we mean by this a sense of space as abstract and homogeneous.

A recent attempt to construct a sociology of memory is found in Connerton's *How Societies Remember* (1989). He distinguishes between *incorporating* and *inscribing* practices and considers their relationship to how memory is sedimented in the bodily postures of those living in particular societies. Incorporating practices are messages which are imparted by means of people's current bodily activity, the transmission only occurring when their bodies are so present. Inscribing practices are the modern devices for storing and retrieving information, photographs, print, alphabets, indexes, tapes, etc – memory as store *contra* Bergson. These practices trap and hold information long after the human organism has stopped informing (and see Ong 1982 on the related differences between oral and literate cultures, as well as Fentress and Wickham 1992: 97).

He analyses a variety of incorporating practices – especially the memorization of culturally specific bodily postures and their significance for communal memory. He also notes that the transition from an oral to a literate culture is a transition from incorporating to inscribing practices and depends upon various kinds of literacy. But in each case part of what is

passed on, and part of what does the passing on is a set of bodily
procedures, techniques and gestures. The past is passed on to us not
merely in what we think or in what we do but literally in *how* we do it: how
we sit when we write, how we stand, how we eat, how we travel and so on.

   This in turn relates to further debates over the nature of memory. We
have already implicitly rejected the notion that memory is something which
is physically locatable in the brain and that it only requires some kind of
activation for it to be released (see Arcaya 1992). Partly we have
emphasized the embodied basis of memory. And partly Middleton and
Edwards have highlighted how 'remembering and forgetting are integral
with social practices that carry with them, in important ways, a culturally
evolved legacy of conduct and invention, both material and social, central
to the conduct of daily life' (1990: 1). This is a crucially important point
which has been demonstrated through many studies conducted in diverse
disciplines. The following are some of the analyses in which the irreducibly
social nature of memory is demonstrated: oral history (Thompson 1988);
the study of folklore (Middleton and Edwards 1990: 3–4); the historical
geography of townscapes and landscapes (Lowenthal and Binney 1981;
Lowenthal 1985); media and communication studies (Nerone and Wartella
1989); sociological and anthropological analyses of 'communities of
memory', of communities united by their past (Bellah et al 1985; Fentress
and Wickham 1992 on 'social memory'); the anthropology of 'systematic
forgetting' (Douglas 1986); the cultural analysis of heritage and museums
(Hewison 1987; Lumley 1988); the geography and sociology of knowledge
(Abercrombie et al 1990; Thrift 1985); and the social psychology of
memory. The last of these disciplines, at least as conceived of by Middleton
and Edwards, concerns itself with a range of pertinent topics (1990): how
people remember together, such as when looking together at family
photographs; how people have to work at producing a shared memory; the
social practices of commemoration where some event or person is ascribed
historical significance and the commemoration silences contrary interpretations of the past; the social processes which reinforce memory; the
rhetorical organization of remembering and forgetting; and the nature of
institutional memory and its effects, not merely on a generalized future,
but on the very constitution of present and future subjects. The upshot of
these elements of a social psychology of collective remembering is that
there is no single, de-contextualised memory separate from the range of
contexts and commemorations, pragmatics and rhetorics, in which people
have been and are engaging.

   Memory is thus irreducibly social and non-individual. But Connerton's
argument had also showed that such social processes of remembering and
forgetting revolve around bodies. Part of what is remembered are ways of
sitting and standing, looking and lounging, hearing and hoping, ruminating
and recollecting, which are embodied. To say that they are embodied is not
to say that they are reducible to biological bodily rhythms. But it is to say
that such rhythms are part of what is worked upon in these various social

contexts; and that what is remembered are certain bodily configurations, especially as they relate to the senses, to sight, touch, hearing, smell and so on, as in Proust's phrase 'our arms and legs are full of torpid memories' (quoted in Lowenthal 1985: 203). Memories presuppose such senses but such senses are themselves socially and discursively constructed. And in particular, as Radley argues, memories are constructed around artefacts – machines, household objects, buildings, streets, tools, walls, fields and so on (1990; some of which themselves possess memories). He summarizes:

> remembering is something which occurs in a world of things, as well as words, and that artefacts play a central role in the memories of cultures and individuals . . . In the very variability of objects, in the ordinariness of their consumption and in the sensory richness of relationships people enjoy through them, they are fitted to be later re-framed as material images for reflection and recall. (Radley 1990: 57–8)

Artefacts are moreover sensed through bodies but how this sensing occurs and the impact that it has results from complex, historically changing processes of social production, communication and signification. In the final section of this chapter we will analyse how these processes of production, communication and signification are currently undergoing substantial transformation. Disorganized capitalism is ushering in some major changes in time, history and memory, changes which can be cryptically summarized as the move to time as simultaneously instantaneous *and* evolutionary.

DISORGANIZED CAPITALISM AND TIME

We can begin here again with Giddens. For him there are three time-scales to consider: the *durée* of daily-time; the *Dasein* of life-time; and the *longue durée* of history (1981: 19–20). Each presupposes or implies the others and he is interested in how each is bound up with the structural practices of social systems. However, these are very much time-scales in the middle ground, between the imperceptibly fast changes of quantum physics, on the one hand, and the unimaginably slow investigations of astronomy or biological evolution, on the other (see Adam 1990: 165). Giddens' time-scales miss both of these other scales.

Indeed if we consider science and technology as social structural practices, then they have two characteristics, neither of which fits into Giddens' time-scales. First, science and technology have resulted from a very long, imperceptibly changing process, occurring over thousands of years, and involving various forms of evolutionary adaptation. The 'mastery of nature' has been a centuries-long process. It was not planned or designed but has happened as the outcome of millions of small changes and tiny advances, which in a non-deterministic fashion resulted in massive transformations of the relationship of humans and 'nature' (as we now are able to appreciate; see Adam 1990: 86–7).

And second, such transformations have resulted in a contemporary science and technology based upon time-frames that lie beyond conscious human experience:

> If telephones, telex and fax machines have reduced the response time from months, weeks and days to seconds, the computer has contracted them down to nanoseconds. The time-frame of a computer relates to event times of a billionth of a second. (Adam 1990: 140)

Rifkin notes that nearly 50 per cent of American workers use electronic equipment based on such nanoseconds while at work (1987: 14). It follows that when many important activities take place below the threshold of human consciousness, then social time as structured by the clock becomes progressively less relevant to the contemporary organization of human society. Never before has time been organized at a speed beyond the realm of human consciousness. Rifkin talks of how computers in the next century will be able to make decisions in nanosecond time. Hence:

> The events being processed in the computer world exist in a time realm that we will never be able to experience. The new 'computime' represents the final abstraction of time and its complete separation from human experience and rhythms of nature. (Rifkin 1987: 15)

So there are two transformations of time which have taken place: the realization of an immensely long, imperceptibly changing, *evolutionary* or glacial time; and of a time so brief, so *instantaneous* that it cannot be experienced or observed. Clock-time lies in the middle and it is clock-time that has been the organizing principle of modernity. To the extent that we are passing into the post-modern, to disorganized capitalism, then we are moving to time as glacial or evolutionary and to a time that is instantaneous.

We have encountered some of these issues before in this book. In particular in chapter 2 we discussed D. Harvey's dystopic scenario in which the acceleration of subjects and objects, as a consequence of time-space compression, produces an emptying out of both objects and subjects (1989). Harvey and others argue that with such accelerated mobility through time and space, all objects, including townscapes and landscapes, have become homogenized, flattened and disposable, while social relationships are empty, meaningless and lack long-term commitment. We have countered such a pessimistic scenario in a variety of ways, particularly in chapter 3 in elaborating the importance of reflexivity and especially the non-cognitive aesthetic-expressive dimensions of the reflexive self.

However, what we did not consider was how such notions of reflexivity are specifically linked to various aspects of time and to their transformations under disorganized capitalism. Both instantaneous time and glacial time are centrally important to the emergence of reflexive subjects, particularly in their aesthetic and expressive moments.

In the case of the former the instantaneous character of contemporary time certainly facilitates its *use* by powerful organizations which often result in a flattening and a disembedding of social relations. But the use of instantaneous time can also be enabling for ordinary subjects. They can view and evaluate different cultures at the flick of a switch, or via high speed (or almost instantaneous) transport. This enables the rapid and extensive juxtaposition of, and comparison between, different cultures and places. And this in turn facilitates people's ability to manipulate these different cultures and their symbolization. Part then of contemporary reflexivity involves time- and space-travel in a variety of 'real' and simulated forms. Such reflexivity is made possible by the reification of time and its instantaneity.

But a second element of contemporary culture is a reflexive awareness of the long-term relationship between humans, animals and the rest of 'nature'. In such a reflexive consciousness it is held, first, that humans are no longer simply superior to all elements of 'nature'; second, that humans have an especial responsibility for ensuring the long-term survival not only of themselves but also of many other species; third, that there is and should be a long-term historical relationship between humans and nature; and fourth, that how this relationship develops in the future is something that can only be evaluated after many generations, when for example it is seen what the effects are of ozone depletion (see Yearley 1991). Thus this glacial notion of time is one in which the relation between humans and nature is very long-term and evolutionary. It moves back out of immediate human history and forwards into a wholly unspecifiable future.

We will now elaborate on these two kinds of post-modern time, time under disorganized capitalism, beginning with instantaneous time. We will consider the many ways in which it seems that the future is dissolving into the present, that 'we want the future now' has become emblematic of a panic about the 'future' and a search for the instantaneous (see Adam 1990: 140). Subsequently in this chapter evolutionary time will be examined.

A useful starting point is Giddens' discussion of the transformations brought about in the modern world by the development of its media, initially printing and then the electronic signal (1991a: 24–7). Printing was enormously significant because such materials could cover space much more easily than hand-written materials. Printing enabled the increasingly simultaneous consumption of the same item (beginning with the Gutenberg Bible) and has led to the stunning proliferation of cultural forms and their increasing disposability. The quantity of printed materials has doubled every fifteen years or so since Gutenberg first appeared (Giddens 1991a: 25). But Giddens also notes the important interdependence between mass printed media and electronic communication. From very early on, the former was dependent on the latter, especially with the growth of newspapers and their conception of 'news'. Although early newspapers played a significant role in separating space from place, this process only became nationally and then globally important with the integration of printed and electronic media. Before then 'news' stories described events which were close-at-hand. The more distant an event, the later it would appear, especially if the 'news' had to be carried across oceans by slow-moving ships. It was the telegraph, later the telephone, and then the computer, which meant that it was the 'event' that governed inclusion, rather than the place in which it occurred. Newspapers thus came to consist of the reporting of very many events, chosen principally in terms of their newsworthy value and not their location.

There are thus two dramatically distinct features of contemporary media. One is what Giddens calls the *collage* effect, that once events have become more important than location, then the presentation in the media takes the form of the juxtaposition of stories and items that share nothing in common except that they are 'newsworthy' (1991a: 26). Stories from many different places occur alongside each other in a chaotic and arbitrary fashion, such stories serving to abstract events from context and narrative. The experience of news is thus a temporally and spatially confused collage – a collage in which time as instantaneous is paramount. Second, the mediated experience of disorganized capitalism involves the 'intrusion of distant events into everyday consciousness' (Giddens 1991a: 27). Events often of an appallingly tragic character are dramatically brought into people's everyday experience. There is thus a literal time-space *compression* as this collage of disconnected stories intrude and shape everyday life. And instantaneously people are 'transported' from one tragedy to another in ways which seem out of control. This then appears to be a world full of risks and where there is little likelihood of even understanding the temporally organized processes which culminate in the newsworthy tragedies that are routinely represented every day.

The collage and compression effects are in turn connected to the development of the so-called three-minute culture, that those watching TV or the VCR tend to hop from channel to channel and that they rarely spend time in following through a lengthy programme. Indeed many programmes are now made to mimic such a pattern, being made up of a collage of visual and aural images, a stream of 'sound bites', each lasting a very short time and having no particular connection with those coming before and after. This instantaneous conception of time can be characterized as 'video-time'.

Another way of expressing this is in terms of the changing attitude to waiting. We have already noted Frankenberg's discussion of medicine as a 'waiting culture' – in order to maintain social order and restore natural order, patients are removed from their normal temporalities and placed within a new space where the time organization of others can be easily imposed upon them (1988: 148). And it is patients who wait, often hours, while the medical staff do not (although interestingly medical staff have little time that is not itself regulated partly by subordinates).

But we can generalize from this and suggest that the capacity to wait is an integral part of growing up and becoming human (Adam 1990: 124–5). Young adults must develop a certain trust in the future – that there is a 'future' and that it has some 'reality'. Deferred gratification then is most likely when future rewards are reasonably certain and partly under a person's control. This kind of waiting is most likely amongst the 'structurally strong class'. Deferred gratification involves people having a trusting relationship to the future and this will characterize those whose position is powerful within the social structure (see Adam 1990: 124–5). However, various kinds of evidence suggest that there may have been a decline in the significance of such deferred gratification, even amongst those who are in a structurally strong position. Instantaneous time dissolves the future – 'I want the future now' as the T-shirt expresses it, although interestingly hunting and gathering societies may exhibit a similar orientation to immediate gratification. Nowotny writes:

> we are about to abolish the *category* of the future and replace it with that *of the extended present* . . . The category of the future is shrinking towards becoming a mere extension of the present because science and technology have successfully reduced the distance that is needed to accommodate their own products. (1985: 14–15)

Thus as a result of the need for instantaneous responses, particularly because of the telephone, telex, fax, electronic signals and so on, the future appears to dissolve and it no longer functions as something in which people appear to trust. There are two consequences. First, as we discussed in chapter 3, the objective time of modernity gradually gives way to a set of personalized, subjective temporalities which are self-generated and involve what Giddens calls 'life-calendars' (Giddens 1991a: ch 6). Trust and commitment over time are less geared to institutions and more to how individuals create their own subjective time of life narratives.

Second, the lack of trust in the future means that it is increasingly likely that gratification will not be deferred. Clearly though there are here marked differences between Western economies, with the Anglo-Saxon countries, rather than Japan or Germany, placing a stronger emphasis upon instantaneous time. The following are some indicators that disorganized capitalism, especially in north America and parts of Europe, does indeed involve a collapse of a waiting culture and the permeation of instantaneous time. There are the increased rates of divorce and other forms of household dissolution as well as the marked rise in the willingness of especially women to undertake affairs within marriage (see Lawson 1989). Likewise conservative critics have suggested that there is a reduced sense of trust, loyalty and commitment of families over generations, that family relationships are much more disposable (see Lasch 1980). And more generally, products and images are increasingly disposable in a 'throwaway society' in which there is a strong emphasis upon the volatility and ephemerality in fashions, products, labour processes, ideas and images (D. Harvey 1989: 285–6; Toffler 1970). There is a heightened 'temporariness' of products, values and personal relationships, where the 'temporary contract' is everything (Lyotard 1984: 66; D. Harvey 1989: 113, 286). This in turn relates to an accelerating turnover-time and the proliferation of new products and of flexible forms of technology (Piore and Sabel 1984). Except in Japanese plants there is the decline in long-term jobs and careers and an increased tendency for short-term labour contracts (D. Harvey 1989: 287). There is the growth of 24-hour trading so that investors and dealers never have to wait for the buying and selling of securities and foreign exchange (see chapter 11 below). There are extraordinary increases in the availability of products so that one does not have to wait to travel anywhere in order to consume some new style or fashion (see D. Harvey 1989: 299 on the 'emporium of styles' in US cities). Or rather 'there is no fashion, only fashions' since there are 'no rules, only choices' (see Featherstone 1991: 83). Political preferences are increasingly volatile, so that in Britain up to two-fifths of the electorate change who they vote for between elections (Sarlvik and Crewe 1983). And as economies become sign-based the turnover-time of such signs and hence of such products is extraordinarily rapid, and in cases almost instantaneous (D. Harvey 1989: 288). More generally, there is an increased sense of speed in social life which at least for Virilio replaces the clear distances of time and space, or rather the 'violence of speed' whether of the military, the media or of cities transcends and destroys place (1986).

This constitutes a striking set of changes, which in turn have significant implications for the nature of subjectivity. The profound emphasis upon instantaneous time means that the time-space paths of individuals are desynchronized. There is a greatly increased variation in different people's times. They are less collectively organized and structured as mass consumption patterns are replaced by more varied and segmented patterns. There are a number of indicators of such time-space desynchronization which again is more marked in the UK and USA: the increased significance of grazing, that is not eating at fixed meal times in the same place in the company of one's family or workmates; the growth of 'free and independent travellers' who specifically resist mass travel in a group where everyone has to engage in common activities at fixed times; the development of flexitime, so that groups of employees no longer start and stop work at the same time; and the growth of the VCR which means that TV programmes can be stored, repeated and broken up, so that no sense remains of the authentic, shared watching of a particular programme. This in turn may well be linked to the emphasis placed on so-called quality time by those whose lives demonstrate exceptionally complex time-space paths. It is precisely because of the very high levels of time-space desynchronization between two or more people that efforts are made to ensure short but sweet moments of uninterrupted 'presence-availability'.

We have so far connected instantaneous time to a lack of confidence about the future. But there is another side to this which we have not yet discussed and that is the remarkable appeal of the past. Once upon a time such nostalgia was formally confined to particular times and places, although Nietzsche amongst others warned how an excess of remembrance can smother creativity. Likewise in the first half of nineteenth-century France there was much medical dissection of the pathology of 'nostalgia'. This was taken to be an excess of desire for the past and a refusal to live in the present as that time which anticipates the future (see Roth 1992). Gradually over the century such a nostalgia was turned into a thing of the past, as progress, mobility and science transformed the contours of industrial society.

Now again it seems nostalgia is everywhere, engulfing almost every experience and artefact from the past, even the 'dark satanic mills' of the industrial revolution or 1950s juke boxes. Lowenthal characterizes such nostalgia as 'memory with the pain taken out' (1985: 8). And Hewison has argued that Britain has come to specialize not on manufacturing goods but rather on manufacturing nostalgia or heritage (1987). And such institutionalized heritage functions to deflect attention in a systematic way from the forms of social deprivation and inequality in the present (see Urry 1990c: ch 8 for a review of this argument). This nostalgia is for an idealized past, for a sanitized version not of history but of heritage. Lowenthal suggests that there is almost a mental complaint:

> Once the menace or the solace of a small elite, nostalgia now attracts or afflicts most levels of society. Ancestor-hunters search archives for their roots; millions throng to historic houses; antiques engross the middle class; souvenirs flood consumer markets . . . 'A growing rebellion against the *present*, and an increased longing for the past', are said to exemplify the post-war mood. (1985: 11)

Michael Wood likewise suggests that until the 1970s nostalgia trips were 'surreptitious and ambivalent' because people did not want to lose their hold on the present and a modernist belief in the future. But:

> Now that the present seems so full of woe . . . the profusion and frankness of our nostalgia [suggests] . . . a general abdication, an actual desertion from the present. (1974: 346)

There are a number of aspects identifiable here: the loss of trust in the future as it is undermined by instantaneous time and the proliferation of incalculable risks; the belief that social life in the present is profoundly disappointing and that in important ways the past was preferable to the present – there really was a golden age; the increased aesthetic sensibility to old places, crafts, houses, countryside and so on, so that almost everything that is old is thought to be valuable whether it is an old master or an old cake tin; the need nevertheless for a certain re-presentation of the past – to construct a cleaned-up heritage look suitable for the gaze of tourists; the interpretation of history through artefacts – an artefactual history – which in part conceals what the underlying social relations were and may write out the history of struggle which is often how social groups do remember socially (such as British miners and 1926); an increased significance of pastiche rather than parody as the past is sought through images and stereotypes which render the 'real' past unobtainable and replace narrative by spectacle; the belief that once history is 'heritage', that once the past has been commodified, it is made safe, sterile and shorn of its capacity to generate risk and danger, subversion and seduction; and the overall loss of belief in a historical subject that in seeking its own redemption will effect a universal redemption of humankind (see Relph 1976; Lowenthal 1985; Lowenthal and Binney 1981; Hewison 1987; Vergo 1989; Corner and Harvey 1991; Morris 1991; Roth 1992; Fentress and Wickham 1992).

Although this critique of heritage is well taken especially in Wright, there are some further points to note. First, quite a lot of heritage conservation has in fact resulted from popular resistance to demolishing derelict buildings or technologies; that people have reflexively sought to save 'their history'. Second, some heritage sites do indeed recognize the history of struggle and opposition, albeit in a somewhat romanticized fashion. Third, it must also be appreciated that people's understanding of history is anyway scarcely undistorted in the absence of the heritage industry – there is hardly such a strong distinction to be made between 'real history' and 'false heritage'. Fourth, the heritage critique rests upon a rather simple view of the nation and of what might reproduce such a nation – so that heritage in Scotland is linked to a much more open, pluralistic and fluid future than is the case in England (see Morris 1991). And finally, it is necessary to investigate how people actively use such sites as bases for reminiscence – as Mellor says, 'as the point of departure for their own memories of a way of life in which economic hardship and exploited labour were offset by a sense of community, neighbourliness and mutuality' (1991: 100). As Lowenthal concludes his magisterial text on *The Past is a Foreign Country*:

> Some preservers believe they save the real past by preventing it from being made over. But we cannot avoid remaking our heritage, for every act of recognition alters what survives. We can use the past fruitfully only when we realise that to inherit is also to transform . . . We must concede the ancients their place . . . But their place is not simply back there, in a separate and foreign country. (1985: 412)

Finally here, in the analysis of instantaneous time we shall return to Adam (1990: ch 7). She points out that humans come to understand themselves and their position in the world through metaphor. In pre-modern times the predominant metaphor was that of the animal, which was both familiar and distinct. In modern times the predominant metaphors have been the clock and various kinds of machinery and equipment. In the last few decades the limitations of these modern metaphors have become apparent, and she particularly criticizes the metaphor of the photographic lens. In its place she suggests two metaphors, the instantaneous time of the computer, and the hologram (see Rifkin 1987 on the former). We have already considered the former but the latter is perhaps less obvious. Holography is based on the principles of non-sequentiality, the individual-whole relationship and a multiperspectival focus. The information stored is not located in the individual parts but in their interference pattern: 'Any one part of a hologram contains, implies, and resonates information of the whole. The focus here is not on individual particles in motion, crossing time and space in succession, but on all of the information gathered up simultaneously' (Adam 1990: 159). The word hologram means 'writing the whole'. This makes the language of causal determinism inappropriate. The connections within a hologram are simultaneous and everything implies everything else. Holographic principles are particularly well-suited to a theory of instantaneous time.

We suggested earlier that there are two components of post-modern time, the instantaneous and the evolutionary. We will now turn to the latter but will deal with this rather briefly since more extensive discussion is developed in the following two chapters. There are three components of evolutionary time (see Rifkin 1987: Part 5 on the 'democratization of time').

First, Giddens suggests that the emptying of time and space establishes something of a single world, in which through the extraordinary institutions of the global media, people have begun at least to imagine themselves as part of a single 'community'. He says that 'humankind in some respects becomes a "we", facing problems and opportunities where there are no "others" ' (1991a: 27). We will examine such globalization further in chapter 11, particularly in the context of global environmental change. One consequence is that there is a re-evaluation of nature. This is increasingly viewed as much less disposable and indeed humans are thought to have an especial responsibility for its preservation. But this in turn entails the taking of a very long-term perspective, certainly one extending way beyond the lifetime of anyone presently living. As a consequence of such an imagination the interests of future generations are being partly considered and it is believed, particularly under the impact of new age and Green philosophy, that contemporary humans have an especial responsibility to take the longest of time horizons – to consider the evolutionary impact upon humans (and other sentient beings) of current and future forms of environmental degradation. This appears to be novel. In Bourdieu's classic study, the Kabyle demonstrate a particular awareness of the rhythms of nature (1990). But this is the outcome, not of an orientation into the almost unimaginable future, but of a relatively short time horizon and a kind of submission to the passage of time. Although the Kabyle demonstrate a dependence upon and solidarity towards nature, there is a nonchalant indifference towards time. This is a far cry from contemporary evolutionary time.

Second, there is a reassessment of place and various forms of resistance to the 'placelessness' generated by the modes of instantaneous time we have just adumbrated. Attempts are made to remake spaces as sites for 'strolling' and 'living in', not merely for passing through as fast as possible.

This seems to presuppose a glacial sense of time, to feel the weight of history, of all those memories of *that* place, and to believe that it will still be there in its essence in many generations' time. This attachment to place can occur in relationship to where one was born or brought up, to one's place of current residence, or to anywhere that one visits. Relph says that its phenomenology results from:

> improving geographical and social knowledge and especially because of a growing intensity of involvement and commitment. The result of such a growing attachment, imbued as it is with a sense of continuity, is the feeling that this place has endured and will persist as a distinctive entity even though the world around may change. (1976: 31)

Or as Lefebvre suggests, certain kinds of space unleash desire and this stems from two logics, of visualization and metaphorization (1991: 97–9). Time by contrast is not desired. One is not seduced by time. Relph also notes that places need not be positively viewed. There can be a 'drudgery of place', the sense of being inexorably tied to a particular place which cannot be escaped from and which seems to have been forever unchanging (certainly relatively compared with other places that are known about). Some places are heavy with time, but not necessarily those which have been subject to museumification (see Lowenthal 1985: 243–4).

Strolling in such places is almost itself subversive. The flâneur both seeks the essence of a place while at the same time consuming it – there is both consumption and subversion (Game 1991: 150). This way of walking, as though one had 'all the time in the world', 'is oppositional to the counting of time, Taylorism, the production process . . . scrutinising, detective work, and dreaming set the *flâneur* apart from the rush-hour crowd' (Game 1991: 150). It also seems that some places particularly invite visiting in order to stroll; they are as Sennett puts it 'places full of time' (1991: ch 7). It is like walking 'out of time' (see E. Wilson 1992 for a recent analysis of the flâneuse).

And finally, although we have noted the by-now well-known criticisms of the 'heritage industry', what those critics tend to ignore is how some re-presentations of history stemmed from popular resistance, from the fact that people were operating with a glacial conception of time (see Urry 1990c: ch 8). For example, the National Trust with over 2 million members is the largest mass organization in Britain and advocates a more or less unchanging Englishness. Much of the early conservation movement in the 1960s was plebeian in character, concerned to preserve railway engines, industrial archaeology sites, steam traction engines and so on. The preservation of some derelict coalmines in Wales resulted from pressure from local groups of miners and their families who sought to hold on to aspects of 'their' history, history here being long-term and involving projection from the past through the present way into the future. In Lancashire there has even been a campaign to conserve a slag heap from an extinct coal mine. These are all attempts then to assert a glacial conception of time, to challenge the profoundly disruptive effects of instantaneous time by reflexive subjects.

In conclusion, while the conflicts of modernity were fought out around the significance of clock-time, around efforts to expand or contract the length and sequencing of waged-labour, conflicts within disorganized capitalism have more focussed upon contradictory temporal principles, between concepts of time as instantaneous and as glacial. Such conflicts are fought at different spatial levels, from the local to the global, as we will see in chapter 11. Indeed we might speculatively suggest that one of the processes which activated the momentous recent transformations of eastern Europe was the inability of such countries to cope with the combined consequences of instantaneous and glacial time. Eastern Europe was stuck in modernist clock-time. The various countries were unable to respond either to the extraordinary speeding up of time and space especially as represented by instantaneous fashion, image and the micro-computer, or to the long-term concern with nature, the environment and the reassertion of history and place. Such countries thus seem in a time-warp, in a forced modernization around clock-time (note of course the appeal of scientific management to Lenin), and recent global processes have made such islands of simply modernist time unsustainable.

Before going on to consider globalization directly in chapter 11 one aspect of spatial-temporal change which has been briefly encountered in this chapter, namely the social organization and consequences of different modes of overcoming the friction of distance through travel, will be analysed.

PART 4

GLOBALIZATION AND MODERNITY

10

MOBILITY, MODERNITY AND PLACE

TRAVEL AND MODERNITY

Modern society is a society on the move. Central to the idea of modernity is that of movement, that modern societies have brought about some striking changes in the nature and experience of motion or travel. This has been explored by a number of seminal commentators who have discussed how modern cities have entailed quite new forms and experiences of travel, such as Baudelaire on the Haussmannization of Paris, Simmel and Benjamin on the rush of life in a metropolis such as Berlin, and Le Corbusier on the effects of the automobile on the urban experience (see Berman 1983, as well as Lash and Friedman 1992). There has been some analysis of the changing nature of transport between towns and cities, particularly following on the development of the railway (see MacKenzie and Richards 1986; Schivelbusch 1980; Thrift 1990b). Also there is some general analysis of the impact of new technologies of transportation and communication, especially those of the late nineteenth and early nineteenth centuries which dramatically increased 'time-space distanciation' (see chapter 2, as well as Kern 1983).

However, this literature does not connect together the changing forms of transportation *between* urban areas with the more general debates on the nature of modernity. Yet in many ways the modern world is inconceivable without these new forms of long-distance transportation and travel. It is not the pedestrian flâneur who is emblematic of modernity but rather the train passenger, car driver and jet plane passenger.

Moreover, in much of the writing about those types of travel there is a technological determinism. Since each new system of transport appears in retrospect to be technologically superior to its predecessor, so it is argued that people quickly and readily found ways to travel which took full advantage of each latest technology. However, this is simply not the case.

As important as new transportation technologies have been, it is organizational innovations which have, in certain cases only, ensured that the new technologies have been economically successful and culturally emblematic of the modern world. Some examples of new technologies which illustrate the importance of organizational innovation include: the early railways where the railway companies did not at first realize the potential leisure and holiday possibilities of the new technology; the railways and steamships in the late nineteenth century which required the innovation of Thomas Cook's voucher system to develop their international market potential; the jet engine which required the innovation of the inclusive holiday organized by the tour operators to be fully successful; and Concorde which was a superior technology but where no corresponding innovation occurred within the travel industry. Transportation technologies therefore necessitate corresponding organizational transformations in order to be successful and to become dominant within a given historical period.

Another way of putting this is to emphasize the crucial significance of the *social* organization of travel. This is after all a huge industry, and it is the industry which serves to organize the *modern experience*. None of the accounts of organized capitalism or Fordism consider the changing ways in which travel is socially organized, a matter which as we have just seen is far more than merely a question of new transportation technologies. Travel should not be seen as merely a 'derived demand'.

One interesting point to note is that the company which is conventionally taken to stand for twentieth-century organized capitalism, namely Ford, actually made *cars* – that is, means of transportation. But the crucial question to ask is why did people come to think, on the incredible scale that has occurred, that journeys by car were necessary, desirable and safe? How were those car journeys socially organized, involving as they did novel and potentially risky ways of transcending space? And what has been the relationship between those journeys and those undertaken by other means of transport or other forms of communication, especially those not involving transformed presence-availability through actual mobility? Following Luhmann we know of the importance of communication but this is only half the story (see 1989). It is also necessary to consider the nature of mobility, this being understood as a generic category subsuming various modes of transportation, commuting, travel and tourism, and of its interrelationships with diverse forms of communication.

Thus there are two points to emphasize here: first, that the paradigmatic modern experience is that of rapid mobility often across long distances; and second, that this mobility is not something that has simply existed but it had to be developed and *organized*. And in some ways the 'social organization of the experience of modernity' is as important an achievement of Western capitalism as is the social organization of the production of manufactured goods. Indeed in some ways it is more significant since in the longer term it has affected everybody, unlike manufacturing whose impact is relatively confined to the maximum of 50 per cent of the workforce actually employed in manufacturing in most of the advanced societies.

Why then has there been so little investigation of mobility, of these diverse forms of transportation and travel? This neglect stems from certain academic prejudices: of analysing manufacturing rather than services, of production rather than consumption, of 'work' rather than 'leisure', of structure rather than mobility, and of work-related mobility rather than leisure-mobility, of seeing it as essentially derived from other more substantial processes. The absence of a sociology of travel illustrates the salience of these various priorities within the 'academy'.

Some of these limitations are now coming to be evident, especially within the new 'urban studies' literature. The causes and consequences of mobility are increasingly seen as central determinants of the nature of urban life, especially though for various categories of the middle class. This has been classically shown in the case of nineteenth-century Paris and twentieth-century Los Angeles (see Berman 1983 on the former; Soja 1989 and Davis 1990 on the latter). But there are two further aspects of the study of mobility that have not been much investigated and which need analysis: the social organization of mobility *between* urban areas; and the effects of such movement on people's subjectivity.

First, certain organizational innovations have transformed the nature of travel in ways which have often been highly socialized. Some examples of this include Thomas Cook and Son who beginning in the 1840s were the first major travel agent and tour operator (see Brendon 1991); the growth of monumental city centre hotels in the late nineteenth century normally located by major railway stations (see Mennell 1985); the inter-war development of holiday camps providing far superior facilities for mass tourists (see Ward and Hardy 1986); and the post-war growth of packaged holidays that made foreign travel available to the mass market in northern Europe (see Urry 1990c).

The recent work on risk can begin to provide the explanation of why these innovations have been so significant. As we saw in chapter 3 one of the key features of modernity is that social relations are disembedded from local contexts of action (see Giddens 1991a: 209). Disembedding means the 'lifting out' of social relations from local involvements and their recombination across larger spans of time and space. Such disembedding depends upon trust. People need to have faith in institutions or processes of which they possess only limited knowledge. Trust arises from the development of expert or professional knowledge, which gives people faith, including the forms of transport which convey them through time-space. Mobility depends upon the development of trust in professional experts who have devised systems of mass travel and transport which at least initially limit the risks involved.

In the next section we will describe the role of Thomas and John Cook in the middle to late nineteenth century. It was they who first constructed professional expertise in travel and tourism, expertise which made journeys relatively risk-free. Many of the early travellers with Thomas Cook eloquently describe his role in reducing risk and generating trust, even where the travel involved what now seem to be quite staggering feats of endurance, danger and uncertainty. Sontag similarly writes of how photography is a risk-reducing stratagem enabling people: 'to take possession of space in which they are insecure . . . The very activity of taking pictures is soothing and assuages general feelings of disorientation . . . Unsure of other responses, they take a picture' (1979: 9–10).

Giddens makes some further comments about the growth of this kind of professional expertise. First, it involves a de-skilling of day-to-day activity. In the case of travel many people have lost that knowledge of local routes and environments which enabled often quite extraordinary distances to be travelled by foot (this is well shown in the diaries of the Lake District poets). Second though, there is no straightforward 'colonization of the life-world' by such expert systems. There is always a tension between expert knowledge and that held by lay actors. In the case of travel the availability of an enormous written literature and many clubs and societies means that people are by no means only dependent upon travel industry professionals for appropriate information. Third, it also does not follow that impersonal forms of knowledge simply dominate personal experience. Rather the very nature of the person or the personal is transformed in modernity. This can be seen in a number of ways: that trust is not something simply given but has to be worked at and continually negotiated and contested; that in modernity people have to learn to 'open' out to others who are often geographically very distant – to develop something of a cosmopolitan attitude; and that the self participates in the collective forms of reflexive knowledge that modern societies have about themselves. Giddens concludes: 'We can live "in" the world of modernity much more comprehensively than was ever possible before the advent of modern systems of representation, transportation and communication' (1991a: 211).

Further, living 'in' the world of modernity is even more complex than this account suggests, since these modern systems generate quite novel forms of experience which cannot be reduced to concepts of time-space distanciation. Rapid forms of mobility have radical effects on how people actually *experience* the modern world, on the very production of subjectivity. These effects include the way that landscapes and townscapes have come to be typically viewed as through a frame; that landscape consists of a series of swiftly passing panoramas; that nature can and should be subdued, or flattened or even bypassed; that new public areas should develop, such as railway stations, airports, hotels and so on, where novel norms of social life apply; that mobility has to be socially organized and involves various forms of surveillance and regulation (especially true with car travel); that new forms of social distance have to be learnt within the confined contexts of mobility (generalization of Simmel's blasé attitude); that social life has to be timetabled and hence the importance of clock-time, the telephone, diaries, secretaries, the Filofax, answermachines and so on; that people come to gaze at many different places which can be compared and juxtaposed with each other; and that multitudinous 'place-myths' develop which organize people's knowledge of themselves and of their social world (see Shields 1991a; Ousby 1990; MacKenzie and Richards 1986; Schivelbusch 1980; Urry 1990c; Morris 1990; Rojek 1993).

Mobility is therefore responsible for altering how people appear to experience the modern world, changing both their forms of subjectivity and sociability and their aesthetic appreciation of nature, landscapes, townscapes and other societies. Such mobility according to MacCannell has the effect of legitimating modern society, of making it appear in a benign and accessible form (1976). Many of the objects of the tourist gaze are functionally equivalent to the objects of religious pilgrimage in traditional society. When people travel (make a pilgrimage) to the great tourist sites of the modern world, MacCannell suggests that they are in effect worshipping their own society.

However, there is one crucial aspect of the modern which MacCannell ignores, namely reflexivity. We have discussed in chapter 3 how a central aspect of contemporary societies is that people are able to monitor and evaluate their society and its place within the world, both historically and geographically. The more that societies modernize, the greater the ability of increasingly knowledgeable subjects to reflect upon their social conditions of existence. We have characterized this as 'reflexive modernization'.

We have also argued that such reflexivity is not only cognitive or normative but also aesthetic. This involves the proliferation of images and symbols operating at the level of feeling and consolidated around judgments of taste and distinction about different natures and different societies. Such distinctions presuppose the extraordinary growth of mobility, both within and between nation-states. This can be described as the development of an aesthetic 'cosmopolitanism' rather than a normative and cognitive 'emancipation'. Such a cosmopolitanism presupposes extensive patterns of mobility, a stance of openness to other and a willingness to take risks, and an ability to reflect upon and judge aesthetically between different natures, places and societies, both now and in the past. Indeed the present fascination with history (the 'heritage industry') is not only the product of the capitalist commodification of history but also an element of an aesthetic reflexivity.

We have therefore argued: first, that in the 'West' over the course of the nineteenth and twentieth centuries a reflexivity about the value of different physical and social environments has been established (see Ousby 1990); second, that this reflexivity is partly based upon aesthetic judgments and stems from the proliferation of many forms of real and simulated mobility; third, that this mobility has served to authorize an increased stance of cosmopolitanism – an ability to experience, to discriminate and to risk different natures and societies, historically and geographically; and fourth, that the social organization of travel and tourism has facilitated and structured such a cosmopolitanism. Mobility, especially that which is non-routine and non-work related, is thus not the trivial and peripheral activity which it has been presumed to be within the academy. It is central to aesthetic reflexivity and becomes ever more important as 'culture', 'history' and the 'environment' are increasingly central elements of contemporary north Atlantic rim societies.

We will now consider whether there are changes taking place in contemporary tourism and travel and hence in the cosmopolitan attitude. This issue will be approached obliquely via Bauman's analysis of the role of knowledge and intellectuals in modernity and postmodernity (1987). In modernity the emphases are upon an orderly totality, the search for control and an increasing and irreversible knowledge of the natural order. Intellectual work is that of 'legislating', making authoritative statements which arbitrate. This authority to arbitrate is legitimized by superior knowledge. Various procedural rules ensure truth, moral judgment and artistic taste. Modernity produces intellectuals as 'legislators', experts who, as we saw above, minimize risk and generate trust for the mass of the population.

Postmodernity by contrast proclaims the end of certainty. There are an unlimited number of models of order, each of which makes sense in terms of the practices which validate it. Validation is particular to a given practice, including modernity's own criteria which can be seen to be historically specific. Systems of knowledge can only be evaluated from within, from inside a given, local or specific framework (Bauman 1987). Intellectual work is no longer that of a legislator but of an 'interpreter'. It consists of translating statements, facilitating communication and preventing the distortion of meaning. What remains for intellectuals to do is to interpret meanings for those outside and to mediate communication between different provinces of meaning. Systems of meaning are moreover roughly equivalent to each other, not higher or lower in some hierarchy of truth, value or aesthetics.

How does this shift relate to the previous discussion of modernity and mobility? First, there have been comparable changes in the forms of professional expertise supplied by the tourism and travel industry. There has been a shift away from the didactic legislator who instructed visitors where to look, what to look for, and when to look, the attitude as found in Baedeker's guides, Michelin's guides or the Guide Bleu (see Barthes 1972). Instead visitors are encouraged to look with interest on an enormous diversity of artefacts, cultures and systems of meaning. None are presumed to be superior and the main role of the 'expert' is to interpret them for the visitor. Indeed whole new bodies of expertise have developed which are precisely concerned with 'interpretation' (see for example the journal *Heritage Interpretation*). At the same time it is presumed that everyone can gain some benefit from travel. No longer is it assumed that only certain kinds of people have the prior knowledge, values or aesthetic insight to benefit from mobility. Provided people can pay, everyone (in certain north Atlantic countries and Japan) is entitled to travel and to engage in for example the democratic and promiscuous practices of photography (see Sontag 1979). Likewise travellers can visit museums which these days may contain artefacts of almost every sort, from mundane household objects to instruments of torture, from representations of manual work to those of elite occupations (see Urry 1990c: ch 6). In each case the professionals are more concerned to interpret, and not to evaluate.

Thus far there are grounds for thinking that the shift from modernity to postmodernity is partially at least reflected in developments in travel and tourism. However, what will be explored below is whether the historic shifts in mobility patterns appear to correlate with the more wide-ranging changes from organized to disorganized capitalism. Does the social organization of travel parallel the shifts which take place in other spheres of economic and social life?

To begin with it should be noted that the study of mobility demonstrates the implausibility of the conventionally understood distinction between production and consumption and the allocation of personal travel and transport to the latter category. Mobility can only be understood as consumption on the dubious grounds that production exclusively refers to the manufacture of material goods. There are three problems with this: first, such an allocation ignores what goods are in fact used for – that is, what is *produced* as a result and how this may in fact be a service to be consumed (such as a meal, a journey, an entertainment); second, there are a variety of 'productions' or 'products' involved in any economic activity, including at least material objects, services, data, ideas and images; and third, 'mobility' not only is a service to be consumed but also may involve all of these different 'products', especially the production of images.

What then about the shift from organized capitalism to disorganized capitalism? Have there been particular changes in the social organization of mobility which mirror or even presage changes which have taken place in other spheres or sectors of north Atlantic societies? In Lash and Urry (1987) we argued that capitalism moved through a series of historical stages: liberal, organized and disorganized. Each of these appears to be associated with a particular dominant configuration of travel and tourism. These are set out below, together with the pattern identifiable in pre-capitalist societies, in table 10.1.

Paralleling these developments in travel have been some associated developments in the nature of 'hospitality'. Heal suggests that open hospitality is practised in those societies characterized by a presumed naturalness of the host–guest relationship, a belief that the outsider is deserving of special generosity, an elite ethos in which honour attaches to acts of beneficence, an ideology of generosity to all comers, and a social system in which gift-exchange transactions remain structurally significant (1990: 389). In the early modern period in England (1400–1700) she shows

Table 10.1   *Capitalism, tourism and travel*

Stage	Configuration
Pre-capitalism	Organized exploration
Liberal capitalism	Individual travel by the rich
Organized capitalism	Organized mass tourism
Disorganized capitalism	The 'end of tourism'

that there was a relatively sophisticated law of generosity to defined guests, but increasingly there was separation between hospitality to the prosperous and alms given to the poor. And most of the other conditions of open hospitality were much less visible in England than elsewhere. Already a fairly extensive system of inns and alehouses had developed by the end of the sixteenth century. Hospitality was becoming commercialized and being taken out of the context of the household (Heal 1990: ch 5). Heal argues that this resulted from the existence in England of an economic and social structure which proved very responsive to the forces of the market, even to the marketizing of hospitality.

If then pre-capitalist societies contain a mixture of open and commercialized hospitality, liberal capitalism ushers in a much more commercialized pattern, linked especially to the railway. In London for example many grand hotels were constructed in the late nineteenth century. And these were very much public places open to all with money. They were public places for wealthy men and women, to see and be seen in. Such hotels necessitated new forms of rationalized organization so that meals could be produced much more rapidly (see Mennell 1985: ch 6 on the innovations introduced by Escoffier). By the end of the century organized mass tourism was well on its way in Britain. Some key organizational innovations will be described in the next section, as hospitality and travel became not merely commercialized but packaged and organized. In the third section the nature of such services in disorganized capitalism will be outlined. It will be shown that if disorganized capitalism involves the dominance of non-material forms of production (especially images), then in many ways this is what tourism has always involved. Does this therefore mean that tourism presages disorganized capitalism? Indeed is it therefore the 'industry' which is paradigmatic of disorganized capitalism as automobiles were of organized capitalism? If disorganized capitalism involves the predominance of culture, consumption, the global, the local and concern for the environment, then all these characterize contemporary travel and hospitality. Disorganized capitalism then seems to be the epoch in which as the specificity of tourism dissolves, so it comes to structure and hegemonize contemporary social and cultural experience. Disorganized capitalism then involves the 'end of tourism'. People are tourists most of the time, whether they are literally mobile or only experience simulated mobility through the incredible fluidity of multiple signs and electronic images.

What are the effects of such processes, of the 'end of tourism'? (We are not suggesting of course that mass tourism is no longer important.) On the one hand, contemporary techniques are such that everywhere can be manufactured, that simulacra of almost every sort of place can be produced and are, and that people are surrounded by an increasingly similar network of signs which are manufactured and remanufactured according to the dictates of the market. These processes appear homogenizing, reducing differences between places through the proliferation of essentially the same signs and images. Yet on the other hand, although it is true that images of place are endlessly manufactured, what is produced is a quite striking diversity, what one might call a 'manufactured diversity'. And people are not simply 'cultural dopes' since they have to do more work, semiotic work, in making sense of what Featherstone terms 'the aesthetic-ization of everyday life . . . the rapid flow of signs and images which saturate the fabric of everyday life' (1991: 67). Consumption becomes more skilled as in a sense everyone becomes a hermeneutist, reading and interpreting the extraordinarily rich and diverse array of signs and images which can be assembled and reassembled almost instantaneously.

THE EMERGENCE OF ORGANIZED TOURISM

The growth of organized or mass travel and tourism in the late nineteenth century was only possible because of a number of economic, technical and social developments. In Britain these included rising real incomes; rapid urbanization with pronounced levels of class segregation; new transportation technologies such as the railway and the steamship; the systematizat-ing of work and the increased regulation of the hours and conditions of labour; novel methods of facilitating and organizing travel; and the development of a number of romanticized 'place-myths' to attract potential travellers.

Travel therefore came to be both organizationally possible and desired by large numbers of people, beginning with the more affluent sections of the English working class. Beginning in industrial Lancashire in the second half of the nineteenth century, there was the extensive development of the habit of taking seaside holidays. Particularly important in enabling this pattern to develop and in providing an organizational form which per-mitted local communities to travel and stay together were voluntary organizations, of pubs, churches and clubs (see Urry 1990c: ch 2). Walton summarizes: 'The unique Lancashire holiday system was thus based on working-class solidarity in retaining and extending the customary holidays . . . Only in Lancashire . . . did whole towns go on holiday, and find resorts able to look after their needs' (1978: 39; and see 1983).

It is well known that marked distinctions of social tone came to be established between various resorts. Different 'place-myths' served to construct a new cultural geography of Britain. Places became identified with the nature not of their permanent population but of their transient visitors (see Perkin 1976; Shields 1991a; as well as Thrift 1990b on the massive changes in travel and transportation in the nineteenth century).

However, in the following we shall concentrate not on the relatively well-examined development of seaside resorts but rather on how middle- and upper-class travel came to be organized. Attention will be focussed upon two developments: the origins of mass overseas travel via what we would now call travel agents and tour operators; and the manner in which place-myths came to be constructed around literary and natural phenomena.

Probably the most impressive economic organization to emerge in nineteenth-century Britain was Thomas Cook and Son, which began in effect in 1841. By 1868 Cook's had organized the travel of some 2m people (and it is now the largest travel organization in the world). There is some justification for suggesting that twentieth-century organized capitalism might be better described as 'Cookism' rather than 'Fordism'. In the following we shall summarize some aspects of the development of one of the most important organizations of the last century and a half. It pioneered ways of organizing travel which have literally made modernity possible. As Brendon says, Thomas Cook generated 'a mass movement of human beings which dwarfs the great migrations of the past and sustains the largest industry in the world' (1991: 3).

There had of course been travel well before Cook's, most noticeably medieval pilgrimages and the European Grand Tour (see Urry 1990c: 4–5; Ousby 1990; Brendon 1991: ch 1; Towner 1985). Nevertheless the number of 'tourists' (a term dating from the later eighteenth century and implying a circular journey; see Ousby 1990: 18) rapidly developed after the end of the Napoleonic wars. But in many ways it is the year *1841* that deserves to be remembered as marking the beginning of modern mass travel, even of modernity as a sociological-geographical phenomenon (see Brendon 1991: 12). This was the year in which a *national* railway timetable, Bradshaw, first appeared. The first European hotel built as an integral part of a railway station was opened in York. The company that is now Cunard started the first Atlantic steamship service. The Wells Fargo Company, which became part of American Express, began in 1841. And most important of all, the very first 'tour' was organized by Thomas Cook, taking some 400 or 500 'excursionists' by train from Leicester to a temperance meeting in Loughborough and back again. The previous decade had also seen both the entry of the term 'sightseeing' into the English language and the crucial invention of the camera.

Cook realized very rapidly the potential of the railway. At the end of the meeting in Loughborough he called for one more cheer for 'Teetotalism and Railwayism' (Brendon 1991: 8). He saw the railway as a democratic and progressive force: 'Railway travelling is travelling for the Million; the humble may travel, the rich may travel . . . To travel by train is to enjoy republican liberty and monarchical security' (quoted in Brendon 1991: 16). However, this democratic revolution required new forms of social organization. The railway companies did not at first realize the economic potential of the mass, low-income passenger market. And although 1842 saw the establishment of the Railway Clearing House, and 1844 the passing of Gladstone's Railway Act which obliged the railway companies to make provision for the 'labouring classes', it required a specialist to organize journeys over several lines and to issue tickets at favourable rates. This is what Cook achieved: to simplify, popularize and cheapen travel, beginning with his first professional excursion to Caernarvon, Snowdon and Liverpool in 1845. Brendon notes that he soon attracted titles such as 'the eponymous hero . . . of travel' and the 'Emperor of Tourists' (1991: 17). There were large increases in the share of railway traffic accounted for by second- and third-class passengers (see Thrift 1990b: 464).

Cook saw travel as a crucial part of the 'rational recreation' movement, to provide wholesome and enjoyable activities as an alternative to drink and the pub. Travel 'provides food for the mind; . . . it promotes universal brotherhood . . . and . . . the broad distinctions of classes are removed without violence or any objectionable means' (quoted in Brendon 1991: 31–2).

He also began to realize that tourism requires certain myths to attract visitors. Cook commenced various 'Tartan tours' in 1846 following on from the remarkable popularity of the novels and poems of Sir Walter Scott. Cook commented that Scott 'gave a *sentiment* to Scotland as a tourist country' (quoted in Brendon 1991: 38). Cook also began to provide handbooks indicating the kinds of things that people should look at and how they should be interpreted, sometimes even the novel that should be read before experiencing a particular sight. Cook's tartan tours also on occasions drew on certain kinds of nostalgia, especially for the old coaching days before the age of the steam railway.

We will now summarize certain further innovations and developments initiated by Cook's which served to produce what might be called 'organized tourism' by the beginning of the twentieth century in Britain.

First, Cook made a major contribution to the success of the Great Exhibition of 1851. This can be interpreted as the first national tourist event ever staged. A staggering 6m visits were made to see the 38,000 exhibits in the Crystal Palace, although the population at the time was only 18m. Cook organized the travel of 165,000 (see Brendon 1991: ch 4 on the following). This was the first occasion that large numbers of working-class people had travelled by train, as 'excursionists', and in particular travelled to London. Since this Great Exhibition occurred only three years after 1848 there was anxiety about the temporary presence in the capital of large numbers of northern workers. However, the event passed without confrontation so demonstrating the way that mass mobility was becoming normal in a modern society. Ousby suggests that Cook and his excursionists were 'demonstrating their readiness to become tourists instead of revolutionaries' (1990: 91). Cook wrote in 1854: 'To remain stationary in these times of change, when all the world is on the move, would be a crime.

Hurrah for the Trip – the cheap, cheap Trip!' (quoted in Brendon 1991: 65). One important effect was that some at least of the barriers between social classes became less marked. Tourism necessarily brought about an intermingling of social classes, something Cook thought entirely beneficial. He considered that opportunity of free movement was a centrally important human freedom. Also Cook's was particularly important in facilitating the travel of large numbers of women in Victorian Britain. Amongst those undertaking Cook's tours women outnumbered men. His company often enabled single women to travel unchaperoned.

Second, Cook had also initiated organized travel overseas beginning with visits to Paris, Brussels and Cologne. In Paris Cook considered that Haussmann's building of a modern city had produced a very attractive tourist site (see Brendon 1991: 78). Cook also did much to domesticate the Swiss Alps after they had been popularized by the Romantics and then by John Ruskin, who referred to the Alps as the 'link between heaven and earth', the 'seen walls of lost Eden' (quoted in Brendon 1991: 81). Hotels were developed which were clean and commodious, and Switzerland was turned into an institution. Cook's tourism helped to produce the clean, well-ordered and efficient modern Switzerland. Interestingly though such tours of Switzerland produced outraged responses from the London establishment. Terms of abuse for such tourists included 'Cook's Vandals', 'Cook's Hordes', a 'low, vulgar' mob, like 'mental patients' and like 'convicts' who could no longer be sent to Australia. Leading intellectuals such as Macaulay and Ruskin joined in the snobbish abuse (see Brendon 1991: 89–95). However, from the 1860s onwards Cook and Son began to arrange the travel for wealthier clients, particularly as the places visited became ever more exotic, and the class prejudice abated. Thomas Cook's son John was the main orchestrator of the 'voyage from vulgarity' as the firm came to organize tourism throughout the world (Brendon 1991: 183).

Third, Cook's was responsible for a number of innovations which transformed travel from something that was individually arranged and full of risks and uncertainty into one of the most organized and rationalized of human activities based on considerable professional expertise. Cook's innovations included the provision in advance of tickets for different forms of transport or for transport in different countries; the supplying of guides and other material indicating appropriate sites and scenes to view; the initiation of conducted tours first in Britain and then in Europe and finally worldwide; the negotiation of block bookings and payment by a single bill for transportation and later for accommodation; the development of the railway coupon, paper tickets bound together so enabling passengers to book and pay for their entire journey in advance; the similar hotel coupon bought in advance in one's own currency and accepted by establishments approved by Cook's; the initiation of Circular Notes which were exchangeable at hotels, banks and ticket agents and were an ancestor of traveller's cheques; the organization of luggage so that it was sent in advance and did not have to travel with the passenger across Europe; and the initiation of

Independent Inclusive Travel with an all-inclusive modestly priced tariff and the itinerary organized in advance. Mark Twain no less pronounced that:

> In bygone times travel in Europe was made hateful and humiliating by the wanton difficulties, hindrances, annoyances, and vexations put upon it by ignorant, stupid and disobliging transportation officials . . . But Cook has remedied all these things and made travel simple, easy, and a pleasure. (Quoted in Brendon 1991: 247; and see 110, 163, 168, 253)

So far then we have shown that some striking changes took place in the social organization of travel. We have additionally noted that Cook's was also concerned to draw upon the historical, literary and cultural myths surrounding particular places. This issue will now be discussed in more detail, via the example of Stratford-upon-Avon which has been part of the English tourist map for two centuries. How did that come about? How and why do certain kinds of myth come to attach themselves to particular places? How are processes of wider communication responsible for transforming patterns of travel?

Stratford-upon-Avon has become a staggeringly successful tourist centre. It is the home of an organized evangelical religion, what Holderness terms 'bardolatry' or the worship of Shakespeare (1988; and see Ousby 1990: ch 1). Though there had been a few isolated prophets, bardolatry scarcely existed before 1769 when David Garrick organized the first Shakespeare Jubilee in Stratford. Unlike some of his contemporaries Shakespeare had been buried in an obscure grave in Stratford Church, while the Puritanism of the early seventeenth century meant that his plays were not performed even in Stratford.

It was only in the eighteenth century that his plays came to be widely staged. And it was then that some of the key features of the bardolatrous pilgrimage were established. These resulted from opportunism, greed and free competition between local entrepreneurs. As Holderness says: 'The past itself was the site of a furious battle between competing appropriators, rival enterprises within a cultural industry' (1988: 5). The reverential pilgrims found that, although the medieval streets were still preserved, the illumination of a timeless genius was fatally flawed by forgery and fabrication. Examples of fabrication and the generation of apocryphal stories included the identification of the house said to be that lived in by Shakespeare's mother; falsely identifying chairs reputed to be Shakespeare's; the invention of the story of the Bard's death following a drinking bout with fellow poets; the identification of a particular tree that he supposedly spent a night under after an earlier drinking bout; the story of his arrest for poaching deer; the identification of his birthplace and Anne Hathaway's cottage although both buildings have been reconstructed on a number of occasions (see Ousby 1990: ch 1; Holderness 1988 on the 'bardolatrous trade').

By the twentieth century the Shakespeare Birthplace Trust had eliminated the most blatant of these fabrications through monopolizing the forms of representation of 'Shakespeare'. Together with the Royal Shakespeare Company and the research institute, the Shakespeare Centre, it has come to provide an authoritative construction of 'Stratford-upon-Avon'. Shakespeare's birthplace has become sacralized, a hugely significant object of worship and pilgrimage. Tourists to Stratford engage in a ritualized passage to a sacred site in search of a particular mythical figure, namely William Shakespeare. And in searching for that myth the tourist encounters merely a set of reconstructed buildings lodged in between all the characteristic features of late twentieth-century life.

One of these buildings is known the world over as Anne Hathaway's cottage. There are two problems with this name: first, Anne Hathaway may or may not have lived here; and second, she may or may not have married 'Shakespeare' (Holderness 1988: 6). But this building has been an object of pilgrimage and worship for generations. And this is part of the reason why its value is assured. It is not that this particular building necessarily did have any particular connection with anyone called 'Shakespeare'. It is rather that it has been presumed for many years to have such a connection and the building continues to be celebrated because millions of other people have done so in the past. The building is a sign which stands for all those other tourists who have similarly worshipped the same building and have engaged in the same acts of pilgrimage. Moreover, such buildings represent an unimpeded image of an idealized historical past. The buildings of Stratford stand for an 'idealised "English" past, picturesque and untroubled, [which] is thus embodied and incorporated into commodities for sale to national and international markets' (Holderness 1988: 6).

It is thus clear that the history of Stratford is incomprehensible without the process by which a particular Shakespeare-myth has come to be constructed and sold to tourists in Britain and worldwide. The maintenance of this shrine to Britain's greatest writer is hugely dependent upon tourism. Culture and tourism are inseparable. And this is reinforced by some further points made by Holderness: first, that much of our contemporary knowledge of Elizabethan theatres has been provided by overseas travellers (or tourists) who handed down the understanding of the Elizabethan 'Golden Age' to later scholars; second, the establishment from the 1570s onwards of purpose-built theatres in and around London presupposed that considerable numbers of tourists would be drawn to the metropolis – where drama had become the prestigious possession of the national state; and third, Shakespeare belonged to a class of entrepreneurs within the culture industries concerned to separate theatre (high culture) off from social life and hence to produce tourism as a necessary adjunct of culture. Holderness summarizes:

> That class helped to establish a cultural pattern in which every spectator is encouraged to become a tourist: who may well undertake a lengthy journey to a

metropolitan theatre, who is required to attend at the dramatic event with reverence . . . and who returns with a souvenir programme as a mnemonic preservation of a sacred experience. (1988: 10)

These days such a person is more likely to return with a souvenir T-shirt of an important cultural event.

During the late eighteenth and nineteenth centuries numerous other place-myths developed. They became attached to particular kinds of social space, spaces that could only exist with large numbers of visitors (such as the London theatres mentioned above). The characters of such spaces were premised upon the tourist gaze, that they were to be gazed upon with curiosity by many outsiders who had often travelled long distances to gain a view. It is a characteristic of modernity that many social spaces develop which are wholly or partly dependent upon visitors; and those visitors are attracted by the place-myths that surround and construct such spaces, that transform material objects into cultural objects. Such places may be central to the culture of a society, such as London or even Stratford-upon-Avon, or they may be attached to otherwise peripheral spaces, what Shields terms 'places on the margin' (1991a).

Examples of such place-myths which have developed over the past couple of centuries in Britain include those attached to various country houses, such as Blenheim or Chatsworth, which were said to be too commercialized even in the *eighteenth* century (Ousby 1990: ch 2); various ruins such as Stonehenge or the Gothic remains of places like Fountains Abbey which became very popular in the Victorian period (Ousby 1990: ch 3); the resort of Brighton whose place-myth consists of royal scandal, the beach as a zone of carnival and pleasure, and dirty weekends, excitement and violence (see Shields 1991a: ch 2); the Lake District which is both a literary shrine like Stratford and also a shrine to the sublime quality of nature – *Wordsworth's Guide to the Lakes* symbolizing both aspects (see Wordsworth 1951; Ousby 1990: ch 4; Andrew 1989: ch 7); and much more recently the 'North' of England which represents the working class, community, industry, outdoor pursuits – with the development of urban and industrial tourism and even a 'real' Coronation Street to visit (see Urry 1990c: ch 6; Shields 1991a: ch 5).

So far we have outlined some of the mechanisms which led to the nature of twentieth-century tourism. We will now summarize some of the key elements of such an 'organized tourism' mainly drawing on British material. In order to simplify presentation we will consider firstly working-class domestic tourism, and then middle- and upper-class foreign tourism (noting that such a distinction leaves out various other elements). Since much of the working-class pattern revolves around the seaside resort the account of this will be very brief because much of the material is summarized elsewhere (see Hern 1967; Walvin 1978; Walton 1978; Walton 1983; Ward and Hardy 1986; Urry 1990c; Cross 1990; Shields 1991a).

The first point to note is that the seaside holiday had emerged in the late nineteenth century in the context of the rationalization of work by employers. Work was developing into more of a time-bound and space-bound activity, separated off from play, religion and festivity. Work developed into a differentiated sphere, valued for its own sake and not seen merely as a remedy for idleness. The emerging industrialists struggled to impose more of a discipline on their newly constructed labour force (see Pollard 1965). Tough and unfamiliar rules of attendance and punctuality were introduced, with various fines and punishments. Campaigns were mounted against drinking, idleness, blood sports and holidays. Many fairs were abandoned as the ideas of 'rational recreation' became more widespread (see Rojek 1993).

As work was rationalized so the hours of work were gradually reduced. Particularly important was the attainment of the half-day holiday, something that became celebrated as 'la semaine anglaisc' (Phelps-Brown 1968: 173). The achievement of longer breaks, of week-long holidays (normally unpaid), was pioneered in the north of England, especially Lancashire. Employers in part came to decide that: 'The total closure of a mill at a customary holiday was preferable to constant disruption throughout the summer, and there were advantages in channelling holiday observances into certain agreed periods' (Walton 1981: 255).

However, it is clear that the main reason for the gradual extension of a specific time-period of the week-long break came from the workforce, especially from its more affluent sections. They saw such a time-period as providing the context in which they could develop their autonomous forms of recreation – and as Walton argues: 'Custom dictated that holidays should be taken *en masse* and celebrated by the whole community' (1978: 35). During the twentieth century there was strong pressure from the unions to implement holidays with pay. Although some agreements had been signed by 1920 little further progress was made in extending this in the inter-war period. Various private members' bills failed until a Select Committee was set up in 1937 and a bill passed in 1938 (although its impact was mainly in the post-war period; see Urry 1990c: 26–7).

By the 1940s then a major tourist industry had developed in Britain which had become particularly 'geared to dealing with people *en masse* and had become highly efficient and organized at attracting and coping with armies of working people from the cities' (Walvin 1978: 107; and see Brunner 1945). There was widespread acceptance of the view that going on holiday was good for one, that it was the basis of personal replenishment. Holidays had become almost a marker of citizenship, a *right* to relaxation and pleasure (see Cross 1990: 9).

The holiday experience was remarkably regulated. The holiday was based on the time-zone of a week (see Colson 1926). It was almost impossible to book mid-week. Visitors were informed when they were to eat, what they would eat and exactly when they could use different facilities. This organization was taken to the furthest limits in the holiday *camp*, particularly with the 'luxury' camps started by Butlins in 1936. Relatively luxurious facilities were provided, what Ray Gosling calls a 'veritable Beveridge of leisure' (Ward and Hardy 1986: 60). Interestingly though when the first camp was opened the visitors appeared bored and Butlin concluded that holidaymakers needed organization. The famous Redcoats were invented – they would 'lead, advise, explain, comfort, help out, and generally make themselves the closest thing to holiday angels on earth' (quoted in Ward and Hardy 1986: 63). Ward and Hardy concluded that 'from one camp to the next the mix was identical – the same pattern of entertainment, the same diet, the same type of accommodation, the same weekly routine' (1986: 161).

We will now illustrate these various points by referrring to the Mass Observation research carried out in 1937–8 in Blackpool, the closest there is to empirical research on 'organized tourism' (see Cross 1990). Blackpool was the world's first specialized working-class resort. It claimed 7m visitors a year in the 1930s, making it the largest resort in Britain and probably in the world at the time. The August Bank Holiday in 1937 saw the arrival of an astonishing 425 special trains (see Walton 1990). More significantly though most of the population of what was called 'Worktown' (Bolton in fact) spent their week-long holiday nearby at Blackpool. Mass Observation summarizes:

> Although over 50 per cent before the holidays say they want something different, less than 10 per cent in practice break away from the conventional industrial holiday which for most means Blackpool . . . The Worktowner . . . goes to the places where the crowds are . . . Blackpool is the most crowded and noisiest resort . . . Going to Blackpool for holidays is becoming as much a habit as going into a town-centre pub on a Saturday night. (Cross 1990: 49)

Extraordinary numbers of people sat in very little space on the beach. And contrary to the place-image of Blackpool it was 'Merriment and noise, not sex' that people were seeking on their visits there (Cross 1990: 191).

Another feature of Blackpool was the amusement park. Blackpool's most extensive was the Pleasure Beach to the south of the centre, in part designed by Joseph Emberton. He commented as follows:

> The origin of the amusement park is in the village fair . . . the village fair was mobile and therefore simple in structure. But with the arrival of transport the inlander began to visit resorts, and it was now possible to introduce something more advanced in structure. The fair, a relic of the Middle Ages, was noisy and filthy. Our problem is that of clearing-up, *of putting order into chaos*. (Quoted in Cross 1990: 98; emphasis added)

We will now turn to middle- and upper-class travel and tourism. Particular attention will be devoted to the inter-war period when the myth of individual travel finally collapsed under the weight of organized tourism. In the British case one could identify 1915 as a key date. This is when the British government introduced the modern passport with the passport photograph. Although this now seems an inevitable component of mobility it caused shock and scandal at the time. As Fussell notes:

There are other unprecedented contributors to the modern neurosis . . . But the passport picture is perhaps the most egregious little modernism . . . The tradition of the passport picture as a demeaning and shame-making corollary of modern experience has been constant since 1915. (1980: 26–7)

Fussell goes on to describe how much of the inter-war literature was concerned with the problem of mobility across frontiers and the uncertainties engendered about the passport and its picture. The general sense of frontiers as menacing formed a large part of the inter-war imagination, as especially writers and their friends travelled by train across Europe and by liner across the Atlantic (see 1980: 24–37). Indeed Fussell suggests that since frontiers imply fragmentation and division, shifting around and repositioning, so 'modern' literature implies 'a concern with current space instead of time or tradition. All imply an awareness of reality as disjointed, dissociated, fractured (1980: 36).

Many literary works in the inter-war period were permeated by the 'travel spirit', and to a lesser extent with lamenting the shift from such travel to mere tourism. Some of the many examples where the 'travel spirit' can be found include Conrad's *The Rover*, Isherwood's *Goodbye to Berlin* and *Mr Norris Changes Trains*, Forster's *Passage to India*, Sassoon's *The Heart's Journey*, Greene's *Stamboul Train*, Orwell's *Down and Out in Paris and London* and *Homage to Catalonia*, Hemingway's *Green Hills of Africa*, and Macaulay's *Going Abroad* (see Fussell 1980 for much more elaboration). These writers in part are concerned to capture the nature of pre-modern travel, although many of the literary metaphors of the time were based on the modern forms of transport, of railways and steamships.

Indeed Fussell sees steamship travel and the grand hotels as the final expression of individual travel which was soon displaced by the plane and the airport designed in the international modern style (see Mennell 1985; and Watkins 1984 on hotels). Fussell sees the high point of organized tourism to be 1957 when safe and efficient uniform international jet service becomes firmly established (1980: 45; the first packaged air holiday occurred in 1949). It is the moment when everything is provided for the passive consumer who does not need to do any work (or *travail*) – the 'travel sense of place was going to yield to the touristic phenomenon of placelessness' (1980: 70). The packaged or inclusive tour was the ultimate in such organized tourism.

TOURIST SERVICES AND DISORGANIZED CAPITALISM

We have already noted that from the 1950s to the 1980s organized tourism took the form of the packaged or inclusive holiday to the Mediterranean. This holiday pattern had a tremendous impact in Britain because of the early emergence of integrated companies, the tour operators, who made spectacular use of two new technologies, jet transport and computerized booking systems (see Urry 1990c: 48). In 1980 about 5m such holidays were sold in Britain. This figure reached a peak of 11m before dipping to 9m by the end of the 1980s. The British tour operators had thus created an exceptionally successful mass market for overseas tourism. They were able to sell their holidays considerably below the prices charged by similar companies in other European countries with the result that such holidays were far more common in Britain than elsewhere (see Milner 1987; Harlow 1990).

However, the recent drop in the number of packaged holidays sold not only in Britain but also on the continent, and symbolically shown by the spectacular collapse of the International Leisure Group (ILG) in March 1991, is symptomatic of a more general cultural shift. There seems to have been a move away from the organized tourism characteristic of the modern period, to a much more differentiated and fragmented pattern of mobility which one could almost describe as the 'end of tourism' per se. ILG was a company which together with its subsidiaries, Intasun and Club 18–30, had become synonymous with the cheap packaged holiday.

The 'end of tourism' may seem an improbable claim, given the size and scale of the travel and hospitality industries worldwide (so much so that in Blackburn in Lancashire a Chaplain for Tourism and Leisure has recently been appointed!). Certainly by the end of the century, tourism will be the largest industry in the world in terms of both employment and share of world trade (although some of the estimates of tourism-related employment are without doubt over-ambitious; see Johnson and Thomas 1990 for a recent review). There has been an annual growth in international arrivals of 4 per cent throughout the 1980s (see Latham 1990).

The suggestion that there may be an 'end of tourism' stems from an analysis of the social relations actually involved in tourism. In chapter 5 it was argued that the cultural industries are characterized by an exchange of finance for intellectual property rights. It is this exchange that gives to those industries some common characteristics and which structure many of the typical disputes and conflicts of interest that arise. In particular as we saw such industries are characterized by high levels of design-intensivity.

The travel and tourist industries are similarly design-intensive and hence proliferate signs and images. There are three principal exchange relationships: the exchange of finance for temporary rights to occupy mobile property; the exchange of finance for temporary possession of accommodation and facilities located away from people's normal place of residence and work; and the exchange of finance for visual property.

The first of these is what is involved in travel. Passengers purchase rights to occupy a certain normally small space which is then propelled from one place to another. The rights are like those involved in renting accommodation, except that the space is not static and the length of time involved is always short and recognized by both parties as temporary. Sometimes what is rented is a specific space (reserved cabin) and sometimes merely a space within a mobile area (unreserved bus seat).

The second exchange relationship occurs where finance is exchanged for temporary rights of possession of spaces away from home, such as hotel beds, restaurant tables or chairlifts. Again it is recognized that the possession is short-term and temporary, while the quality of the rented space may be superior to that available at home. The availability of such spaces has occurred through the reorganization of private and public spaces, as we noted in the first section when discussing the marketization of hospitality.

The third exchange occurs where finance is exchanged for visual property, for being able to look at and record to memory landscapes and townscapes even though one does not actually own the property being looked at or even have temporary rights of possession. Elsewhere it has been argued that it is this ability to 'gaze' at unfamiliar sights that is the defining characteristic of tourism (see Urry 1990c). Tourism presupposes the exchange of finance for temporary visual property which visitors can acquire when they have temporary rights of posssession of spaces away from home.

This set of distinctions has been introduced in order to explain why we might be moving towards the 'end of tourism'. The first kind of exchange has recently become much more common. In recent years there has been a very marked increase in the number of journeys that people take and in their length. Some of the factors bringing this about include the increased size of urban areas and hence of commuting distances; the development of long-distance commuting; the huge growth of business and conference travel; the growth in car ownership and of car journeys; and the development of high-speed trains and jet planes which have significantly reduced journey times (increased time-space compression). The effect of all this means that travelling on holiday has become a much less significant event and does not serve to demarcate off being a tourist from many other kinds of social activity which also involve travel.

The second kind of exchange has become somewhat more common, particularly with the growth of visits for business, conference and academic purposes.

However, the most significant change has occurred with regard to the third form of exchange, of finance for visual property. Here there has been a quite stunning transformation. The development of the mass media has led to the massive proliferation of visual images and to the 'aestheticization of everyday life' (see Featherstone 1991). The purchase of images has become extraordinarily widespread and means that the purchase and consumption of visual property is in no way confined to specific tourist practices. Almost all aspects of social life have been aestheticized. This means that visual consumption can occur in many different contexts, shopping, eating and drinking, sport, leisure, education, culture and so on. To take one paradigmatic example, the publicity material for the West Edmonton shopping mall in Canada demonstrates this very clearly:

> Imagine visiting Disneyland, Malibu Beach, Bourbon Street, the San Diego Zoo, Rodeo Drive in Beverly Hills and Australia's Great Barrier Reef . . . in one weekend and under one roof . . . Billed as the world's largest shopping

complex of its kind, the Mall covers 110 acres and features 628 stores, 110 restaurants, 19 theatres . . . a five-acre water park with a glass dome that is over 19 storeys high . . . Contemplate the Mall's indoor lake complete with four submarines . . . Fantasyland Hotel has given its rooms a variety of themes: one floor holds Classical Roman rooms, another '1001 Nights' Arabian rooms, Polynesian rooms . . . (Travel Alberta undated)

In recent years visual consumption has become exceptionally more widespread and pervasive. This reflects what elsewhere we have termed 'de-differentiation'. The modern period was one of vertical and horizontal differentiation, the development of many separate institutional, normative and aesthetic spheres, each with their specific conventions and modes of evaluation and with multiple separations (and legislating hierarchies) of high and low culture, science and life, auratic art and popular pleasures and so on (see Urry 1990c: 83–5; Lash 1990b).

Postmodernity involves de-differentiation. There is a breakdown of the distinctiveness of each sphere and of the criteria which legislate within each vertical dimension. There is implosion as a result of the pervasive effects of the media and the aestheticization of everyday life. Cultural spheres are much less auratic. There is a shift from contemplation to consumption, or from 'high culture' to the 'high street' (we are grateful to N. Whiteley here). Some of the differences between the cultural object and the audience dissolve as legislation is replaced by interpretation. And finally postmodernity problematizes the relationship between representations and reality. Since what we increasingly consume are signs or images, so there is no simple 'reality' separate from such modes of representation. What is consumed in tourism are visual signs and sometimes simulacrum; and this is what is consumed when we are supposedly not acting as tourists at all.

The significance of visual consumption can be seen in the pervasive tendency to produce 'themed' environments, such as the townscapes of elsewhereness found in the West Edmonton mall. Eco terms these apparently real and authentic environments 'travels in hyper-reality' (1986). The surfaces of such places appear more 'real' than the original. Eco summarizes: 'Disneyland tells us that technology can give us more reality than nature can' (1986: 44). Two contexts in which such simulated reality is commonplace are shopping centres and world fairs. In both people are encouraged to gaze upon and collect the signs and images of many cultures – to act as tourists, in other words (see Shields 1991b; Urry 1990c: ch 7). This is made possible by the most extreme form of 'time-space compression', what one might term global miniaturization.

Contributing to this proliferation of images has been the huge growth in choice for consumers. This can be seen by briefly considering the extraordinary development over the past few decades of the social practice of eating out, partly of course resulting from changes in social class and gender relations (as we saw in chapters 6 and 7). Twenty or thirty years ago this practice tended to be confined for most people to the holiday period.

Apart from work canteens it was fairly rare for people to go out to restaurants for pleasure unless they were on holiday. Now this practice has become commonplace in the 'West', having been taken to the furthest extreme in the USA (the contrast with eastern European countries is particularly noticeable). There is one restaurant for every 1,000 people in the average American city, with around 10,000 restaurants in Chicago, for example (Pillsbury 1990: 6; and see Finkelstein 1989 more generally). The number of restaurants in the USA doubled between the 1960s and the 1980s (Pillsbury 1990: 103). Likewise there are said to be at least 100 different restaurant cuisines in the typical American city. As Pillsbury says: 'The great migrations, the acculturalization process, and the food technology explosion have brought exotic new foods to virtually all communities at low cost' (1990: 130). Many of these new cuisines have been tried out first in California which has provided a kind of testing ground for cuisines even when they are apparently based on other regions of north America (see Pillsbury 1990: 86 on the very varied restaurant activity ratios in different American cities).

This range of consumer alternatives can also be seen in the extraordinary number of countries that can now be visited throughout the world, particularly because of the role of international agencies, such as the World Bank, the Inter-American Development Bank, the United Nations Development Programme, the Organization of American States, and the European Community (Pearce 1989: 45–8). Choice can also be seen in the remarkable range of holidays that can now be taken even within say Britain. These include Xenophobic Weekends, Bleary Breaks, Murder Weekends, Bureaucratic Breaks, Soccer Weekends, City Breaks in Wigan, Boring Weekends in Grantham and visits to 'Belfast – a Hibernian Rio'! And finally, over the past few decades there has been an incredible increase in the range of museums to visit, either while away or within one's own area. It seems that a new museum opened every week or so in Britain in the 1980s. Some of the more improbable museums worldwide include a pencil museum in Keswick, Auschwitz, the Leprosy Museum in Bergen, a dental museum in London, a shoe museum in Street, a chemical museum in Widnes, a prisoner-of-war museum in Singapore, Granada's Coronation Street museum in Manchester, as well as a possible museum on Robben Island featuring Nelson Mandela's former prison cell (see Urry 1990c: ch 6; Rojek 1993).

Partly this proliferation of choice stems from certain kinds of resistance on the part of consumers. The mass holiday in which all consumers were treated as relatively similar has apparently declined in popularity. Poon for example talks of the shift from 'old tourism', which involved packaging and standardization, to 'new tourism', which is segmented, flexible and customized (1989). The Marketing Director of British Airways writes for instance of 'the *end of mass marketing* in the travel business . . . we are going to be much more sophisticated in the way we *segment* our market' (quoted in Poon 1989: 94; see Pearce 1989: ch 4).

This shift away from mass packaged tourism might be said to reflect the rather broader change towards 'post-Fordist' consumption. Table 10.2 shows how this can be characterized, as well as giving examples drawn from the tourism industry. Clearly there are many examples which illustrate the claim that tourist developments are increasingly taking a 'post-Fordist' pattern. We will consider three here: the development of 'alternative tourism' in some developing countries; the emergence of the what might be called the 'post-tourist'; and the recent transformation of Thomas Cook as the company has sought to 'think globally, and act locally'.

Table 10.2   *Post-Fordism and tourism*

Post-Fordist consumption	Tourist examples
Consumers increasingly dominant and producers have to be much more consumer-oriented	Rejection of certain forms of mass tourism (holiday camp and cheaper packaged holidays) and increased diversity of preferences
Greater volatility of consumer preferences	Fewer repeat visits and the proliferation of alternative sights and attractions
Increased market segmentation	The multiplication of types of holiday and visitor attractions based on lifestyle research
The growth of a consumers' movement	Much more information provided about alternative holidays and attractions through the media
The development of many new products, each of which has a shorter life	The rapid turnover of tourist sites and experiences because of fashion changes
Increased preferences expressed for non-mass forms of production/consumption	The growth of 'green tourism' and of forms of refreshment and accommodation which are individually tailored to the consumer (such as country house hotels)
Consumption as less and less 'functional' and increasingly aestheticized	The 'de-differentiation' of tourism from leisure, culture, retailing, education, sport, hobbies

First, opponents of high-volume, large-scale tourist development have recently come to recommend 'alternative' tourism for developing countries, whose economic, social and environmental fabric has been most devastated by mass tourism. Such alternative tourism has a number of emphases: on values of self-determination, authenticity, social harmony and preservation of the existing environment; on a fairer partnership between local people and entrepreneurs *and* outside agencies; on a smaller scale of development and greater use of local techniques, materials, architectural styles and skills; and on giving back to the area facilities, resources and quality of the environment from the rewards which the tourism will generate (see Pearce 1989: 101–6). Countries where such developments have become of some importance include guest house development in Papua New Guinea, bungalows in French Polynesia, 'eco-tourism' in Belize and 'integrated rural tourism' in Senegal. Rather more generally certain environmental effects of mass tourism, particularly the coastline of high-rise hotels and apartments, is now heavily criticized. In Spain for example the authorities are seeking to prevent future developments close to the coastline and indeed to demolish those buildings put up without appropriate planning permission. Many countries have now come to see that more environmentally conscious wealthier tourists actually seem to be attracted by developments which do not involve obvious social and environmental destruction. This is even now happening in what was the Mediterranean site most renowned for the devastating effects of mass tourism, namely Majorca. Tourists from other countries can in effect be part of the reflexive processes within a society and contribute to the partially conscious evaluation of its future trajectory. Organizations such as Tourism Concern or Green Flag International are endeavouring to induce in tourists a reflexivity about their holiday choices, to evaluate the impact of tourism upon the physical, built and 'natural' environment. It is hoped that tour operators in particular will respond by selecting destinations which minimize such deleterious impacts.

Second, it has been suggested that a component of contemporary tourism consists of a cultural paradigm which can be termed 'post-tourism' (Urry 1990c: ch 5 for more detail). There are a number of components of such a paradigm. The post-tourist does not have to leave his or her house in order to see many of the typical objects of the tourist gaze. With TV and the VCR most such objects can be gazed upon, compared, contextualized and gazed upon again. The typical tourist experience is anyway to see *named* scenes through a *frame*, but this can now be experienced in one's living room at the flick of a switch, and it can be repeated again and again. It can be suggested that there is little difference between seeing a particular view through the viewfinder of one's camera and through the television set. The latter of course causes far less environmental damage. Tourism through virtual reality may be the twenty-first-century solution.

Moreover, the post-tourist is aware of change and delights in the multitude of choice. He or she is freed from the constraints of high culture on the one hand, or low culture on the other. The post-tourist delights in being able to move easily from one to the other and in the contrasts between the two. For the post-tourist all the world is literally and metaphorically a stage. He or she can find pleasure in the multitude of games that can be played and in the paradox of choices between them. There is no need to make a fetish out of the correct evaluation, and everything is there to be interpreted. Indeed most important of all, the post-tourist knows that he or she is a tourist, and that tourism is merely a series of games with multiple texts and no single authentic experience. The post-tourist knows that he or she will have to queue time and time again, that there will be difficulties of foreign exchange, that the glossy brochure is a piece of pop culture, that the apparently authentic local entertainment is as socially contrived as the ethnic bar, and that the quaint traditional fishing village could not survive without the income from tourism. The post-tourist is ironic and cool, self-conscious and role-distanced. Simple pleasures of the sort that were once experienced at the 'unsophisticated' seaside, whether at Clacton or the Costa Brava, become harder to experience.

Finally, we will return to Thomas Cook and briefly consider how it is attempting to think globally and act locally (see Brendon 1991: ch 19). Cook's had maintained its tradition of public service throughout the 1950s and 1960s. The company was run by conservative managers who had risen up through the company and were highly knowledgeable about travel, but not about finance or marketing. Cook's failed to develop a credit card (unlike American Express); the company did not manage to compete with the increasingly large package holiday competitors (such as Thomson which first appeared in Britain in 1965); and Cook's failed to integrate vertically by buying up airlines or even investing in 'time charters'. By 1970 the state-owned Cook's was coming under heavy criticism, for its rigid civil-service style of rank and promotion, for its lack of modern technology, and for its non-commercial image. Against this however, Cook's had a reputation for reliability, for service, for staff commitment, training and loyalty, and for professionalism. The Midland Bank bought Cook's in 1972 particularly for what was at the time the seventh most recognizable trademark in the world (Cook's was sold in 1992 because of the huge difficulties of its parent company).

Many changes have been put into effect in the past two decades, particularly in terms of technology. Travel is an information-rich industry and yet in the 1970s Cook's still operated with exceptionally cumbersome bureaucratic procedures. In 1980 Cook's introduced a Travel Information Bank which now gives all branches access to 40,000 computerized pages of up-to-minute travel data. Other computer systems include a private data communications system, a computerized hotel reservation system, and an automatic sales system. The previously nineteen grades of status were reduced to four. Cook's is now a global company with a network based in 140 countries. A new global management system has been developed, to foster both cohesion and devolution. Control is maintained from the centre by means of standardized computer equipment but regional managers are said to be able to exert local initiative. Cook's still attempts to provide customized holidays for individual customers living in particular places. In the future much of this customizing will be effected by the individual holidaymaker who will sit in front of a computer terminal, see videos of possible destinations, and then make choices which will be processed automatically.

It now seems that Cook's decision not to integrate vertically has in fact been a wise one. It has specialized in the retailing and financing of travel, or more precisely of information about travel. Most of the time it has not owned hotels, airlines or other forms of transport.

CONCLUSION

Two ideas discussed elsewhere in this book are that of 'time-space compression', and the simultaneous 'visualization' and 're-enchantment' of consumption. Such notions are both centrally important to the analysis of travel and tourism. 'Time-space compression' is the sense of overwhelming change in space-time dimensionality discussed in chapter 2. In the nineteenth century, Heine for example talked of the tremendous foreboding that he experienced with the opening of the rail link between Paris and Rouen: 'Even the elementary concepts of time and space have begun to vacillate. Space is killed by the railways. I feel as if the mountains and forests of all countries were advancing on Paris' (see D. Harvey 1990: 426). A commentator in Britain said that: 'As distances were thus annihilated, the surface of our country would, as it were, shrivel in size until it became not much bigger than one immense city' (see D. Harvey 1990: 426). By the late twentieth century it is not only a question of time-space compression through actual travel that has been annihilating space but also simulated travel and the extraordinary proliferation and circulation of image and sign. Such signs and images are overwhelmingly visual and come to be attached to all sorts of objects and services. Consumption then is 'symbolic', not simply or predominantly functional or determined by price. Shields characterizes this as the 're-enchantment' of commodities – that mass produced commodities reacquire the aura of symbolization (see 1991b).

There are three points to note here. First, many of the symbols which 'enchant' commodities are connected with place and travel, and this is so because of the central importance of visual or iconic symbolization to contemporary consumption. It should incidentally be noted that the premises of travel agents have been visually redesigned to look much less like banks and more like fashionable furniture shops (and indeed are often now called travel *shops*).

Second, consumers are less taken in by the illusions of mass consumerism than once was the case. We have already adumbrated the nature of the post-tourist. Likewise we may hypothesize the post-shopper, who is partly ironic or cool, able to play at the multiple games of consumption and aware of the arbitrary nature of exchange-value (see Shields 1991b). Consumers are bombarded with images which reflect 'time-space compression' – a 'manufactured diversity'; they have to become skilled at interpreting such images, doing semiotic work; and they are increasingly reflexive about their society, its products and images, albeit images which are themselves part of what one might term a semiotic society.

And third, the reactions to the progressive annihilation of temporal and spatial barriers are complex and do not simply entail their embrace. Harvey suggests that the more global interrelations become, so the world's population increasingly clings to place and neighbourhood, to region and ethnicity, to tradition and heritage. However cosmopolitan people apparently are:

> There is still an insistent urge to look for roots where image streams accelerate and become more and more placeless . . . The forebodings generated out of the sense of social space imploding in upon us . . . translates into a crisis of identity. Who are we and to what space/place do we belong? (D. Harvey 1990: 427)

Time and space, identity and image have thus been ineluctably transformed by these various forms of mobility during modernity and postmodernity.

11

GLOBALIZATION AND LOCALIZATION

There was this Englishman who worked in the London office of a multinational corporation based in the United States. He drove home one evening in his Japanese car. His wife, who worked in a firm which imported German kitchen equipment, was already at home. Her small Italian car was often quicker through the traffic. After a meal which included New Zealand lamb, Californian carrots, Mexican honey, French cheese and Spanish wine, they settled down to watch a programme on their television set, which had been made in Finland. The programme was a retrospective celebration of the war to recapture the Falkland Islands. As they watched it they felt warmly patriotic, and very proud to be British. (R. Williams 1983: 177)

This chapter is concerned with the argument of Raymond Williams, and also that of Daniel Bell, that contemporary nation-states are now too small for the big problems of contemporary social life and too big for the small problems (R. Williams 1983: 197–9; Bell 1987: 116). In particular, we will address a set of issues that has been encountered in various places in this book, the nature of the global relations which characterize the contemporary world and their implications for nations, regions and localities. Mostly this discussion has focussed upon economic transformations and we will provide our own analysis of economic change in the first section on money and finance. However, we will mainly be concerned with the global implications of two other crucially significant areas of contemporary analysis: the question of the environment and the ramifications of 'thinking globally and acting locally'; and the nature and implications of a 'global culture' for nationality and locality.

It is clear that in recent years major changes have occurred which have increased the *global* character of the relationships affecting these various domains of human practice. There has been the growth of 'global governance', so that it is increasingly difficult to think of the nation-state as still the appropriate power-container of important economic and social relationships (Held 1991; Giddens 1981). Chernobyl showed that environmental disasters know no national boundaries; the 1973 oil price increase demonstrated that national economic policies cannot be conducted independently of international transformations; and the latest Olympic Games show that up to one-half of the world's population could imagine themselves as part of the same 'cultural' experience. These developments raise two questions. First, just what happens to conventional theories which are largely organized around the key concept 'society'? Are there 'societies' and if so what are they? And indeed are there national economies any more? Is there still a *British* economy? Second, even so, may the importance of international/global processes have been somewhat overstated? Are there not *two* parallel processes here proceeding side-by-side, of globalization and localization? And if that is so then what are the implications for the kind of appropriate theory that ought to be developed?

It has been presumed in the past two centuries in the 'West' that societies are coterminous with nation-states and that a democratic state comprises a community which governs itself and determines its own future (Held 1991, 1993). A democratic state presupposed a 'national community of fate'. Various recent transformations have rendered such a community (or society) as no longer sovereign (see on the following Appadurai 1990; Crook et al 1992; Held 1991; Jacques 1990; Jessop 1992; Keohane 1984; Sklair 1990).

These transformations include, first, the development of transnational practices which transcend individual nation-states through generating immense flows of capital, money, goods, services, people, information, technologies, policies, ideas, images and regulations. Such transnational practices or flows do not simply derive from single countries, nor even from one particular geographical area. Such economic, political and cultural practices are relatively independent of each individual nation-state.

Second, these practices do not of course originate from all parts of the world equally. Globalization is really advanced capitalist globalization, since a hegemonic role is played by the north Atlantic rim countries and Japan in the development of these non-national transnational practices. Such transnational practices depend upon particular localized sites for their development and influence (Hollywood, City of London).

Third, national governments are increasingly unable to control cross-border flows generated by these transnational practices. Because of global interdependence there is a decrease in the effectiveness of policy instruments which would enable states to control activities which occur within their borders. Territories are less obviously governed by nation-states, which have tended to reduce the range and type of activities undertaken. There has been a marked 'hollowing' out of the state.

Fourth, within such a highly interconnected global order, many of the traditional domains of state activity cannot be fulfilled without international collaboration. This involves dealing both bilaterally with other states and more importantly with transnational practices. Accordingly states have had to increase the level of their political integration with other states in order to offset the destabilizing consequences of global interconnectedness. Examples include GATT, the IMF, the World Bank, the OAS, the EC and OPEC.

Fifth, a putative pattern of global governance has developed, with transnational bureaucracies, international representative organizations and very many international agencies. The rights and obligations, powers and capacities of states ave been redefined. Held summarizes: 'The state's capacities have been both curtailed and expanded, allowing it to continue to perform a range of functions, which cannot be sustained any longer in isolation from global or regional relations and processes' (1991: 208).

Sixth, as a result a range of different kinds of socio-spatial entities are emerging which are not nation-state societies of the north Atlantic sort. There are societies which are not coterminous with the nation-state; there are nation-states that are barely societies; and there are societies that are not states in the 'conventional' sense. No longer are nation-states obvious and legitimate sources of authority over civil society. In the future many different kinds of socio-spatial grouping will emerge which will not fit into the nation-state society framework. And of course away from the north Atlantic rim, the nation-state model has never been dominant.

Finally, the Westphalian model of democracy, that the world consists of and is divided into sovereign states with no superior authority, is becoming outmoded and may be replaced with a model of cosmopolitan democracy (see Held 1993). In this the basic building blocks will be groups and associations, produced by a global order consisting of multiple and overlapping networks of power, and which have access to a cosmopolitan civil society.

These are clearly a wide-ranging set of transformations, produced by various global flows. Luard has gone on to suggest that if there are no longer coherent national societies then an 'international society' is coming into existence (1990). Two processes have combined to reduce the differences between 'societies' and such an 'international society'. First, contemporary 'societies' are just so diverse in terms of beliefs, conditions, interests and the ways of life found within them, that it is hard to say that they have any common characteristics. Second, there is the apparent reduction in 'size' of international society through 'time-space compression' of various flows, which greatly enhances people's interconnectedness *and* their consciousness of this interconnectedness. Such an international society is characterized by the following features: that power is both dispersed yet where found is highly concentrated; that there are relatively few formal relationships between individuals so that the authority exercised by international organizations remains fairly weak and unpredictable; that there is an undeveloped sense of solidarity especially that fostered vis-à-vis others; that there are few international organizations to which people feel allegiance or loyalty; and that there is little consensus about the society and how it may develop. These features would also of course characterize many 'national' societies, such as the contemporary USA or the former USSR. What is important to note is that it is increasingly difficult to identify clearly identifiable and discrete societies, that some hybrid forms of society which are neither national nor global are developing, and that there is an increasing interconnectedness of societies worldwide which render as outdated certain theories of democratic rights.

The best example of these developments is post-1992 Europe. The EC is not a conventional nation-state since, among other features of supposed states, it does not possess centralized powers of physical coercion or concentrated-coercive powers of military organization (see Mann 1986: 26–7 on this distinction). But in certain respects the EC has similarities with the way that some national societies have been developing, societies characterized by diverse, complex and only partially overlapping networks of power (see Bryant 1991). 1992 represents an ambitious effort to combine a neo-liberalist deregulation of non-market impediments to trade (through the four freedoms), together with an older Federalist European project of establishing a powerful regional bloc (see Ross 1992: 56).

Two points about the EC should be noted. First, it possesses powers to constrain individual societies (increasingly with 'qualified majority' voting) and to pronounce as illegal the actions of individual states. There has been an accretion of powers hitherto located in national parliaments (such as policies with regard to competition, trade, exchange rates, science, technology and research: see Cooke 1990; Held 1991). However, many of these national powers had already been weakened through the emergence of the inter-state and global flows discussed elsewhere in this book. At the same time national states will acquire new powers over their neighbours through various EC directives. In the late 1980s Jacques Delors began trying to fill in the new European space with a set of clear European state-building policies. As Ross argues: 'The new Europe would be an "organized space" between its nations and the global market' (1992: 62). To an extent some of the 1992 changes with regard to financial flows will actually increase state regulation over money and finance, compared with the exceptional level of deregulation of the 1980s (especially of course in the UK; see Leyshon and Thrift 1992).

Second, the EC increasingly acts at the behest of individual regions or localities, some of whom deal direct with Brussels/Strasbourg and bypass the individual society/nation-state. Around fifty Eurocities and separate German Länder are directly represented at the level of the EC. In some cases regions in different societies have formed coalitions to present a stronger case to the EC for sectoral support. Some indication of this can also be seen in the advocacy by the German Greens of the need to establish a neutral and decentralized 'Europe of the regions', or as the SNP (Scottish National Party) argues for 'independence within Europe'. An interesting illustration of these trends can be seen in the 'Four Motors' agreement of 1988 to develop economic co-operation between Baden-Württemberg, Rhône-Alps, Lombardy and Catalonia (see Cooke 1990). Dawkins argues that 1992:

> will only work on the back of co-operation between regions, irrespective of what passes between national capitals. Ironically, the creation of a single market is encouraging the region . . . to try to pull more decision-making power from a central government which it has always felt has interfered too much in local affairs. (1990; see *Regional Studies* 26 (4): 1992 for analysis of 1992 and its effects on regional development)

The principle of subsidiarity is one which directly poses the issue of regional/local powers as opposed to the powers of national states (and especially the Council of Ministers). What is emerging in Europe, at least after the Single European Market Agreement, is a new form of political domination and representation. This can be described as a 'disorganized state': pluralist with many different groups represented; fragmented with no single centre of authority (Commission, Council of Ministers, Parliament); competitive with different levels, agencies and institutions openly competing for policies and funds; anti-corporatist with no strong peak organizations, particularly not labour; and regionalist with strong interfaces between the centre and the 'regions' (see Ross 1992 on the 'variable geometry' of 'Europeanization').

Finally here, we will consider the importance of these regional and local processes by briefly returning to the issue of flexible specialization. Hirst and Zeitlin (1990) argue that *The End of Organized Capitalism* suffered from three particular deficiencies with regard to this thesis: that flexible specialization should not have been seen as reactive but as something that is actively and strategically devised; that as a strategy it is generated within particular *local* areas through inter-firm patterns of cooperation; and that ignoring the Italian case, with its weak macro-economic policies, it means that there is a failure to analyse the case of successful establishment of localized patterns of inter-firm collaboration.

Their argument demonstrates that important economic effects follow from processes which are essentially local or at least non-national (as is argued in *The End of Organized Capitalism*). Hirst and Zeitlin go on to argue that there have to be 'political, normative and organizational means to create relationships which foster [local] cooperation and coordination' (1990: 44). They talk of the need to institutionalize trust and coordination between locally proximate companies. Appropriate policy thus necessitates a local or 'regional . . . "public sphere" in which firms, labour interests, officials and politicians can interact and cooperate' (1990: 44).

However, there are two deficiencies of their enthusiastic embrace of flexible specialization: over-emphasizing the cooperative character of such local relationships; and minimizing the role of global economic and political changes which have made some such flexibly specialized localities possible (for more debate on local policy responses see Harloe et al 1990). Also to be noted is the way in which the literature on flexible specialization is itself important in helping to generate new localities characterized by such practices – a good example of reflexive modernization.

However, their main emphasis is on the importance of local processes. They provide *prima facie* grounds for thinking that localization is centrally important in contemporary societies. The following are some of the processes that appear to be heightening significant differences between local areas or localities: the increased ability of large companies to subdivide their operations and to locate different activities within different labour markets; the breaking up of previously relatively coherent regional economies; the competition between local states for jobs, the growth of international differences and the localizing of regional policy; the decreasing tendency for voting patterns to be nationally determined and the increased importance of so-called 'neighbourhood' effects; the enduring significance of symbols of place and location, particularly with the decline in the popularity of the international modern style of architecture; and the resurgence of locally oriented culture and politics (shown in the UK according to Hebdige 1990 in both the miners' strike and acid house parties, Hebdige 1990, but see Robins 1989a). These considerations do not imply that localities are necessarily unified, or that the outcomes are exactly what local residents had demanded. Broadly speaking one can say that local powers tend to be reactive, to resist decisions from centres, and to devise institutional and policy responses through identifying niches in existing forms of social organization.

Amin and Thrift also point out that the local and the global intersect in different ways in different places, and that there is great spatial variability in the robustness of the local conditions which permit growth (1992). In other words, global processes can in a sense be pinned down in certain localities and hence can become the basis for self-sustaining growth in those places. They also note that the conditions which permit local agglomerations to develop are increasingly understood to be as much social/cultural as they are economic/institutional. This can be seen in three ways (see Amin and Thrift 1992 on the following).

First, there is a problem of interpretation. The globalization of certain sectors means that entrepreneurs in specific localities need to develop means of interpreting and representing such global processes. A local production complex can provide the context within which discourses and accounts develop by which these apparently distant systems (cf Giddens' expert systems) can be made sense of and interpreted. Second, localities provide contexts for social interaction. And such interaction is needed to gather information, to make agreements and coalitions, to reinforce relations of trust or implicit contract, and to develop rules of acceptable behaviour. And third, places enable product and process innovation to take place in relatively decentralized systems. Localities enable entrepreneurs where there is a critical mass of knowledgeable people to enable gaps in the market to be identified, new uses of technology to be developed, and rapid responses to be initiated.

In this book we have outlined many ways in which economic change is being socially-spatially transformed. In the first section we will briefly analyse one further aspect of the socio-spatial transformation of the economic, that is of money itself. It will be shown that such transformations of money and finance involve a complex dialectic of global *and* local processes – that the globalization of finance itself rests upon particular localizations, especially on how the City of London in the past provided the context for localized interpretation, interaction and innovation in financial services (see Amin and Thrift 1992 also on the following).

MONEY AND FINANCE

We will begin here by adopting and developing Susan Strange's distinction between relational and structural power (1988). The former refers to the classic neo-Weberian paradigm of the power of agent A to get B to do something that would not otherwise take place. The latter is the power to shape the overall structures within which states, political, economic and cultural institutions, and national classes and so on have to operate and make decisions. In the later nineteenth century structural power was centred in Britain; in the inter-war period there was no hegemon and this it is said explains the particular intensity of the depression; in the post-1945 settlement structural power was centred in the USA – it was the hegemon through the particular combination of coercion and consensus; while in the current fin-de-siècle structural power is not centred in and working through any particular country. It is free-floating and serves to dislocate or disorganize all societies, although obviously some much more than others (for a useful review, see Foster 1989). Disorganized capitalism is thus *dis*organized because there is no single hegemon (Gilpin 1987). No one country exerts structural power and as a result certain 'international public goods' may not be supplied. There is no particular reason in a new world order for particular countries to take responsibility, or indeed to have the individual powers, to deal with the global problems that will be periodically generated (such as the break-up of the Soviet Union, let alone the implosion of Yugoslavia). Indeed one might define disorganized capitalism as being constituted by 'global problems and only local solutions'.

Particularly important for Strange is not the structural power over the economy, but the more specific structural power over *credit*. This is distinct not only from control over production but also from the role of money merely as a means of circulation (1988: 30; and see Altvater 1990). It is this power to create credit that has been the major basis for de-territorializing (or de-nationalizing) the world economy. What has been set up is a system of credit, separate and de-synchronized from the global system of production. This global credit system is unregulated, governed through the market, unlike the role of money as a means of circulation which can be more effectively subject to national and international rules and regulations (see Altvater 1990: 23). Moreover, this global credit system is predominantly private. Its growth has generated a striking new privatization of the world economy on a scale which dominates any of the forms of publicly available money (such as the IMF or the World Bank). The market for credit, and especially for new financial innovations, and the private hierarchies of the credit-creating enterprises dominate the public hierarchies of national and international regulation. These new global forms of credit are thus out of the control of nation-states, but they nevertheless exert structural power over each of them (see Leyshon and Thrift 1992).

The contrast with organized capitalism is striking. Such north Atlantic societies had been characterized by an integrated circuit of finance capital (Lash and Urry 1987: ch 7). It was based upon the substantial dominance of banking groups over industry and from their custodianship of the national currency and economy. Elites were organized into specific groups with particular banks at their centre and they competed to influence the national state (see Scott and Griff 1984 on the UK). This pattern was found within each of the major nation-states in the north Atlantic rim.

Now with disorganization finance and industry have both been internationalized. But what is striking is that they have been internationalized as separate and relatively uncoordinated circuits of capital. So they are de-synchronized and in no sense come together at the boundaries of individual nation-states. No longer are there separate and rival empires competing with each other within a national territory (again see Scott and Griff 1984 on the UK).

Some of the developments in the internationalization of credit and finance have included the emergence of international branch networks by American, European and Japanese banks; the formation of international banking groups in the early 1970s; the establishment of international consortia banks to serve a particular area or industry; the erosion of most of the differences between banks and other financial institutions via various kinds of deregulation; extensive merger and takeover activity between banks and other financial bodies; and the formation of new international financial conglomerates.

A number of conditions dating from the early 1960s provided the basis for these developments. First, there was the tremendous expansion of investment by US companies in Europe, particularly as many European countries were at the time developing active regional policies designed to attract inward investment to their peripheral regions. The overall global stock of foreign direct investment worldwide grew rapidly between 1960 and 1978, as well in the later 1980s (Gill and Law 1988: 193).

Second, there were gaps in the regulatory framework at the time (see Strange 1988: 104–5). The US government did not seek to regulate dollar deposits held with US branches offshore, especially those held in London. And the Bank of England, while controlling financial transactions conducted in sterling, did not seek to regulate the activities of British and foreign banks in London that were conducted in dollars. Thus the growth of Eurodollars was facilitated by this lack of regulation by either the US or UK authorities. This was particularly marked in the case of the USA where there was a general indifference to and official lack of interest in financial activities conducted outside US territory. The US government could have exercised all sorts of powers (such as reserve requirements) but did not do so, according to Strange, because of 'the American concept of the role of government and the prime importance given to behaviour within the United States or behaviour directly and visibly affecting the economy or society of the United States' (1986: 51).

And third, there were more general economic developments which facilitated the internationalization of credit and finance. These included the growth of an international division of labour which necessitated extensive cross-investments including the very rapidly expanding European market; the need for financing the merger boom in the later 1960s; the financing of trade with newly industrialized countries (NICs) and with eastern Europe; the oil crisis of 1973 which generated extraordinarily increased revenues in London; the freeing of exchange rates, the establishment of a paper-dollar system, and the relaxation of exchange controls; the derestriction and deregulation of domestic banks and of other financial institutions (such as building societies in the UK or savings and loans in the USA); and the extensive growth in short-term trading in options and futures (see Brett 1983; Evans 1985; Strange 1986, 1988; Lash and Urry 1987; Budd and Whimster 1992).

So far then we have noted a range of factors which generated the internationalization of finance and credit. However, in the 1960s and 1970s this was particularly focussed upon the development of the Eurodollar market in *London*. Hence globalization presupposed localization. The following are some of the the factors that led to the City of London becoming the centre for the development of the Eurocurrency market: it was very long-established with procedures thought to guarantee trust and confidence; there was great expertise available particularly in financing overseas investment; it was not so tied into 'its' national industry by comparison with say West German finance; and it was less regulated by government compared with some other offshore financial centres (Ingham 1984; Strange 1986: 106; Evans 1985: 108–9). The Chairman of New York's Citibank explained why London became the centre of the Eurodollar market: 'The Eurodollar market exists in London because people believe that the British government is not about to close it down. That's the basic reason and it took you a thousand years of history' (Ingham 1984: 41).

In other words, the development of global financial processes presupposed particular local configurations, in this case a thousand years of the history of the City of London. Until the early 1980s all of the City's financial markets were concentrated within an inner square containing a highly intense transaction network (see Pryke 1991; Amin and Thrift 1992 on the following). It was spatial proximity which helped to sustain trust. Everyone was within walking distance and this was not just convenient but ensured control. It was also a place with a very strong conception of time, with enormously powerful 'invented traditions'. These were the traditions of a financial aristocracy, of Englishness and of male clubbiness. What had developed since the coffee houses of the eighteenth century was a unique space, suffused with power and tradition. And this was such a close or intimate space that it was largely sustained through unwritten rules ('My word is my bond' – later to be replaced by 'My word is my junk bond'!) rather than through heavy-handed confrontation with especially delinquent overseas institutions. Compliance was enforced by word of mouth, a process made possible by the extraordinary compactness of the City. Trust and control followed from place. Unlike almost every other industry there had been no serious temporal and spatial disruption, there was still an 'extended village' and the endless commemoration of history. The old City was thus a localized social and cultural system which served to maximize trust (Pryke 1991: 216–17; Amin and Thrift 1992).

It was because it was such a particular place that it became the location for the Eurocurrency markets. But paradoxically the very growth of those markets began to dissolve this particular place and the forms of control and trust that it presupposed. Before the mid-1970s the Bank of England had operated on the basis of 'I know a bank when I see a bank' (quoted in Pryke 1991: 206). The Bank had dictated both the boundary of the City and the boundary of the people being supervised. Such a system depended upon intense proximity. But from the late 1970s the spatial form of the City, as well as of course its social form, began to change, beginning with the move of Citibank to Aldwych. Pryke summarizes the further spatial changes:

> The City was to become the hub not of a culturally familiar, slow-paced, empire-oriented regime of trade finance but of a new fast-moving capitalism . . . The growth in numbers and size of foreign capital began to threaten the supremacy of the Bank's style of spatial policing, which in many ways required incoming capital to subordinate itself to British rule. (1991: 210)

The number of foreign banks increased from 100 in 1961 to about 450 in the late 1980s, most employing between 50 and 400 staff. This necessitated a spatial transformation of the City. It literally expanded physically, to the west as far as Covent Garden, to the south to the Hay's Wharf development at London Bridge, and it would have expanded to the ill-fated excess of Canary Wharf. Such a planned expansion was facilitated by new technologies of information and 24-hour electronic trading (see King 1990: Part 2 for details). It is interesting to note how the transformation of London has more or less paralleled that of New York – for Canary Wharf read Battery City Park with its World Financial Center. There is a striking similarity in their 'landscapes of power', in vertical as opposed to horizontal vernacular landscapes, as well as in an aestheticization of space since these are partly public places to be consumed by those with appropriate cultural capital (Zukin 1992a).

At the same time there was a social transformation, what Budd and Whimster term the 'tale of two cities'. Stanley summarizes the old City based on the club-like atmosphere:

> The prevalent forms of controlling conduct were moral suasion, raised eyebrows, the stern rebuke over drinks and the prospect of the cold shoulder. (1992: 151)

But all this changed during the 1980s, a period identified as:

> one of panic and hyper-financial activity in which rapid changes in customary practice gave rise to a sense where the only certainty was the instantaneous . . . The homogeneity which had been the principal control mechanism in the City's regulatory position collapsed. (Stanley 1992: 156)

'Greed is good' became the watchword; or as Caryl Churchill expressed it in *Serious Money*:

> Naturally there's a whole lot of greed and
> That's no problem because money buys freedom. (1987: 109)

There was an anomie of affluence as incomes soared. 'Never before had so many unskilled 24 year olds made so much money in so little time' (quoted in Stanley 1992: 142). People were judged by how much and what they could consume. Personal success rather than conformity to the club-like atmosphere of the City became paramount. Illegal actions and the collapse of regulation were commonplace in the state of anomie that characterized the City in the 1980s. Individuals no longer felt constrained by the subcultural codes which the previous club-like atmosphere had sustained. Two effects are worth noting: the value of identifiable fraud increased one hundred-fold compared with 1960 (Stanley 1992: 155–8); and those working in the City generated a huge surge in demand for country houses which increasingly functioned as a positional good, a store of economic, social and cultural value, for the new 'disestablishment' (Thrift and Leyshon 1992).

The effect of these processes in London, as well in the other major financial centres, was to generate extraordinary global flows of money and finance. Every day $600 billion of foreign exchange is traded, an amount equivalent to one year's world trade. By 1989 London had become the leading centre for foreign exchange dealing, although this could change in the 1990s with the continuing growth of Tokyo. It should also be noted that 80 per cent of turnover in London is accounted for by overseas banks (Coakley 1992: 61–2). Likewise the value of bonds, secured against future profits or the like, was worth a staggering $10 trillion in the late 1980s.

This has therefore resulted in an extensive privatization of finance, with the amounts of money circulating dwarfing the sums available to individual governments or to international agencies such as the IMF. This means that individual monetary policies are almost impossible to devise and implement, particularly in the case of the smaller and weaker nations (see Strange 1986: 12–13). There has been a loss of interest rate sovereignty. The enormous foreign exchange markets serve to reduce inflation and interest rate disparities so that investment returns become equalized throughout the major Western economies. In a sense the foreign exchange market now runs a world monetary policy in the global rather than any national interest (see Hutton 1990). It is moreover escalating further and further out of control, generating what Strange terms a 'financial casino', 'an international financial system in which the gamblers in the casino have got out of hand, almost beyond, it seems, the control of government' (1986: 21).

So far we have concentrated upon developments in the world financial system that principally took place between the mid-1960s and mid-1980s, developments most significantly involving the exceptional growth in the amount and mobility of foreign exchange dealing. We will now briefly consider further transformations which have taken place within the last decade, transformations which have generated three world cities, London, New York and Tokyo. Sassen argues that as the world economy has become globalized, so there has been an increased agglomeration of central control functions within a few sites, and in particular within these three cities (1991). Indeed these cities have come to form a crucial interconnectedness, a new urban system resulting from their collective place within the global economy. And this place, their global destiny, derives from monopolizing two kinds of production. These are first, specialized producer services of the sort needed by complex organizations in order to run spatially dispersed networks of plants and offices. And second, there is the 'production' of certain kinds of financial innovation, especially securitization and the initiation of electronic and hence instantaneous exchange dealing on a global scale, especially in international equities (Sassen 1991: 5).

These developments have initiated a shift in the point of gravity of the global economy. In the 1960s and 1970s finance was dominated by large, mainly American transnational banks. Now with the decline in their relative importance and with the development of new financial institutions, it is the urban centres – the global cities – which have become centrally significant. It is three post-industrial *places*, London, New York and Tokyo, rather than the banks which dominate world finance (Sassen 1991: 19).

Although these cities have long been centres for business and finance, they have been transformed in the past decade or so through the transformation of the financial industry. This is now characterized by less regulation, more diversification, greater competition, a more pronounced short-termism, the loss of market share by the banks, and a huge increase in the volume and rapidity of transactions (Sassen 1991: 168). For these cities the value of financial transactions dwarfs that of any other industry and hence the urban form of London, New York or Tokyo cannot be separated from their role in this world financial system. Sassen points out that most analyses of cities have presumed that urban systems are essentially coterminous with nation-states. But recent financial transformations have served to produce an urban system, of London–New York–Tokyo which is global (Sassen 1991: ch 7). It is the *interactions* and connections between these cities and not competition between them which suggest that a global urban system is in the making. These cities contain 'the largest concentrations of leading producer services firms, the top twenty-four securities houses in the world, sixty-three of the top one hundred banks in the world, 84% of global capitalization, and the largest concentrations of a variety of commodity and currency markets' (Sassen 1991: 169). This is a system in which these three global cities are constituted as transnational centres of financial and service activity, cities whose connections with each other are in a way more important than their domestic connections. Sassen suggests that what contributes to growth in the network of global cities may not produce growth within the separate countries (1991: 9). Moreover these connections, although permitted by governments through derestriction and deregulation, are essentially private. Governments participate only to a limited degree in these transactions and hence these cities contain global economic spaces for the operation of both domestic and foreign companies equally. In London for example the number of foreign securities houses has increased from 10 in 1960 to over 120 in the late 1980s, with more than 25 per cent from Japan, including many of the largest ones (King 1990: 94–5). There has been a globalization of security dealing.

It is important to note that 1992 may transform this just-established urban hierarchy based on globalization and localization. If European financial services were to become more integrated it is probable that a pan-European hierarchy would develop. The following are some of the key determinants of the configuration of such a hierarchy: critical mass of services; niche markets; location of corporate consumers; property and other costs; infrastructure including telecommunications and air transport; language; and local business culture (see Begg 1992). Begg's research suggests that London will in fact sustain its position as one of the three nodes of the global financial system, but it will face stiff competition from Paris and Frankfurt. London seems likely to retain its position because of its social/cultural organization; it is the centre of interpretation, of interaction and of product innovation (see Amin and Thrift 1992). Leyshon and Thrift summarize how London reasserted its position in the late 1980s:

> competitive reregulation consolidated the City's position as Europe's premier financial centre, and enabled it to capture a large proportion of financial business flowing into Europe . . . The City's renewed financial preeminence was accomplished through a willingness of the UK state to bend the structure of financial regulation towards the new imperatives of the international financial system. (1992: 58; and see Moran 1991)

The second level in the hierarchy will consist of diversified European centres which will include Amsterdam, Milan, Madrid and possibly Brussels, as well as London, Paris and Frankfurt. At the third level, specialist niche market centres will include Edinburgh, Dublin and Luxembourg. Beyond those levels will be a variety of national and regional centres.

The Single European Market will produce significant rationalization of financial services, external restructuring and mergers, and co-operation across borders (more generally, see Ramsay 1991). Financial institutions under globalization shift from their traditional quasi-administrative role to being straightforwardly competitive (see Begg 1992: 335).

The effect of all this is that there has been a de-nationalization of each economy through the generation of global finance, securitization, the rising costs of capital, and the development of a worldwide debt economy. Money as a means of payment in no sense represents the value created through material processes. Such a debt and paper economy tremendously reduces the powers of both nation-states and international bodies to steer national economies; it generates the new urban system and consequential social polarization; it makes much 'real' investment uneconomic, and channels people and resources into more and more elaborate forms of casino capitalism; and it weakens national labour through money's increasing indifference to sectors or regions or localities (see Sassen 1991; Budd and Whimster 1992).

Indeed more speculatively one could suggest that money has become a kind of free-floating signifier detached from the real processes to which it once referred. Through options, swaps and futures, money is traded for money. Indeed since much of what is exchanged as commodities are future monetary transactions, so what is traded in no sense exists (see Stanley 1992: 149–50). Money is thus an exceptionally important sign interconnecting with countless other signs removed from real or material processes. Money functions as a detached signifier, part of the sign-system of postmodern societies. It is moreover the exchange of such signs which it is argued serve to construct postmodern identities. It is these signs and their exchanges which increasingly constitute some people's reality in the so-called First World (see Baudrillard 1981). When it is said that it is 'money' that makes the world go around, that is not quite right. Both money and the world are constituted as signs or images. Money *is* the world going round faster and faster – a pure simulacrum electronically displayed on the computer screen.

NATURE AND THE ENVIRONMENT

It was a characteristic of organized capitalism that a whole range of economic and social problems was thought to be soluble at the level of the nation-state. Issues of poverty, health and the environment were to be dealt with through national policies, especially through a Keynesian welfare state which could identify and respond to what one might call the risks of organized capitalism. It is now of course well known that such a national state solution is no longer viable, at least in the terms in which it had been originally conceived. Disorganized capitalism disorganizes such a national strategy. And a crucial reason for that is the globalization of processes – which affect the levels of poverty, the standards of health and the nature and quality of the environment. The agenda of the 'state' now includes processes and policies conceived at an inter-state and global level. Contemporary problems and ideally contemporary solutions are global, but also as we shall see they are partly local. Certain aspects of the environment are only comprehensible at the local level; indeed for many people that is all of the environment that they can challenge. It is only local action that can be envisaged and sustained. In this section then, we shall concern ourselves with drawing out some of the complex implications of the redrawing of the global-local nexus. We shall elaborate on some of the implications of the insightful motto of the environmental movement to 'think globally, act locally'.

In mainstream political debate the relationship between what are known as 'society' and 'nature' seems fairly simple to understand. There appear to be two autonomous spheres, of society and of nature, and it is then possible to investigate and to challenge two aspects of that relationship. On the one hand, there are the deleterious effects of various forms of human activity upon the natural environment, such as the way that the increased emission of carbon gases appears to produce global warming (Yearley 1991: ch 1). And on the other hand, there are the consequences of certain environmental changes on human activity, such as the effects of the explosion at Chernobyl in the Ukraine on sheep farming in the English Lake District.

However, the relationship between society and nature is more complex than this. First, human beings should be seen as indissolubly one part or element of nature. In the long process of modernization since the seventeenth century nature came to be seen as something outside society, as a machine rather than an organism. Earlier notions including that of nature as a nurturing mother were lost. Nature has normally been feminized but viewed as something to be used and indeed to be 'raped' (Merchant 1982). Over the modern period that nature was increasingly seen as something that should be subject to human investigation and because of necessity to subordination by human societies. Francis Bacon, who is often credited with developing this viewpoint, summarized as follows: 'For you have but to follow and as it were hound nature in her wanderings, and you will be able, when you like, to lead and drive her afterwards to the same place again' (quoted in Merchant 1982: 168). Nature was seen as waiting to be 'mastered' and many of Bacon's writings emphasized the way in which male science could and should dominate female nature.

The juxtaposition of society and nature reached its full development during the nineteenth century in the 'West'. Nature was degraded into a realm of unfreedom and hostility that needed to be subdued and controlled. Modernity involved the belief that human progress should be measured and evaluated in terms of the human domination of 'nature' rather than through transforming the relationship *between* humans and nature, as Walter Benjamin amongst others advocated. This view that nature should be dominated presupposed the doctrine of *human exception-*

alism: that humans are fundamentally different from and superior to all other species; that people can determine their own destinies and learn whatever is necessary to achieve them; that the world is vast and presents unlimited opportunities; and that the history of human society is one of unending progress. This domination of 'nature' resulted moreover not only from capitalist industrialization but also from intense inter-state competition and the pursuit of maximum economic growth rather than environmental management.

One deficiency of such a doctrine is that strictly speaking there is no single entity which we can designate as 'nature'. The concept can refer to the essential character of something; the underlying force lying behind events in the world; the entirety of animate and inanimate objects; the physical as opposed to the human environment; and the rural or countryside as opposed to the town or city (see Strathern 1992: 172). Even concentrating upon the last three notions, each 'nature' is geographically and historically constituted. Natural limits should not be viewed as fixed and eternal but rather as dependent upon particular historical and geographical determinations. Further, nature should not be viewed as merely setting limits to what humans can achieve. Natures are constraining but also enabling. There are many examples of the relatively beneficial ways in which 'nature' has enabled human activity of a non-environmentally destructive character to occur. 'Nature' should not be seen as something that has to be tamed or 'mastered', or something that is necessarily at odds with human endeavour.

Thus on the one hand, it is necessary to avoid the conservative position that there are absolute natural limits to human endeavour, as found in Malthus for example. There are no absolute limits since 'nature' is historically and geographically dependent upon the social relations within which it is embedded. But on the other hand, one should avoid positing a wholly social constructionist utopianism in which it is thought that nature sets no constraints on human activity. There are clearly dramatic ways in which the physical environment exerts its revenge upon human agency. Benton attempts to avoid both these problematic positions by arguing that: 'What *is* required is the recognition that each form of social/economic life has its own specific mode and dynamic of interrelation with its own specific contextual conditions, resource materials, energy sources and naturally mediated unintended consequences' (1989: 77). Thus there are a variety of forms assumed by the nature/society relationship. This varies both historically and geographically, and later in this section we shall examine how the contemporary globalization of economic and social relationships is currently transforming the society/nature relationship.

In analysing this it is however important to avoid an economic reductionism. 'Society' is not merely a question of the form taken by the economy in a given epoch. There are also, first, the changing *cultural* configurations which define and transform what actually is taken to be 'nature', what is 'natural', in each society, such as the contemporary British view that deciduous rather than coniferous forests are 'natural', or that the discerning consumer should purchase 'natural' products (see Strathern 1992: 173). And second, there are also the changing *political* definitions of how and why certain aspects of the physical and/or built environment either are worth preserving or are deemed suitable for destruction – and this depends upon what can be called the 'politics of nature'.

Thus although there are natures which take their revenge on human societies in often the most dramatic (and deserved!) of ways, it is crucial to acknowledge how such natures are *produced*, economically, culturally and politically, within different epochs. In chapter 3 we analysed Beck's thesis in which it is claimed that in the contemporary 'risk society' nature is exacting a global, undiscriminating revenge. People's appropriation of nature is not something that occurs abstractly. It depends upon the kinds of social activity in which they are engaging and hence on the resulting modes by which they gaze upon and experience nature. The society/nature relationship should thus not be viewed a-historically and a-geographically. 'Nature' thus depends upon historically and geographically specific social practices, including those of recreation and tourism. A. Wilson describes how they have produced a particular 'culture of nature' (1992; and see Romeril 1990; Urry 1992). Wilson demonstrates how tourism has redefined the land as a resource for leisure. It has become one of the most important ways in which the relations between humans and nature are now organized.

One consequence is that what is viewed and criticized as unnatural or environmentally damaging in one era or one society is not necessarily taken as such in another. For example, the rows of terraced housing thrown up during nineteenth-century capitalist industrialization in Britain are now viewed, not as an environmental eyesore, but as quaint, traditional and harbouring patterns of human activity well worth preserving. The 'reading' and production of nature is something that is learnt; and the learning process varies greatly between different societies, different periods and different social groups within any society. Grove-White neatly summarizes this process in the recent period: 'In an important sense, motorways, nuclear power, agriculture and conservation – self-evidently "environmental" as they appear to be now – all had to be *invented* as issues by the environmental movement in the 1970s' (1991: 4; and see Yearley 1991 for a useful summary of the relevant scientific arguments and evidence).

Moreover, many of these developments which we now characterize as environmentally harmful have in a sense been the result of millions of small decisions by individuals and households – to buy a car, to choose central heating, to travel to the Mediterranean, to purchase a refrigerator and so on. Those issues that we now deem to constitute the environmental problem are the result of two processes. On the one hand, there are the millions of individual household decisions which collectively have produced environmental damage and which national states have little or no chance of controlling. And on the other hand, there is a complex social and political process which has successfully created and juxtaposed a number of issues as 'environmental' and has placed them onto various local, national and international agendas albeit with only limited success (see Lowe and Goyder 1983; Lowe and Flynn 1989; Rudig 1986; Rootes 1990 for a variety of data and evidence about environmental politics).

Central to recent changes in the social construction of nature have been transformations in the structural importance and character of consumption. Structurally, Bauman summarizes:

> in present day society, consumer conduct (consumer freedom geared to the consumer market) moves steadily into the position of, simultaneously, the cognitive and moral focus of life, the integrative bond of the society . . . In other words, it moves into the self-same position which in the past – during the 'modern' phase of capitalist society – was occupied by work. (1992: 49)

And as such the pleasure principle becomes dominant. Pleasure seeking is a duty since the consumption of goods and services becomes *the* structural basis of Western societies. And via the global media, discussed in the next section, this principle comes to be extended worldwide.

Social integration thus takes place less through the principles of normalization, confinement and disciplinary power, as described by Foucault or indeed by Bauman in the case of the holocaust (1989). Instead it takes place through the 'seduction' of the market-place, through the mix of feeling and emotions generated by seeing, holding, hearing, testing, smelling and moving through the extraordinary array of goods and services, places and environments that characterize contemporary consumerism organized around a particular 'culture of nature' (see A. Wilson 1992). Such a market-place has in recent years proved to be the arch-enemy of a simple uniformity. The market thrives on variety, diversity and change, on the extraordinarily rapid transformations of recreational pleasure-seeking (see Bauman 1992: ch 2).

This set of changes obviously has enormous implications for nature and the physical environment. The first point is obvious, that the development of an overwhelming global consumerism has the most profound of consequences for the physical environment, and this is reflected in holes in the ozone layer, global warming, acid rain, nuclear power accidents and the destruction of many local environments. Such Western consumerism in which 'nature seems turned into a mere artefact of consumer choice' (Strathern 1992: 197) has been extensively critiqued by the environmental movement – and this is in turn seen as part of the wider critique of modernity itself. In addition, it should be noted that consumerism has also come to be applied *to* the solution of environmental problems, through the development of environmental economics. This argues that a sustainable future can be bought within the market-place, that is through altering the prices of various commodities so that consumption patterns more accurately reflect total costs (see Pearce et al 1989). Consumerism can also involve obtaining or purchasing new parts for the human body, so undermining a clear sense of the natural body inside as opposed to the unnatural body outside (see Strathern 1992).

But there is a further point here. This is that the very development of consumerism itself has helped to generate the current critique of environmental degradation and the cultural focus upon nature. Ecology in part presupposes a certain kind of consumerism. This is because one element of consumerism is a heightened reflexivity about the places and environments, the goods and services that are 'consumed', literally, through a social encounter, or through visual consumption (see Urry 1992). As people reflect upon such consumptions they develop not only a duty to consume but also certain rights, rights of the citizen as consumer. Such rights include the belief that people are entitled to certain qualities of the environment, of air, water and scenery, and that these extend into the future and to other populations.

We will now summarize some transformations in the social construction of nature and its 'consumption' that have become apparent in the past couple of decades, transformations in part generated by the globalization of social and natural relations. These changes raise major questions of social and personal identity resulting from complex forms of social interdependence (see Grove-White 1991; Strathern 1992). Such changes involve the paradox highlighted by Strathern, that in the contemporary period there is an increased focus upon nature, upon valuing the natural and upon 'nature conservation', but that these are themselves cultural constructions. Culture has been necessary to rescue nature in other words. Strathern argues that this produces 'the conceptual collapse of the differences between nature and culture when Nature cannot survive without Cultural intervention' (Strathern 1992: 174).

First then, humans are increasingly viewed culturally as part of nature rather than distinct from and opposed to it. As such it is thought less appropriate for humans simply to 'conquer' nature since they are part of it. And as part of nature humans are thought to have special responsibilities *for* nature, partly because of their unprecedented powers of global destruction. They also have such responsibility because of the particular human capacity to act reflexively (see chapter 3 above). In modernity reflexivity consists of social practices being constantly examined and reformed in the light of incoming information received about those very practices, thus altering their constitution. Giddens says: 'only in the era of modernity is the revision of convention radicalised to apply (in principle) to all aspects of human life, including technological intervention into the material world' (1990: 38–9).

Second, this reflexivity is leading the methods of western science, the embodiment of modernity, to be constructed as no more legitimate an activity than many other social activities, each of which involves different forms of judgment. Science is not viewed as having a *necessarily* civilizing, progressive and emancipatory role in revealing what nature is like. In many cases science and its associated technologies are seen as *the* problem and not the solution. This is especially the case where there are in effect massive and uncontrolled scientific experiments which treat the entire globe (or a fair part of it) as a laboratory (as with toxic waste, agro-chemicals, nuclear power and so on). In the risk society science is seen as producing most of the risks although these are largely invisible to our senses. At the same time, science's loss of automatic social authority weakens the legitimacy even of the environmental (and medical) 'sciences'. This in turn causes a problem for the Green movement since such sciences have of necessity become central to many of the campaigns conducted by the non-governmental organizations (NGOs). Yearley suggests that 'the green movement is peculiarly dependent on science' (1991: 113). The very identification of risk depends upon such science because of the 'disempower-ment of the senses' that chemical and nuclear contamination produces (Beck 1987: 156; Douglas and Wildavsky 1982).

Third, nature is increasingly viewed as 'global' or holistic. The Brundt-land Report talks of 'Our Common Future', partly because of the global character of certain of the threats posed to nature, beginning of course with the 'nuclear' threat. This perception has been assisted by the development of global mass media which have generated an 'imagined community' of all societies inhabiting 'one earth' (cf Friends of *the* Earth). And not only non-human animals but also other components of nature, such as rain forests, are seen as having extensive rights – in the view of some, the same rights as humans (Porritt 1984: 208). Nature has in part come to be culturally viewed as not an object but as a subject. This has been carried to an extreme version in the influential Gaia hypothesis (see Lovelock 1988). This states that the earth should be viewed as a particular kind of subject, as a superorganism. It is argued that life on the planet is coordinated to keep it habitable by Gaia, the earth goddess. For example, the amount of carbon dioxide in the atmosphere has regulated the earth's temperature. This view emphasizes the extraordinary way in which all kinds of phenomena are suffused with life, and that the planet has a kind of global purpose which ought to be 'worshipped'. This is a paradigm case which demonstrates the cultural production of Nature.

Finally, people who are as yet unborn are viewed as having extensive rights of inheritance of a particular quality of the environment, one which is certainly no worse than that which is enjoyed by the world's current population. Notions of this sort have existed before, through for example the idea that farmers should exercise stewardship of their land for later generations. But what is distinctive about the current epoch is that it is believed that future generations *throughout the world* have rights of inheritance of a particular 'nature'. And this is a nature which includes not only the surface of the earth but also a particular condition of the ozone layer. That there might be holes in that layer is of course something which nobody can observe and rests upon the most arcane of scientific theorizing. Realization of the interests of future generations ('our children and their children') will almost certainly harm the interests of significant numbers of the current inhabitants of the earth. The rights are taken to be evolutionary and global and not local, as in previous notions involving the stewardship of nature (see chapter 9 above on evolutionary or glacial notions of time).

It does not follow though from the account so far provided that there is a single environmental or 'Green' politics surrounding 'nature' in the current epoch. This would indeed be foolish – there are for example at least 1400 organizations involved in such politics in Britain. Three levels of environmental politics can be usefully distinguished. First, there is the *preservation* of certain current elements or features of the physical or built environment from change, particularly those resulting from what are taken to be obvious excrescences of 'modernity'. What is protected may well be characterized as 'natural' or 'traditional' but it is in part the product of previous rounds of human intervention.

Second, there are the attempts to *reform* particular kinds of what are deemed to be environmentally damaging social activities, through legislation, taxation or changed consumption patterns. Examples include the development of Green consumerism, differential consumption tax rates, Green parenting, environmental audits by firms and so on. Some of these reforms can however lead to high levels of authoritarian intolerance for those people or organizations who remain 'unreformed'.

And third, there is the proposed *ecological* transformation of industrial societies, of the work ethic, of the nature of Western consumerism, and of the overall mistreatment of the planet. A global crisis produces a global response. Mere preservation or reformism are viewed as a woefully inadequate response to the global crisis whose consequences are particularly devastating in developing countries (see Yearley 1991: ch 5).

Environmental issues are thus being transformed by the globalization of economic, social and political relationships. However, the connections between the environment and globalization are more complex than we have so far suggested. The environmental movement itself has employed the most insightful motto: to 'think globally, act locally'. What does this mean? What kind of reworking of the global-local nexus is involved here? Minimally the motto indicates two processes: first, that many environmental problems at the local level have global origins and hence need international agreements to remedy them (such as acid rain). And second, many such large problems require for their solution localized, decentralized actions from vast numbers of people, many of whom will not actually benefit from such a change (such as reduced use of carbon fuels). We will consider these processes in turn.

The consequence of the first is that there are immense problems of producing appropriate collaboration between individual governments since each may have good reasons to try to free-ride on the presumed actions of others. This can be seen in the current debates about reducing carbon emissions so as to limit global warming. The British government first proposed to limit the *increase* in carbon gases so that by the year 2005 the emissions will return to the level in 1990. But it is very instructive to note that national governments increasingly find themselves having to justify their actions on the environment to others at international gatherings. It is the threat of being shamed by the rest of the international 'community' that has come to constitute the major constraint on national governments. A recent example of this has been the attempted shaming of the British government by the EC over the extraordinary number of 'dirty beaches' in the UK. In such cases it is interesting to note that many people expect the national state to be powerfully enabling and to constrain polluters. The problem here is not the power of the state but its relative weakness.

The second process above raises major problems, that is in ensuring the necessary actions from large numbers of people within localized settings. This can be seen in the classic if criticized account of the 'tragedy of the commons'. Here Hardin argues that there is an area of common land on which herders graze cattle; each herder will seek to maximize the number grazed; eventually the capacity of the common is reached but instead of stability tragedy follows; this is because the positive benefit from grazing further cattle goes to the individual herder while the costs are borne by all; thus it will be rational for each individual to keep enlarging the size of their herds especially since the returns from each head of cattle decline as the numbers increase; hence in the absence of regulation, a state or a set of alternative norms, 'Freedom in the commons brings ruin to all' (Hardin 1968: 1244).

Hardin suggests that this scenario is empirically common. Examples include the way in which the seas are over-fished or that agricultural land is over-fertilized (see Johnston 1989: 118–19). We could also add the example of the Alps (see Kettle 1990). These mountains extend into seven countries but now support a permanent population of only 12m. However, the temporary population is 10 times as large and rising fast. The Alps have been reconstructed as 'a single-commodity colony of lowland Europe. That commodity is . . . "industrial ski-ing" ' (Kettle 1990: 7). There are now an extraordinary 40,000 ski-runs in the Alps, produced by the ripping up of forests, the obliteration of pastures, the diverting of rivers and the concreting over of valleys. One consequence is that a warm winter in the Alps is now the equivalent of a harvest failure elsewhere. There are also major problems of traffic and roads in the area. To a significant extent these major problems in the Alps can only be tackled by extensive collaboration *between* the seven governments, who may well have to constrain the actions of considerable numbers of the residents of those countries. In some ways the Alps serve to construct a 'society' with a common set of problems. It does not coincide with the seven individual nation-states.

However, these are *relatively* straightforward examples of environmental problems which *may* be resolvable locally. For example, the herders may come to understand through iterative processes over time that some kind of regulation is desirable. More complex are those situations where it is necessary for large numbers of people in many distant locations to be willing to act altruistically on behalf of temporally and/or geographically distant populations, without any obvious self-interested benefit. An example is the need to reduce the number of car journeys in order to limit carbon emissions. This is by contrast with say healthy eating where people would appear to benefit individually from a changed diet. In many cases of environmental change people have to act altruistically on behalf of geographically distant populations or populations as yet unborn. The collective good to be produced is invisible in time and/or space. However, what is interesting to consider is whether the global media and supra-national states could come to play a crucially important role in sustaining the notion of a 'global village'. Such a village can facilitate the construction of an imagined community comprised of the earth's present and future population which may endeavour to conserve 'nature', bearing in mind the cultural construction of that nature.

Thus national states are squeezed between global and local processes. So far though we have not said much about globalization. Giddens defines it as the intensification of worldwide social relations which link distant localities in such a way that local happenings are shaped by geographically distant events and vice versa (1990). However, localities are not necessarily rendered homogeneous. Local transformation and the engendering of 'local nationalisms' are, he says, as much part of the processes of globalization as are the lateral extensions of social connections across time and space (1990: 64).

This argument is also emphasized and developed by D. Harvey (1989). For him, as we have seen, the key process affecting cultural and political change is 'time-space compression'. This refers to the way in which changes in the organization of capitalist labour-time have transformed space, subduing all sorts of differences between places and indeed the very certainty of absolute space. Everything depends upon developments elsewhere as the nineteenth and twentieth centuries have brought about a plethora of new technologies of transportation and communication which have subdued and unified space, producing many 'small worlds' or what Appadurai terms 'imagined worlds' (see Appadurai 1990, as well as Lodge 1983). In particular, as we have discussed above, it is signs or images which most exemplify time-space compression. A worldwide industry produces and markets images, not only for products, but also for people, govern-ments, places, universities and so on. There are an extraordinary number and transitoriness of different images, including in recent years those of nature and the natural. Globalization thus involves the circulation of images on a novel global scale; and it involves images which are of the entire globe ('one earth').

Such images or themes have been particularly attached to the country-side. This appears to be especially attractive to many social groups and reflects the anti-urbanism of the environmental movement (see Capra

1982). The countryside appeals for a number of reasons: that one is apparently 'closer' to nature; that there is an absence of crowds; that there is a non-mechanical environment; and that the environment is unplanned, complex and labyrinthine. But of course there is little that is 'natural' about Western agriculture in the countryside: in order to achieve solitude it is necessary to travel long distances to bypass congested sights; the environment is highly mechanized and one only avoids such mechanical sights through the construction of very selective 'landscapes'; and little in the environment is unplanned since in some respects agriculture is one of the most rationalized of industries and subject to extensive external regulation. Indeed Daniels and Cosgrove point out how the rural landscape is like a 'flickering text . . . whose meaning can be created, extended, altered, elaborated and finally obliterated by the touch of a button' (1988: 8). Such images have been important in the construction of various rural or 'wilderness' 'themed' environments which consist of a pastiche of artefacts, sounds, textures, photographic images and so on. They involve a highly constructed 'nature' and almost certainly will produce environmental damage, especially from the viewpoint of scientific conservation. This damage, relative to a particular construction of nature, will result both from a contrived construction of rural themes and from marked increases in the number of visitors which will for example affect the indigenous flora and fauna.

Two additional points need to be made here. First, there are at least two very different kinds of preservation or conservation. On the one hand, there is aesthetic conservation – to conserve in accordance with pre-given conceptions of beauty and the picturesque. On the other, there is scientific conservation – to conserve in accordance with *current* scientific thinking on which elements of the physical environment are worth preserving and how they should be preserved. These notions can stand in stark contrast with each other, especially in the light of greatly increased demands to visit some particular area or site because of changes in aesthetic sensibilities (although they need not conflict as in Wordsworth's 'romantic ecology': see Bate 1991).

But second, scientific conservation itself is not concerned with a pure and unconstructed 'nature'. Plants and animals are not simply 'indigenous' to an area. What is indigenous is not an absolute. The species found in a given area change, depending upon climate, atmosphere, migration, land use and so on. There is no absolute nature – it is specific to historical and geographical determinations. *Relative* to that particular nature, certain sorts of changes are environmentally damaging. But this damage is specific to a given historical and geographical nature and to a particular, and not universal, notion of scientific conservation. Moreover, that 'nature' and that 'science' are themselves embedded within distinct political and cultural contexts.

Moreover, reflexivity now enables the production of simulacra, replications of originals more real, or hyper-real, than the original (Eco 1986).

Almost everything can now be reproduced, including apparently authentic ancient buildings as in Quinlan Terry's neo-classical Richmond development on the banks of the Thames in England; and 'natural' features of the landscape, such as the pink and white terraces which were located above Lake Rotomahana in New Zealand and are to be 'recreated' elsewhere a century after they were destroyed by a volcano (Urry 1990c: 146).

Harvey also argues that globalization generates localization. The 'collapse of spatial barriers does not mean that the significance of space is decreasing' (1989: 293). The less salient the temporal and spatial barriers the greater the sensitivity of firms, of governments and of the general public to variations of place across time and space: 'As spatial barriers diminish so we become much more sensitized to what the world's spaces contain' (D. Harvey 1989: 294). The specificity of place, of its workforce, the character of its entrepreneurialism, its administration, its buildings, its history and especially its physical environment, become *more* important as temporal and spatial barriers collapse. This explains just why places increasingly seek to forge a distinctive image and to create an atmosphere of place, nature and tradition that may prove attractive to capital, to highly skilled prospective employees, and to visitors.

The revised sensibility to the environment, to its social, physical and built character, thus stems from globalization and localization. The former includes both the immensely threatening social relations of technology *and* the rapidly heightened circulation of images. The latter includes both the real threats to localities by new technologies and the proliferation of multiple and competing place-images (see Shields 1991a). It is interesting to note that all sorts of interests are concerned to make places seem *different* from each other and to make them consistent with particular *images* of place. Often of course those efforts are not successful, such as when many high streets contain the same 'tasteful' shops, or when neighbouring resorts develop competing marinas as part of similar sea-defence systems. Such local competitiveness of place partly stems from globalization, from time-space compression of capital and travel, which forces many places to compete to attract investment, workers and visitors. International tourism is a process by which the affluent countries, having mined their own environments, now scavenge the earth to consume those of other people, particularly those environments consistent with images of 'natural', 'unspoilt' and 'Green' (see Crick 1990).

Localities are moreover complex in character. Different social groups have different stakes or interests in a place (see Bagguley et al 1990: ch 5). Some people will benefit more from expanding the employment base, others from increasing the range of shops, others from improving the leisure and entertainment facilities, others from making it safer, others from reconstructing the place's 'heritage', others from improving the physical environment, others from making it healthier, and so on. The interests of individuals and groups are therefore heterogeneous, ranging from the material to the cultural, to the medical and especially to the

304 ECONOMIES OF SIGNS AND SPACE

aesthetic. And of course different groups have different resources to realize such interests within a given locality, to ensure that a nuclear power station should be built, or that a sewage outlet should not be constructed, or that a set of old buildings should be preserved rather than demolished, and so on. Resources include not only money and power but also public opinion and organizational capacities.

But interests in a locality are even more complex than this. First, there are those 'altruistic' pressure groups who may take on what they *presume* to be the interests of other groups or even of the locality as a whole. An example would be to campaign to prevent the building of a power station locally. The effects of such 'altruistic groups' may harm the interests of other individuals and groups. Moreover, there are the interests of those who do not currently live in a place but who may do so, or of those who may visit it. Their interests, especially those of tourists, will not be directly represented in a local area but they clearly possess interests in certain kinds of services and environment. Local groups may well find themselves invoking the apparent interests of these potential residents or visitors in arguing for and developing various kinds of environmental policy.

Two important sets of interests found in a locality are those of 'amenity' and 'security' (Bagguley et al 1990: ch 5). In relationship to the environment both may involve contradictions. 'Amenity' may mean access to the distant countryside, which is often well-protected in the form of 'national parks', but it also involves constructing high speed road and rail links through areas of lesser natural beauty so that access can be more easily enjoyed. 'Security' refers to the capacity to defend or perpetuate a desired or familiar set of conditions, such as the way that a local civic society campaigns to sustain a particular labyrinthine road system within a city centre. Yet environmentally this may cause problems for visitors who will experience a lack of security since they are likely to get lost; and for women who find that such narrow streets contain insecure 'dark corners'.

Four general conclusions follow from this discussion. First, the development of global environmental problems, and especially that of climate change, demonstrates that national governments are often unwilling to act on their own since the actions of any single government will make little direct difference. However, if other states were to act in the same way then the actions of each are essential. States therefore may have a crucial role to play but only if many others can be persuaded (or shamed) to act in similar fashion.

Second, national policies can normally only be successful if large numbers of individuals are persuaded to engage in appropriate actions within their respective local areas. Such actions will only occur if there are forms of local involvement and attachment. However, people's commitments to and interests in their locality are varied and complex and this variety of interests will seriously affect the possibilities of large numbers of people 'acting locally'.

Third, national governments are squeezed between globalization and localization. They are constrained by global changes in the 'risk society' which they cannot individually control; and they have immense difficulties in organizing localities since their attempts may often be challenged and resisted by residents in part because the environment is their locality for many people.

And fourth, different places are not just lived in but are visited. Places are partly made by such visitors. One effect of more visitors may be to improve the campaigning for an improved environment, especially to the extent to which a kind of 'Green tourism' consciousness becomes more common. And yet to the extent to which people increasingly expect to experience a 'natural' environment so tourism will spread into more and more countries and into many different types of environment, especially as there is an exponential growth in the means of image-circulation. There is little prospect of escape, as 'nature' itself is an increasingly valued and sought-after good and image for places subject to intense global competition. A. Wilson argues that a new 'culture of nature' is needed which does not inscribe the land with particular geographies of agriculture, leisure, wilderness and technology (1992: 257).

In the next section we shall consider some further processes which affect localities, namely the extraordinary development of a so-called global culture which is the means by which this global competition is established and sustained.

GLOBAL CULTURE AND NATIONAL CULTURE

There has recently developed a striking explosion of interest in the notion of a 'global culture' (see *Theory, Culture and Society* 1990 in particular). What has fuelled such interest has been the emergence of large international media companies which own media interests in numerous countries normally acquired through predatory merger and takeover strategies; which produce cultural goods for an international market; which operate in a wide variety of different types of media; and which increasingly function to undermine any sense of a national media tied to a particular nation-state (as we saw in chapter 5). Their interests are global and they have done much to generate international markets rather than national markets for their products. They have particularly promoted new technologies such as satellite which have no national boundaries. They have particularly benefited from the general deregulation and the marketization of modern culture in the last two decades. There has been what Thompson terms the 'mediatization' of culture (1990: ch 4; see also Brunn and Leinbach 1991).

In relationship to the obvious power of such companies it is not difficult to hypothesize the weakness of each individual consumer. It seems uncontroversial to suggest that the effect will be to produce mass consumers of the products of such companies on a world scale. *Dallas* and

Dynasty, the Olympics and the Berlin Wall concert, *Neighbours* and *The Muppets* – these appear to have become the global cultural currency of the late twentieth century.

But is it really the case that such a culture produces uniformity? Is there really a new mass culture and mass society? Such a suggestion sits rather oddly with the claims about the *ending* of mass production and consumption argued for by many commentators analysed in Part 2 of this book (see Aglietta 1987; D. Harvey 1989; Altvater 1990). Indeed it may be more plausible to suggest that there is not *a* global culture, but that there are a number of processes which are producing the globalization of culture. Featherstone argues that 'there may be emerging sets of "third cultures", which themselves are conduits for all sorts of cultural flows which cannot be merely understood as the product of bilateral exchanges between nation-states' (1990: 1). The literature on post-modernism would suggest that these globalization processes are leading to the proliferation of multiple popular and local cultures which only in part correspond to or are congruent with dominant ideologies within particular nation-states.

These new global processes have two crucial characteristics. First, as Robertson has consistently argued, they are autonomous from mere inter-state relationships (see 1990 for example). Hence we should employ the term globalization rather than internationalization since the latter implies exchanges between the nation-state (see Featherstone 1990: 6). It should also be noted that the growth of the nation-state was not an impediment to globalization since it was an idea which itself rapidly became globalized. But recently the following global processes have developed: the new forms of communication already mentioned; the development of international travel and of professional 'small worlds' little connected to nation-state relationships; the increasing numbers of international agencies and institutions; the development of global competitions and prizes; the emergence of a small number of languages of communication, most notably English; and the development of much more widely shared notions of citizenship and of political democracy (cf both South Africa and eastern Europe).

Second, these global processes are dominant but in a different sense from that understood in much of the dominant ideology debate (see Abercrombie et al 1980, 1990; Thompson 1990). Contemporary developments do not produce a straightforwardly dominant ideology, that is sets of *ideas* which in some way involve legitimation, dissimulation, unification, fragmentation and reification (see Thompson 1990: 60). Ideologies are characteristic of modernity and there can be a partly rational discourse about those ideas and about their supposedly ideological character (Lash 1990a). And it may be that such ideas did indeed operate to produce coherence amongst the dominant class rather than amongst the whole society, as Abercrombie et al argue (1980).

But with postmodernity it is the global networks of communication and information that are crucial. This has a number of implications: that the symbolic forms transmitted by the technical media of mass communication are central to contemporary cultural forms; that these developments greatly expand ideological scope since they enable symbolic forms to be transmitted to extended audiences dispersed in time and space; they permit new kinds of social interaction, what Thompson terms 'technically mediated quasi-interaction' (1990: 268); and most important of all they produce images and less in the way of ideas, images that are diverse, pluralistic and which overload the viewer. Such images may be used for oppositional movements, such as with regard to environmental issues. Some such images will be highly localized, some will coincide with nation-states, and some may contribute to the assertion of ethnicity. To the extent to which these networks of communication mobilize the cultural paradigm of the postmodern then they much less clearly belong to the previous world of modernity and the critique of ideas and ideologies.

This argument is further developed by Appadurai who attempts to detail five different dimensions of such global cultural flows, dimensions which move in non-isomorphic paths and which challenge simple notions of a cultural centre and a subordinate periphery (1990). These dimensions constitute building blocks for what Appadurai terms 'imagined worlds', the multiple worlds constituted by the historically situated imaginations of persons and groups spread across the globe. Such worlds are fluid and irregularly shaped.

The five dimensions of such global cultural flows are *ethnoscapes* – the moving landscape of tourists, immigrants, refugees, exiles, guestworkers and so on; *technoscapes* – the movements of technologies, high and low, mechanical and informational, across all kinds of boundaries; *finanscapes* – via currency markets, national stock exchanges and commodity specula-tions, there is the movement of vast sums of monies through national turnstiles at bewildering speed; *mediascapes* – the distribution of electronic capabilities to produce and disseminate images and the proliferation of images thereby generated; and *ideoscapes* – concatenations of images often in part linked to the ideologies of states or of movements of opposition, ideas derived in part from the Enlightenment (Appadurai 1990: 296–300).

Our argument here is first, that 'de-territorialization' characterizes all of these spatial landscapes; and second, that in consequence mediascapes are of increasing cultural significance and are swamping ideoscapes (as argued by Thompson 1990). In the rest of this section we will draw out some of the implications of this, especially for nations and the nation-state.

First, if we accept the argument that much of contemporary culture is in some sense postmodern then this means that these mediascapes are global or at least transnational. As Bauman clearly argues: 'The models of postmodernity, unlike the models of modernity, cannot be grounded in the realities of the nation state' (1989: 152). Or as Ohmae expresses it more directly:

On a political map, the boundaries between countries are as clear as ever . . . [But] of all the forces eating them away, perhaps the more persistent is the flow

of information – information that governments previously monopolized . . .
Their monopoly of knowledge about things happening around the world enabled
them to fool, mislead, or control the people . . . Today . . . people everywhere
are more and more able to get the information they want directly from all
corners of the world. (1990: 18–19)

It should of course be noted that the elements that may constitute such a
set of images and information will include those drawn from different
national cultures. But, as A. Smith argues, the 'emerging global culture is
tied to no place or period. It is context-less, a true melange of disparate
components drawn from everywhere and nowhere, borne upon the
modern [postmodern] chariots of global communications systems' (1990:
177). People are increasingly consumers of cultures as well as of products,
and indeed the differences between these are anyway dissolving. Consumers increasingly move on a world stage. Part of the power of the
consumer stems from their lack of allegiance to particular national societies
and their particular products and images (Ohmae 1990: 3–5).

Also, it is necessary to take into account not only the global processes of
production but also the circumstances in which cultural products are
received by audiences. Global programmes, even like *Dallas*, are read
differently in different countries and places. Audiences possess skills in
reading and using programmes, through talk in households and workplaces and through the use of the VCR. At the level of audiences it
is inconceivable that there could be a global culture. Indeed in some
respects there is an increasing contradiction between centralized production (at least in some respects) and more decentralized and fragmented
reception.

Furthermore, a particular role is played by 'cosmopolitans' in the
production of such cultural forms. As Hannerz notes, when the local-
cosmopolitan distinction was initially developed cosmopolitans were seen
as those who lived their lives in the context of a single national society by
contrast with provincial locals (see 1990: 237). This is no longer the case.
Cosmopolitanism involves an intellectual and aesthetic stance of openness
towards divergent experiences from *different* national cultures. There is a
search for and delight in contrasts between societies rather than a longing
for uniformity. Hannerz also talks of the need for the cosmopolitan to be in
'a state of readiness, a personal ability to make one's way into other
cultures, through listening, looking, intuiting and reflecting' (1990: 239).

He draws a strong distinction between cosmopolitans and tourists, citing
the main character in the film *The Accidental Tourist* who wrote travel
books for anti-cosmopolitan tourists, people for whom visiting another
country was largely a spectator sport. However, this contrast is overdrawn
and rests upon the middle-class belief that their orientation to travel is far
more sophisticated than that of mere 'tourists'.

There are two contemporary examples of where something of a greater
cosmopolitanism directly engendered by tourism has helped to produce
significant political shifts. First, in what was 'Eastern Europe' the freedom

to travel to the 'West' (the 'West' as the 'other') was a major demand and an important part of the consumer citizenship claims which destabilized those societies in the past decade or so. Following the collapse of the 'Iron Curtain' huge numbers of east Europeans have been travelling to parts of western Europe, resulting in even greater problems of congestion in proximate areas like Venice. Second, in Britain it is hard to explain the somewhat more positive attitude to some level of European integration without taking into account the enormous flows of British tourists to Europe – a process which has rendered Europe as exotic and cosmopolitan rather than menacing and threatening. Hebdige maintains that a kind of 'mundane cosmopolitanism' is part of most people's everyday experience. People are increasingly world travellers, either directly or via the TV in the sitting room. Hebdige argues that: 'It's part of being "taken for a ride" in and through late-20th century consumer culture. In the 1990s everybody [at least in the 'West'] is more or less cosmopolitan' (1990: 20).

Such a cosmopolitanism can be characterized in terms of the following ideal type. It consists of six features: extensive patterns of real and simulated mobility in which it is thought that one has the right to travel anywhere and to consume at least initially all environments; a curiosity about all places, peoples and cultures and at least a rudimentary ability to map such places and cultures historically, geographically and anthropologically; an openness to other peoples and cultures and a willingness/ability to appreciate some elements of the language/culture of the place that is being visited; a willingness to take risks by virtue of moving outside the tourist environmental bubble; an ability to locate one's own society and its culture in terms of a wide-ranging historical and geographical knowledge, to have some ability to reflect upon and judge aesthetically between different natures, places and societies; and a certain semiotic skill – to be able to interpret tourist signs, to see what they are meant to represent, and indeed to know when they are partly ironic and to be approached coolly or in a detached fashion.

The development of such cosmopolitanism is in turn linked to changes in the nature of citizenship. It has been normal to think of citizenship as being based on the notion that rights are provided by institutions located within territorially demarcated nation-states (see Held 1991). However, a novel kind of 'consumer citizenship' is developing, with four main features. First, people are increasingly citizens by virtue of their ability to purchase goods and services; citizenship is a matter of consumption rather than of political rights and duties (cf John Major's 'citizen's charter'). Second, it is held that people in different societies should have similar rights of access to a wide *diversity* of consumer goods, services and cultural products (see Ohmae 1990). Third, it should be possible for people to be able to travel within all countries as tourists. Those countries which have tried to prevent this (such as China, Albania, Saudi Arabia) are seen as infringing the human rights of foreigners to travel across their territories. And fourth, people from a certain range of societies are seen as having rights of movement and of residence in whichever society they choose to visit as a stranger for whatever periods of time. It is not merely that rights are increasingly global as Held argues, but that those rights include claims to *consume* other cultures and places throughout the world (1991).

However, the development of such putatively global processes does not mean that nationalities have become irrelevant. Most of this chapter has been concerned with the development of processes which have rendered the nation-state as substantially weakened. Nationality though is a different issue. We are now well-aware of the constructed character of many nationalist rituals. But to say that they are constructed, just as 'global cultures' appear to be constructed, is not to suggest that such cultures are in fact equivalent (A. Smith 1990: 178). National cultures are particular, timebound, expressive, and their eclecticism is heavily constrained. Smith notes three crucial components of such nationalities: a sense of continuity between successive generations; shared memories of specific events and personages; and a sense of common destiny on the part of the collectivity sharing those experiences (1990: 179). Indeed he argues that most nationalities have ethnic origins and are therefore in some sense an ethnic grouping or an 'ethnie' (A. Smith 1986). Nationalities are by no means so 'modern' a phenomenon as many commentators have suggested. Particularly significant are the 'legends and landscapes' that give meaning and sense to particular ethnies and hence in some cases to specific nations.

Putative global cultures have by contrast no such collective memories, no succession of generations, no sacred landscapes, and indeed no Golden Age to look back to (see A. Smith 1990). For Smith then the effect of globalization is to reinforce ethnicity and nationality and not to generate a new global culture. It is the new communication networks, as well as the politicization of cultures, the role of intellectuals and the intensification of cultural wars, which all make possible a denser more intense interaction *between* members of a given community and to heighten their competitiveness vis-à-vis other nationalities and ethnies. Now of course many of these ethnies do not coincide with nation-states and so if anything the emergence of such an ethnic revival is a further illustration of the dialectic of globalization and localization (see A. Smith 1984).

There are however a number of further points that Smith does not consider. First, to the extent to which images do indeed become exceptionally important, so ethnies/nationalities will become increasingly constructed through images. Such images are of course circulated, appropriated and manipulated in contemporary culture, and they are particularly circulated for the purposes of international travel and tourism. As ethnies come to be constructed as objects of the 'tourist gaze', often with newly 'invented traditions', this will almost certainly change what the members of particular groups feel about their ethnie identity. They may well consider that the history, memories and places are no longer truly theirs (see Urry 1990c). MacCannell interestingly talks of 'reconstructed ethnicity', an 'ethnicity-for-tourism in which exotic cultures figure as key attractions' (1992: 158). The effect is that tourism 'promotes the restoration, preservation and fictional re-creation of ethnic attributes . . . "Reconstructed Ethnicity" here refers to the kinds of touristic and political/ethnic identities that have emerged in response to pressures from White Culture and tourism' (1992: 159). This is not just ethnicity but a kind of rhetoric, a symbolic expression in a larger system.

There are further important connections between nationality and the nation-state. McCrone notes that the view that 'nation-states, at least in the "developed" world, had economic, political and cultural coherence – that they were self-contained "societies" – has begun to seem less sure' (1992: 2). And this will make certain kinds of nationality empty or vacuous. Indeed McCrone goes on to argue that in the case of Scotland: 'the quest for Scottish cultural independence from a culturally suffocating and homogeneous Anglo-British one ignores the fact that . . . the latter has fragmented' (1992: 193). It has partly fragmented because of the globalizing processes analysed in this chapter; and because of the development of multiple forms of alternative social identity. New kinds of sociation develop whose membership is voluntary and whose commitments are neither ethnic nor national, what have recently been characterized as 'bunds' following Schmalenbach (see Hetherington 1990). Such new sociations result from the 'de-traditionalization' of social life, as people's tastes, values and norms are less determined by 'societal' institutions such as education, royalty, government, family, the law and so on. These new sociations provide important sites whereby new kinds of social identity can be experimented with, and they often provide the context for the learning of new skills.

Finally, we should note how the globalization-localization processes analysed here impact very significantly on women. There is a sense in which their interests might be said to be less 'national' than are those of men (see Enloe 1989, and especially Walby 1990a, for the following). This is so in a variety of respects: women tend to participate less in national as opposed to local politics; they appear to be less militaristic and thus in a sense less nationalistic; they are less likely to kill or threaten to kill others in pursuit of a national identity; they are more likely to join anti-war movements; and they are less a part of the nationally incorporated citizenry of a nation-state, sometimes indeed being more or less excluded from the state. Their interests seem to be both more localist, that is concerned about the quality of local services and environment (especially its safety), and more internationalist, as the female pacificist says in Virginia Woolf's *The Three Guineas*: 'As a woman I have no country. As a woman I want no country. As a woman my country is the whole world' (quoted in Walby 1990a).

Social identity is significantly a question of imagined communities, of imagining oneself to share a common history or destiny or fate with thousands or millions of others that one can never know (see Anderson 1989; and the application to the Scottish case in McCrone 1992). The dialectic of globalization and localization appears to have disrupted the imagined national communities of significant numbers of women in the First World. It is they after all who have had disproportionately to provide humanitarian relief and aid to the victims of ethnic and national struggles.

CONCLUSION

This chapter has attempted to outline a variety of ways in which the relationship of global and local processes is being redrawn, how new global-local nexi are emerging within various spheres of social activity. In that set of developments we have raised various questions about the viability of nationality and the nation-state. We are not suggesting that states do not still possess immense powers. However, one wonders if making or threatening war is the one which they do best. In a way the other problems which confront them are so insuperable, so global and yet involving so many specific local relationships, that gunboat diplomacy, assuming global destruction through nuclear weapons is off the agenda, is a relatively straightforward power to exercise. We have insisted on the multi-layered nature of these processes, ranging through the economic, the political, the cultural and the environmental.

More generally we have outlined what Robins terms 'global-local times', or, as Sony describes their operational strategy, 'global localization' (see Robins 1989a). We have talked about a number of 'locals', from small areas to groupings on the move, to large regions and ethnies. They are all being remade, as new sets of relationships are being constructed at the global level. The task for social science is to make sense of these new kinds of global-local relations and to examine their implications for what we used to examine, namely national societies and economies. In this novel analysis it will be necessary to determine whether the sorts of processes outlined here are cyclical or structural; whether local/global relations are subsets of wider relationships such as the fragmented/the whole or the producer/consumer (see Ohmae 1990); and what the connections are between these processes and the divisions of class, gender and ethnicity, which are normally understood as structured on a national basis. Disorganized capitalism then involves the dissolution of a national community of fate in the north Atlantic rim, of societies which in some sense clearly governed themselves and in which rights, duties and commitments were un-ambiguously owed to the nation-state.

McCrone indeed suggests we are moving into post-nationalist times. This is because nationalism is the gravedigger of many conventional nation-states; because notions of nationality are moving from more ethnic ideas to a more territorial sense (Yugoslavia notwithstanding; see McCrone 1992: 218–19); and because nation-states can no longer govern their borders and prevent the extraordinary flows of ideas, images, capital, technologies, environmental hazards and people that is the contemporary experience. Mobile objects and reflexive subjects produce a disorganized capitalism which involves the dissolution of a national community of fate. Societies no longer obviously govern themselves, and rights, duties and commitments are not simply owed to the nation-states (of the north Atlantic rim).

12

CONCLUSION

Just before the three thousand strong 26th Biannual Congress of German Sociology, Karl Otto Honderich – distinguished Professor at Frankfurt University – penned an unsettling and reverberating *j'accuse* into the pages of *Die Zeit*. Into the pages of this weekly newspaper of intellectual opinion – read by some 400,000 educators, professionals, political policy-makers and others crucially active in 'culture brokerage' and general public sphere responsibility – Honderich (1992) asked if 'sociology had failed Germany'. According to Honderich, sociology had failed Germany in a very specific sense – with its assumptions of a modernizing process, not of *Gemeinschaft*, but of *Gesellschaft*; with its presuppositions of an even more individualized society; with its universalistic claim that social life, indeed the 'life world', was first and foremost a 'learning process'; what the professoriat has offered German public life has been a one-sided sociology of 'the I'.

This was a failure, even a betrayal, of German public life, in that even in the most advanced, even in the 'highest' of modernities, the daily reality of neo-Nazi attacks on asylum seekers, of wave upon wave of immigration, of ethnic cleansing in nearby ex-Yugoslavia, of the improbability of German intervention because of the incomplete repression of collective memory reflected the dogged persistence of 'the we'. What academic theory and cultural analyses had not offered to Germany was a sociology of 'the we'.

And indeed much of this book is dedicated to the development of, in the context of today's global and informationalized age, such a sociology of the 'I'. Where economies of signs and space function as flows the result is individuation. Either this occurs through the emptying out of the shared meanings of 'the we', as the self comes up against an even faster circulation of goods, images, money, ideas and other selves. Or economies of signs and space as flows are part and parcel of the post-material, an informational mode of power/knowledge in which the discourses of the ideoscape and mediascape interpellate selves previously rooted in shared meanings and background practices, and convert these selves into 'I's through the process of individuation, normalization and atomization. Where economies of signs and space function instead as information and communication structures, the outcome is a less unhappy mode of individualization – that of reflexivity in which 'the I' is empowered to take control in regard to the rules and resources of social structure as well as the monitoring of his or her own life narrative. But here the self is again an equally deracinated 'I', cast adrift from community, from the shared meanings and background practices of 'the we'.

But this book has also pointed to a sociology of 'the we'. On the one hand, the same economies of signs and space are the networks, the flows of a 'we' of globalization, and potentially of imagined global communities. Indeed unlike *The End of Organized Capitalism* which was a *cross*-national analysis of social-structural change, this book is an exercise in *inter*-national social analysis. But if our sociology of flows has pointed to the constitution of a global 'we', the sociology of reflexivity, that is of aesthetic or hermeneutic reflexivity, has pointed to possibilities of local versions of 'the we'.

These two embodiments of the 'we' correspond to two very different understandings of the global. One is universalistic, that typically referred to in sociological treatments of globalization. This sort of understanding of the world can be found on the one hand in Marxist world-systems theory (Wallerstein 1990), and on the other in Parsonian functionalism (Robertson 1990). In either case what is assumed is the triumph of the universal over the particular, the development of ever more abstract social relations, a more or less evolutionist, Whig understanding of history and a liberal or proletarian vision of emancipation. Counterposed to this stands the world cast much more in the mould of Heidegger's being-in-the-world (Dreyfus 1991). These are worlds, not of the mediated, but of the immediate. They presume a 'thrownness' into a nexus of shared meanings and practices. These worlds consist not of norms as general rules, but of the non-rule regulated customs or *Sitten* of Hegel's *Sittlichkeit*, of the non-rule regulated (though learned) 'habits' of Bourdieu's 'habitus'. These are worlds in which meaning is achieved by a self which operates, not reflexively, but routinely.

This rooted and Heideggerian phenomenon of 'the we', which is 'worlded' rather than global, seems to open up political space for the new communities, including the 'new social movements'. In its departure from the subject-object assumptions of the abstract 'I', it opens up space as well for ecological thought. But the Heideggerian anti-discursive world of shared meanings, background practices and building, dwelling and thinking is at the same time and proximally the world of racism and ethnic hate. It is not, *pace* Adorno and Bauman, only the 'technology' of bureaucratic reason which was responsible for the Third Reich, but also these very rooted worlds of shared meanings, habits and shibboleths.

This said, does not the very circulation of symbols and selves in international space make possible another more 'cosmopolitan' mode of such rooted being? We encounter today the phenomenon of the 'diaspora'. This is by contrast with the 'melting-pot' where ethnically diverse human beings were melted into a standardized, individuated, *gesellschaftlich* society. In contrast to this the diaspora is at the same time a transplanted community and an integral part of the host society (Bhabha 1990). Hence Salman Rushdie can with conceptual precision refer to himself as 'a

(British) wog'. This sort of cosmopolitanism is vastly other than the pure 'difference' of Marshall Berman's Manhattan of 'all that is solid melts into air' (1983). It is as rooted, as much *Gemeinschaft*, as it is contingency.

Just as loaded, in this recast understanding of the 'we' as the notion of world, is the idea of 'community'. Here again 'community' can be understood, on the one hand as abstract, highly mediated and universal, and on the other as concrete, immediate and particular. What sort of communities find their basis in the socio-cultural geometry of flows described in this book? In the first instance we can see the sort of abstract and mediated 'imagined communities' so artfully delineated by Anderson (1989). His imagined communities are by definition other than ordinary, immediate, communities. And how they are different is made quite clear in his thesis that nationalism's imagined communities are not the stuff of the pre-modern *Gemeinschaft* but quintessentially modern phenomena. Further, Anderson understands their context as involving abstract time, which events happen *in*; abstract space, *in* which places are located; and an abstract social, *in* which people and social relations are located. Nothing could be further from Heidegger's being-in-the-world, in which precisely such Cartesian understandings of time, space and society are castigated as metaphysical obfuscations of being. Nothing also could be further from Alasdair MacIntyre's more immediate communities, in which goods and other meanings are routinely produced in the context of networks of immediately available tools and practices (1981).

But are global versions of Anderson's imagined communities on the one hand, and fully immediate *Gemeinschaften* on Heidegger's (or Tönnies') view on the other, the only alternatives? What about *invented* communities? In a very important sense all communities were at some point invented, even those into whose world we are thrown via our families as very small children. Yet even here two contexts have changed in today's reflexive modernity. The first is that to a greater extent we are not so much thrown into communities, but decide which communities – from youth subcultures to new social movements – we shall throw ourselves into. Second, the invention of communities is a sort of conduct which we more frequently enter into. New communities are being ever more frequently invented, so that such invention of community, such innovation becomes almost chronic. It is no longer the exception, but the rule.

This invention of community or reinvention of self involved in decisions to join new (invented) communities involves aesthetic (hermeneutic) reflexivity. Aesthetic (hermeneutic) reflexivity means making choices about and/or innovating background assumptions and shared practices upon whose bases cognitive and normative reflection is founded. We discussed also in chapter 3 how, unlike cognitive or moral judgment, Kantian aesthetic judgment did not involve the application of a universal rule to a particular case. And how instead, like English Common Law, it involved the application of a previous particular case to a particular. Now if judgment is strictly understood as the application of a universal to a particular, this would not be judgment at all. It would instead be the sort of '*pre*-judgment' of Gadamer's theory of hermeneutics. It would be a question of the non-rule governed *Sitten* of Hegel's ethical life, which are conditions of possibility and 'ethical substance', to any abstract moral rule or judgment.

In this context we can understand the significance of Bourdieu's 'taste communities' in *Distinction* (1984). This book is modelled as we mentioned in chapter 3 on Kant's *Critique of Judgment*. What is at issue is less aesthetic judgment than taste in more prosaic everyday life. And if aesthetic judgments are in important respects already pre-judgments, then so much the more so would be everyday 'judgments' of taste. In Heidegger's being-in-the-world we move into the subject-object categories of cognitive and moral judgment only when there is a breakdown in our shared meanings, only when there is a breakdown in our background practices through which we routinely produce meaning. But (pre-)judgments of taste do not involve this sort of subject-object mode. Such (pre-)judgments are already the background practices, the shared assumptions of taste communities. They are not judgments at all, but *Sitten*, habit. They are not 'rules' or structures about which we can be objective, because we already dwell among them. These pre-judgments are the predispositions, the orientations of the habitus. The habitus *is* these unreflective background practices of the judgments of taste.

The shared, unreflexive orientations and predispositions at issue in Bourdieu's work are the very stuff of (immediate) community. They are at the same time the very stuff of culture. 'Culture' on this count is the immediate, the proximal meanings and practices of place as understood in counterposition to the abstract norms of 'society'. This is of course also what turn-of-the-century German hermeneutics meant by *Kultur* as counterposed to *Zivilisation* of the French Enlightenment and notions of 'society' held by positivists such as Auguste Comte. At stake here was far from just a methodological struggle but also a fundamental disagreement as regards ways of life. At issue was an ideographic mode of life, an ideographic 'ethnomethodology' of everyday life, as counterposed to conduct regulated by an abstract norm-governed social.

In a similar vein, turn-of-the-twenty-first-century Cultural Studies rejects the abstract, impersonal, *gesellschaftlich* rules of the social, but this time for not one, but two alternatives. On the one hand, the abstract blueprint of the social – whether as Marxism, Keynsian welfare-state or rational-choice neo-classicism – is rejected for culture, as the immediate meanings and practices of community. On the other, the social is neglected for culture as the free-floating images of the global mediascape.

The problem is that in contemporary global economies of signs and space, those communities of place and even the invented communities can as easily be race-baiting neo-tribes as they can be new communitarian social movements. 'Neo-tribes' are by definition recently invented communities involving some membership choice. Otherwise they would just be 'tribes'. In general it might be said that 'tame zones' of thickly networked information and communication structures invented communities of the new social movement variety tend to be found, while in sparsely networked 'wild zones' – for example, eastern Germany where aesthetic (and other) resources are thin on the ground – neo-tribes tend to be invented. The point as Bauman (1987) has understood is that such a hermeneutics must also be one of 'translation' to 'the other'. Or as Rorty (1992) has suggested it must be a 'cosmopolitan' hermeneutics between the speech communities of any such neo-tribes. Just as Rorty has counterposed to universalist emancipation such a cosmopolitanism, so would we, along with Bhabha (1990), want to counterpose to abstract and universalist globalization such an *inter*-nationalization of speech communities.

'The we' at issue is not just a phenomenon of ethnic identity and new communitarian social movements but is also integrally involved in work-life, consumption and hence the class structure. Thus 'reflexive production' is only comprehensible in Germany and Japan in terms of information structures rooted in the 'we'. That is, as we pointed out in chapter 4, the 'I' of market governance of Anglo-American production systems has fostered low trust and opportunism, and hindered information flow and knowledge acquisition on the shopfloor. Market governance of labour markets has led in the Anglo-Saxon world to strategic assumptions where capital has opportunistically exploited collectively organized labour when labour-markets are loose and 'labour has exploited capital' when labour-markets have been tight. The outcome of this, in the UK and the USA, was the ultimate revenge of capital on labour and the decimation of union density in the 1980s. The corporatist institutionalization of trust between capital and labour in Germany underlay faster growth and a continued strong presence of unions.

It has further been irrational for the atomized 'I' of the Anglo-American capitalist entrepreneurs to invest in training, in the knowledge that utilitarian labour-power will only go and work for another firm after he or she is trained. On the other hand, this sort of investment is rational for the 'institutionalized we' (as embodied in employers' associations, chambers of commerce and underwritten by the technical colleges) of German capitalists as a group. It is also rational for the individual Japanese firm in so far as its obligational contracting with workers, who work 'in' rather than 'for' the firm, also constitutes an institutionalized 'we'. For them the trust relations between investors and the firm (as well as workers – either as individuals or through works' councils) facilitate information flow to all regions of production systems.

What then are the implications for changing class structure of our analyses of these dialectics between agency and structure, between the 'I' and the 'we'? Marx of course famously and accurately posited that in industrial capitalism class-in-itself or class structure would be more or less determinant of class-for-itself or class consciousness. It has been common for analysts of post-industrialism, of reflexive modernity, to speak of the decline of importance of class structure or consciousness in voting behaviour, the proclivity to join unions, the taking on of a working-class lifestyle and the like. The analyses in this book take this perhaps a step further and suggest an inversion of the Marxist thesis; they suggest that in informationalized and reflexive modernity it is consciousness or reflexivity which is determinant of class structure. This provisional argument can be seen in four ways.

First, access to information and communication networks, as conditions of reflexivity, is a crucial determinant of class position. The 'wild zones' of very sparse lines, flows and networks tend to be where the underclasses, or at least the bottom third, of the 'two-thirds societies' are found. That is, place in the 'mode of information' rather than in the mode of production is the crucial factor in class position. Similarly the unusually densely networked centres of the global cities tend to be where the top fractions, in the corporation headquarters, business and finance and legal services, of today's new informational bourgeoisie are primarily located.

Second, where reflexivity is found will determine the shape of class structure. Thus where information structures favour reflexive production – through their articulation with production systems – in Germany and Japan, industry is competitive and there is a proportionally quite large (industrial) working class. The deficit of reflexivity in production in the UK and USA has via loss in competitiveness led to a class structure in which the rump of a working class is now quite small. Concomitantly the persistence of reflexive consumption in the market-driven Anglo-American world will mean a much larger advanced consumer services sector, including many professionals employed in the expert systems upon which reflexive and individualized consumers are dependent. This will be part of a 'swollen' professional middle class in the Anglo-American world by comparison with corporatist Germany and Japan.

Third, reflexive production in corporatist countries (Germany, Japan) will continue largely to mean the application of information technology in machine building, while in neo-liberal countries (USA, UK, France) it involves working in the informational sectors themselves. The corporatist countries will continue to have a large 'middle mass', of which the highly skilled working class makes up a large part. Neo-liberal nations have a much smaller middle mass – indeed a sizeable portion of the working class proper will work in exporting say Japanese products from inwards investing firms in Britain. Such nations will have exacerbated class polarization of the university-educated information and advanced service sector professionals and a large number of 'junk jobs' in the downgraded services and manufacturing sectors at the bottom end of the social stratification ladder. This will itself be further exacerbated by expected increases in immigration, by the so-called 'browning' of the USA and western Europe.

And finally, the corporatist countries with their large middle mass will continue to have smaller disparities in class stratification. But the same collective institutions that favour growth and class equality – through their reflexive exclusion of 'the other' – create much greater inequalities in regard to gender and ethnicity. Such statist-corporatist measures exclude ethnic minorities from corporate membership and national citizenship altogether. Thus the other side of the high-value-added labour of the corporatist middle mass of men is a low labour force participation rate for women.

In this book we have thus endeavoured to recast the categories by which contemporary societies are to be investigated. There are a number of conceptual innovations which imply the reordering of much of the conventional basis of Western social science.

We noted in the last chapter that the central feature of this social science has been the study of 'societies', each of which is seen as deriving its specific character from the particular relationship of nation and state. It was believed that members of a society share a particular community of fate, that they are governed by a state to which duties and responsibilities are owed and by which certain rights are guaranteed. In the analysis of such 'societies' it is presumed that most aspects of the lives of its members are determined by factors endogenous to the society; and that a fairly clear distinction can be drawn between these endogenous factors and those which are external.

This was a formulation bred from within the north Atlantic rim, since it is mainly there that there have been national societies which had the conceit to believe that they could in some sense govern themselves. And likewise a vibrant social science focussed around the concept of relatively autonomous societies was produced from within those societies of conceit, from Scotland in the eighteenth century (Millar, Ferguson), Britain in the mid-nineteenth century (Marx, Engels, Spencer), Germany and France at the turn of the century (Weber, Simmel, Durkheim, Mauss), the USA in the twentieth century (Mead, Parson, Merton), and so on.

Now we are a little wiser. Issues of economic and social development for the vast majority of the world's population reveal anything but self-determination and autonomy. Likewise, the startling emergence of global environmental issues which know no national boundary, of 'risk societies', have shown that there is in a sense the 'end of the social'. By this we mean the end of societies with endogenously determined 'social structures'. We have analysed in this book the processes which have deconstructed such endogenously determined societies. But this end of the social has in turn been brought about by some exceptionally powerful processes. The concept which we have adopted to analyse these processes is that of the flow. Castells states: 'There is a shift, in fact, away from the centrality of the organizational unit to the network of information and decision. In other words, *flows, rather than organizations*, become the units of work, decision, and output accounting (1989: 142).

In this book we analysed not social structures but flows; and we showed that those flows are not just of people, although the flows of migrants, tourists and refugees are now at record figures, but also of ideas, images, technologies and capital. Our analysis of these economies of signs and space has been focussed upon the overlapping, non-isomorphic patterns of such flows, their organization through time and space, their overlapping effects within particular sites, and the relative causal influence of different flows in different historical epochs. We have considered some of the ways that such flows both subvert endogenously determined social structures (such as the emptying out of the ghetto) *and* provide the preconditions for heightened reflexivity (such as the cultural construction of nature).

Of course the critique of the concept of society has been developed elsewhere. In recent years a number of commentators have suggested that the concept is unhelpful, but there has been relatively little systematic attempt to replace it, Mann's being the most important (see 1986). We have endeavoured to develop some of the categories by which to investigate what Castells has characterized as the 'transformation of the flows of power into the power of flows' (1989: 171).

So far we have suggested that social science has been organized in terms of the concept of the individual 'society'. There has though been an alternative approach which has talked very generally about certain categories of society, such as industrial, capitalist, organized capitalist, late capitalist, post-industrial, post-Fordist and so on. Although some of these categories are helpful they lead analysts to minimize really important differences between societies, both historically and in the contemporary world. In this book we have demonstrated that there are major differences in the form of accumulation and in the pattern of services as between Germany, Japan, certain Scandinavian countries, and the UK and USA. Indeed as with *The End of Organized Capitalism* we tried to demonstrate the importance of 'cross-societal' analysis, to show that there are major differences between apparently similar advanced capitalist societies. But we have not engaged in such comparative analysis simply to show that there are differences between societies because that would have been to return to the kind of 'society-centric' formulation criticized above. Rather we have shown that such differences are the complex product of the interplay between each society's history *and* the current flows of capital, technologies, people, ideas and images, where those flows are also seen as having a history and a geography and where there are certain local nodes in particular societies involved in the propagation or reproduction of particular flows.

So although in a loose sense we might wish to characterize a number of societies mainly in the north Atlantic rim as the product of 'disorganized capitalism', that they are post-industrial, postmodern and post-Fordist, there are some striking differences between them. However, there is not a complete arbitrariness of form. For example, there are three main routes to reflexive accumulation, the Japanese, the German and the advanced sectors model.

This though leads onto a further theme, namely the importance attached to individual and institutionalized reflexivity. In relationship to accumulation the processes by which information was generated, distributed and passed on were shown to be of central importance. We saw not only significant differences between the three routes to reflexive accumulation but also that the kind of information itself differed, being much more practical in the German case, more abstract in the advanced sectors, and more the result of shopfloor discussion in the Japanese case.

So how reflexivity is systematized varies between what appear to be similar societies. Although they are all loosely post-industrial, Germany remains peculiarly retarded in its development. This is partly because of its family structures (a weak development of 'public patriarchy'; see Walby 1990b), and partly because of the very success of German manufacturing based upon training and craft apprenticeships. The US and UK are more obviously post-industrial and postmodern, while Scandinavia has developed as a kind of public post-industrial society. In the UK and US the growth of advanced producer and consumer service industries and hence the huge institutionalization of reflexivity has produced an economy in which services dominate manufacturing. In such societies individual reflexivity is institutionalized through the development of various complex services including even 'therapy services' (see Giddens 1991a, 1992).

Overall we have emphasized that reflexivity is not merely a matter of cognition or of ethics, but also of aesthetics. Such aesthetic or hermeneutic reflexivity, in its interpretive relation to social conditions and the self, is active in production and consumption, in critique and as a foundation for community. More generally, the development of multiple forms of a modernizing reflexivity counters the postmodern dystopia favoured by some analysts. There are of course some immensely powerful transformations of mobility in disorganized capitalism – indeed this book is a systematic attempt to chart these – but the processes involved are more contradictory than the 'dystopic' postmodern account would suggest. Not only are there mobile objects, and this includes capital, technologies, labour-power and images, but there are also reflexive subjects, individually able to monitor their actions and increasingly embedded within systems which are themselves reflexive, cognitively, morally or aesthetically.

The term 'disorganized capitalism' has been employed here. It is not a characterization of individual societies but refers rather to the entire epoch in which a number of putative trends have been developing. There is an asymmetry about organized and disorganized capitalism.

The former refers to individual societies, to a particular configuration of economic, social, political and cultural relations at the level of the *individual* society. It refers to the no more than a dozen or so organized capitalist societies, which were all located within the north Atlantic rim. Although there were some substantial differences between them, as we analysed in *The End of Organized Capitalism*, each of them was characterizable as an organized capitalist society. Beyond them there were scores of other 'more-or-less' societies in colonial and semi-colonial relations with this organized core.

Disorganized capitalism is an epoch in which various processes and flows have transformed this pattern of a dozen or so organized capitalist societies constituting the core within the north Atlantic rim. The processes and flows which have ushered in such a disorganized capitalism include the following: the flowing of capital and technologies to 170 or so individual 'self-governing' capitalist countries each concerned to defend 'its' territory; time-space compression in financial markets and the development of a system of global cities; the growth in importance of internationalized producer services; the generalization of risks which know no national boundaries and of the fear of such risks; the putative globalizing of culture and communication structures partly breaking free of particular territories; the proliferation of forms of reflexivity, individual and institutionalized, cognitive and especially aesthetic; huge increases of personal mobility across the globe, of tourists, migrants and refugees; the development of a service class with cosmopolitan tastes especially for endlessly 'fashionable' consumer services provided by one or other category of migrant; the declining effectivity and legitimacy of nation-states which are unable to control such disorganized capitalist flows; and the emergence of 'neo-worlds', the kinds of socially and regionally re-engineered cultural spaces which are the typical homelands for cosmopolitan postmodern individuals (see Luke 1992 on the last; examples include the art world, the financial world, the drug world, the advertising world, as well as the academic world parodied in Lodge 1983). Luke summarizes the shifts involved: from place to flow, from spaces to streams, from organized hierarchies to disorganiz-ation (1992). Social classes, which are conventionally taken as focussed around place, national spaces and organized hierarchies, are one of the victims of such disorganization. They are simultaneously localized and globalized, transformed by the flows of people, images and information. Classes in the sense of hierarchically organized national entities are rapidly disssolving, at the very same time that social and spatial inequalities rapidly increase.

What then are the consequences of such forms of disorganization for social and political life at the turn of the millennium? Do the flows of social life provide such rich possibilities that apocalyptic terrors of the future are unjustified and inappropriate? The marriage of the computer and the telecommunications revolution results in movements of information at the speed of light and to enormous audiences, and this might be thought to decentralize both knowledge and power and to enable 'new sociations' to develop away from the 'traditional' institutions of social life (see Hetherington 1990). Wriston argues how:

> an international communications system, incorporating technologies from mobile telephones to communication satellites, deprives governments of the

ability to keep secrets from the world, or from their own people, [hence] power changes hands [since] the world is watching, and the power of world opinion is transmitted and focussed and reported by the telecom network. (1992: 575–6)

The 'de-traditionalization' of the British monarchy is perhaps the clearest example of this. Another instance is the way in which, prior to the Gulf War, Kuwait was transformed from a place in space to be annexed by Iraq into a flow as its assets were transformed into streams of electronic communication on the screens of the world's financial institutions (see Luke 1992).

Or alternatively will these flows create nightmare scenarios, of increasingly extensive 'wild zones' consisting of collapsing empires (USSR), imploding nation-states (Yugoslavia), ungovernable First World cities (Los Angeles), tracts of desertification (southeast Africa) and countries dominated by narco-capitalism (Colombia; see Luke 1992). Such wild zones are characterized by a collapsing (or collapsed) civil society, a weakly developed 'civilizing process', and flight to 'tame zones' for those that are able to escape. Such tame zones are areas of economic, political and cultural security, often with strong boundaries separating them off from the wild zones of disorganized capitalism (see Luke 1992; as well as chapter 6 above). Such divisions can of course be seen within local areas where electronic surveillance techniques keep the one-thirds and the two-thirds societies apart.

So there are quite different possibilities envisaged here, of a kind of disorganized decentralization, or an apocalypse now; of a generally benign redistribution of information, knowledge and power, or a terrifying crisis of ungovernability spreading over significant parts of the globe. There are many aspects of these contrasting visions. We will note three, those focussed around information, the state and place.

The growth of information may be seen as liberating or as repressive. On the one hand, the use of new forms of information technology may facilitate the development of small communitarian public spheres. A new logic of place and practical will-formation could develop on the basis of decentralized data banks, interactive communication systems and community-based multi-media centres (see Castells 1989: 352). New sociations can generate new skills and new loci of power away from the traditional institutions of class, family, education, politics, monarchy and so on.

Or on the other hand, information technology can lead to new forms of control and erode the critical crafts of reading and writing. What Agger terms 'fast capitalism' undermines the power of the book and a kind of Foucauldian power/knowledge dystopia may develop in which even moral and practical knowledge is transformed into cognitive and technical systems which normalize and regulate what was previously private (including the private and critical activity of book reading: see Agger 1989; Webster and Robins 1989: 340–1). A visual culture is publicly controllable in a way in which a literary culture is not.

Likewise the potential evolution of the state can be viewed positively or negatively. The modernist nation-state, which resulted in the achievements of both liberal and social democracy *and* of the 'holocaust', is being 'hollowed out' (as we saw in the preceding chapter; see Jessop 1992; Bauman 1989). Its powers are being delegated upwards to supraregional or international bodies, downwards to regional or local states or to the private sector, inwards to alternative elements controlling the means of physical coercion, and outwards to relatively autonomous cross-national alliances. Such a hollowed-out state has its powers weakened at the same time that its legitimacy is challenged. This occurs partly because of its shortcomings in the face of the flows previously discussed and especially its inability to control the information flows within its national boundaries, and partly because it has difficulty in justifying its actions as being in accordance with the apparently omnipotent 'market' (see Ohmae 1990). So states are faced by a tremendous postmodern complexity. Partly this might be seen positively, as indicating the demise of the kinds of bureaucratically organized states which have waged wars, incarcerated citizens and administered large populations for most of this century. The demise of the nation-state might favour the proliferation of local and regional states which could more effectively respond to the wishes of its citizens, a much more localist and pluralist democracy (see Held 1993). Or such developments might be viewed as reinforcing a nightmarish dystopia. The absence of a national context for policy will result in enormous social and spatial inequalities, of ungovernable wild zones next to highly disciplined tame zones, where each reinforces the other, and where there is no strong national authority able to impose more uniform civilized conditions of existence. The absence of national social classes means that there is little to counter such disorganization. At the same time the cosmopolitan participants in various neo-worlds can speed between the tame zones leaving other travellers to make out in the wild zones, perhaps encountering each other in 'empty meeting grounds' (see MacCannell 1992).

Finally, flows impact most significantly on places. How can spatial meanings be attached to or develop within an experience in which 'the space of flows . . . supersedes the space of places'? (Henderson and Castells 1987: 7; and see Watts 1992). Do places vanish, rendered invisible by the overwhelming rush of capital, images, ideas, technologies and people? Does not this intense mobility of objects and subjects produce placelessness, where only the most superficial of differences stand out against the onward rush of flows? Meyrowitz suggests that many people:

> no longer seem to 'know their place' because the traditionally interlocking components of 'place' have been split apart by electronic media . . . Our world may suddenly seem senseless to many people because, for the first time in modern history, it is relatively placeless. (1985: 309)

Alternatively it may be argued these flows are themselves organized, they are not literally undiscriminating, and so places attract and they repel.

Of course by place we mean in part image but even so places might not be seen as simply swamped by a meaningless placenessness. They are remade or reimagined, often to attract flows of tourists or entrepreneurs (a tame zone), or to repel migrants or low-wage capital (to a wild zone). But places have always been remade. There is nothing surprising about this. What is distinct about the contemporary remaking of place are the following: the importance of image and especially of an (aesthetic) reflexivity of place; the impact of global flows and especially of information, image and voluntary visitors which cause places to be remade with increasing rapidity; and the relative weakness of national states (and national classes) in the face of such flows and their effects on the extraordinary remaking of place. As Marx might have said more generally, 'all that is built or all that is "natural" melts into image' in the contemporary global economies of signs and space.

BIBLIOGRAPHY

Abegglen, J. and Stalk, G. (1985) *Kaisha: The Japanese Corporation*. New York: Basic Books

Abercrombie, N. (1990) 'Flexible specialization in the publishing industry'. Unpublished paper, Department of Sociology, Lancaster University

Abercrombie, N. (1991) 'The privilege of the producer', pp. 171–85 in R. Keat and N. Abercrombie (eds), *Enterprise Culture*. London: Routledge

Abercrombie, N., Hill, S. and Turner, B. (1980) *The Dominant Ideology Thesis*. London: Allen & Unwin

Abercrombie, N., Hill, S. and Turner, B. (eds) (1990) *Dominant Ideologies*. London: Unwin Hyman

Abler, R.F. (1991) 'Hardware, software and brainware: mapping and understanding telecommunications technologies', pp. 31–48 in S. Brunn and T. Leinbach (eds), *Collapsing Time and Space*. London: Harper Collins

Ackroyd, S., Hughes, J. and Soothill, K. (1989) 'Public sector services and their management', *Journal of Management Studies*, 26: 603–20

Adam, B. (1990) *Time and Social Theory*. Cambridge: Polity

Adorno, T. (1970) *Ästhetische Theorie*. Frankfurt: Suhrkamp

Adorno, T. and Horkheimer, M. (1972) *Dialectic of Enlightenment*. New York: Herder & Herder

Agent Interview (1989) Interview with a London literary agent and senior commissioning editor with a newly established and fashionable London trade publisher, London, November

Agger, B. (1989) *Fast Capitalism*. Urbana, Ill.: University of Illinois Press

Aglietta, M. (1987) *A Theory of Capitalist Regulation: The US Experience*. London: Verso

Aksoy, A. and Robins, K. (1992) 'Hollywood for the twenty-first century: global competition for critical mass in image markets', *Cambridge Journal of Economics*, 16: 1–22

Allen, J. (1988) 'Towards a post-industrial economy', pp. 91–135 in J. Allen and D. Massey (eds), *The Economy in Question*. London: Sage

Altvater, E. (1990) 'Fordist and post-Fordist international division of labour and monetary regimes'. Paper, Pathways to Industrialization and Regional Development in the 1990s Conference, UCLA, 14–18 March

Amin, A. and Robins, K. (1990) 'The re-emergence of regional economies? The mythical geography of flexible accumulation', *Environment and Planning D: Society and Space*, 8: 7–34

Amin, A. and Thrift, N. (1992) 'Neo-Marshallian nodes in global governance', *International Journal of Urban and Regional Research*, 16: 571–87

Anderson, P. (1989) *Imagined Communities*. London: Verso

Andrew, M. (1989) *The Search for the Picturesque*. Aldershot: Scolar Press

Angel, D. (1989) 'The labor market for engineers in the US semi-conductor industry', *Economic Geography*, 65: 99–112

Angel, D. (1990) 'New firm formation in the semi-conductor industry: elements of a flexible manufacturing system', *Regional Studies*, 24: 211–21

Aoki, M. (1987) 'The Japanese firm in transition', pp. 263–88 in K. Yamamura and Y. Yasuba (eds), *The Political Economy of Japan*, Vol 1, *The Domestic Transformation*. Stanford, Calif.: Stanford University Press

Aoki, M. (1988) *Information, Incentives and Bargaining in the Japanese Economy*. Cambridge: Cambridge University Press

Aoki, M. (1989) 'The nature of the Japanese firm as a nexus of employment and financial contracts: an overview', *Journal of the Japanese and International Economies*, 3: 345–66

Aoki, M. (1990) 'The participatory generation of information rents and the theory of the firm', pp. 26–52 in M. Aoki, B. Gustafsson and O. Williamson (eds), *The Firm as a Nexus of Treaties*. London: Sage

Appadurai, A. (1990) 'Disjuncture and difference in the global cultural economy', *Theory, Culture and Society*, 7: 295–310

Arcaya, J. (1992) 'Why is time not included in modern theories of memory?', *Time and Society*, 1: 301–14

Argyris, C. (1972) *The Applicability of Organizational Sociology*. Cambridge: Cambridge University Press

Asanuma, B. (1989) 'Manufacturer–supplier relationships in Japan and the concept of relation-specific skill', *Journal of the Japanese and International Economies*, 3: 1–30

Ashworth, G. and Voogd, H. (1990) *Selling the City*. London: Belhaven

Bagguley, P., Mark Lawson, J., Shapiro, D., Urry, J., Walby, S. and Warde, A. (1990) *Restructuring: Place, Class and Gender*. London: Sage

Balaczs, G. (1991) 'Comment on compte des pauvres: la construction statistique de l'objet pauvreté', paper for Poverty, Immigration and Urban Marginality in the Advanced Societies Conference, Paris, 10–11 May

Banham, R. (1971) *Los Angeles: The Architecture of Four Ecologies*. New York: Harper & Row

Barley, S., Freeman, J. and Hybels, R. (1991) 'Strategic alliances in commercial biotechnology', paper for 10th European Group for Organization Studies (EGOS) Colloquium, Vienna, 15–17 July

Barou, J. (1982) 'Immigration and urban social policy in France: the experience of Paris', pp. 137–49 in J. Solomos (ed), *Migrant Workers in Metropolitan Cities*. Strasbourg: European Science Foundation

Barthes, R. (1972) *Mythologies*. London: Cape

Bassett, K. and Harloe, M. (1990) 'Swindon: the rise and decline of a growth coalition', pp. 42–61 in M. Harloe, C. Pickvance and J. Urry (eds), *Localities, Policies and Politics*. London: Unwin Hyman

Bassett, K., Boddy, M., Harloe, M. and Lovering, J. (1989) 'Living in the fast lane: economic and social change in Swindon', pp. 45–85 in P. Cooke (ed), *Localities*. London: Unwin Hyman

Bate, J. (1991) *Romantic Ecology*. London: Routledge

Baudrillard, J. (1981) *For a Critique of the Political Economy of the Sign*. St Louis: Telos Press

Bauman, Z. (1987) *Legislators and Interpreters*. Cambridge: Polity

Bauman, Z. (1989) *Modernity and the Holocaust*. Cambridge: Polity Press

Bauman, Z. (1992) *Intimations of Postmodernity*. London: Routledge

Beck, L.W. (1965) 'Kant's two conceptions of the will in their political context', pp. 215–29 in L.W. Beck, *Studies in the Philosophy of Kant*. Indianapolis: Bobbs-Merrill

Beck, U. (1987) 'The anthropological shock: Chernobyl and the contours of the risk society', *Berkeley Journal of Sociology*, 32: 153–65

Beck, U. (1991) 'Die blaue Blume der Moderne', *Der Spiegel*, 33: 50–1

Beck, U. (1992a) *Risk Society: Towards a New Modernity*, tr M. Ritter. London: Sage

Beck, U. (1992b) 'From industrial society to risk society: questions of survival, structure and ecological enlightenment', *Theory, Culture and Society*, 9: 97–123

Beckenbach, N. (1991) *Industriesoziologie*. Berlin: De Gruyter

Begg, I. (1992) 'The spatial impact of completion of the internal market for financial services', *Regional Studies*, 26: 333–47

Begg, I. and Cameron, G. (1988) 'High technology location and the urban areas of Great Britain', *Urban Studies*, 25: 361–79

Bell, D. (1973) *The Coming of Post-Industrial Society*. London: Heinemann
Bell, D. (1979) *The Cultural Contradictions of Capitalism*. 2nd edition. London: Heinemann
Bell, D. (1987) 'The world and the United States in 2013', *Daedalus*, 116 (3): 1–31
Bellah, R., Madsen, R., Sullivan, W., Swidler, A. and Tipton, S. (1985) *Habits of the Heart*.
    Berkeley, Calif.: University of California Press
Benjamin, W. (1973) 'The work of art in an age of mechanical reproduction', pp. 219–54 in
    W. Benjamin, *Illuminations*. London: Fontana
Benteler, P. (1991) 'Betriebliche Binnenstruktur und berufliche Bildung', pp. 91–101 in U.
    Laur-Ernst (ed), *Neue Fabrikstrukturen*. Bonn: Bundesinstitut für Berufsbildung
Benton, T. (1989) 'Marxism and natural limits: an ecological critique and reconstruction',
    New Left Review, 178: 51–86
Berendt, J. (1984) *The Jazz Book*. London: Paladin
Bergson, H. (1950) *Time and Free Will*. London: Allen & Unwin
Bergson, L. (1913) *Creative Evolution*. London: Macmillan
Berking, H. and Neckel, S. (1990) 'Die Politik der Lebensstile in einem Berliner Bezirk: Zu
    einigen Formen nachtraditionaler Vergemeinschaftung', *Soziale Welt*, 7: 481–500
Berman, M. (1983) *All that is Solid Melts into Air*. London: Verso
Bernschneider, W., Schindler, G. and Schüller, J. (1991) 'Industriepolitik in Baden-
    Württemberg und Bayern', pp. 57–73 in U. Jürgens and W. Krumbein (eds), *Industriepoli-
    tische Strategien*. Berlin: Sigma
Bernstein, I. (1960) *The Lean Years: A History of the American Worker, 1920–1933*. Boston:
    Houghton Mifflin
Berque, A. (1982) *Vivre l'espace au Japon*. Paris: Presses Universitaires de France
Bhabha, H.K. (ed), (1990) *Nation and Narration*. London: Routledge
Bianchini, F. (1991) 'Alternative cities', *Marxism Today*, June: 36–8
Blackburn, P., Coombs, R. and Green, K. (1985) *Technology, Economic Growth and the
    Labour Process*. New York: St Martin's Press
Bluestone, B. and Harrison, B. (1982) *The Deindustrialization of America*. New York: Basic
    Books
Boase, M. (1989) Interview with Martin Boase, an Advertising Executive, BMP DDB
    Needham, London, 16 August
Boltanski, L. (1987) *Making of a Class: Cadres in French Society*. Cambridge: Cambridge
    University Press
Boltanski, L. and Thevenot, L. (1988) *Les économies de grandeur*. Paris: Presses Universit-
    aires de France
Bordwell, D., Staiger, J. and Thompson, K. (1985) *The Classical Hollywood Cinema*. New
    York: Columbia University Press
Bourdieu, P. (1984) *Distinction*. London: Routledge
Bourdieu, P. (1987) 'Legitimation and structured interests in Weber's sociology of religion',
    pp. 119–36 in S. Whimster and S. Lash (eds), *Max Weber: Rationality and Modernity*.
    London: Allen & Unwin
Bourdieu, P. (1990) 'Time perspectives in the Kabyle', pp. 219–37 in J. Hassard (ed), *The
    Sociology of Time*. London: Macmillan
Bourdieu, P. and Darbel, A. (1969) *L'amour de l'art: les musées d'art européens et leur public*.
    Paris: Editions de Minuit
Bourgois, P. (1991) 'In search of respect: the new service economy and the crack alternative
    in Spanish Harlem', paper for Poverty, Immigration and Urban Marginality Working
    Conference, Maison Suger, Paris, 10–11 May
Boyer, R. (1986) 'Rapport salarial, croissance et crise', pp. 11–33 in R. Boyer (ed), *La
    flexibilité du travail en Europe*. Paris: Découverte
Brabourne, J. (1989) Interview with Lord Brabourne, Honorary President, British Film
    Technicians and Producers Association, London, 11 July
Brater, M. (1991) 'Ende des Taylorismus: Paradigmawechsel in der Berufspädagogik?', pp.
    83–99 in U. Laur-Ernst (ed), *Neue Fabrikstrukturen: Veränderte Qualifikationen*. Bonn:
    Bundesinstitut für Berufsbildung

Bratton, J. (1991) 'Japanization at work: the case of engineering plants in Leeds', *Work, Employment and Society*, 5: 377–95

Braverman, H. (1974) *Labor and Monopoly Capital*. New York: Monthly Review Press

Brendon, P. (1991) *Thomas Cook: 150 Years of Popular Tourism*. London: Secker & Warburg

Brett, E. (1983) *International Money and Capitalist Crisis*. London: Heinemann

Brint, S. (1988) 'The upper professionals of the "dual city": a high command of commerce, culture and civic regulation', paper for Dual City Working Group, New York, 11–12 December

Brown, P. and Scase, R. (1991) 'Social change and economic disadvantage in Britain', pp. 1–22 in P. Brown and R. Scase (eds), *Poor Work, Disadvantage and the Division of Labour*. Milton Keynes: Open University Press

Brunello, G. (1988) 'Transfers of employees between Japanese manufacturing enterprises', *British Journal of Industrial Relations*, 26: 119–32

Brunn, S. and Leinbach, T. (1991) 'Introduction', pp. xv–xxvi in S. Brunn and T. Leinbach (eds), *Collapsing Time and Space: Geographic Aspects of Communication and Information*. London: Harper Collins

Brunner, E. (1945) *Holidaymaking and the Holiday Trades*. Oxford: Oxford University Press

Brusco, S. (1990) 'Small firms and the provision of real services', discussion paper for Flexible Specialization in Europe Workshop, ILO, Zurich, 25–6 October

Brusco, S. and Righi, E. (1989) 'Local government, industrial policy and social consensus: the case of Modena (Italy)', *Economy and Society*, 18: 405–24

Bryant, C. (1991) 'Europe and the European Community', *Sociology*, 25: 189–207

Budd, L. and Whimster, S. (1992) *Global Finance and Urban Living: The Case of London*. London: Routledge

Budzinski, M. and Clemens, K. (1991) *Rausland, oder: Menschenrechte für alle*. Göttingen: Lamuv Verlag

Burrage, M. (1972) 'Democracy and the mystery of the crafts: observations on work relationships in America and Britain', *Daedalus*, 101: 141–62

Burton, D. (1992) 'Banks go to Market'. PhD dissertation, Department of Sociology, Lancaster University

Busch, K. (1989) 'Nation-state and European integration: structural problems in the process of economic integration within the European Community', pp. 123–53 in M. Gottdiener and N. Komninos (eds), *Capitalist Development and Crisis Theory*. Basingstoke: Macmillan

Butterwegge, C. and H. Isola (eds), (1990) *Rechtsextremismus im vereinigten Deutschland*. Berlin: LinksDruck Verlag

Campbell, J., Hollingsworth, J.R. and Lindberg, L. (eds) (1991) *Governance of the American Economy*. Cambridge: Cambridge University Press

Campbell, A., Sorge, A. and Warner, M. (1988) 'Manufacturing products with micro-electronics: sectoral strengths and the social construction of actors in Britain and Germany', paper for The Impacts of Structural and Technological Change on the Labour Market, Research Unit Labour Market and Employment (IIM), Wissenschaftszentrum (WZB), Berlin, 20–1 October

Capra, F. (1982) *The Turning Point*. London: Wildwood House

Cargill T. and Royama, S. (1988) *The Transition of Finance in Japan and the United States*. Stanford, Calif.: Hoover Institution

Carlzon, J. (1987) *Moments of Truth*. Cambridge, Mass.: Ballinger

Casey, B. (1991) 'Recent developments in the German apprenticeship system', *British Journal of Industrial Relations*, 29: 205–22

Castells, M. (1989) *The Informational City*. Oxford: Blackwell

Castles, S. and Kosack, G. (1973) *Immigrant Workers and Class Structure in Western Europe*. London: Oxford University Press

Cawson, A. (1989) 'Sectoral governance in consumer electronics in Britain and France', paper for Comparing Capitalist Economies: the Governance of Economic Sectors Conference, Bellagio, Italy, 31 May

Champagne, P. (1989) *Faire l'opinion publique*. Paris: Editions de Minuit

Cheng, M.T. (1991) 'The Japanese permanent employment system', *Work and Occupations*, 18: 148–71

Churchill, C. (1987) *Serious Money*. London: Methuen

Clairmonte, F. and Cavanagh, J. (1984) 'Transnational corporations and services: the final frontier', *Trade and Development*, 5· 215–73

Coakley, J. (1992) 'London as an international financial centre', pp. 52–72 in L. Budd and S. Whimster (eds), *Global Finance and Urban Living*. London: Routledge

Coffey, W.J. (1992) 'The role of producer services in systems of flexible production', pp. 133–46 in H. Ernste and V. Meier (eds), *Regional Development and Contemporary Industrial Response: Extending Flexible Specialization*. London: Belhaven

Cohen, S. and Zysman, J. (1987) *Manufacturing Matters*. New York: Basic Books

Cole, R. (1971) *Japanese Blue Collar*. Berkeley, Calif.: University of California Press

Cole, R. (1989) *Strategies for Learning: Small Group Activities in American, Japanese and Swedish Industry*. Berkeley, Calif.: University of California Press

Coleman, J. (1990) *Foundations of Social Theory*. Cambridge, Mass.: Harvard University Press

Collins, J. (1989) *Uncommon Cultures*. New York: Routledge

Colson, F. (1926) *The Week*. Cambridge: Cambridge University Press

Commission of the European Communities (1990) *European Economy: Social Europe. The Impact of the Internal Market by Industrial Sector: The Challenge for the Member States*. Brussels: Commission of the European Communities

Connerton, P. (1989) *How Societies Remember*. Cambridge: Cambridge University Press

Cooke, P. (1988) 'Flexible integration, scope economies and strategic alliances: social and spatial mediations', *Environment and Planning D: Society and Space*, 6: 281–300

Cooke, P. (ed), (1989) *Localities*. London: Unwin Hyman

Cooke, P. (1990) 'Globalization of economic organization and the emergence of regional interstate partnerships', paper for Structural Change in the West Conference, Cambridge, September

Cooke, P. and Wells, P. (1991) 'Uneasy alliances: the spatial development of computing and communication markets', *Regional Studies*, 25: 345–54

Coriat, B. (1976) *Science, technique et capital*. Paris: Seuil

Coriat, B. (1979) *L'Atelier et le chronomètre*. Paris: Bourgois

Coriat, B. (1985) 'L'accord de 1984 dans l'automobile et la nouvelle stratégie syndicale', *Travail*, 9: 21–26

Coriat, B. (1990) *L'atelier et le robot: essai sur le fordisme et la production de mass à l'âge de l'électronique*. Paris: Bourgois

Coriat, B. (1991) *Penser à l'envers: travail et organisation dans l'entreprise japonaise*. Paris: Bourgois

Corner, J. and Harvey, S. (eds), (1991) *Enterprise and Heritage*. London: Routledge

Cornford, J. and Robins, K. (1992) 'Development strategies in the audiovisual industries: the case of northeast England', *Regional Studies*, 26: 421–35

Coser, L., Kadushin, C. and Powell, W. (1982) *Books: The Culture and Commerce of Publishing*. New York: Basic Books

Cousins, C. (1986) 'The labour process in the state welfare sector', pp. 85–108 in D. Knights, and H. Willmott (eds), *Managing the Labour Process*. London: Gower

Cousins, C. (1987) *Controlling Social Welfare*. Brighton: Wheatsheaf

Coveney, P. and Highfield, R. (1991) *The Arrow of Time*. London: Flamingo

Crang, P. (1993) 'A new service society: on the geographies of service employment'. PhD dissertation, Department of Geography, University of Cambridge

Crick, M. (1990) 'Tourist, locals and anthropologists: quizzical reflections on "otherness" in tourist encounters and in tourism research', paper for the World Congress of Sociology, Madrid, July

Crook, S., Pakulski, J. and Waters, M. (1992) *Postmodernization: Change in Advanced Society*. London: Sage

Cross, G. (1990) *Worktowners at Blackpool: Mass-Observation and Popular Leisure in the 1930s*. London: Routledge

Cross, M. (1987) 'Migrant workers in western European cities: forms of inequality and strategies for policy', *Migration*, 2: 3–15

Cross, M. and Etzinger, H. (1988) 'Caribbean minorities in Britain and the Netherlands: comparative questions', pp. 3–15 in M. Cross and H. Etzinger (eds), *Lost Illusions: Caribbean Minorities in Britain and the Netherlands*. London: Routledge

Cross, M. and Johnson, M. (1988) 'Mobility denied: Afro-Caribbean labour and the British economy', pp. 73–105 in M. Cross and H. Etzinger (eds), *Lost Illusions: Caribbean Minorities in Britain and the Netherlands*. London: Routledge

Crouch, C. (1977) *Class Conflict and the Industrial Relations Crisis*. London: Heinemann

Crouch, C. and Finegold, D. (1991) 'Comparative occupational training systems: the role of employers associations and trade unions', European Group of Organizational Studies Conference, Vienna, July

Curtis, S. (1989) *The Geography of Public Welfare Provision*. London: Routledge

Daniel, W. and Milward, N. (1984) *Workplace Industrial Relations in Britain*. London: Heinemann Educational Books

Daniels, P. (1985) *Service Industries: A Geographical Appraisal*. London: Methuen

Daniels, P. (1987) 'The geography of services', *Progress in Human Geography*, 11: 433–47

Daniels, P. (1991) 'Internationalization, telecommunications and metropolitan development: the role of producer services', pp. 149–69 in S. Brunn and T. Leinbach (eds), *Collapsing Time and Space*. London: Harper Collins

Daniels, S. and Cosgrove, D. (1988) 'Introduction: iconography and landscape', pp. 1–10 in D. Cosgrove and S. Daniels (eds), *The Iconography of Landscape*. Cambridge: Cambridge University Press

Dankbaar, B. (1989) 'Sectoral governance in the automobile industries of West Germany, Great Britain and France', discussion paper for Comparing Capitalist Economies: Variations in the Governance of Sectors Conference. Bellagio, Italy

Davidoff, L. (1973) *The Best Circles*. London: Croom Helm

Davis, M. (1990) *City of Quartz*. London: Verso

Dawkins, W. (1990) 'Rhone-Alps', *Financial Times*, 27 March

de Jong, M., Machielse, K. and de Ruitjer, P. (1992) 'Producer services and flexible networks in the Netherlands', pp. 147–62 in H. Ernste and V. Meier (eds), *Regional Development and Contemporary Industrial Response*. London: Belhaven

de Jong, W. (1989) 'The development of inter-ethnic relations in an old district of Rotterdam between 1970 and 1985', *Ethnic and Racial Studies*, 12: 257–78

Deleuze, G. (1972) *Proust and Signs*. New York: Braziller

Demes, H. (1989) 'Die pyramidenförmige Struktur der japanischen Automobilindustrie und die Zusammenarbeit zwischen Endherstellern und Zuliefern', pp. 251–97 in N. Altmann and D. Sauer (eds), *Systemische Rationalisierung und Zulieferindustrie*. Frankfurt: Campus

Department of the Environment (1990). *Tourism and the Inner City*. London: HMSO

Department of Trade and Industry Official (1989) Interview with a civil servant charged with cinema industry, London, 15 July

Deutschmann, C. (1986) 'Economic restructuring and company unionism: the Japanese model', discussion paper for Research Unit Labour Market and Employment, Wissenschaftszentrum, Berlin

Deutschmann, C. and Weber, C. (1987) 'Das japanische "Arbeitsbienen"-Syndrom: Auswirkungen der Rundum-Nutzung der Arbeitskraft', discussion paper, Wissenschaftszentrum, Berlin.

Donovan, P. (1990a) 'Industry shuns Southeast', *The Guardian*, 15 January

Donovan, P. (1990b) 'The tragic truth behind an urban disaster story', *The Guardian*, 20 January

Dore, R. (1973) *British Factory – Japanese Factory*. Berkeley, Calif.: University of California Press

Dore, R. (1986) *Flexible Rigidities: Industrial Policy and Structural Adjustment in the Japanese Economy, 1970–1980*. Stanford, Calif.: Stanford University Press

Dore, R. (1987) *Taking Japan Seriously*. London: Athlone

Dore, R. (1989) 'Where we are now: musings of an evolutionist', *Work, Employment and Society*, 3: 425–46

Douglas, M. (1986) *How Institutions Think*. London: Routledge

Douglas, M. and Wildavsky, A. (1982) *Risk and Culture*. Los Angeles: University of California Press

Dreyfus, H. (1991) *Being-in-the-World: A Comment on Heidegger's 'Being and Time'*. Cambridge, Mass.: MIT Press

Dubofsky, M. (1968) *When Workers Organize: New York City in the Progressive Era*. Amherst, Mass.: University of Massachusetts Press

Dunning, J. and McQueen, M. (1981) *Transnational Corporations in International Tourism*. New York: UN Centre on Transnational Corporations

Durkheim, E. (1947) *The Elementary Forms of the Religious Life*. London: Allen & Unwin

Durkheim, E. and Mauss, M. (1970) *Primitive Classifications*. London: Cohen & West

Eaglcton, T. (1989) *The Ideology of the Aesthetic*. Oxford: Blackwell

Eco, U. (1976) *A Theory of Semiotics*. Bloomington, Ind.: Indiana University Press

Eco, U. (1986). *Travels in Hyper-Reality*. London: Picador

Economic Development, Wigan (undated) *I've never been to Wigan but I know what it's like*. Wigan: Economic Development Office

Eder, K. (1988) *Die Vergesellschaftung der Natur*. Frankfurt: Suhrkamp

Elias, N. (1992) *Time: An Essay*. Oxford: Blackwell

Enloe, C. (1989) *Bananas, Beaches and Bases: Making Feminist Sense of International Politics*. London: Pandora

Erbe, M. (1987) 'Berlin im Kaiserreich (1871–1918)', pp. 691–796 in W. Ribbe (ed), *Geschichte Berlins, Zweiter Band, Von der Märzrevolution bis zur Gegenwart*. Munich: Beck

Erikson, E. (1963) *Childhood and Society*. New York: Norton

Esping-Andersen, G. (1990) *The Three Worlds of Welfare Capitalism*. Cambridge: Polity

Evans, T. (1985) 'Money makes the world go round', *Capital and Class*, 24: 99–124

Evans-Pritchard, E. (1940) *The Nuer*. Oxford: Oxford University Press

Fainstein, S. and Fainstein, N. (1989) 'The racial dimension in urban political economy', *Urban Affairs Quarterly*, 25: 187–99

Family Firm Editor (1990) Interview with a senior publisher with a position on the board of a long-established British family firm, recently acquired by an American company, London, January

Featherstone, M. (1990) 'Global culture: an introduction', *Theory, Culture and Society*, 7: 1–14

Featherstone, M. (1991) *Consumer Culture and Postmodernism*. London: Sage

Feldman, R. (1986) *Japanese Financial Markets*. Cambridge, Mass.: MIT Press

Fentress, J. and Wickham, C. (1992) *Social Memory*. Oxford: Blackwell

Fevre, R. (1991) 'Emerging alternatives to full-time and permanent employment', pp. 56–70 in P. Brown and R. Scase (eds), *Poor Work*. Milton Keynes: Open University Press

Finkelstein, J. (1989) *Dining Out: A Sociology of Modern Manners*. Cambridge: Polity

Flecker, J., Thompson, P. and Wallace, T. (1991) 'Taking control: an analysis of the organizational consequences of mergers and acquisitions in the UK and Austria', paper for 10th European Group for Organization Studies (EGOS) Colloquium, Vienna, 15–17 July

Fletcher, W. (1989) Interview with Winston Fletcher of the advertising firm Delaney Fletcher Slaymaker Delaney/Bozell, London, 31 August

Flora, P. and Heidenheimer, A. (eds), (1981) *The Development of Welfare States in Europe and America*. London: Transaction Books

Florida, R. and Kenney, M. (1990) *The Breakthrough Illusion: Corporate America's Failure to move from Innovation to Mass Production*. New York: Basic Books

Fogelson, R. (1971) *Violence as Protest: A Study of Riots and Ghettos*. Garden City, N.Y.: Doubleday

Foster, J. (1989) 'The uncoupling of the world order: a survey of global crisis theories', pp. 99–122 in M. Gottdiener and N. Komninos (eds), *Capitalist Regulation Development and Crisis Theory*. Basingstoke: Macmillan

Foucault, M. (1984) *Histoire de la sexualité*, Vol. 2, *L'Usage des plaisirs*. Paris: Gallimard

Frankenberg, R. (1988) ' "Your time or mine?" An anthropological view of the tragic temporal contradictions of biomedical practice', pp. 118–53 in M. Young and T. Schuller (eds), *The Rhythms of Society*. London: Routledge

Frieden, B. and Sagalyn, L. (1989). *Downtown Inc.: How America Rebuilds Cities*. Cambridge, Mass.: MIT Press

Funke, H. (1991) *'Jetzt sind wir dran': Nationalismus im geeinten Deutschland*. Berlin: Aktion Suehnezeichen/Frieden-dienste

Fussell, P. (1980) *Abroad: British Literary Travelling between the Wars*. Oxford: Oxford University Press

Gabriel, Y. (1988) *Working Lives in Catering*. London: Routledge

Gadamer, H.-G. (1955) 'Bemerkungen über den Barock', pp. 61–71 in E. Castelli (ed), *Retorica e Barocco*. Rome: Fratelli Bocca Editori

Game, A. (1991) *Undoing the Social*. Milton Keynes: Open University Press

Gans, P. (1990) 'Changes in the structure of the foreign population of West Germany since 1980', *Migration*, 7: 25–49

Ganssmann, H. (1990) 'Ein Versuch über Arbeit', unpublished mimeo, Institut für Soziologie, Freie Universität Berlin

Ganssmann, H. (1991) 'Der nationale Sozialstaat und die Wirtschaft der neuen Bundesländer', paper, Freie Universität Berlin, October

Garnham, N. (1990) *Capitalism and Communication*. London: Sage

Garnsey, E. and Roberts, J. (1991) 'High technology acquisition and anti-synergy', paper for 10th European Group for Organization Studies (EGOS) Colloquium, Vienna, 15–17 July

Gershuny, J. (1978) *After Industrial Society? The Emerging Self-Service Economy*. London: Macmillan

Gershuny, J. and Miles, I. (1983) *The New Service Economy*. London: Pinter

Ghirardo, D. (1988) 'See-through cities: Houston and Los Angeles', paper for ICA Conference on the City, London, October

Giarini, O. (ed), (1987) *The Emerging Service Economy*. Oxford: Pergamon

Giddens, A. (1981) *A Contemporary Critique of Historical Materialism*. London: Macmillan

Giddens, A. (1984) *The Constitution of Society*. Cambridge: Polity

Giddens, A. (1985) *The Nation-State and Violence*. Cambridge: Polity

Giddens, A. (1990) *The Consequences of Modernity*. Cambridge: Polity

Giddens, A. (1991a) *Modernity and Self-Identity*. Cambridge: Polity

Giddens, A. (1991b) 'Structuration theory: past, present and future', pp. 201–21 in C. Bryant and D. Jary (eds), *Giddens' Theory of Structuration*. London: Routledge

Giddens, A. (1992) *The Transformation of Intimacy*. Cambridge: Polity

Gill, S. and Law, D. (1988) *The Global Political Economy*. Hemel Hempstead: Harvester-Wheatsheaf

Gilpin, R. (1987) *The Political Economy of International Relations*. Princeton: Princeton University Press

Glasmeier, A. (1985) 'Innovative manufacturing industries: spatial incidence in the United States', pp. 55–80 in M. Castells (ed), *High Technology, Space and Society*. Newbury Park, Calif.: Sage

Glasmeier, A. (1988) 'Factors governing the development of high tech industry agglomerations: a tale of three cities', *Regional Studies*, 22: 287–301

Goe, W.R. (1990) 'Producer services, trade and the social division of labor', *Regional Studies*, 24: 327–42

Goffman, E. (1968) *Asylums*. Harmondsworth: Penguin

Gould, P. (1991) 'Dynamic structures of geographic space', pp. 3–30 in S. Brunn and T. Leinbach (eds), *Collapsing Space and Time*. London: Harper Collins

Grabher, G. (1989) 'Industrielle Innovation ohne institutionelle Innovation? Der Umbau des

Montankomplexes im Ruhrgebiet', paper for Unit Labour Market and Employment, Wissenschaftszentrum (WZB), Berlin

Grabher, G. (1990) 'On the weakness of strong ties: the ambivalent role of inter-firm relations in the decline and reorganization of the Ruhr', paper for Unit Labour Market and Employment (IIM), Wissenschaftszentrum (WZB), Berlin

Granovetter, M. (1974) *Getting a Job: A Study of Contacts and Careers*. Cambridge, Mass.: Harvard University Press

Granovetter, M. (1985) 'Economic action and social structure: the problem of embeddedness', *American Journal of Sociology*, 91: 481–510

Granovetter, M. (1990) 'Entrepreneurship, development and the emergence of firms'. discussion paper, FS I, Wissensschaftszentrum, Berlin

Grant, W. (1991) 'Globalization and Comparative Economic Governance', paper for Comparing Capitalist Economies: Modes of Economic Governance Conference, Switzerland, April

Green, A. (1992) 'Post-compulsory education and training in Europe: integrated systems and the roles of the social partners', paper for British Sociological Association Annual Conference, Kent University, Canterbury, 6–9 April

Gregory, D. (1985) 'Suspended animation: the stasis of diffusion theory', pp. 296–336 in D. Gregory and J. Urry (eds), *Social Relations and Spatial Structures*. London: Macmillan

Grill, D. and Sontheimer, M. (1991) 'Der Zug der Vergessen', *Die Zeit*, 39 (19 September): 13–16

Grove-White, R. (1991) 'The emerging shape of environmental conflict in the 1990s', Royal Society of Arts Lecture, 13 February

Gutman, A. (1991) 'Communitarian critics of liberalism', pp. 384–400 in S. Lash (ed), *Post-Structuralist and Post-Modernist Sociology*. Aldershot: Edward Elgar

Gutman, H. (1976) *The Black Family in Slavery and Freedom*. New York: Pantheon

Habermas, J. (1973) *Legitimation Crisis*. London: Heinemann.

Habermas, J. (1981) *Theorie des kommunikativen Handels*. Frankfurt: Suhrkamp

Habermas, J. (1984) *The Theory of Communicative Action*, Vol. 1. Cambridge: Polity

Habermas, J. (1987) *The Philosophical Discourse of Modernity*. Cambridge: Polity

Haller, M. (1990) 'The challenge for comparative sociology in the transformation of Europe', *International Sociology*, 5: 183–204

Hannerz, U. (1990) 'Cosmopolitans and locals in world culture', *Theory, Culture and Society*, 7: 237–252

Hardin, R. (1968) 'The tragedy of the commons: the population problem has no technical solution; it requires a fundamental extension in morality', *Science*, 162: 1243–8

Harloe, M., Pickvance, C. and Urry, J. (eds), (1990) *Place, Policy and Politics: Do Localities Matter?* London: Unwin Hyman

Harlow, J. (1990) 'Britain heads the Euro holiday league', *Daily Telegraph*, 8 September

Harrington, M. (1962) The Other America: Poverty in the United States. New York: Macmillan

Harrison, B. and Bluestone, B. (1988) *The Great U-Turn*. New York: Basic Books

Harvey, D. (1989) *The Condition of Postmodernity*. Oxford: Blackwell

Harvey, D. (1990) 'Between space and time: reflections on the geographical imagination', *Annals of the Association of American Geographers*, 80: 418–34

Harvey, S. (1989) 'Deregulation, innovation and Channel Four', *Screen*, 30: 57–72

Hassard, J. (1990) 'Introduction', pp. 1–20 in *The Sociology of Time*. London: Macmillan

Hassard, J., Rowlinson, M. and McArdle, I. (1991) 'Competitive strategies for changing markets: process and product quality in the electronics industry', paper for 10th European Group for Organization Studies (EGOS) Colloquium, Vienna, 15–17 July

Hausler, J. (1992) 'Adapting to an uncertain environment: R&D in the west German machinery industry', pp. 97–112 in H. Ernste and V. Meier (eds), *Regional Development and Contemporary Industrial Response: Extending Flexible Specialisation*. London: Belhaven

Hawking, S. (1988) *A Short History of Time*. London: Bantam

Hayek, F. (1944) *The Road to Serfdom*. London: Routledge & Kegan Paul

Heal, F. (1990) *Hospitality in Early Modern England*. Oxford: Clarendon

Heald, S. (1991) 'Tobacco, time and the household economy in two Kenyan societies: the Teso and the Kuria', *Comparative Studies in Society and History*, 33: 130–57

Hebdige, D. (1990) 'Fax to the future', *Marxism Today*, January: 18–23

Heclo, H. (1974) *Modern Social Politics in Britain and Sweden*. New Haven, Conn.: Yale University Press

Heidegger, M. (1977) *The Question Concerning Technology and Other Essays*. New York: Harper & Row

Heidegger, M. (1978) *Being and Time*. Oxford: Blackwell

Held, D. (1991) 'Democracy, the nation-state and the global system', pp. 197–235 in D. Held (ed), *Political Theory Today*. Cambridge: Polity

Held, D. (ed), (1993) *Prospects for Democracy*. Cambridge: Polity

Henderson, J. (1989) *The Globalization of High Technology Production*. London: Routledge

Henderson, J. and Castells, M. (1987) 'Introduction', pp. 1–17 in J. Henderson and M. Castells (eds), *Global Restructuring and Territorial Development*. Beverly Hills, Calif.: Sage

Hepworth, M. (1991) 'Information technology and the global restructuring of capital markets', pp. 132–48 in S. Brunn and T. Leinbach (eds), *Collapsing Time and Space*. London: Harper Collins

Hern, A. (1967) *The Seaside Holiday*. London: Cresset

Herrigel, G. (1988) 'Industrial order in the machine tool industry: a comparison of the US and Germany', paper for Comparing Capitalist Economies: Variations in the Governance of Sectors Conference, Madison, Wisconsin

Hetherington, K. (1990) 'The homecoming of the stranger: new social movements or new sociations', Lancaster Regionalism Group Working Paper No. 39, Department of Sociology, Lancaster University

Hewison, R. (1987) *The Heritage Industry*. London: Methuen

Hill, R.C. (1989) 'Comparing transnational production systems: the automobile industry in the USA and Japan', *International Journal of Urban and Regional Research*, 13: 462–80

Hill, S. (1990) 'Management and the flexible firm: the total quality model', paper, Department of Sociology, London School of Economics, September

Hirsch, P. (1990) 'Processing fads and fashions: an organization-set analysis of cultural industry systems', pp. 127–139 in S. Frith and A. Goodwin (eds), *On Record*. London: Routledge

Hirschhorn, L. (1985) 'Information technology and the new services game', pp. 172–89 in M. Castells (ed), *High Technology*. London: Sage

Hirst, P. and Zeitlin, J. (eds), (1989) *Reversing Industrial Decline?* Oxford: Berg

Hirst, P. and Zeitlin, J. (1990) 'Flexible specialization vs post-fordism: theory, evidence and policy implications', paper for Pathways to Industrialization and Regional Development in the 1990s Conference, UCLA, 14–18 March

Hochschild, A. (1983) *The Managed Heart*. Berkeley, Calif.: University of California Press

Hoenekopp, E. (1991) 'Ost–West Wanderungen: Ursachen und Entwicklungstendenzen: Bundesrepublik Deutschland und Österreich', *Bundesarbeitsblatt*, 1: 115–33

Hoffmann, J. (1991) 'Innovationsforderung in Berlin und Baden-Württemberg: zum regionalen Eigenleben technologie-politischer Konzepte', pp. 64–97 in U. Jürgens and W. Krumbein (eds), *Industriepolitische Strategien*. Berlin: Sigma

Hofmann-Axthelm, D. (1992) 'Identity and reality: the end of the philosophical immigration officer', pp. 196–217 in S. Lash and J. Friedman (eds), *Modernity and Identity*. Oxford: Blackwell

Hohfeld, W. (1914) *Fundamental Legal Conceptions*. New Haven, Conn.: Yale University Press

Holderness, G. (1988) 'Bardolatry: or, The cultural materialist's guide to Stratford-upon-

Avon', pp. 1–15 in G. Holderness (ed), *The Shakespeare Myth*. Manchester: Manchester University Press

Holloway, S. (1990) 'Urban economic structure and the urban underclass: an examination of two problematic social phenomena', *Urban Geography*, 11: 319–46

Honderich, K.O. (1992) 'Hat die Soziologie Deutschland versagt?' *Die Zeit*, 24 September

Horne, J. (1985) *Japan's Financial Markets*. London: Allen & Unwin

Huber, B. and K. Unger (1982) 'Politische und rechtliche Determinanten der Ausländerbeschäftigung in der Bundesrepublik Deutschland', pp. 102–87 in H.J. Hoffmann-Nowotny and K.O. Honderich (eds), *Ausländer in der Bundesrepublik Deutschland und in der Schweiz*. Frankfurt: Campus

Hughes, M.A. (1989) 'Misspeaking truth to power: a geographical perspective on the underclass fallacy', *Economic Geography*, 65: 187–207

Hughes, M.A. (1990) 'Formation of the impacted ghetto: evidence from large metropolitan areas, 1970–1980', *Urban Geography*, 11: 265–84

Hurtz, A. (1991) 'Thesen über zu erwartende Qualifikationsveranderungen bei der Einführung rechnerintegrierter Formen der Produktion', pp. 125–31 in M. Laur-Ernst (ed), *Neue Fabrikstrukturen*. Bonn: Bundesinstitut für Berufsbildung

Husbands, C. (1991) 'The mainstream right and the politics of immigration in France: major developments in the 1980s', *Ethnic and Racial Studies*, 14: 170–198

Hutton, T. and Ley, D. (1987) 'Location, linkages and labor: the downtown complex of corporate activities in a medium-size city, Vancouver, British Columbia', *Economic Geography*, 63: 126–41

Hutton, W. (1990) 'A world without borders . . . but would the UK economy still be on the margins?', *The Guardian*, 6 June

Illeris, S. (1989a) 'Producer services: the key sector for future economic development', *Entrepreneurship and Regional Development*, 1: 267–74

Illeris, S (1989b) *Services and Regions in Europe*. Aldershot: Fast Report, Avebury

Ingham, G. (1984) *Capitalism Divided*. London: Macmillan

Irigaray, L. (1985) *Speculum of the Other Women*. Ithaca, NY: Cornell University Press

Jaccard, P. (1960) *Histoire sociale du travail, de l'antiquité à nos jours*. Paris: Payot

Jacques, M. (1990) 'After communism', *Marxism Today*, January: 34–9

Jakobsen, O. (1960) 'Linguistics and poetics', pp. 350–58 in T. Sebeok (ed), *Style in Language*. Cambridge, Mass.: Harvard University Press

Jameson, F. (1981) *The Political Unconscious: Narrative as a Socially Symbolic Act*. London: Methuen

Jameson, F. (1984) 'Postmodernism or the cultural logic of late capitalism', *New Left Review*, 146: 53–92

Jameson, F. (1988) 'Cognitive mapping', pp. 347–57 in C. Nelson and L. Grossberg (eds), *Marxism and the Interpretation of Culture*. London: Macmillan

Janelle, D.G. (1991) 'Global interdependence and its consequences', pp. 49–81 in S. Brunn and T. Leinbach (eds), *Collapsing Time and Space*. London: Harper Collins

Jargowsky, P. and Bane, M.J. (1991) 'Ghetto poverty in the United States, 1970–1980', pp. 235–73 in C. Jencks and P. Peterson (eds), *The Urban Underclass*. Washington, DC: Brookings Institution

Jencks, C. (1991) 'Is the American underclass growing?', pp. 28–101 in C. Jencks and P. Peterson (eds), *The Urban Underclass*. Washington, DC: Brookings Institution

Jessop, B. (1992) 'The Schumpeterian workfare state', Lancaster Regionalism Group Working Paper No. 43, Department of Sociology, Lancaster University

Johnson, K. and Mignot, K. (1982) 'Marketing trade unionism to service industries: an historical analysis of the hotel industry', *Services Industries Journal*, 2: 5–23

Johnson, P. and Thomas, B. (1990) 'Employment in tourism', *Industrial Relations Journal*, 21: 36–48

Johnston, R. (1989) *Environmental Problems*. London: Belhaven

Jones, P. and North, J. (1991) 'Japanese motor industry transplants: the west European dimension', *Economic Geography*, 67: 105–23

Jürgens, U. (1990) 'The transfer of Japanese management concepts in the international automobile industry', pp. 204–18 in S. Wood (ed), *The Transformation of Work?* London: Unwin Hyman

Jürgens, U. (1991a) 'The changing contours of work in the car industry', paper, Abteilung Regulierung von Arbeit: Technik-Arbeit-Umwelt, Wissenszentrum (WZB), Berlin

Jürgens, U. (1991b) 'Internationalization strategies of Japanese and German automobile companies', paper for Production Strategies and Industrial Relations in the Process of Internationalization Symposium, Tohoku University, Sendai, Japan, 14–18 October

Jürgens, U. and Reutter, W. (1989) 'Verringerung der Fertigungstiefe und betriebliche Interessenvertretung in der deutschen Automobilindustrie', pp. 119–53 in N. Altmann and D. Sauer (eds), *Systematische Rationalisierung und Zulieferindustrie*, Frankfurt: Campus

Jürgens, U., Dohse, K. and Malsch, T. (1986) 'New production concepts in West German car plants', pp. 258–81 in Tolliday, S. and Zeitlin, J. (eds), *Between Fordism and Flexibility*. Oxford: Blackwell

Jürgens, U., Malsch, T. and Dohse, K. (1989) *Moderne Zeiten in der Automobilfabrik*. Berlin: Springer

Kanter, R.M. (1984) 'Variations in managerial career structures in hi-tech firms', pp. 109–31 in P. Osterman (ed), *Internal Labor Markets*. Cambridge, Mass.: MIT Press

Kasarda, J. (1990) 'Structural factors affecting the location and timing of urban underclass growth', *Urban Geography*, 11: 234–64

Kawasaki, S. and McMillan, J. (1987) 'The design of contracts: evidence from Japanese subcontracting', *Journal of the Japanese and International Economies*, 1: 327–49

Kealy, E. (1990) 'From craft to art: the case of sound mixers and popular music', pp. 207–20 in S. Frith and A. Goodwin (eds), *On Record*. London: Routledge

Keane, J. (1984) *Capitalism and Public Life*. Cambridge: Cambridge University Press

Keat, R. and Abercrombie, N. (eds) (1991) *Enterprise Culture*. London: Routledge

Keohane, R. (1984) *After Hegemony*. Princeton: Princeton University Press

Kern, H. and Schumann M. (1984) *Das Ende der Arbeitsteilung? Rationalisierung in der industriellen Produktion*. Munich: Beck

Kern, S. (1983) *The Culture of Time and Space, 1880–1914*. London: Weidenfeld & Nicolson

Kettle, M. (1990) 'Slippery slopes', *Marxism Today*, 7 January

King, A. (1990) *Global Cities*. London: Routledge

King, S. (1988) 'Stephen King, advertising executive', *Campaign*, 16 September

Knox, P. (1990) 'The new poor and a new urban geography', *Urban Geography*, 11: 213–16

Kochan, T. (ed), (1985) Challenges and Choices Facing American Labor. Cambridge, Mass.: MIT Press

Kochan, T., Katz, H. and McKensie, W. (1986) *The Transformation of American Industrial Relations*. New York: Basic Books

Kocka, J. (1969) *Unternehmensverwaltung und Angestelltenschaft am Beispiel Siemens, 1847–1914*. Stuttgart: Klett-Cotta

Kocka, J. (1987) 'Bürgertum und Bürgerlichkeit als Probleme der deutschen Geschichte vom späten 18. zum frühen 20. Jahrhundert', pp. 21–63 in J. Kocka (ed), *Bürger und Bürgerlichkeit im 19. Jahrhundert*. Göttingen: Vandenhoeck & Ruprecht

Koehler, H. (1987) 'Berlin in der Weimarer Republik, 1918–1932', pp. 797–923 in W. Ribbe (ed), *Geschichte Berlins*, Zweiter Band, *Von der Märzrevolution bis zur Gegenwart*. Munich: Beck

Koenig, P., W. Ammann and Mehrlaender, U. (1988) *Berufswahl und handwerkliche Berufsausbildung türkischer Jugendlicher: Ergebnisse eines Modelprojektes*. Bonn: Verlag Neue Gesellschaft

Koike, K. (1984) 'Skill formation systems in the US and Japan', pp. 47–75 in M. Aoki (ed), *The Economic Analysis of the Japanese Firm*. North Holland: Elsevier

Koike, K. (1987a) 'Human resource development and labor–management relations', pp. 289–330 in K. Yamamura and Y. Yasuba (eds), *The Political Economy of Japan*. Stanford, Calif.: Stanford University Press

Koike, K. (1987b) 'Skill formation systems: a Thai–Japan comparison', *Journal of the Japanese and International Economies*, 1: 408–40

Koike, K. (1988) *Understanding Industrial Relations in Modern Japan*. London: Macmillan

Koritz, D. (1991) 'Restructuring or *de*structuring? De-industrialization in two industrial heartland cities', *Urban Affairs Quarterly*, 26: 497–511

Körner, S. (1955) *Kant*. Harmondsworth: Penguin

Laing, D. (1989) Interview with D. Laing, Editor of *Music Week*, London, 11 July

Lamont, M. (1992) *Money, Morals and Manners: The Culture of the French and of the Upper American Middle Class*. Chicago: University of Chicago Press

Lane, C. (1988) 'Industrial change in Europe: the pursuit of flexible specialization in Britain and West Germany', *Work, Employment and Society*, 2: 141–68

Lasch, C. (1980) *The Culture of Narcissism*. London: Sphere

Lash, S. (1988) 'Discourse or figure? Postmodernism as a regime of signification', *Theory, Culture and Society*, 5: 311–36

Lash, S. (1990a) 'Coercion as ideology: the German case', pp. 65–97 in N. Abercrombie, S. Hill and B. Turner (eds), *Dominant Ideologies*. London: Unwin Hyman

Lash, S. (1990b) *Sociology of Postmodernism*. London: Routledge

Lash, S. (1991) 'Disintegrating Firms', *Socialist Review*, 21: 99–110

Lash, S. and Friedman, J. (eds), (1992) *Modernity and Identity*. Oxford: Blackwell

Lash, S. and Urry, J. (1987) *The End of Organized Capitalism*. Cambridge: Polity

Latham, J. (1990) 'Statistical trends in tourism and hotel accommodation, up to 1988', pp. 117–28 in C. Cooper (ed), *Progress in Tourism, Recreation and Hospitality Management*, Vol. 2. London: Belhaven

Law, R. and Wolch, J. (1991) 'Homelessness and Economic Restructuring', *Urban Geography*, 12: 105–36

Lawson, A. (1989) *Adultery: An Analysis of Love and Betrayal*. Oxford: Blackwell

Leborgne, D. and Lipietz, A. (1990) 'Open issues and fallacies of post-Fordism', paper for Pathways to Industrialization and Regional Development in the 1990s Conference, UCLA, 14–18 March

Lee, C. (1984) 'The service sector, regional specialization and economic growth in the Victorian economy', *Journal of Historical Geography*, 10: 139–55

Lefebvre, H. (1991) *The Production of Space*. Oxford: Blackwell

Leithauser, G. (1986) 'Des flexibilités . . . et pourtant une crise: la République Fédérale d'Allemagne', pp. 181–205 in R. Boyer (ed), *La flexibilité du travail en Europe*. Paris: Editions de la Découverte

Lepenies, W. (1989) *Die Drei Kulturen: Soziologie zwischen Literatur und Wissenschaft*. Munich: Hanser

Levi-Strauss, C. (1950) *Marcel Mauss*. London: Routledge

Lewis, J. and Townshend, A. (eds), (1989) *The North–South Divide*. London: Paul Chapman

Lewis, O. (1961) *The Children of Sanchez*. New York: Random House

Leyshon, A. and Thrift, N. (1992) 'Liberalization and consolidation: the Single European Market and the remaking of European financial capital', *Environment and Planning A*, 24: 49–81

Limage, L.J. (1987) 'Economic recession and migrant/minority youth in Western Europe and the United States', *International Migration Review*, 25: 399–409

Lincoln, J., Hanada, M. and McBride, K. (1986) 'Organizational structures in Japanese and US manufacturing', *Administrative Science Quarterly*, 31: 338–64

Lipietz, A. (1984) 'Mondialisation de la crise générale du fordisme', *Les Temps Modernes*, 41: 696–736

Lipietz, A. (1992) *Towards a New Economic Order: Post-Fordism, Ecology and Democracy*. Cambridge: Polity

Lively, P. (1991) *City of the Mind*. London: Deutsch

Lockett, R. (1989) Interview with Roy Lockett, Deputy General Secretary, Association of Cinema and Television Technicians, London, 12 July

Lodge, D. (1983) *Small World*. Harmondsworth: Penguin

Lovelock, J. (1988) *Gaia: A New Look at Life on Earth*. Oxford: Oxford University Press
Lowe, P. and Flynn, A. (1989) 'Environmental politics and policy in the 1980s', pp. 255–79 in J. Moran (ed), *The Political Geography of Contemporary Britain*. London: Macmillan
Lowe, P. and Goyder, J. (1983) *Environmental Groups in Politics*. London: Allen & Unwin
Lowenthal, D. (1985) *The Past is a Foreign Country*. Cambridge: Cambridge University Press
Lowenthal, D. and Binney, M. (eds), (1981) *Our Past Before Us: Do We Save It?* London: Temple Smith
Luard, I. (1990) *International Society*. London: Macmillan
Luhmann, N. (1982) *The Differentiation of Society*. New York: Columbia University Press
Luhmann, N. (1986) *Love as Passion*. Cambridge: Polity Press
Luhmann, N. (1989) *Ecological Communication*. Cambridge: Polity
Luke, T. (1992) 'New world order or neo-world orders: power politics and ideology in the informationalizing global order', paper for Theory, Culture and Society 10th Anniversary Conference, Champion, Pennsylvania, 16–19 August
Lumley, R. (ed), (1988) *The Museum Time-Machine*. London: Routledge
Lury, C. (1990) 'Flexible specialization in the advertising industry', paper, Department of Sociology, Lancaster University
Lury, C. (1993) *Cultural Rights*. London: Routledge
Lutz, B. and Veltz, P. (1989) 'Maschinenbauer versus Informatiker – Gesellschaftliche Einflüsse auf die fertigungstechnische Entwicklung: Deutschland und Frankreich', pp. 215–72 in K. Duell and B. Lutz (eds), *Technikentwicklung und Arbeitsteilung im internationalen Vergleich*. Frankfurt: Campus
Lyotard, J. (1984) *The Postmodern Condition*. Manchester: Manchester University Press
MacCannell, D. (1976) *The Tourist*. London: Macmillan
MacCannell, D. (1992) *Empty Meeting Grounds: Tourist Papers*. London: Routledge
MacIntyre, A. (1981) *After Virtue*. London: Duckworth
MacIntyre, A. (1988) *Whose Justice? Which Rationality?* London: Duckworth
MacKenzie, J. and Richards, J. (1986) *The Railway Station: A Social History*. Oxford: Oxford University Press
McCrone, D. (1992) *Understanding Scotland*. London: Routledge
Maffesoli, M. (1991) *Les temps des tribus: le déclin de l'individualisme dans les sociétés de masse*. Paris: Livre de Poche
Mahnkopf, B. (1989) 'Gewerkschaftspolitik und Weiterbildung: Chancen und Risiken einer qualifikationsorientierten Modernisierung gewerkschaftlicher (Tarif-)Politik', discussion paper for FS I, *Arbeitsmarkt und Beschäftigung*, Wissenschaftszentrum, Berlin
Mahnkopf, B. (1990) 'Training, further training and collective bargaining in the Federal Republic of Germany', Report for OECD Directorate for Social Affairs, Manpower and Education, Wissenschaftszentrum, Berlin
Mahnkopf, B. (1991) 'Vorwärts in der Vergangenheit? Pessimistische Spekulationen über die Zukunft der Gewerkschaften in der neuen Bundesrepublik', pp. 269–94 in U. Busch, M. Heine, H. Herr, A. Westphal (eds), *Wirtschaftspolitische Konsequenzen der deutschen Vereinigung*. Frankfurt: Campus
Mahnkopf, B. (1992) 'Towards a skill-oriented modernization of trade union policy', pp. 143–60 in E. Matzner (ed), *Feasible Full Employment: On the Socio-Economics of Comparative Institutional Advantage*. Aldershot: Edward Elgar
Maier, H. (1987) 'Das Modell Baden-Württemberg: Über institutionelle Voraussetzungen differenzierter Qualitätsproduktion', paper for Unit Labour Market and Employment, Wissenschaftszentrum, Berlin
Mair, A., Florida, R. and Kenney, M. (1990) 'The new geography of automobile production: Japanese transplants in North America', *Economic Geography*, 66: 352–73
Malecki, E. (1985) 'Industrial location and corporate organization in high technology industries', *Economic Geography*, 61: 345–69
Malsch, T. (1987) 'Arbeit und Kommunikation im informatisierten Produktionsprozess', paper for International Institute for Comparative Social Research/Labour Policy, Wissenschaftszentrum, Berlin

Malsch, T. and Weissbach, H.-J. (1987) 'Informationstechnologien zwischen Zentralsteurung und Selbstregulation', paper for International Institute for Comparative Social Research/ Labour Policy, Wissenschaftszentrum, Berlin

Mann, M. (1986) *The Sources of Social Power.* Cambridge: Cambridge University Press

Mark Lawson, J., Savage, M. and Warde, A. (1985) 'Gender and local politics: struggles over welfare policies, 1918–1939', pp. 195–215 in L. Murgatroyd, M. Savage, D. Shapiro, J. Urry, S. Walby and A. Warde, *Localities, Class and Gender.* London: Pion

Marketing Director (1989) Interview with the Marketing Director of a newly established, small but expanding publishing firm with good literary reputation, London, December

Markusen, A. and Bloch, R. (1985) 'Defensive cities: military spending, high technology and human settlements', pp. 106–20 in M. Castells (ed), *High Technology, Space and Society.* Beverly Hills, Calif.: Sage

Mars, G. (1984) *The World of Waiters.* London: Allen & Unwin

Marsden, D. and Ryan, P. (1990) 'Institutional aspects of youth employment and training policy in Britain', *British Journal of Industrial Relations,* 28: 351–69

Marshall, G. (1986) 'The workplace culture of a licensed restaurant', *Theory, Culture and Society,* 3: 33–48

Martin, B. (1981) *A Sociology of Contemporary Cultural Change.* Oxford: Blackwell

Martin, R. (1989) 'The political economy of Britain's north–south divide', pp. 20–60 in J. Lewis and A. Townshend (eds), *The North–South Divide.* London: Paul Chapman

Marx, K. (1976) *Capital,* Vol. 1. Harmondsworth: Penguin

Marx, K. and Engels, F. (1976) *Collected Works,* Vol. 6. London: Lawrence & Wishart

Massey, D. (1984) *Spatial Divisions of Labour.* London: Macmillan

Massey, D. (1991) 'A global sense of place', *Marxism Today,* June: 24–9

Massey, D. and Meegan, R. (1982) *The Anatomy of Job Loss.* London: Methuen

Maurice, M. and Sorge, A. (1990) 'Industrielle Entwicklung und Innovationsfähigkeit der Werkzeugmaschinenhersteller in Frankreich und der Bundesrepublik Deutschland: Gesellschaftliche Analyse der Beziehungen zwischen Qualifikation und Wirtschaftsstruktur', discussion paper for Labour Market and Employment Unit, Wissenschaftszentrum, Berlin

Maurice, M., Sellier, F. and Silvestre, J.-J. (1982) *Politique d'éducation et organisation industrielle en France et en Allemagne.* Paris: Presses Universitaires de France

Mauss, M. (1979a) 'Body techniques', pp. 95–123 in *Sociology and Psychology.* London: Routledge (originally published, 1934)

Mauss, M. (1979b) 'A category of the human mind: the notion of the person, the notion of "self" ', pp. 57–94 in *Sociology and Psychology.* London: Routledge (originally published, 1938)

Mehrlaender, U. (1983) *Türkische Jugendliche: Keine beruflichen Chancen in Deutschland?* Bonn: Verlag Neue Gesellschaft

Mehrlaender, U. (1984) 'Turkish youth: occupational opportunities in the Federal Republic of Germany', *Environment and Planning C, Government and Policy,* 2: 375–81

Mehrlaender, U. (1987) 'Sociological aspects of migration policy: the case of the Federal Republic of Germany', *International Migration Review,* 21: 87–95

Mellor, A. (1991) 'Enterprise and heritage in the dock', pp. 93–115 in J. Corner and S. Hervey (eds), *Enterprise and Heritage.* London: Routledge

Melucci, A. (1989) *Nomads of the Present.* London: Radius

Mennell, S. (1985) *All Manners of Food.* Oxford: Blackwell

Merchant, C. (1982) *The Death of Nature.* London: Wildwood

Meyer-Dohm, P. (1991) 'Zum Verhältnis von Erstausbildung und Weiterbildung im Betrieb', paper for Symposium: Bildung und Beschäftigung in Japan und Deutschland: Neue Anforderungen in den neunziger Jahren, Deutsch-Japanisches-Zentrum, Berlin, 2 December

Meyrowitz, J. (1985) *No Sense of Place.* Oxford: Oxford University Press

Middlemas, K. (1975) *Politics in Industrial Society.* London: Deutsch

Middleton, D. and Edwards, D. (1990) 'Introduction', pp. 1–22 in D. Middleton and D. Edwards (eds), *Collective Remembering*. London: Sage

Miller, D. (1987) *Material Culture and Mass Consumption*. Oxford: Blackwell

Milner, M. (1987) 'Where the squeeze is not only on holidaymakers', *The Guardian*, 20 August

Minces, J. (1973) *Les travailleurs étrangers en France*. Paris: Seuil

Mitter, S. (1986) 'Industrial restructuring and manufacturing homework: immigrant women in the UK clothing industry', *Capital and Class*, 27: 37–80

Mommsen, W. (ed), (1981) *The Emergence of the Welfare State in Britain and Germany, 1850–1950*. London: Croom Helm

Monden, Y. (1983) *Toyota Production System*. Atlanta, Ga.: Institute of Industrial Engineers

Moore, T. and Laramore, A. (1990) 'Industrial change and urban joblessness: an assessment of the mismatch hypothesis', *Urban Affairs Quarterly*, 25: 640–58

Moran, M. (1991) *The Politics of the Financial Services Revolution: The USA, the UK and Japan*. London: Macmillan

Morgan, K. and Sayer, A. (1988) *Microcircuits of Capital*. Cambridge: Polity

Morishima, M. (1991) 'Information Sharing and Firm Performance in Japan', *Industrial Relations*, 30: 37–61

Morokvasic, M. (1991) 'Die Kehrseite der Mode: Migranten als Flexibilisierungsquelle in der Pariser Bekleidungsproduktion: ein Vergleich mit Berlin', *Prokla*, 83 June: 264–84

Morokvasic, M., Waldinger, R. and Phizacklea, A. (1990) 'Business on the ragged edge: immigrants and minority business in the garment industries of Paris, London and New York', pp 157–76 in R. Waldinger, H. Aldrich and R. Ward (eds), *Ethnic Entrepreneurs*. London: Sage

Morpurgo, J. (1979) *Allen Lane: King Penguin*. London: Hutchinson

Morris, A. (1991) 'Popping the cork: history, heritage and the stately home in the Scottish borders', pp. 141–51 in G. Day and G. Rees (eds), *Regions, Nations and European Integration*. Cardiff: University of Wales Press

Morris, M. (1990) 'Metamorphoses at Sydney Tower', *New Formations*, 11: 5–18

Morten, J. (1989) Interview with John Morten, General Secretary, Musicians Union, London, 11 July

Moulaert, F., Chikhaoui, Y. and Djellal, F. (1991) 'Locational behaviour of French high-tech consultancy firms', International Journal of Urban and Regional Research, 15: 5–23

Moulaert, F., Martinelli, F. and Djellal, F. (1989) 'The functional and spatial division of labour of information technology consultancy firms in Europe', International Symposium on Regulation, Innovation and Spatial Development, Cardiff, September

Moynihan, D.P. (1965) *The Negro Family: A Case for National Action*. Washington, DC: US Department of Labor

Mulgan, G. (1989) 'The changing shape of the city', pp. 262–78 in S. Hall and M. Jacques, (eds), *New Times*. London: Lawrence & Wishart

Mulgan, G. (1991) *Communication and Control: Networks and the New Economics of Communication*. Cambridge: Polity

Mullins, P. (1991) 'Tourism urbanization', *International Journal of Urban and Regional Research*, 15: 326–42

Mumford, L. (1960) 'Universal city', in C. Kraeling and R. Adams (eds), *City Invisible*. Chicago: University of Chicago Press

Murakami, Y. (1987) 'The Japanese model of political economy', pp. 33–91 in K. Yamamura and Y. Yasuba (eds), *Political Economy of Japan*. Stanford, Calif.: Stanford University Press

Myerscough, J. (1988) *The Economic Importance of the Arts in Britain*. London: Policy Studies Institute

Needelmann, B. (1988) ' "Psychologismus", oder Soziologie der Emotionen? Max Webers Kritik an der Soziologie Georg Simmels', pp. 11–35 in O. Rammstedt (ed), *Simmel und die fruhen Soziologie*. Frankfurt: Suhrkamp

Nerone, J. and Wartella, E. (1989) 'Introduction' to Special Issue on Social Memory, *Communication*, 11: 85–8

Neumann, L. (1992) 'Decentralization and Privatization in Hungary', pp. 233–46 in H. Ernste and V. Meier (eds), *Regional Development and Contemporary Industrial Response*. London: Belhaven

Nguyen, D.T. (1992) 'The spatialization of metric time', *Time and Society*, 1: 29–50

Nietzsche, F. (1956) *The Genealogy of Morals*. New York: Anchor Books

Nowotny, H. (1975) 'Time structuring and time measurement: on the interrelation between timekeepers and social time', pp. 325–42 in J. Fraser and N. Lawrence (eds), *The Study of Time*. Berlin: Springer-Verlag

Nowotny, H. (1985) 'From the future to the extended present: time in social systems', pp. 1–21 in G. Kirsch, P. Nijkamp and K. Zimmerman (eds), *Time Preferences: An Interdisciplinary Theoretical and Empirical Approach*. Berlin: Wissenschaftszentrum

Noyelle, T. (1986) 'Services and the world economy: towards a new international division of labour', ESRC Workshop on Localities in an International Economy, Cardiff, September

Noyelle, T. and Dutka, A. (1988) *International Trade in Business Services*. Cambridge, Mass.: Ballinger

Noyelle, T. and Stanback, T. (1985) *The Economic Transformation of American Cities*. Totowa, NJ: Rowman & Allanheld

Oakey, R. and Cooper, S. (1989) 'High technology industry: agglomeration and the potential for peripherally sited small firms', *Regional Studies*, 23: 347–60

O'Brien, P. (1989) 'Steel: the United States and Japan since World War II', paper for Comparing Capitalist Economies: The Governance of Economic Sectors Conference, Bellagio, May

Offe, C. (1981) 'The attribution of public status to interest groups: observation on the West German Case', pp. 123–58 in S. Berger (ed), *Organizing Interests in Western Europe*. Cambridge: Cambridge University Press

Offe, C. (1984) *Contradictions of the Welfare State*. London: Hutchinson

Offe, C. (1985) *Disorganized Capitalism*. Cambridge: Polity

Ohmae, K. (1990) *The Borderless World*. London: Collins

Ong, W. (1982) *Orality and Literacy*. London: Methuen

O'Reagan, K. and Quigley, J. (1991) 'Labor market access and labor market outcomes for urban youth', *Regional Science and Urban Economics*, 21: 277–93

Orru, M., Hamilton, G. and Suzuki, M. (1989) 'Patterns of inter-firm control in Japanese business', *Organization Studies*, 10: 549–74.

Ousby, I. (1990) *The Englishman's England*. Cambridge: Cambridge University Press

Parsons, T. (1937) *The Structure of Social Action*. New York: McGraw Hill

Parsons, T. (1968) *The Structure of Social Action*. 2nd edition. New York: Free Press

Patrick, H. and Rohlen, T. (1987) 'Small-scale family enterprises', pp. 331–84 in K. Yamamura and T. Yasuba (eds), *Political Economy of Japan*. Stanford, Calif.: Stanford University Press

Pearce, D. (1989) *Tourist Development*. Harlow: Longman

Pearce, D., Barbier, D. and Markandya, A. (1989) *Blueprint for a Green Economy*. London: Earthscan

Peck, J. (1991) 'The politics of training in Britain: contradictions in the TEC initiative', *Capital and Class*, 44: 23–34

Penn, R. (1990) 'Changing patterns of employment in Rochdale, 1981–1984: "Post-industrialism" or "resurgent industrialism"? Evidence from the Social Change and Economic Life Initiative', Working Paper WP51, Department of Sociology, Lancaster University

Percy, S. and Lamb, H. (1987) 'The squalor behind the bright fast food lights', *The Guardian*, 22 August

Perkin, H. (1976) 'The "social tone" of Victorian seaside resorts in the Northwest', *Northern History*, 2: 180–94

Peterson, P. (1991) 'The urban underclass and the poverty paradox', pp. 3–27 in C. Jencks and P. Peterson (eds), *The Urban Underclass*. Washington, DC: Brookings Institution

Phelps-Brown, E. (1968) *A Century of Pay*. London: Macmillan

Phizacklea, A. (1990) *Unpacking the Fashion Industry*. London: Routledge

Pillsbury, R. (1990) *From Boarding House to Bistro*. Boston: Unwin Hyman

Pinch, S. (1989) 'The restructuring thesis and the study of public services', *Environment and Planning A*, 21: 905–26

Pine, R. (1987) *Management of Technical Change in the Catering Industry*. Aldershot: Avebury

Piore, M. and Sabel, C. (1984) *The Second Industrial Divide*. New York: Basic Books

Plaschkes, O. (1989) Interview with Otto Plaschkes, Chief Executive, British Film and Television Producers Association, London, 14 July

Pollard, S. (1965) *The Genesis of Modern Management*. London: Edward Arnold

Poon, A. (1989) 'Competitive strategies for a "new tourism" ', pp. 91–102 in C. Cooper (ed), *Progress in Tourism, Recreation and Hospitality Management*, Vol. 1. London: Belhaven

Porritt, J. (1984) *Seeing Green: The Politics of Ecology Explained*. Oxford: Blackwell

Porter, V. (1985) *On Cinema*. London: Pluto Press

Porter, V. (1989) Interviewed at the Polytechnic of Central London. July

Portes, A. and Bach, R. (1985) *Latin Journey: Cuban and Mexican Immigrants in the United States*. Berkeley, Calif.: University of California Press

Portes, A. and Jensen, J. (1989) 'The enclave and the entrants: patterns of ethnic enterprise in Miami before and after Mariel', *American Sociological Review*, 54: 929–49

Poster, M. (1990) *The Mode of Information*. Cambridge: Polity

Pryke, M. (1991) 'An international city going "global": spatial change in the City of London', *Environment and Planning D: Society and Space*, 9: 197–222

Radley, A. (1990) 'Artefacts, memory and a sense of the past', pp. 46–59 in D. Middleton and D. Edwards (eds), *Collective Remembering*. London: Sage

Ramsay, H. (1991) 'The community, the multinational, its workers and their charter: a modern tale of industrial democracy', *Work, Employment and Society*, 4: 541–66

Ratcliffe, I. (1988) 'Race, class and residence: Afro-Caribbean households in Britain', pp. 126–46 in M. Cross and H. Etzinger (eds), *Lost Illusions*. London: Routledge

Razin, E. (1988) 'Entrepreneurship among foreign immigrants in the Los Angeles and San Francisco metropolitan regions', *Urban Geography*, 9: 283–301

Relph, E. (1976) *Place and Placelessness*. London: Pion

Rex, J. and Moore, R. (1967) *Race, Community and Conflict*. Oxford: Oxford University Press

Reynolds, B. (1989) *The Hundred Best Companies to work for in the UK*. London: Fontana/ Collins

Reynolds, H. (1988) ' "Leisure revolution": prime engineer of regional recovery', *Daily Telegraph*, 2 December

Riddle, D. (1986) *Service-Led Growth: The Role of the Service Sector in World Development*. New York: Praeger

Rifkin, J. (1987) *Time Wars: The Primary Conflict in Human History*. New York: Henry Holt

Rights and Contract Manager (1989) Interview with the Rights and Contracts Manager of a new, small, but high profile general publishing company, London, December

Ritzer, G. (1992) *The McDonaldization of Society*. London: Sage

Robertson, R. (1990) 'Mapping the global condition: globalization as the central concept', *Theory, Culture and Society*, 7: 15–30

Robins, K. (1989a) 'Global times', *Marxism Today*, December: 20–7

Robins, K. (1989b) 'Reimagined communities? European image spaces beyond fordism', *Cultural Studies*, 3: 150–62

Rojek, C. (1993) *Ways of Escape*. London: Macmillan

Romeril, M. (1990) 'Tourism: the environmental dimension', pp. 103–13 in C. Cooper (ed), *Progress in Tourism, Recreation and Hospitality Management*, Vol 1. London: Belhaven

Rootes, C. (1990) 'The future of the "new politics": a European perspective', *Social Alternatives*, 8: 7–12

Rorty, R. (1992) 'Cosmopolitanism without emancipation: a response to Lyotard', pp. 59–72 in S. Lash and J. Friedman (eds), *Modernity and Identity*. Oxford: Blackwell

Rose, H. (1980) 'Blacks and Cubans in metropolitan Miami's changing economy', *Urban Geography*, 10: 464–86

Ross, G. (1992) 'Confronting the New Europe', *New Left Review*, 191: 49–68

Roth, M. (1992) 'The time of nostalgia: medicine, history and normality in 19th-century France', *Time and Society*, 2: 271–86

Roy, D. (1990) 'Time and job satisfaction', pp. 155–67 in J. Hassard (ed), *The Sociology of Time*. London: Macmillan

Rudig, W. (1986) 'Nuclear power: an international comparison of public protest in the USA, Great Britain, France and West Germany', pp. 364–417 in R. Williams and S. Mills (eds), *Public Acceptance of New Technologies*. London: Croom Helm

Saatchi & Saatchi (1987) *Annual Report and Accounts: Year ended 30 September 1987*. London: Saatchi & Saatchi

Sabel, C. (1982) *Work and Politics*. Cambridge: Cambridge University Press

Sabel, C. (1990) 'Skills without a place: the reorganization of the corporation and the experience of work', paper for British Sociological Association Annual Conference, Guildford, Surrey, 2–5 April

Sabel, C., Herrigel, G. et al (1987) 'Regional prosperities compared: Massachusetts and Baden-Württemberg in the 1980s', discussion paper ILM-IIM, Wissenschaftszentrum, Berlin

Sako, M. (1988) 'Neither markets nor hierarchies: a comparative study of the printed circuit board industry in Britain and Japan', paper for Comparing Capitalist Economies: the Governance of Economic Sectors Colloquium, Madison, Wisconsin, May

Sakson, A. (1991) 'Die neueren Wanderungsbewegungen polnischer Arbeitskräfte: eine Dokumentation', *Prokla*, 83: 285–90

Sarlvik, B. and Crewe, I. (1983) *Decade of Dealignment*. Cambridge: Cambridge University Press

Sassen, S. (1988) *The Mobility of Labour and Capital*. Cambridge: Cambridge University Press

Sassen, S. (1991) *The Global City*. Princeton: Princeton University Press

Savage, M., Barlow, J., Dickens, P. and Fielding, T. (1992) *Property, Bureaucracy and Culture*. London: Routledge

Saxenian, A. (1985) 'Silicon Valley and Route 128: regional prototypes or historical exceptions?', pp. 81–105 in M. Castells (ed), *High Technology*. Beverly Hills, Calif.: Sage

Saxenian, A. (1989) 'The Cheshire cat's grin: innovation, regional development and the Cambridge case', *Economy and Society*, 18: 448–77

Sayad, A. (1977) 'Les trois âges de l'immigration algériennes', *Actes de la recherche en sciences sociales*, 15: 59–81

Sayer, A. (1986) 'New developments in manufacturing: the just-in-time system', *Capital and Class*, 30: 43–72

Scaping, Peter (1989) Interview with Peter Scaping, Executive officer, British Phonographic Industry (trade association of record companies), London, 19 July

Schivelbusch, W. (1980) *The Railway Journey: Trains and Travel in the Nineteenth Century*. Oxford: Blackwell

Schlegel, J. (1991) 'Introductory address: Das deutsche Bildungs- und Beschäftigungssystem', Symposium, Deutsch-Japanisches-Zentrum, Berlin, 1–3 December

Schmitter, P. (1979) 'Still the century of corporatism?', pp. 7–52 in P. Schmitter and G. Lehmbruch (eds), *Trends toward Corporatist Intermediation*. London: Sage

Schmitter, P. (1981) 'Interest intermediation and regime governability in contemporary western Europe and north America', pp. 287–330 in S. Berger (ed), *Organizing Interests in Western Europe*. Cambridge: Cambridge University Press

Schmitter, P. (1982) 'Reflections on where the theory of neo-corporatism has gone and where the praxis of neo-corporatism may be going', pp. 259–280 in G. Lehmbruch and P. Schmitter (eds), *Patterns of Corporatist Policy-Making*. London: Sage

Schmitter, P. (1988) 'Sectors in modern capitalism: modes of governance and variations in performance', paper for Colloquium Comparing Capitalist Economies, Madison, Wisconsin, May

Schneider, M. and Phelan, T. (1990) 'Blacks and jobs: never the twain shall meet?', *Urban Affairs Quarterly*, 26: 299–312

Schoeneberg, U. (1982) 'Bestimmungsgründe der Integration und Assimilation ausländischer Arbeitnehmer in der Bundesrepublik Deutschland und der Schweiz', in H.J. Hoffmann-Nowotny and K.O. Honderich (eds), *Ausländer in der Bundesrepublik Deutschland und in der Schweiz*. Frankfurt: Campus

Schwengel, H. (1990) 'British Enterprise Culture and German *Kulturgesellschaft*', pp. 136–50 in R. Keat and N. Abercrombie (eds), *Enterprise Culture*. London: Routledge

Scott, A. (1986) 'Industrial organization and location: division of labor, the firm and spatial process', *Economic Geography*, 62: 215–31

Scott, A. (1988a) *Metropolis: from the division of labor to urban form*. Berkeley, Calif.: University of California Press

Scott, A. (1988b) *New Industrial Spaces*. London: Pion

Scott, J. and Griff, C. (1984) *Directors of Industry*. Cambridge: Polity

Sengenberger, W. (1988) 'Flexibility in the labour market: internal versus external adjustments in international comparison', paper for Structural and Technological Change on the Labour Market Conference, Wissenschaftszentrum, Berlin

Senior Contract Manager (1989) Interview with a Senior Contract Manager with 30 years' experience in a number of well-known publishing houses; now with long-established house recently acquired by a US company, London, October

Sennett, R. (1991) *The Conscience of the Eye*. London: Faber & Faber

Shapiro, D., Abercrombie, N., Lash, S. and Lury, C. (1992) 'Flexible specialization in the culture industries', pp. 179–94 in H. Ernste and V. Meier (eds), *Regional Development and Contemporary Industrial Response*. London: Belhaven

Sheard, P. (1989) 'The Japanese general trading company as an aspect of inter-firm risk-sharing', *Journal of the Japanese and International Economies*, 3: 308–22

Shelp, R. (1982) *Beyond Industrialization*. New York: Praeger

Shields, R. (1991a) *Places on the Margin*. London: Routledge

Shields, R. (1991b) 'The individual, consumption cultures and the fate of community', paper for British Sociological Association Conference, Manchester, April

Shimokawa, K. (1986) 'Product and labour strategies in Japan', pp. 224–43 in S. Tolliday and J. Zeitlin (eds), *Between Fordism and Flexibility*. Oxford: Blackwell

Silverstone, R., Hirsch, E. and Morley, D. (1990) 'Information and communication technologies and the moral economy of the household', CRICT Discussion Paper, Brunel University, October

Simmel, G. (1950) *The Sociology of Georg Simmel*, ed K.H. Wolff. New York: Free Press

Simmel, G. (1990) *Vom Wesen der Moderne: Essays zur Philosophie und Aesthetik*. Hamburg: Junius Verlag

Sisson, K. (1987) *The Management of Collective Bargaining*. Oxford: Blackwell

Sklair, L. (1990) *Sociology of the Global System*. Hemel Hempstead: Harvester

Skocpol, T. (1991) 'Targeting within universalism: politically viable policies to combat poverty in the United States', pp. 411–26 in C. Jencks and P. Peterson (eds), *The Urban Underclass*. Washington, DC: Brookings Institution

Smart, J. (1963) *Philosophy and Scientific Realism*. London: Routledge

Smith, A. (1984) 'Ethnic myths and ethnic revivals', *European Journal of Sociology*, 25: 283–305

Smith, A. (1986) *The Ethnic Origins of Nations*. Oxford: Blackwell

Smith, A. (1990) 'Towards a global culture?', *Theory, Culture and Society*, 7: 171–92

Smith, S. (1989) Interview with Steve Smith, Chief Executive, British Record Retailers Trade Association and former producer, London, 19 July

Smith, S.L., Dickson, K. and Smith, H. (1990) ' "How was it for them?" High technology research collaboration and the constraints of "disorganized capitalism" ', paper for British Sociological Association Annual Conference, Guildford, April

Soja, E. (1989) *Postmodern Geographies*. London: Verso

Soja, E., Morales, R. and Wolff, G. (1983) 'Urban restructuring: an analysis of social and spatial change in Los Angeles', *Economic Geography*, 59: 195–230

Sontag, S. (1979) *On Photography*. Harmondsworth: Penguin

Sorge, A. (1991) 'Strategic fit and the societal effect: interpreting cross-national comparisons of technology, organization and human resources', *Organization Studies*, 12: 161–90

Sorge, A. and Streeck, W. (1987) 'Industrial relations and technical change: the case for an extended perspective', pp. 19–47 in R. Hyman and W. Streeck (eds), *New Technology and Industrial Relations*. Oxford: Blackwell

Sorokin, P. (1937) *Social and Cultural Dynamics*, Vol 2. New York: American Books

Sorokin, P. and Merton, R. (1937) 'Social time: a methodological and functional analysis', *American Journal of Sociology*, 42: 615–29

Stanback, T. (1985) 'The changing fortunes of metropolitan economies', pp. 122–42 in M. Castells (ed), *High Technology, Space and Society*. Beverly Hills, Calif.: Sage

Stanley, C. (1992) 'Cultural contradictions in the legitimation of market practice', pp. 142–70 in L. Budd and S. Whimster (eds), *Global Finance and Urban Living*. London: Routledge

Stinchcombe, A. (1959) 'Bureaucratic and craft administration of production', *Administrative Science Quarterly*, 4: 168–87

Stolting, E. (1991) 'Festung Europa: Grenzziehungen in der Ost-West-Migration', *Prokla*, 83: 249–63

Storper, M. and Christopherson, S. (1987) 'The city as studio; the world as back lot: the impact of vertical disintegration on the location of the motion picture industry', *Environment and Planning D: Society and Space*, 4: 305–20

Storper, M. and Harrison, B. (1990) 'Flexibility, hierarchy and regional development: the changing structure of industrial production systems and their forms of governance', discussion paper, D902, School of Architecture and Urban Planning, UCLA, Los Angeles

Storper, M. and Walker, R. (1989) *The Capitalist Imperative*. Oxford: Blackwell

Strange, S. (1986) *Casino Capitalism*. Oxford: Blackwell

Strange, S. (1988) *States and Markets*. London: Pinter

Strathern, M. (1992) *After Nature: English Kinship in the Late Twentieth Century*. Cambridge: Cambridge University Press

Streeck, W. (1982) 'Organizational consequences of neo-corporatist cooperation in West German labour unions', pp. 29–82 in G. Lehmbruch and P. Schmitter (eds), *Patterns of Corporatist Policy-Making*. London: Sage

Streeck, W. (1989) 'Skills and the limits of neo-liberalism: the enterprise of the future as a place of learning', *Work, Employment and Society*, 3: 89–104

Streeck, W. et al (1987a) 'The role of the social partners in vocational training and further training in the Federal Republic of Germany'. Labour Market and Employment Unit, Wissenschaftszentrum, Berlin, 112pp

Streeck, W., Hilbert, J., van Keyelaer, K., Maier, F. and Weber, H. (1987b) *Steuerung und Regulierung der beruflichen Bildung*. Berlin: Sigma.

Stubbs, R. (1989) Interview with Roger Stubbs, Senior Marketing Executive of EMI Records, London, 14 July

Suzuki, Y. (ed), (1987) *The Japanese Financial System*. Oxford: Clarendon

Takagayi, S. (1988) 'Recent developments in Japan's bond and money markets', *Journal of the Japanese and International Economies*, 2: 63–91

Taylor, C. (1989) *Sources of the Self: The Making of Modern Identity*. Cambridge: Cambridge University Press

Tenbrock, F. (1991a) 'Eine Chance für America', *Die Zeit*, 43 (18 October): 39–40

Tenbrock, F. (1991b) 'Jenseits von Schwarz und Weiss', *Die Zeit*, 42 (11 October): 41–2

Thompson, E. (1967) 'Time, work-discipline and industrial capitalism', *Past and Present*, 36: 57–97

Thompson, J. (1990) *Ideology and Modern Culture*. Cambridge: Polity

Thompson, P. (1988) *The Voice of the Past: Oral History*. Oxford: Oxford University Press

Thrift, N. (1985) 'Flies and germs: a geography of knowledge', pp. 366–403 in D. Gregory and J. Urry (eds), *Social Relations and Spatial Structures*. London: Macmillan

Thrift, N. (1990a) 'The making of a capitalist time consciousness', pp. 105–29 in J. Hassard (ed), *The Sociology of Time*. London: Macmillan

Thrift, N. (1990b) 'Transportation and communication, 1730–1914', pp. 453–86 in R. Dodgson and R. Butlin (eds), *An Historical Geography of England and Wales*. 2nd edition. London: Academic Press

Thrift, N. and Leyshon, A. (1992) 'In the wake of money: the City of London and the accumulation of capital', pp. 282–311 in L. Budd and S. Whimster (eds), *Global Finance and Urban Living*. London: Routledge

Toffler, A. (1970) *Future Shock*. New York: Random House

Touraine, A. (1974) *The Post-Industrial Society*. New York: Wildwood Press

Towner, J. (1985) 'The Grand Tour: a key phase in the history of tourism', *Annals of Tourism Research*, 15: 47–62

Townsend, P., Corrigan, P. and Kowarzik, U. (1987) *Poverty and Labour in London*. London: Low Pay Unit

Travel Alberta (undated) *West Edmonton Mall*. Edmonton: Alberta Tourism

Traxler, F. and Unger, B. (1989) 'Industry or infrastructure? A cross-national comparison of governance, its determinants and economic consequences in the dairy industry', paper for Comparing Capitalist Economies Conference, Bellagio, Italy, May–June

Tremblay, P. (1990) 'The corporate structure of multinational enterprises in tourism: transaction costs and information', paper for World Congress of Sociology, Madrid, August

Turner, V. (1969) *The Ritual Process: Structure and Anti Structure*. London: Allen Lane

Uekusa, M. (1987) 'Industrial organization: the 1970s to the present', pp. 469–515 in K. Yamamura and Y. Yasuba (eds), *Political Economy of Japan*. Stanford, Calif.: Stanford University Press

Urry, J. (1985) 'Social relations, space and time', pp. 20–48 in D. Gregory and J. Urry (eds), *Social Relations and Spatial Structures*. London: Macmillan

Urry, J. (1987) 'Some social and spatial aspects of services', *Society and Space*, 5: 5–26

Urry, J. (1990a) 'Conclusion: places and policies', pp. 187–204 in M. Harloe, C. Pickvance, J. Urry (eds), *Place, Policy, and Politics*. London: Unwin Hyman

Urry, J. (1990b) 'Lancaster: small firms, tourism and the "locality" ', pp. 146–64 in M. Harloe, C. Pickvance, J. Urry (eds), *Place, Policy, and Politics*. London: Unwin Hyman

Urry, J. (1990c) *The Tourist Gaze*. London: Sage

Urry, J. (1991) 'Time and space in Giddens' social theory', pp. 160–75 in C. Bryant and D. Jary (eds), *Giddens' Theory of Structuration*. London: Routledge

Urry, J. (1992) 'The tourist gaze and the "environment" ', *Theory, Culture and Society*, 9: 1–26

Veblen, T. (1953) *The Theory of the Leisure Class*. New York: Mentor

Vergo, P. (ed), (1989) *The New Museology*. London: Reaktion

Virilio, P. (1986) *Speed and Politics*. New York: Semiotext

Wacquant, L. (1989) 'The ghetto, the state and the new capitalist economy', *Dissent*, Fall: 508–20.

Wacquant L. (1991) 'From "black metropolis" to "hyper-ghetto": race, state and economy in the transformation of the black ghetto in the post-fordist era', paper for Poverty, Immigration and Urban Marginality in the Advanced Societies Working Conference, Paris, 10–11 May

Walby, S. (1990a) 'Woman and nation', *International Journal of Comparative Sociology*, 32: 81–100

Walby, S. (1990b) *Theorizing Patriarchy*. Oxford: Blackwell

Walby, S., Greenwell, J., Mackay, L. and Soothill, K. (1994) *Medicine and Nursing: Professions in a Changing Health Service*. London: Sage

Waldinger, R. (1986–7) 'Changing ladders and musical chairs: ethnicity and opportunity in post-industrial New York', *Politics and Society*, 15: 369–402

Waldinger, R. (1989) 'Immigration and urban change', *Annual Review of Sociology*, 15: 44–69

Walker, R. (1985) 'Is there a service economy? The changing capitalist division of labor', *Science and Society*, 49: 42–83

Walker, R. (1988) 'The geographical organization of production-systems', *Environment and Planning D: Society and Space*, 6: 377–408

Wallerstein, I. (1990) 'Culture as the ideological battleground of the modern world-system', *Theory, Culture and Society*, 7: 31–56

Walton, J. (1978) *The Blackpool Landlady*. Manchester: Manchester University Press

Walton, J. (1981) 'The demand for working class seaside holidays in Victorian England', *Economic History Review*, 34: 249–65

Walton, J. (1983) *The English Seaside Resort: A Social History, 1750–1914*. Leicester: Leicester University Press

Walton, J. (1990) 'Afterword: Mass Observation's Blackpool and some alternatives', pp. 229–40 in G. Cross (ed), *Worktowners at Blackpool: Mass-Observation and Popular Leisure in the 1930s*. London: Routledge

Walvin, J. (1978) *Beside the Seaside*. London: Allen Lane

Ward, C. and Hardy, D. (1986) *Goodnight Campers! The History of the British Holiday Camp*. London: Mansell

Ward, R. and Cross, M. (1991) 'Race, employment and economic change', pp. 116–31 in P. Brown and R. Scase (eds), *Poor Work*. Milton Keynes: Open University Press

Warren, P. (1989) Interview with Peter Warren of J. Walter Thompson advertising agency, London, 20 August

Watkins, D. (1984) *Grand Hotel: the Golden Age of Palace Hotels*. London: Dent

Watts, M. (1992) 'Space for everything (a commentary)', *Cultural Anthropology*, 7: 115–29

Weber, M. (1930) *The Protestant Ethic and the Spirit of Capitalism*. London: Unwin Hyman

Weber, M. (1972) *Wirtschaft und Gesellschaft: Grundriss der verstehenden Soziologie. Studienausgabe, besorgt von J. Winckelmann*. Tübingen: Mohr (Paul Siebeck)

Webster, F. and Robins, K. (1989) 'Plan and control: towards a cultural history of the information society', *Theory and Society*, 18: 323–51

Weir, M. (1991) *Politics and Jobs: the Boundaries of Employment Policy in the United States*. Princeton, NJ: Princeton University Press

Weiss, J. (1987) 'On the irreversibility of Western rationalization and Max Weber's alleged fatalism', pp. 154–63 in S. Whimster and S. Lash (eds), *Max Weber: Rationality and Modernity*. London: Allen & Unwin

Wenders, W. (1991) 'Inflation der Bilder', *Tip*, 19/91 (12–25 September): 26–31

Whiteley, N. (1987) *Pop Design: Modernism to Mod*. London: Design Council

Whitley, R. (1990) 'Eastern Asian enterprise structures and the comparative analysis of forms of business organization', *Organization Studies*, 11: 47–74

Whitley, R. (1991) 'The social construction of business systems in east Asia', *Organization Studies*, 12: 1–28

Whyte, W. (1948) *Human Relations in the Restaurant Industry*. New York: McGraw

Wieworka, J. (1991) 'Popular and political racism in Europe: unity and diversity', paper for British Sociological Association Annual Conference, Kent University, Canterbury, April

Williams, K., Williams, J., Haslam, C. and Wardlow, A. (1989) 'Facing up to manufacturing failure', pp. 71–94 in P. Hirst, and J. Zeitlin, (eds), *Reversing Industrial Decline*. Oxford: Berg

Williams, R. (1983) *Towards 2000*. London: Chatto & Windus

Williamson, O. (1975) *Markets and Hierarchies: Analysis and Antitrust Implications*. New York: Free Press

Williamson, O. (1985) *The Economic Institutions of Capitalism*. New York: Free Press

Willis, P. (1977) *Learning to Labour: How Working Class Kids get Working Class Jobs*. Aldershot: Gower

Wilpert, C. (1991) 'Migration and ethnicity in a non-immigration country: foreigners in a united Germany', *New Community*, 18: 49–62

Wilson, A. (1992) *The Culture of Nature*. Oxford: Blackwell
Wilson, E. (1992) 'The invisible flâneur', *New Left Review*, 191: 90–110
Wilson, W.J. (1978) *The Declining Significance of Race*. Chicago: University of Chicago Press
Wilson, W.J. (1987) *The Truly Disadvantaged: The Inner City, the Underclass and Public Policy*. Chicago: University of Chicago Press
Wilson, W.J. (1991a) 'Public policy research and "The Truly Disadvantaged" ', pp. 460–81 in C. Jencks and P. Peterson (eds), *The Urban Underclass*. Washington, DC: Brookings Institution
Wilson, W.J. (1991b) 'Studying inner-city social dislocations: the challenge of public agenda research', *American Sociological Review*, 56: 1–14
Wolch, J. (1991) 'Urban homelessness: an agenda for research', *Urban Geography*, 12: 99–104
Wood, M. (1974) 'Nostalgia or never: you can't go home again', *New Society*, 7 November
Wood, S. (1989a) 'The Japanese management model, tacit skills in shop floor participation', *Work and Occupations*, 6: 446–60
Wood, S. (1989b) 'The transformation of work?', pp. 1–43 in S. Wood (ed), *The Transformation of Work?* London: Unwin Hyman
Wood, S. (1991) Untitled mimeo on work organization in Japan, London School of Economics, London
Wordsworth, W. (1951) *A Guide through the District of the Lakes*. London: Hart-Davis
Wouters, C. (1989) 'The sociology of emotions and flight attendants: Hochschild's *Managed Heart*', *Theory, Culture and Society*, 6: 95–124
Wriston, W. (1992) 'The twilight of sovereignty', *Royal Society of Arts Journal*, 140 (August–September): 567–77
Yearley, S. (1991) *The Green Case*. London: Harper Collins
Zolberg, A. (1991) 'Stranger encounters', pp. 178–93 in P. Simon and I. Simon-Barrouh (eds), *Les étrangers dans la ville*. Paris: L'Harmattan
Zukin, S. (1988) *Loft Living*. London: Radius
Zukin, S. (1992a), 'Postmodern urban landscapes: mapping culture and power', pp. 221–47 in S. Lash and J. Friedman (eds), *Modernity and Identity*. Oxford: Blackwell
Zukin, S. (1992b) 'The city as a landscape of power: London and New York as global financial capitals', pp. 195–223 in L. Budd and S. Whimster (eds), *Global Finance and Urban Living*. London: Routledge

INDEX